The Clinical Legal Education Handbook

OBServing Law – IALS Open Book Service for Law

The Clinical Legal Education Handbook

Edited by Linden Thomas and Nick Johnson

Institute of Advanced Legal Studies
University of London Press
2020

Institute of Advanced Legal Studies
University of London
Charles Clore House
17 Russell Square
London WC1B 5DR
https://ials.sas.ac.uk

University of London Press
Senate House
Malet Street
London WC1E 7HU
https://sas.ac.uk/publications/

Contents

List of abbreviations

ABA	American Bar Association
AQS	Advice Quality Standard
ASA	Advice Services Alliance
BIBA	British Institute of Insurance Brokers
BSB	Bar Standards Board
CAFCASS	Children and Family Court Advisory and Support Service
CDD	Customer due diligence
CILEx	Chartered Institute of Legal Executives
CLE	clinical legal education
CLEA	Clinical Legal Education Association
CLEO	Clinical Legal Education Organisation
CLOCK	Community Legal Outreach Collaboration Keele
COFA	Compliance Officer for Finance and Administration
COLP	Compliance Officer for Legal Practice
CPD	continuing professional development
DBS	Disclosure and Barring Service
DPA	Data Protection Act 2018
DPB	designated professional body
DQR	designated qualifying regulator
EA	Equality Act 2010
ECF	exceptional case funding
ESA	Employment and Support Allowance
EULA	end user licence agreement
FCA	Financial Conduct Authority
FHDRA	first hearing and dispute resolution appointment
FSMA	Financial Services and Markets Act 2000
FTE	full-time equivalent
GAJE	Global Alliance for Justice Education
GDPR	General Data Protection Regulation
HEI	Higher Education Institution
IRAC	issue, rule, application, conclusion
KIS	Key Information Set
LAA	Legal Aid Agency

LAFQAS	Legal Aid Franchise Quality Assurance Standard
LASPO	Legal Aid, Sentencing and Punishment of Offenders Act 2012
LERN	Legal Education Research Network
LETR	Legal Education Training Review
LO	learning outcome
LPP	legal professional privilege
LSA	Legal Services Act 2007
LSB	Legal Services Board
LSC	Legal Services Commission
MCT	multiple choice test
MTCs	Minimum Terms and Conditions
NINSO	Northumbria Internet and Society Research Interest Group
ODR	online dispute resolution
OFT	Office of Fair Trading
OISC	Office of the Immigration Services Commissioner
PFRs	Practice Framework Rules
PII	professional indemnity insurance
PIP	Personal Independent Payment
PLE	public legal education
POCA	Proceeds of Crime Act 2002
PSU	Personal Support Unit (known as Support Through Court since late 2019)
QAA	Quality Assurance Agency
QWE	qualifying work experience
REL	Registered European Lawyer
RFL	Registered Foreign Lawyer
SAAS	Software-as-a-Service
SCL	Society for Computers and Law
SIIR	Solicitors Indemnity Insurance Rules
SLF	student law firm
SQM	Specialist Quality Mark
SRA	Solicitors Regulation Authority
STC	Support Through Court
TACT	Terrorism Act 2000
VLC	virtual law clinic

Notes on contributors

Lydia Bleasdale is an Associate Professor at the School of Law, University of Leeds, where she is also Director of Community Engagement.

Vivien Cochrane is a solicitor in the Criminal Litigation team at Kingsley Napley in London. She has over ten years' experience of advising clients in cases covering the full spectrum of criminality and has been involved in some of the most high profile and novel criminal cases in recent history.

Rachel Dunn is a Senior Lecturer at Northumbria Law School.

John Fitzpatrick is an emeritus professor of law in the University of Kent, and was Director of the Kent Law Clinic from 1992 to 2018. He previously worked as a caseworker and solicitor in community law centres in Brixton and Hammersmith.

Richard Grimes is a solicitor, a visiting professor at Charles University, Prague and an independent access to justice and legal education consultant. He was formerly Director of Clinical Programmes at the University of York.

Lee Hansen is a Lecturer and Deputy Director of the Essex Law Clinic at the University of Essex. Lee has a background in legal practice in Community Legal Centres in Australia.

Will Hayes is a barrister in the Criminal Litigation team at Kingsley Napley in London. He has extensive experience of representing clients in a vast range of complex and high profile criminal cases at all stages of proceedings, from interviews under caution at the commencement of police investigations right through to cases before the Court of Appeal.

Nick Johnson teaches law at De Montfort University and sits as a Tribunal Judge in the Social Entitlement Chamber. He qualified as a solicitor in 1993 and has taught law for more than 20 years. From 2006 to 2018, he led Nottingham Law School's Legal Advice Centre.

Vinny Kennedy is a Solicitor and Senior Lecturer at Northumbria University Newcastle and a former Supervising Solicitor for the student Law Clinic at Sheffield Hallam University.

Jane Krishnadas is a Senior Lecturer in Law and the Conceptor and Convenor of the Community Legal Outreach Collaboration, Keele (CLOCK) at Keele University School of Law.

LawWorks (the Solicitors Pro Bono Group) is a charity working in England and Wales to connect volunteer lawyers with people in need of legal advice, who are not eligible for legal aid and cannot afford to pay and with the not-for-profit organisations that support them.

Tony Martin is a solicitor and Head of Clinics at BPP University Pro Bono Centre. He is also a freelance trainer and Chair of Hammersmith and Fulham Law Centre.

Hugh McFaul is a Senior Lecturer in Law and Co-Director of the Open Justice Centre at The Open University.

Tribe Mkwebu is a Senior Lecturer in Law at Northumbria Law School, University of Northumbria. He is also a Clinic Supervisor within the University's Student Law Office.

Donald Nicolson is Professor of Law and Director of the University of Essex Law Clinic and was founding Director of Law Clinics at the Universities of Strathclyde and Bristol. He is on the editorial board of *Legal Ethics* and *the International Journal of the Legal Profession* and a trustee of the Clinical Legal Education Organisation.

Julie Price is a Professor in Law in the School of Law and Politics at Cardiff University and heads the Cardiff Law School Pro Bono "Law in the Real World" schemes.

Frances Ridout is a Senior Lecturer and Supervising Barrister at Queen Mary University of London. She is the Director (Clinical Legal Education) of the Queen Mary Legal Advice Centre.

Beverley Rizzotto is a senior lecturer and manager of the Legal Advice Centre at the University of Wolverhampton. She is also a practising solicitor in the West Midlands region.

Victoria Roper is a Senior Lecturer at Northumbria University, Newcastle upon Tyne. She is a Trustee of the UK Clinical Legal Education Organisation (CLEO), a Senior Fellow of the HEA and a member of national Education and Training Committee of the Law Society for England and Wales.

Francine Ryan is a Senior Lecturer and Director of the Open Justice Centre at The Open University. She is also responsible for the operation and supervision of the Open Justice Law Clinic.

Michael Sales is a software developer with over 15 years' experience in public and private sector roles, currently working at Newcastle University providing web and collaborative development support to the university research community.

Christopher Simmonds is a Senior Lecturer at Northumbria Law School.

Rachel Stalker is a Senior Lecturer and Solicitor in the School of Law at Liverpool John Moores University. She established the pro bono Legal Advice Centre in 2014 and coordinates its continuing work.

Ann Thanaraj is the founder and host of 'Lawyering in a Digital Age: Equipping students for technologically advancing practice of law', an international initiative which brings together a global audience to shape the direction of legal education fit for a digital age; Ann is also Head of Online Learning at Teesside University and former Head of Law at University of Cumbria.

Linden Thomas is a Senior Lecturer and Supervising Solicitor of the pro bono programmes at the University of Birmingham Law School. She also manages the School's Centre for Professional Legal Education and Research (CEPLER) and is Co-Chair of the Clinical Legal Education Organisation.

Lucy Yeatman is a Lecturer in Law at the University of Liverpool and an in-house solicitor specialising in family law at the Liverpool Law Clinic.

Introduction

Linden Thomas

The inception of this Handbook can be traced back to the Clinical Legal Education Organisation[1] conference in June 2016, where I presented an early draft of a paper in which I argued that law clinics were in a regulatory black hole.[2] The paper was born out of the frustrations I experienced as a newcomer to clinical legal education (CLE), trying to navigate my way through the regulatory maze in which the rules governing the provision of pro bono services by university law clinics seemed, to me, to be hidden.

Despite CLE having gone through a period of significant and sustained growth in the preceding years,[3] I had not been able to locate any accessible source of guidance setting out why it was that I was allowed to provide legal advice to members of the public on behalf of my institution, or whether there might be any restrictions on me doing so.

The information I needed to know was all in the public domain. However, I found myself having to piece it together bit by bit, drawing on a wide range of different sources in order to do so, which was both time-consuming and frustrating. It was also a little daunting, not least because I felt it would have been all too easy to be ignorant of the existence of certain legislative limitations on the type of legal services I could provide, some of which carry criminal sanctions for breach. No guidance published by the regulator at that time seemed to have been drafted with the growing number of universities acting as a forum for pro bono legal services provision in mind.

From the discussion that followed my presentation, it became clear that I was not the only person to have had this experience. Like me, many clinicians had come straight out of private practice, where someone else had had overall responsibility for compliance and had put in place the processes and procedures to be followed. With no obvious source of guidance, many of us found ourselves navigating new waters and wondering what we didn't know

---

1   The Clinical Legal Education Organisation (CLEO) is a charity that provides encouragement, expertise and support to develop clinical legal education in UK law schools. See **Part 6** for further details.

2   This was later published in the following article: Linden Thomas, 'Law clinics in England and Wales: A regulatory black hole' (2017) *The Law Teacher*, early online publication <https://www.tandfonline.com/doi/full/10.1080/03069400.2017.1322858> accessed 23 July 2019.

3   A 2014 report published by LawWorks revealed that by the end of 2013, at least 70 per cent of all UK law schools were delivering some form of pro bono or clinical legal education. See D Carney, F Dignan, R Grimes, G Kelly and R Parker, *The LawWorks Law School and Pro Bono Clinic Report 2014* (LawWorks, 2014) <https://www.LawWorks.org.uk/solicitors-and-volunteers/resources/LawWorks-law-school-pro-bono-and-clinics-report-2014> accessed 22 August 2019.

that we didn't know. I therefore offered to write a short guide, setting out what I had learnt. In response, I received an outpouring of offers from other clinicians volunteering to write about aspects of setting up, running and delivering law clinics that they had particular knowledge and experience of. Thus, the idea to pull these contributions together into this *Clinical Legal Education Handbook* was formed.

From its earliest stages then, the Handbook has been a wholly collaborative effort and is a testament to the generous and cooperative nature of the CLE community. The structure and contents were informed by a group of nearly 20 clinicians working in law schools the length and breadth of the country, many of whom went on to write sections for the final version.

The Handbook is intended to be a practical guide that will be of use to clinicians, whether they are new to CLE and trying to work out where and how to begin, or have been working in the field for some time and wish to develop a new project or else find themselves encountering a new challenge in an established clinic and in need of a steer as to how to respond.

There is one health warning about this book that it is incumbent upon me to set out here. One of the (many) virtues of a law clinic is that it is versatile: there are as many different models of clinic as there are clinics.[4] Each one is tailored to meet the specific requirements of the environment in which it is set. A clinic's structure and design will depend upon a multiplicity of factors, including the institution in which it is hosted, the resources it has available to it, the client need it is intended to meet and the educational objectives it proposes to realise. Consequently, there is seldom a 'one size fits all' approach to ensuring regulatory and legislative compliance, and so the contents of the Handbook should not be relied on as a substitute for independent legal advice where it is required.

Precisely which policy or practice ought to be introduced to any clinic will be influenced, among other things, by institutional policy, processes and attitude to risk. However, I hope the Handbook will address the abovementioned concern reported by clinicians that they 'don't know what they don't know', and that the explanations and recommendations within these pages will help you to feel more comfortable and confident in spotting potential areas of risk and making informed decisions as to whether and when you need to seek further guidance on the application of particular rules or laws in their own context.

The Handbook consists of seven parts. **Part 1: Law clinics: What, why and how?** puts CLE into context. It proposes an inclusive definition of CLE and offers guidance on:

---

4   For more on the many and varied models of clinic, see **Part 1**.

- how best to make the business case for your clinic
- what to consider in order to ensure your clinic is properly funded and that the requirements of key stakeholders are realised
- the practical details that ought to be taken into account when determining how to set up a new clinic.

Part 1 also offers a comparative overview of five different live client clinics and concludes with a number of case studies, which demonstrate the breadth of clinical models available to choose from.

Part 2: Regulatory framework offers guidance on the regulatory and legislative framework which impacts on the way that clinics are established and run.[5] As is inevitably the case when one writes about law and regulation, nothing stands still. At the time of writing,[6] the Solicitors Regulation Authority (SRA) has released a new set of Standards and Regulations[7] which will replace the 2011 SRA Handbook[8] on 25 November 2019.

To the extent possible and in order to ensure that this Handbook remains a useful resource for as long as possible, the sections in Part 2 reflect the position under the incoming Standards and Regulations and the accompanying guidance that has been published to date. References to the equivalent 2011 Handbook rules are also included for completeness. Any legislative and regulatory developments, or associated guidance, released into the public domain on or after 22 August 2019 will not be reflected.

In **Part 3: Assessment in clinics: Principles, practice and progress**, Grimes and Rizzotto offer guidance for anyone contemplating how they might assess participation in their law clinic. They consider what is meant by assessment, why we might assess clinic work and what methods can be used to do so. They also explore the purpose and value of feedback and the role it has to play in ensuring continuous development for supervisors and students alike.

In **Part 4: Research on clinical legal education**, Mkwebu explores the fertile ground for research that CLE provides. In a detailed literature review, he offers an in-depth analysis of research carried out in the field to date and organises the literature on CLE into five themes:

---

5   **Part 2** focuses predominantly on the position in England and Wales. Therefore, readers in other jurisdictions will need to check the situation under the applicable laws and regulations.

6   August 2019.

7   SRA, Standards and Regulations (20 March 2019) <https://www.sra.org.uk/sra/policy/future/resources.page#resources> accessed 23 July 2019.

8   The SRA Handbook was introduced in 2011 and has been subject to a number of revisions. Solicitors Regulation Authority, *Handbook* (6 December 2018, version 21) <https://www.sra.org.uk/handbook/> accessed 23 July 2019.

- emotional wellbeing of students and academic staff
- reflection and assessment
- skills development and employability
- the social justice mission
- the regulatory framework.

In doing so, he presents a comprehensive yet accessible introduction for newcomers to CLE into the breadth of literature available. He also identifies gaps in the literature, which may serve as a roadmap for those clinicians – both experienced and new – seeking direction as to where to focus their own future research activity.

Part 5: Precedent documents and resources contains a bank of documents kindly shared by a number of universities and individuals, which you are welcome to adopt and tailor as required to suit your own context. The documents have been grouped into the following five categories:

- contracts and handbooks
- policies and procedures
- checklists and practice documents
- learning and teaching
- other useful resources.

Contained in **Part 6: Glossary of clinical legal education networks**, these are a list of networks that provide an incredibly valuable forum for sharing of good practice in relation to CLE and all that it encompasses. Events and conferences organised by such networks can offer sources of inspiration for new models of clinic, information about innovations both in method and mode of delivery, insights into the latest research and an opportunity for shared learning about good pedagogy,[9] among many other things. We hope including this glossary will enable those who are new to CLE to access these networks and begin to benefit from all that they have to bestow at an early stage in their clinical careers.

I referred earlier in this introduction to that unsettling sense of not knowing what one doesn't know, and my hope that this Handbook will go some way to remedying this for those with responsibility for running law clinics. However, there are some lessons that simply have to be learnt through experience. Indeed, isn't that precisely what CLE is all about?

---

9   For those interested in learning more pedagogical approaches to CLE teaching, there are a wealth of materials available. Some such sources are referenced in the literature review in **Part 4**. See also, for example, David McQuoid-Mason and Robin Palmer, *African Law Clinicians' Manual* (Open Society Foundation, 2013, 2nd edn) available at <http://www.cleo-uk.org>.

Therefore, included in the postscript to this Handbook at **Part 7: 'Things I wish I'd known before I started doing clinical legal education'** are reflections from clinicians who have been involved in CLE for some time. I hope you will enjoy reading their words of wisdom as much as I did.

Before I bring this Introduction to a close, there are a number of people to whom I wish to offer my thanks for their assistance in turning the idea for this Handbook into a reality.

First, thank you to the many contributors for offering your time and expertise for the benefit of the clinical community.

Thank you also to our publisher, the Institute of Advanced Legal Studies, for your support (and patience) and for recognising the merit in making this Handbook available as an open access resource.

A particular thank you also to Richard Grimes, who not only wrote some parts of this Handbook, but also offered feedback on a number of sections. You remain a fountain of knowledge and most valued champion for all things CLE.

Last, but by no means least, by far the biggest thanks must go to my co-editor, Nick Johnson. It has been a pleasure working with you and I can say with absolute certainty that this book would not have been what it is without your help and support. Thank you.

I will conclude by saying simply that I hope that you, the users of this Handbook, find it to be a valuable resource that informs and enables your clinical practice, so that you may focus your energies where they are most valuable: delivering high quality legal education and promoting access to justice.

Linden Thomas

August 2019

Part 1
Law clinics: What, why and how?

Part 1
Law clinics: What, why and how?

Lydia Bleasdale, Beverley Rizzotto, Rachel Stalker, Lucy Yeatman, Hugh McFaul, Francine Ryan, Nick Johnson and Linden Thomas

What is clinical legal education?

Defining 'clinical legal education' (CLE), or a 'clinic', is not straightforward, as it takes many forms. To borrow a metaphor,[1] one can conceive of CLE as a *cathedral* on the one hand, or a *bazaar* on the other.

Treating a clinic as a *cathedral* – defining very narrowly what its architecture must look like, what resources and materials it must have available, who may enter and what activities must be conducted therein – is to discourage the maverick creative spark which is so often the very hallmark of CLE.

A richer approach, better reflecting realities, is to imagine a clinic instead as a *bazaar* – open to all who wish to both enhance legal education and seek to improve access to justice for the wider public. Some 'stalls' may appear more frequently than others, and each will conduct their business in a unique way, but each stallholder's underlying ethos is broadly similar.

Although it may not be easy to come up with a comprehensive definition of CLE, there are two common denominators for all clinics:

- the delivery of a legal service (actual or simulated)
- the participation of law students (and possibly others), acting under professional supervision where necessary.

For the purposes of this Handbook, by 'clinical legal education' we mean any clinic activity (as defined above), whether accredited or extra-curricular:

> in which each student takes responsibility for legal or law-related work for a client (whether real or simulated) in collaboration with a supervisor. Structures enable each student to receive feedback on their contributions and to take the opportunity to learn from their experiences through reflecting on matters including their interactions with the client, their colleagues and their supervisor

---

1   Eric S Raymond, *The cathedral and the bazaar: Musings on Linux and Open Source by an accidental revolutionary* (O'Reilly Media, 1999).

as well as the ethical dimensions of the issues raised and the impact of the law and legal processes.[2]

While many university law clinics will follow similar models, they will vary to differing degrees in terms of focus and method of delivery. In the remainder of Part 1, reference to a 'clinic' indicates a university clinic involving real clients unless otherwise stated. Such clinics involve the provision of some combination of legal information, advice, casework and/or representation to clients on an individual basis.

There are currently approximately 229 live client clinics operating in the UK, around two-fifths of which are university law clinics.[3] We provide examples of different models of clinic in further detail later on in Part 1.

Many clinics will also encompass other types of projects, which are aimed at delivering general public education and/or increasing legal empowerment in the wider local community or for a particular community group, rather than advising on and/or resolving clients' individual legal problems through a live client clinic run by the university. Examples of such activity include:

- public legal education, such as 'Streetlaw' (also commonly referred to as 'Street Law')[4]
- research and reporting projects, often carried out for non-governmental or not-for-profit organisations
- externships, which see students volunteer with and under the supervision of third party advice agencies.

Further examples of each of the above are provided later in Part 1. However, the majority of Part 1 and indeed, this Handbook, focuses on university-led, live client clinics rather than public legal education-oriented programmes, or programmes run and supervised externally to universities. This in part reflects the relative complexity involved in establishing a university-led clinic and also the popularity of this model.

---

2   Jeff Giddings, *Promoting justice through clinical legal education* (Justice Press, 2013), p. 14.

3   LawWorks, *LawWorks Clinics Network Report April 2017–March 2018*, published December 2018 <https://www.lawworks.org.uk/sites/default/files/files/LW-Clinics-Report-2017-18-web.pdf> accessed 3 July 2019.

4   See, for example: Richard Grimes, David McQuoid-Mason, Ed O'Brien and Judy Zimmer, 'Street Law and social justice education' in Frank S Bloch (ed), *The global clinical movement: Educating lawyers for social justice* (Oxford University Press, 2011); and Seán Arthurs, Melinda Cooperman, Jessica Gallagher, Freda Grealy, John Lunney, Rob Marrs and Richard Roe, 'From zero to 60: Building belief, capacity and community in Street Law instructors in one weekend' (2017) *International Journal of Clinical Legal Education* 4(2), 118–241.

Designing your live client clinic

There are many different models of live client clinic, with various combinations of supervision, management and insurance being possible across all of these models. All of these options are equally valid and will depend entirely on the administrative, strategic and financial considerations unique to the school where a clinic may be established. When considering how a new clinic should be managed, and where it ought to be located, you would be well advised to consider Donald Nicolson's matrix for plotting clinical models.[5]

Nicolson considers there to be two dimensions to the development of clinics:

- The 'organisational dimension', which is broadly concerned with how clinics are run, including whether student engagement within them is compulsory, whether the activities are assessed, and whether clinics are primarily focused upon social justice or upon student learning.[6]
- The 'activities dimension', which includes considerations such as the physical location of the clinic (in the community or on campus), whether the service offered includes generalist legal advice or more specialist legal advice, and whether the service includes an element of educating the public about their legal rights, as opposed to focusing only upon advising on existing problems.[7]

Where a particular law school chooses to sit within this matrix will be determined by a range of considerations, some of which are likely to be beyond the direct control of those establishing the clinic. For example, the decision may be influenced by the extent of available professional supervision, the extent of existing legal provision within the community, the location of the campus, its accessibility and its associated suitability for an on-campus service, and the basis on which funding is provided in support of such activities.

Nevertheless, many aspects of the clinical strategy will be within the control of those establishing the clinic itself, and it is important to consider the following issues.

Who do you want to work with, and why?

If operating a clinic on campus, are you happy to receive client referrals from other organisations? If so, will these be from any organisation, and will this be on a formal or an 'as and when' basis? How would a more formal arrangement

---

5   Donald Nicolson, '"Our roots began in South Africa": Modelling law clinics to maximise social justice ends' (2016) *International Journal of Clinical Legal Education* 23(3), 87–136.

6   Ibid at p. 87.

7   Ibid at p. 88.

work, and how would you avoid creating extra work for those agencies through the referral system?

If you are partnering with external agencies and running a clinic off campus, will you be selective about who you partner with? If so, on what basis? Will you only partner with established agencies (who potentially offer a larger pool of clients, due to being more embedded), or will you partner with those who are newer (who potentially offer fewer clients to start with, but who may offer the opportunity to work collaboratively on a new and exciting project)? Will you work with charities and third sector agencies only, or would you consider statutory bodies, such as local councils?

How will the insurance be arranged?

Consider if arranging insurance might it be easier under one model than under another. For example, if students are to be trained and supervised by an external body, it is feasible to suggest that insurance ought to come from that body. Conversely, if the students are being trained and supervised by staff internal to the university, there is a strong case for saying the university's insurance ought to cover those activities (rather than, for example, additional insurance being bought in by the law school).

For further guidance on insurance, see **Part 2.3** of this Handbook.

Health and safety policies within the university

These should not restrict you from engaging with a particular model of clinic, but you will need to be mindful of them and engage with the relevant unit of the university in order to ensure policies are complied with (whether the clinic is based within the law school, or operates off campus).

Will you offer appointments?

Or would you prefer to run the clinic on a drop-in basis?

Will your clinic offer advice and/or form-filling only, or representation as well?

In non-contentious matters, will the clinic draft and/or negotiate documentation on the client's behalf? The type of service you offer may be influenced by the regulatory position of those supervising the clinic work.

See **Part Two** for further guidance on the regulatory status of solicitors and barristers working in university law schools.

How will you incorporate flexibility within the clinic, not only for clients and lawyers but also for students?

Can you be flexible about when and where the clinics take place, to allow for different people to get involved at different times? For example, family clinics might best be held in the middle of the day, when those seeking advice about domestic violence matters may be more able to leave the house.

Can some clinics be held in the daytime in order to allow all parties with caring responsibilities to have their evenings free? Can part-time students participate in clinics or will appointment times clash with teaching times? Can client interviews be conducted via Skype or telephone?

Once these intended outcomes – perhaps best framed within the context of a clinic (or law school) strategy – are clear, the model can then follow.

However, the model will not solely depend upon the intended outcomes for the law school, but also upon factors which are, to a greater or lesser extent, outside of the control of those formulating the clinic. For example, it might be that in order to meet the intended objectives, a large-scale in-house clinic suite of office and client interviewing space would be preferable. However, this might be unreasonable to consider and/or suggest in light of available law school finances. In short, the intended outcomes must be pragmatically aligned with what is feasible within a particular law school's context.

Business case for a clinic

Clinics can be expensive to operate, with costs varying according to the model adopted, the insurance arrangements in place, the extent of the service offered, the scale of the activity and the staffing and supervisory arrangements.[8] However, there are numerous universal benefits to engaging in clinical activities, and these should be clearly articulated to those whose approval for investment in clinical work must be gained.

Internal stakeholders

Within the university, those who must approve the costs associated with the clinic potentially include a Head of School and/or Head of Faculty, university in-house legal team, university insurance officer, and senior management teams.

The need to make the case to some of these parties might be more obvious in some instances than in others: Heads of School and/or Faculty are likely to

---

8   More detailed guidance on the costs involved in establishing and resourcing a clinic are addressed later in Part 1.

have the final say as to whether or not staff resources (e.g. workload time, new appointments), other financial resources (e.g. travel costs, postage costs), and/or physical resources (e.g. computers, office space) can be allocated to clinical activities. Equally, however, a university insurance department might wish to understand why clinic activities should and need to be covered.

The following points could be of assistance when making the business case within the university.

Development of student skills and awareness

Depending upon the model of clinic adopted, skills that students can gain through involvement with a clinic include researching, drafting, interviewing, note-taking, form-filling, listening, team-working, time management, client care, and/or verbal presentations, alongside gaining broader educational benefits, such as the potential to enhance their substantive legal knowledge, emotional intelligence, ethical awareness and professional responsibility.[9]

Clinic work also affords students an opportunity to gain confidence through situations that might take them outside of their comfort zones. Students can gain a greater understanding of the law and of access to justice, potentially including areas of law that are not part of the core curriculum. They can also gain exposure to clients with whom they might ordinarily have little or no contact, thereby ensuring their legal education provides them with insight into the practical effects of the law on differing sections of society, and helping to prepare them for a variety of workplaces with diverse client groups/service users. All of these gains arguably illustrate why CLE ought to form part of a law school's offering.

Professional insight

Students can gain greater 'hands-on' insight into the legal profession, including (depending upon the clinic supervision model) through working with members of that profession. This, coupled with the development of the skills outlined above, can feed into the university's employability strategy.

---

9   See, for example: Kevin Kerrigan and Victoria Murray (eds), *A student guide to clinical legal education and pro bono* (MacMillan Education, 2011); Jonny Hall and Kevin Kerrigan, 'Clinic and the wider law curriculum' (2011) *International Journal of Clinical Legal Education* 15, 25–37; Colin James and Felicity Wardhaugh, 'Enhancing emotional competencies with law students' (2016) *International Journal of Clinical Legal Education*, 23(4), 53–88; Ann Thanaraj, 'Understanding how a law clinic can contribute towards students' development of professional responsibility' (2016) *International Journal of Clinical Legal Education* 23(4), 89–135; Carol Boothby and Cath Sylvester, 'Getting the fish to see the water: An investigation into students' perceptions of learning writing skills in academic modules and in a final year real client legal clinic module' (2017) *The Law Teacher* 51:2, 123–37; Donald Nicholson, '"Education, education, education": Legal, moral and clinical' (2008) *The Law Teacher* 42(2), 145–72; and Colin James, 'Lawyers' wellbeing and professional legal education' (2008) *The Law Teacher* 42(1), 85–97.

Community engagement

Clinics afford an opportunity to embed university activities within the community, a matter of increasing strategic importance.[10] Although university strategies commonly reference the importance of internationalisation, many will also have a civic mission and will therefore recognise the importance of contributing positively to the local community. Clinics can assist with this, particularly where advice is given to clients beyond the university community of staff and students.

Student wellbeing

Some commentators draw a link between wellbeing and altruism,[11] which (again depending upon the model of clinic adopted, specifically whether it is assessed or co-curricular) might support pro bono activities within law schools. Given the importance of student wellbeing and the national focus on this matter,[12] this is another positive aspect of clinical work that might be emphasised at university level.

Student recruitment

With the majority of law schools now offering some form of pro bono work[13] there is arguably a legitimate expectation on the part of students that these opportunities will exist at law school. It may therefore be a deciding factor in a student's choice of one institution over another, thereby adding a commercial justification.

Routes to qualification as a solicitor

The current proposals for the Solicitors Qualifying Examination (SQE) expressly

---

10   See, for example, <https://www.universitiesuk.ac.uk/blog/Pages/Acting-locally-universities-reconnecting-with-communities.aspx> accessed 15 August 2019.

11   See, for example, DLA Piper's former head of pro bono, Amy Heading <https://www.youtube.com/watch?v=_FQqlvmXSJI> accessed 15 August 2019.

12   See, for example, Universities UK, *Student mental wellbeing in higher education: Good practice guide*   <https://www.universitiesuk.ac.uk/policy-and-analysis/reports/Documents/2015/student-mental-wellbeing-in-he.pdf> accessed 16 August 2019; Times Higher Education, *Student experience survey 2017: Investigating well-being at university* (26 March 2017) <https://www.timeshighereducation.com/student/blogs/student-experience-survey-2017-investigating-well-being-university> accessed 16 August 2019.

13   A 2014 study found that at least 70 per cent of law schools in the UK had pro bono/clinical initiatives: see Damian Carney, Frank Dignan, Richard Grimes, Grace Kelly and Rebecca Parker, *The LawWorks Law School Pro Bono and Clinic Report 2014* <https://www.lawworks.org.uk/sites/default/files/LawWorks-student-pro-bono-report%202014.pdf> accessed 3 July 2019. The most recent LawWorks report (**note 3**) reports a net gain in the number of clinics in their network in the year 2017–18. It is not specified whether these are based in universities or not, and not all university law clinics join the LawWorks network. However, it is likely that the percentage of law schools that offer pro bono work will have increased since 2014 and constitutes the majority.

state that experience in a law clinic might be counted as part of the requisite two-year qualifying work experience needed to qualify as a solicitor under the new regime.[14]

Furthermore, Stage 2 of the SQE will assess students on Client Interviewing, Advocacy/Persuasive Oral Communication, Case and Matter Analysis, Legal Research and Written Advice and Legal Drafting – most of which, if not all, can be experienced in clinic.

Again, in order to ensure consistent and competitive admission rates, universities have a commercial interest in providing adequate resourcing for clinics in order to maximise opportunities for those students who wish to qualify as a solicitor upon graduation.

For further guidance on clinics and qualifying work experience under the SQE, see **Part 2.9**.

Research and CLE

Clinics offer rich research opportunities for staff involved in areas such as social justice and pedagogy. Such research projects can often be pursued in collaboration with students, other schools and departments internally, and universities and third sector partners externally. Clinics can therefore align with and enhance the research agendas of many law schools.

Further detail on CLE and research is contained in **Part 4** of this Handbook.

External stakeholders

The business case for clinics might also need to be made outside of the university, particularly where the clinics will rely (wholly, or in part) upon supervision from external lawyers or other partners. Although lawyers will often have some understanding of the benefits of undertaking pro bono work, it can be helpful to illustrate two particular benefits to them (personally and collectively) when attempting to secure their involvement:

1. **Working with students**
   - Undertaking clinic work with students is of dual benefit to lawyers:
     - There exists the opportunity to familiarise oneself with students who, in the near future, may wish to apply for employment in the legal

---

14   See 'A new route to qualification: The Solicitors Qualifying Examination (SQE)', April 2017, p.   10   <https://www.sra.org.uk/globalassets/documents/sra/consultations/sqe-summary-document.pdf?version=4a1ad1> accessed 19 February 2020. The SQE will be a centralised examination, to be launched in 2021, which those wishing to be admitted as a solicitor will need to pass.

sector. Working with them in clinics gives lawyers the opportunity to engage with potential applicants, which could be useful to both the lawyer and the applicant during later recruitment stages.

–   Whether the clinic students wish to become lawyers or not, clinics offer an opportunity for lawyers to support and influence the next generation of the workforce. Lawyers at Leeds University's clinic, for example, often report gaining enjoyment from doing so, and from being able to work with a different set of people to those they usually encounter. They report the optimism, excitement and genuine interest in the law on the part of students as something that they take pleasure in seeing and helping to develop.

2. Working with clients

•   Allied to the previous point about working with students, lawyers will often particularly enjoy working with clinic clients, especially if the clients they usually encounter in their day job are of a different background and have different types of queries to the clients they deal with in the clinic. Working in clinics, even if they are advising within their usual area(s) of practice, provides for some diversity in their working lives and can even enhance the skill sets of more junior lawyers, in particular. For example, lawyers working for firms that tend to act for corporate and commercial clients may get the opportunity to act for individual clients through the clinic, thereby developing their own practice experience.

Finally, where the clinic takes place within an existing advice agency, or where students work solely off site and are supervised and trained by external partners, the business case must also be made to the host agency or organisation. When seeking to place volunteers within any type of agency, these placements come with associated costs. As far as external partners are concerned, the following factors can be persuasive:

•   Provided you are not competing with existing services, but rather are complementing those in existence and perhaps filling a need that the host agency cannot meet (and is not going to be able to meet in the foreseeable future),[15] the service offered can alleviate pressures on them.

•   For some partners, working with students is an opportunity to showcase the areas of law in which they work, with a view to encouraging students to consider potential future employment in these areas of law. For example, one project, working with a council's welfare rights

---

15   For example, if an organisation cannot provide advice in the area of family law – and does not foresee employing advisers to do so – then a clinic service operating within that area would potentially be welcomed as 'filling a gap'.

unit, found that the unit's director was particularly keen to highlight the availability of paid roles in the welfare rights field: it is seemingly very difficult to recruit suitable people into welfare rights law, and this pro bono collaboration provided a way of showcasing the area to potential future employees.

- The provision by an external partner of premises from which to operate a clinic can be a crucial benefit for the university, particularly where rent would otherwise cause costs to rocket and potentially render a clinic inoperable. However, creating and building upon long-term partnerships can achieve benefits for both parties, such as increasing the footfall in a shopping centre by holding the clinic in a designated unit, and developing other ways in which partners can work together that are mutually beneficial. This may not be related to the clinic at all, but the aim is to forge a working relationship between the university and external partner to ensure that smaller individual agreements (the lease of premises at a reduced rent) remain in place.

When seeking to form relationships with external parties – whether lawyers or agencies – there are some things you can do to both generate these initial conversations, and increase the possibility of them bearing fruit:

- **Use your students**: they will be your best ambassadors! Consider involving them in pitches, if possible, and encourage them to suggest firms with whom they undertake work experience to get involved with the clinics. Students will also have their own networks, which can be beneficial to the clinic, so encourage them to look out for pro bono opportunities. For example, the University of Birmingham recently launched a clinic in conjunction with a charity following an introduction from a student who had volunteered with the organisation.

- **Keep in touch with graduates of the law school**: they could one day become your clinic volunteers. Similarly, make use of your university's alumni network, if it has one, as well as sites such as LinkedIn, Twitter and Facebook (both to contact known graduates and to advertise volunteering opportunities).

- **Nominate, nominate, nominate**: once you have a project, consider nominating it for any local, national and/or university awards for collaborative working, student volunteering, etc. These awards are a welcome boost to any team, and even being shortlisted is excellent publicity for both the law school and any external partners. New potential partners will be keen on such positive publicity.

- **Try to avoid requiring huge amounts of time from legal practitioners**: particularly as the end of the financial year approaches. Advance scheduling can mitigate the risk of over-reliance on a busy external practitioner or of supervisors having to decline to attend due to pressure of work. For example, the clinic at Liverpool John Moores University agrees the schedule for appointments and drop-in clinics with its external supervising solicitors in the summer prior to the start of the next academic year, rather than trying to source supervisors on an ad hoc basis as and when client enquiries are received once term is underway.

- **Set up a clinic advisory board representing all stakeholders** both within and outside the university: this can provide invaluable guidance and advice to clinicians, as well as helping to inform annual clinic strategies.
- **Undertake annual reviews with partners**: this can help to ensure that expectations are being met on each side, and to jointly devise plans for the forthcoming year.

How to set up a clinic

Once an appropriate model has been identified, to ensure the smooth running of your project you need to put in place regulation and compliance, financial issues and staffing resources, student training, office processes and appropriate signposting or referral practices.

Regulation and compliance

There are a number of practical regulatory and compliance issues to consider when setting up a clinic. For example:

- Who will supervise the work done in the clinic and what type of work are they authorised to do?
- Are there any legislative or regulatory restrictions or limitations on the type of service you intend to offer?
- What insurance arrangements do you need to put into place?
- What client care processes do you need to introduce?
- How will you ensure that client and student data is kept safe and secure?

All of the above regulatory and compliance issues and more are dealt with in detail in **Part 2**.

Financial issues and staffing resources

As outlined above, when establishing – or for that matter expanding – a university law clinic, except in the most unusual cases there will be cost and resource implications for the institution hosting the project. Law schools are typically perceived as cost-efficient departments, offering a popular subject at low cost and ultimately making a significant contribution to the financial health of the institutions of which they are a part. For those seeking to establish or develop a clinic, the cost of the project will be uppermost in the minds of those who will either approve or reject the proposal.

Many law schools in other jurisdictions, especially the USA, have relied on substantial charitable donations to establish and run law clinics. The fact that clinics can meet both educational and social justice objectives make them a prime focus for donations. Most UK universities now have substantial teams of staff devoted to seeking donations, often from wealthy alumni who are keen to give something back to their former university or college. Other sources of funding, such as (at the time of writing) EU funding, or support from charitable trusts, such as the Legal Education Foundation, can also make a substantial contribution to the work of a clinic.

While such external support is welcome, it is important to note that even the most substantial donation is only likely to support a project in the short term or provide a specific resource. Further, gifts or grants may come with strings attached, and the process of accounting for how such money has been spent can itself be time-consuming and costly. Ultimately, most sustainable clinic projects have direct financial support from their institutions.

For law school heads and those they report to within the university structure, clinics are often seen as a substantial drain on resources.[16] Most university law schools work on a financial model that considers them as making an income from students, research grants, etc. and then making a specific contribution to the institution to support central services such as estate, administration, library and so on. For law schools, given their comparatively low cost base, such contributions are often substantially higher than from others, such as science and technology departments. Therefore, arguing for even relatively small sums to establish clinics locally within schools must be set against the background of local management's need to meet a school's contribution.

Against this background it is important for those seeking finance to stress the business case for clinics, as outlined above. Given that clinics can be significant factors in student recruitment and, as suggested above, can have a substantial impact on raising the profile of a law school, being able to offer prospective students the opportunity to gain experience in a clinic will appeal to most law school management teams, particularly in the light of greater competition among universities for students at all levels.

---

16   Mutaz Qafisheh, 'The role of legal clinics in leading legal education: A model from the Middle East' (2012) *Legal Education Review* 22(1), 177–98; John B Mitchell, 'And then suddenly Seattle University was on its way to a parallel, interactive curriculum' (1995) *Clinical Law Review* 2(1), 1–36, 5 (see also **Part 4**).

It should also be noted that although law school finances can vary substantially, depending on student recruitment from year to year, there is an element of stability in that most students in the public university sector continue for three years. As it can take several years to establish and develop a clinic, it is recommended that any bid for funding should look for at least three years' initial funding, which can be justified on the basis that this reflects a natural financial cycle.

When discussing financial requirements, much focus is often on the obvious costs that a clinic gives rise to, such as office equipment, physical space, the cost of practising certificates and matters such as phone calls, copying or stationery costs. Further, depending on the area of practice and the status of the clinic, there may be additional costs in professional indemnity insurance, IT and case management systems or know-how databases where user licences do not cover clinical activity. Of course, these cannot be ignored. Undoubtedly, though, the most significant resource for which money is needed is staff time. When considering financial issues, and seeking to establish or develop a service, it is vital that you clearly and realistically cost the amount of staff time needed to ensure the service is properly set up.

While clinics have often been established by academics simply using their own time to set up and run a project, this model is unlikely to be sustainable. Unless an institution is willing to invest the cost of staff time into establishing a clinic, either employing an individual specifically for that purpose or allocating a fixed level of staff time to run a clinic – or both – it is unlikely that such projects will endure. Even where external volunteer lawyers are relied upon to supervise work done in the clinic there will need to be some allocation of university staff time to manage those relationships and oversee the operation of the clinic. Staff who develop clinics without some form of significant timetable relief or time allocation will often find themselves having to discontinue a project to meet teaching or research commitments or otherwise risk career progression by continuing.[17]

Assuming there is a recognition that staff time needs to be made available, there is likely to be significant discussion as to the grade and status of such staff. Most clinics require a high level of administrative support, both during and often outside of term-time depending on the nature of the service provided. To ensure compliance with professional requirements, that client data remains protected and that confidentiality is preserved, it is likely the administrative function will need to be separated from the main school/department administrative team, whether or not it is undertaken by separate people.

---

17   Margaret M Barry, 'Clinical legal education in the law university: Goals and challenges' (2007) *International Journal of Clinical Legal Education* 7, 27–50.

There will therefore be a clear need for staff to provide this support and, in many cases, law schools will look to place this responsibility on professional clinic supervisors, perhaps providing some additional administrative support from within the faculty. The arguments as to the employment status of those working in clinics is well-rehearsed elsewhere.[18] It is worth bearing in mind that merging the role of administrator and case supervisor and employing staff on non-academic contracts may have a significant impact on the nature of the service provided. Employing someone without an educational background on a non-academic contract may mean that educational objectives are seen as secondary to service provision. What are clearly financial decisions – i.e. to employ a supervisor on a non-academic contract – can have a significant impact on the nature of project that emerges. You should also consider what career progression opportunities will be available to those engaged to run clinics on non-academic contracts.

Further, if new staff are recruited, job descriptions will be required. In costing a role, institutions will have job evaluation processes. When employing staff on professional support grades rather than academic contracts, such evaluations may result in staff being on lower pay grades and less favourable terms and conditions, as there may not be a recognition of the important teaching role a supervisor plays even in 'not for academic credit' clinics. Ideally, it is suggested, staff recruited should be on academic contracts, ensuring that clinic staff feel fairly treated as well as ensuring a link between clinic and non-clinic academic staff in a department, which may be difficult to sustain if clinic and traditional academic staff are employed on different terms.

If clinic staff are academics, you will need to consider how annual leave works among those engaged in the clinic. If the service offered is all year round and all staff are employed on academic contracts, which may have provision for staff to take leave over the summer, some variation to these provisions may be needed.

Further, it is worth giving consideration to time allocation for clinic time, especially where students are working for credit in a clinic. Time for more traditional forms of delivery, such as lectures and seminars, will probably be allocated to academic staff on the basis of a staffing formula allocating staff time for preparation, face-to-face teaching, assessment, etc. It is important to identify at an early stage the necessary resource commitment and funding for a clinic, particularly one that is for credit, and for a clear decision on the way in which staff time is to be credited.

---

18   David A Santacroce et al, 'The status of clinical faculty in the legal academy: Report of the Task Force on the status of clinicians and the legal academy' (2012) *Journal of the Legal Profession* 36 (2), 353.

To this end, there may be something to be gained, when considering how to allocate staff time, from looking at the way in which supervisory time in other disciplines is credited in staff work plans. Supervisor time in laboratories (science subjects) or studios (say, in fashion, art and design) will be allocated to academic and professional staff in a way that may mirror the type of supervision undertaken in a clinic. Law school managers may not be familiar with these ways of deploying staff time and it may be worth researching this within an institution to see what precedents there are. Of course, the level and nature of the supervision will vary depending on the subject; law students may well require closer and more intense supervision than art and design students. However, other departments may provide a useful starting point in considering this issue.

Finally, some thought may be given to how other income could be obtained for clinics. For some, which are set up as alternative business structures (see **Part 2.2**), there is a clear opportunity to charge fees, although this would need to fit with any charitable objectives. In addition, clients may wish to make small donations; again, few large clinics are likely to be able to rely on such income to replace core institutional funding.

Student training

There is no definitive guide that you must follow to ensure that student volunteers have the correct level of training to hit the ground running and begin their journey within clinical legal education. It will very much depend on a number of factors:

- **Clinic model that is in operation:** The more responsibility the student volunteers are given, for example conducting interviews and providing face-to-face advice (albeit under supervision), the more demanding the level of training that may be required.

- **Level of study of the volunteer:** Most undergraduate law degrees tend towards the theoretical and academic, with no emphasis on practical legal skills. Therefore students may begin volunteering with little or no legal work experience. Such a student would need more training and guidance, for example, than a post-graduate student working towards the Legal Practice Course diploma or equivalent, where practical legal skills are integrated into the course and their assessments.

- **Role of the student within the clinic:** As there is not a single model of clinic, the roles and responsibilities of student volunteers can differ within each model framework. Models that encourage students to take a more active role within the running of a clinic will of course need training on how to conduct themselves in fulfilling such a role, rather than just being given information about how the clinic operates.

- **Individual student needs and confidence levels:** When they first begin to volunteer, many students lack confidence and experience not just within the legal profession, but also within the work environment. Training will need to reflect this, by catering for all students and promoting inclusive learning. In order to achieve such an aim, it is useful for students to 'learn by doing' through engaging in practical activities such as role plays and mock interviews. Such training methods provide a good opportunity for students to get to know their fellow volunteers, and less confident students can then be identified and provided with additional support as necessary.

Students will benefit from training in the following areas:

- knowledge and understanding of the university's clinic, the services it provides and how it operates
- professional ethics and conduct[19]
- interviewing and advising
- communication skills.

Knowledge and understanding of the clinic

In order for students to be able to effectively carry out their role, whether as part of an assessed or extra-curricular activity, the service provided by the clinic – and how it operates – are fundamental pieces of information of which the student must be aware.

Training sessions can be an opportunity for new volunteers to access materials and precedents that they will come into contact with and use in the clinic, and to learn about their role within the clinic environment and what they will be expected to do. Many clinics operate in accordance with a handbook or manual. LawWorks provides a template of a handbook to members, which can be tailored to suit each clinic.[20] London South Bank University also developed a handbook specifically for drop-in clinics, and has made it available for others to adopt.[21] It provides an overview of the service they offer, information concerning the role and responsibilities of student volunteers, and resources they utilise. **Part 5.1** of this Handbook also contains a selection of precedent documents that a clinic can adopt and which can be used for training purposes.

19   This is obviously a wide area, and at a minimum student volunteers should understand the importance of client care and confidentiality, as well as the Principles contained in the Solicitors Regulation Authority Standards and Regulations and the Code of Conduct for Individuals.

20   LawWorks provides members with a wealth of information and materials to use at the clinic, including a template for a handbook, which includes a framework of how the clinic operates, rules and procedures and the student process.

21   <https://www.lsbu.ac.uk/__data/assets/pdf_file/0020/17291/lsbu-drop-in-clinic-manual.pdf> accessed 16 August 2019.

Students may be obliged to read and sign an agreement of cooperation in accordance with the clinic handbook, as this can demonstrate the importance and legitimacy of the volunteering role that they are undertaking; again, **Part 5.1** contains specimen draft agreements.

Setting boundaries for students to operate within the clinic environment is a way of managing expectations they may have in performing their role, and meeting the service users' expectations as to the service they provide. Enquiries can be dealt with accordingly, and if the student has been given proper training on, for example, the types of legal issue the clinic can deal with, they will know whether they need to take initial details from the client, or should try to signpost the client to other services if the clinic cannot assist.

If students are expected to signpost service users to other agencies or services that may be able to assist them when the clinic cannot, they should also be provided with an overview of local services that are available, and what issues each service can assist with. At the University of Wolverhampton, students are informed about such services with reference to the Wolverhampton Information and Advice Directory.[22] As part of their training, students are also provided with information about how to find a solicitor to assist with their issue, and whether legal aid may be available.

Further guidance on signposting and referrals is contained in **Part 2.6**.

Professional ethics and conduct

There has been much debate as to whether the subject of professional ethics in law should be incorporated into the undergraduate curriculum.[23] This is not presently compulsory until students undertake postgraduate-level vocational courses.[24] With the implementation of the SQE[25] those wishing to qualify as a solicitor will be required to address principles of professional conduct at Stage 1. Therefore, those law schools that wish to map their law degree on to the SQE requirements may well choose to incorporate professional ethics into undergraduate-level teaching.

---

22   Produced by the City of Wolverhampton Council to provide advisers with information about services and organisations in the Wolverhampton area that can give support and assistance to people in respect of welfare benefits, debt, housing and employment issues <https://www.wolverhampton.gov.uk/benefits/benefits-universal-credit-welfare-reform/wolverhampton-information-and-advice-directory> accessed 16 August 2019

23   H Brayne, N Duncan and R Grimes, *Clinical legal education: Active learning in your law school* (Blackstone Press, 1998).

24   The Legal Practice Course for aspiring solicitors and the Bar Professional Training Course for aspiring barristers.

25   <https://www.sra.org.uk/home/hot-topics/solicitors-qualifying-examination/> accessed 19 February 2020.

For student volunteers within a clinic dealing with real clients, an understanding of professional ethics – in particular client care and confidentiality – is crucial in order for them to actively apply such principles in the cases that they are engaged with. In order to ensure that students see the link between the ethical principles and the situations they may find themselves in within the clinic, it is recommended that the training includes some form of discussion or activity where students can apply such principles to fictional examples. This will help students to embed their learning and provide them with an opportunity to recognise, question and explore ethical dilemmas they may encounter when dealing with a client's matter.

Interviewing and advising

At most clinics, interviewing and advising will be an essential part of the service, and thus is a fundamental skill that students will practise through their experiential learning process as a volunteer.

When formulating a training session on interviewing and advising, consideration should be given to, but not limited to, the following:

- communication skills (including listening skills)
- preparation for the interview
- structure of the interview
- questioning techniques and the types of questions that should be asked (for example, when to use open questions and when to use closed questions)
- what kind of information needs to be elicited
- note-taking
- closing the interview.

Given that an underlying notion of clinical legal education is for students to learn 'on the job' and learn about the law by seeing it in action,[26] you should encourage experiential learning and practical activities within the training programme. Following the theory of andragogy, coined by Knowles (1985), 'adult learners' in higher education are usually learning for a purpose and will benefit from working in groups.[27] This can begin at the training stage, by involving students in their own training through use of role play, discussion and peer assessment. This also provides a valuable platform from which student volunteers can practise their interviewing skills, gaining confidence prior to interviewing real clients.

---

26   R Burridge, K Hinett, A Paliwala and T Varnava, *Effective learning and teaching in law* (Kogan Page, 2002).

27   W Kidd and G Czerniawski, *Successful Teaching 14-19: Theory, Practice and Reflection* (1st edn, Sage, 2010), p. 122.

This is best served as one of the final activities or sessions of training, when the students are familiar with the set-up of the clinic, expectations of them as a volunteer and the structure of the interview. It also provides the coordinator or manager with an opportunity to get to know the students, and to pair/group students accordingly, depending upon experience, level of study or confidence – or a combination of all of the above.

With regards to interviewing skills, some university clinics adopt a 'scaffolding' approach to the teaching and training of students. Students are first encouraged to consider through group discussion what makes for a good interview in terms of preparing both the environment and the interviewer, before building upon this discussion and – with the use of short videos of a 'good' interview and a 'poor' interview – prompting further discussion.[28] Role play, peer assessment and feedback would follow, allowing the student volunteers opportunity to practise their interviewing skills using a set pro forma (see **Part 5.3.4** for an interview aide memoire), prior to interviewing clients at the clinic.

Communication skills

As part of their role as clinic volunteers, it is essential for students to demonstrate and develop excellent communication skills. Such skills go beyond oral skills and conversing with clients, supervisors and fellow students. Many clinics operate their advice service by providing written advice, and thus it is often the students who will draft such letters. Students will therefore require some training on the principles of good written advice.

In such cases, as well as role play and other oral-based activities, it is good practice to incorporate written tasks into training sessions, and to provide students with hints and feedback as to good practice in letter drafting. For example, an activity could consist of students being given a set of simple client instructions and a summary of the law – perhaps from various sources[29] – that they would then use to draft a letter using lay terminology. A model answer could then be distributed, which students could use for self-assessment or peer assessment prior to being given generic feedback.

Supervision

Whatever your model of clinic is, students working on live client cases need to be closely supervised. It is this element of supervision that makes the work of the clinic labour-intensive and therefore expensive to deliver compared to traditional teaching methods such as lectures and seminars.

28   For example, see the interview techniques video produced by the University of Wolverhampton's Legal Advice Centre: <https://www.youtube.com/watch?v=yKkn3toIQJs&feature=youtu.be> accessed 16 August 2019.

29   For example, a summary of the law and the relevant statutory provisions.

When planning a clinic you need to think about how student work will be supervised and who will do this. Some clinics will have a dedicated member of staff whose role is solely to supervise the students and manage the day-to-day running of the clinic, while some clinics rely on practitioners who volunteer their time in order to ensure that students are providing the correct advice to their clients. Often, clinics will operate using a hybrid of both methods.

There are differing views on the level of supervision that students should be given when conducting clinical legal activities. It has been argued that a greater emphasis on students taking responsibility for their own learning is the best preparation they can undertake for the learning that they will eventually do in practice.[30] Some clinicians will not advocate this approach, for the reason that a balance needs to be struck between the benefit to the student in engaging in practical legal education, and the need for members of the community to be provided with sound and accurate legal advice which will not put them (or any potential case that they may have) at a detriment. Those supervising will also need to bear in mind their professional obligations, which are dealt with in **Part 2**.

The more experience the students have of working in the clinic the lighter touch the supervision can potentially be, and it is possible to make good use of peer learning by putting students into pairs or groups with mixed levels of experience. Some universities (such as the University of York) have developed a practice where postgraduate students of the clinical LLM are used for this purpose, and to assist in supervision.

When planning supervision, think about whether this will be done in small groups or in pairs, whether supervisors meet students face-to-face or give written feedback on their work. For example, how many drafts of a letter are you able to look at before it goes out to the client? If you only allow one draft, will the supervising lawyer then spend an inordinate amount of time rewriting letters? If you allow up to four or five drafts then will the client have to wait too long for their letter? There may be instances where supervisors have to intervene and assume ultimate responsibility for delivering timely advice to the client, and this should be considered when determining how many client matters a clinic can take on at any one time, to be commensurate with the time that a supervisor has to provide such a service.

When starting out with a new clinic, be realistic about how many students and client matters one member of staff can supervise, and be realistic with external volunteers about the amount of time needed to give feedback on student work.

---

30   Steven T Maher, 'The praise of folly: A defense of practice supervision in clinical legal education' (1990) 69 *Nebraska Law Review* 537.

Office processes and practical arrangements

Premises need not be large but they must be lockable and secure to protect client confidentiality and data protection obligations, while at the same time allowing students to be safely supervised. Hardcopy client records and/or sensitive data relating to students or clients will need to be stored in a locked cabinet in a locked room in order to comply with the requirements of the General Data Protection Regulation (for more on this, see **Part 2.14**). Means by which students are permitted access to the premises and to client data should be strictly controlled and form part of student training and/or your clinic handbook. IT systems will also need to be secure.

It is advisable to liaise with your data protection officers and security team to let them know when and where your clinic runs, and you should also be aware of your university's public liability insurance and out of hours working policies, or any other policies that may govern staff and students conducting activities with members of the public on or off university premises. Risk assessments of premises used for the clinic should be undertaken in accordance with the policies of your university's health and safety department.

Furthermore, clinics should be prepared for clients – and student volunteers – notifying the clinic prior to their appointment or participation in the clinic that they have a disability, which means they would have difficulty evacuating the premises in the event of a fire. Again, you should consult your university's policies to ensure that your practices comply with the requirements of the Equality Act 2010 and any associated/additional policies your institution may have. This is addressed in further detail below.

Disability

As clinics operate within universities and other higher education providers, they are subject to the same duties under the Equality Act 2010 (EA) as the institutions of which they are a part. In summary, these duties include:

- Eliminating unlawful discrimination, harassment and victimisation and other conduct prohibited by the EA.
- Advancing equality of opportunity between people from different groups. This involves considering the need to:
  - remove or minimise disadvantages suffered by people due to their protected characteristics
  - meeting the needs of people with protected characteristics
  - encourage people with protected characteristics to participate in public life or in other activities where their participation is low.

- Fostering good relations between people from different groups.[31]

Further, universities are bound by specific provisions of the EA that require, among other things, for a provider not to discriminate in the way it provides education or access to any of the services it provides. As disability is a protected characteristic under the EA, you should take into account the need to make reasonable adjustments.[32]

In terms of the provision of services, it is also incumbent on clinics to consider their EA duties in terms of providing services to members of the public. This requires clinics to ensure that their service provision does not discriminate against those with disabilities or other protected characteristics, and that reasonable adjustments are made in terms of service provision.

Clinics that are part of a university must also consider the issue of disability for staff, supervisors (if external) and students. For the former, this is clearly part of the employment relationship and will need to be addressed within the wider context of their relationship with their employer. For external supervisors and students, the issue may be different.

Disability and service provision

Some clients of a university law clinic will have some form of disability. To ensure that those with a disability can be properly accommodated, it is useful to build into your procedures provision for clients to be able to identify themselves as having a disability and to provide an indication of what sort of adjustment they may need. In addition to the duties outlined above, university clinics are service providers for the purposes of the EA and therefore must ensure they do not discriminate by failing to make reasonable adjustments in the provision of a service.[33]

Issues such as physical access to facilities will clearly need to be considered, ensuring that alternative space can be used if clients have difficulty accessing buildings. This may present problems for small clinics operating out of makeshift accommodation.

Other examples of adjustments might include:

- making written material available in different forms for those clients who are sight-impaired
- providing an induction loop or similar for those with hearing problems
- ensuring that physical surroundings are appropriate for those with conditions such as autistic spectrum disorder or a physical impairment.

31 EA 2010, s 149.

32 Ibid, s 91(2)(a).

33 Ibid, s 29. Note these provisions also apply to other protected characteristics.

Universities will have equality and diversity teams that should be able to offer some form of support to clinics in terms of advice and guidance. For a clear idea of what is required by law, the Equality and Human Rights Commission publishes statutory guidance to those providing services, which should be considered by any clinic providing a service to the public.[34]

Disability and students

Most staff supervising in clinics, especially academic staff, will be familiar with the need to ensure that students with disabilities are accommodated in terms of the provision of education, e.g. through physical adjustments, provision of materials in different forms and provision made for assessments. As well as ensuring that recruitment processes do not discriminate where a clinic selects its students, it is vital to ensure that students with disabilities are able to participate to the same extent as those without.

Equality and Human Rights Commission guidance in this area is relatively limited[35] and provides little direction. It is likely, though, that students with disabilities will have some agreed adjustments already in place with the university, and you should think about obtaining details of these. As with clients, issues such as access to facilities, providing documents in written form and assisting with a hearing disability are clear areas to be mindful of. The same can be said of external supervisors who work with a clinic.

Further, it is important to consider student training when dealing with interaction with disabled clients. Issues can, of course, be dealt with on a case-by-case basis; however, good practice in this area is to ensure that disability, discrimination and the issue of equality in general is dealt with at students' initial training/induction, at least insofar as indicating what steps can be taken to ensure that the EA duties are observed.

Safeguarding and vulnerability

Vulnerability as a legal concept is outlined in the Safeguarding Vulnerable Groups Act 2006. In general terms, someone is vulnerable either if they are a minor or if for physical or mental health reasons they are unable to look after themselves.

While universities, unlike schools and further education colleges, do not have specific statutory requirements imposed on them in relation to vulnerable

---

34   <https://www.equalityhumanrights.com/sites/default/files/what-equality-law-means-for-your-business-2018.pdf> accessed 2 August 2019.

35   <https://www.equalityhumanrights.com/en/advice-and-guidance/higher-education-providers-guidance>
accessed 2 August 2019.

adults, a common law duty of care requires them to ensure that when dealing with minors and vulnerable adults, sufficient attention is paid to the issue of vulnerability.

A general consideration of universities' obligations is beyond the scope of this section; however, universities are likely to have policies in place dealing with vulnerability, particularly as many will work with those who are under 18 in such things as access schemes or summer schools. Further, many students will undertake placements with organisations working with children or adults and with those working in partnership where students are undertaking work with vulnerable groups. Those supervising law students on placement with outside organisations should check their own institution's policies and processes to ensure that students are properly trained to deal with vulnerability, and issues such as reporting concerns.

For in-house clinics, it is possible that the issue of vulnerability will be raised if:

- a student adviser is considered vulnerable – where this is because the student has a disability, you need to consider issues associated with disability (see above)
- the clinic works with vulnerable clients or clients associated with vulnerable people
- the clinic works with children, for example at a school and/or college.

It is important to ensure that, in circumstances where student advisers may be dealing with a vulnerable client, sufficient regard is paid to any adjustments to deal with the identified vulnerability.

Undoubtedly, services exist that cater for the needs of vulnerable clients and provide students with excellent experience in dealing with such issues (see Manchester University's clinic[36]). The Law Society provides an excellent practice note[37] giving guidance on dealing with vulnerable clients, which will guide supervisors in appropriate cases. When identifying a potentially vulnerable client, you may also need to consider the level of experience of the students working with that client.

Further, if working regularly with vulnerable groups it may be necessary to provide guidance on how to deal with concerns relating to abuse, and reporting such concerns. This clearly raises issues associated with client confidentiality and will involve very careful consideration of whether it is necessary to report or not.

---

36   <https://www.socialsciences.manchester.ac.uk/legal-advice-centre/services/practice-areas/mental-incapacity/> accessed 2 August 2019.

37   <https://www.lawsociety.org.uk/support-services/advice/practice-notes/meeting-the-needs-of-vulnerable-clients-july-2015/> accessed 2 August 2019.

Student safeguarding

Most students will not meet the criteria for being 'vulnerable' in terms of the above definition. However, consideration needs to be given to ensuring student safety when students are working in a clinic.

The responsibility for students' welfare when engaged in clinic work remains with the clinic itself, and regular risk assessments should be undertaken and recorded to see if working practices provide enough security for students. Risks will often be specific to particular clinics depending on their physical surroundings and their client group. For example, some clinics provide students with panic alarms, but not all will consider this necessary.

Further, it is probably wise for a clinic to have a clear social media policy and ensure students are aware of the importance of protecting themselves online and maintaining personal (as well as client) privacy.

Clinics should ensure that proper safeguards are put in place when working with external partners. Again, many universities will have clear policies on steps to be taken when working with external agents and it may be that a university volunteering office/department can provide some support in ensuring formalities are complied with. At the very least, it is suggested that where students are working for an external provider as their volunteer under an arrangement agreed through the clinic, the relevant supervisor ensures that liability insurance is in place to cover the students and any third parties when volunteering. Any concerns as to student wellbeing on such externships should be recorded and followed up.

Further, any students working with minors or vulnerable people will probably be required to have a Disclosure and Barring Service check. Whether a check is required, or the level of check required, may depend on factors such as the requirements of a partner organisation and the extent of contact and supervision.

Most universities will have a safeguarding officer who should be able to provide guidance and support on the steps you should take in any situation.

To summarise, ensuring that the clinic follows its own university's policy and brings in the expertise available in the institution should ensure student safety and avoid difficulties for clinic supervisors.

Signposting and referrals

Demand for clinic services is increasing year on year, and once up and running, most clinics can expect to receive more enquiries than they are able to accommodate. Your clinic may already be full, may not be running at the time of the enquiry, may deal only with enquiries from the local area or might not deal with the area of law needed by the enquirer. Clinics should not be surprised to receive enquiries from beyond their city or even county, and which do not relate to any issue of law advertised by the clinic. Some people who are desperate for advice and unable to pay for a solicitor will contact any free resource in a 'scattergun' approach, in the hope that if the organisation they contact cannot help them, they may at least be able to suggest someone who can.

Guidance on effective signposting and referrals is contained in **Part 2.6**.

Live client clinic case studies

Table 1 below describes and contrasts five different live client clinics run at four different universities. The descriptions are intended to briefly summarise the work done and the different structures and systems in place at each, illustrating the variety of different ways in which clinics can operate and the different considerations to be taken into account when setting up a new clinic. Once again, it is not an exhaustive list.

Each of the clinics contained within the table forms part of a wider programme of clinical activity. A summary of those programmes is set out below for context.

University of Leeds School of Law

The University of Leeds has a number of pro bono opportunities, some of which are research projects,[38] collaborative StreetLaw projects[39] and projects working with litigants in person.[40] Two other projects are more typical clinics falling within the definition ascribed earlier, run by two members of staff at the law school:[41] pop-up clinics[42] and a welfare rights clinic. These are addressed in the table below.

---

38 <https://www.law.leeds.ac.uk/about/extra/cerebra-pro-bono-research-programme> accessed September 2017.

39 <https://essl.leeds.ac.uk/law/news/article/450/streetlaw-becomes-streetleeds-as-new-collaborative-community-project-is-launched-in-leeds> accessed February 2020.

40 <https://www.supportthroughcourt.org/volunteer/court-volunteering/> accessed February 2020.

41 A full-time clinics coordinator and an academic member of staff with workload allocation whose primary responsibilities are to provide strategic oversight and development.

42 <https://essl.leeds.ac.uk/law/news/article/179/legal-advice-clinics-launched> accessed February 2020.

Liverpool John Moores University

Liverpool John Moores University set up its extra-curricular Legal Advice Centre (LAC) in 2014, after Rachel Stalker joined the School of Law and was tasked with coordinating the school's pro bono work. The LAC was shortlisted in 2015 for the LawWorks and Attorney General Student Pro Bono Awards (Best Contribution by a Law School and Best New Student Pro Bono Activity).

The LAC offers clients a typical advice-only model: a fact-finding interview run by a pair of students, supervised by a solicitor, with written advice following two weeks later. Advice is offered for family law, employment law, civil litigation, wills and administration and property law. Liverpool John Moores University is also part of the CLOCK scheme run from Keele University, and engages in research activity with local law firms and its local law society.

The school found that it could not cater for family law clients – family law being the biggest area of demand. Those approaching the school for advice in this area often had urgent issues or court dates and so could not await an appointment and/or written advice provided at a later date. The family law drop-in clinic was therefore set up in 2015[43] and is discussed in the table below.[44]

University of Liverpool

Liverpool Law Clinic[45] is a well-established clinic and is a good example of how a service can grow over time. The Law Department has been offering undergraduate students clinic opportunities since 2007 and Liverpool Law Clinic is a fully functioning pro bono legal practice embedded in the Liverpool Law School. It offers final-year law students direct experience of representing real clients under the supervision of the clinic's in-house legal team of qualified lawyers.

Nearly all of the students who participate in the clinic do so on taught modules as part of the final year of the undergraduate LLB. The clinic has a particular specialism in immigration and asylum law, and has a statelessness project supported by a charitable funder. It has different models of working, offering opportunities to assist with full representation, as well as advice-only work. Solicitors in the clinic run weekly outreach advice services in the Alder Hey Children's Hospital and in the Liverpool Family Court. Students assist solicitors

---

43   <https://www.ljmu.ac.uk/about-us/faculties/faculty-of-business-and-law/school-of-law/legal-advice-centre/clinics accessed February 2020.

44   As outlined earlier in **Part 1**, those interested in setting up drop-in clinics should also refer to the excellent manual created by London South Bank University: <https://www1.lsbu.ac.uk/ahs/downloads/law/lsbu-drop-in-clinic-manual-v1> accessed 16 August 2019.

45   <https://www.liverpool.ac.uk/law/liverpool-law-clinic/> accessed 16 August 2019.

to interview clients and provide verbal advice, which is followed up by an advice letter, researched and drafted by the students.

In addition:

- The Liverpool Law Clinic works with external solicitors from a large number of firms in the Merseyside area, and also runs a summer placement scheme in June every year: in 2016–17 nearly 200 final-year students took clinic modules.
- The clinic also offers opportunities for students to volunteer on projects working with solicitors in Liverpool – for example, groups of Liverpool Law Clinic students assisted with the Hillsborough Enquiry, the Orgreave Campaign and the campaign for fresh inquests into the Birmingham Pub Bombings (the latter alongside the Liverpool John Moores University LAC).
- The Law Department runs a welfare rights project in partnership with Law Centres and Citizens Advice, and in 2017–18 delivered a new module, Access to Justice, where students are trained to assist with disability benefits applications and are placed with Citizens Advice.

The clinic has dedicated space in the university, including interview rooms, an admin office, student PC suites and a seminar room. Students are required to do all casework in clinic rooms to protect confidentiality, and the university has invested in an online case management system called Advice Pro.

University of Wolverhampton

The University of Wolverhampton has operated its Legal Advice Centre (LAC) since 2011 when Mumtaz Hussain, Head of Professional and Postgraduate Studies at the university, set up the initiative within the Law School. The model used by the university is a general advice-only service, and the LAC takes enquiries from members of the public who call in person, or contact the clinic via the enquiry form on the university's Legal Advice Centre webpage.[46]

Students work in pairs during a fact-finding interview, supervised by the LAC manager or other academic at the university, later providing either written advice or a follow-up appointment (at the client's preference), generally seven to 21 days after the initial interview. The advice is aimed to inform the client of the law that is relevant to their legal issue, and identify possible courses of action, while also signposting the client to other services where they may be able to seek further help, or solve their legal problem.

---

46   <https://www.wlv.ac.uk/legaladvice> accessed 16 August 2019.

The LAC utilises Intralinks[47] to manage client files, where the students can access case information securely, and share research and draft client letters of advice with each other and the case file supervisor. The students are encouraged to take on as much responsibility as they feel able to, including answering telephone enquiries, dealing with email enquiries, signposting without supervision (for matters that the clinic cannot deal with) and handling drop-in enquiries (taking initial contact details and explaining how the LAC works).

The LAC is currently working on new ideas and models to provide greater access to justice, and ensure students at the university are exposed to a range of legal areas and issues. A pilot family law session took place in March 2019, which involved students shadowing an external practitioner at a pro bono family law clinic where members of the public attended the LAC for free, 20-minute consultations. Family law clinics were held previously on an ad hoc basis, and proved to be successful.

Since the pilot in March, a family law clinic has been held every month to date (July 2019) and over the course of the five two-hour long sessions, 34 people have been provided with assistance with their legal issues, ranging from separation and divorce to child custody arrangements. While this number might seem small, all but one of the sessions was completely full, with the attending solicitor being fully engaged for the whole two-hour slot.

---

47   A cloud-based management system that is kindly made available free of charge through LawWorks membership, and allows a legal clinic to manage client files effectively. More detail on Intralinks is contained in **Part 2.12**.

Table 1: Practical examples of five live client clinics

	University of Leeds: Pop-up clinics	University of Leeds: Welfare rights project	Liverpool John Moores University: Drop-in clinics	University of Liverpool	University of Wolverhampton
On or off campus?	Off campus, in locations already known and trusted by clients, including a Citizens Advice, a charity and a grassroots community development trust.	Off campus, at Leeds City Council's Welfare Rights Unit, in an area just outside the city centre.	On campus.	Both: • The law clinic offers advice and representation from bespoke premises in the Law Department • Law clinic staff also offer advice services in the Alder Hey Children's Hospital and Liverpool Family Court.	Off campus. The Legal Advice Centre (LAC) has its own unit in the City's Mander Shopping Centre, which is leased by the university.
Supervision?	Provided by solicitors external to the law school, with insurance being provided either by their firms or by LawWorks. Each solicitor is allocated to a clinic that provides advice in their specialism.	Training and the day-to-day supervision of students taking part in the project is provided by Leeds City Council's Welfare Rights Unit staff. The law school's full-time clinical legal education co-ordinator also provides administrative support to the project, e.g. by arranging the rota of student volunteers.	External solicitors with expertise in family law supervise the advice given. University staff coordinate students and triage cases.	Internal lawyers have conduct of cases, coordinate services, train and supervise students. External volunteer lawyers also assist with advice services and supervise student work.	The LAC is coordinated by the LAC manager, who is a qualified solicitor and oversees all cases, and supervises some, along with four other academics at the university. On occasion, assistance is provided by external solicitors from two local law firms, who provide solicitors on a pro bono basis to supervise students during the advice session, and provide them with feedback on their research and the advice session itself.

	University of Leeds: Pop-up clinics	University of Leeds: Welfare rights project	Liverpool John Moores University: Drop-in clinics	University of Liverpool	University of Wolverhampton
Area of law covered?	Family, housing, employment and small business law.	Personal Independent Payment (PIP) applications and Employment and Support Allowance (ESA) applications.	Family law.	Immigration, family, community care, education, disability benefits.	Employment law matters, probate issues, property (usually neighbour disputes or ownership issues), consumer rights and civil litigation (such as personal injury). Business law-related matters, for example partnership law.
Assessed or co-curricular?	Voluntary, no academic credit.		Voluntary, no academic credit.	Both: the majority of students in the law clinic are on credit-bearing modules, but we also have a growing number of projects for which students can volunteer.	Both: generally, students are not assessed, and volunteer in addition to their studies. Since October 2017, however, some third-year undergraduates are assessed as part of a new compulsory Practical Legal Skills module. The assessment takes the form of a reflective oral assessment about their experience at the LAC, and a written assessment providing detailed research and analysis of an area of law that they encountered at the LAC.

	University of Leeds: Pop-up clinics	University of Leeds: Welfare rights project	Liverpool John Moores University: Drop-in clinics	University of Liverpool	University of Wolverhampton
Selection of students?	Students apply via a written application form, with shortlisted students being interviewed for approximately 10 minutes each.		Lottery open to students of all levels who are interested in volunteering. More places made available for Level 4 students.	Places are limited: first come, first served on a module selection exercise. Voluntary projects vary but normally a combination of first come, first served and interviewing.	Students apply via a covering letter and CV, although opportunities are afforded to all Level 5, 6 and postgraduate students. They are all interviewed by the LAC manager prior to completing training.
How many students involved?	Approximately 20 per academic year.	15 undergraduate students.	We train a rota of 16 undergraduate and postgraduate students with four students attending each clinic.	Approximately 300 students a year.	For the academic year 2018/19, there were a total of 46 students, of which 16 were volunteers and 30 undertaking placements as part of assessed modules. Students were mostly undergraduates, with around only 15% of students taking the GDL/CPE, LPC or CILEx courses.
Time commitment required from students?	Depending upon their timetables and other commitments, a student volunteer would be expected to cover at least four clinics in an academic year.	Volunteers typically cover around four clinics per academic year: within that clinic they would see two clients on a one-to-one basis within a three-hour period.	All students attend at least two clinics a year: each clinic session runs for 90 minutes.	Normal requirements of a 15-credit taught module. Students have some workshops and some formal supervision meetings, and are expected to spend a substantial amount of time on independent study.	Students are asked to volunteer for a minimum of two hours per week (excluding research on cases, which is completed in their own time). Students therefore generally volunteer 32 hours over the course of 16 weeks across semester one and semester two.

	University of Leeds: Pop-up clinics	University of Leeds: Welfare rights project	Liverpool John Moores University: Drop-in clinics	University of Liverpool	University of Wolverhampton
How are students trained?	Covers taking notes; completing an advice session pro forma (which includes sections on the nature of the client's problem and the advice that was given by the advising solicitor); and general client care. The training is provided by the two staff who run the law school's clinics. The client care aspect of the training includes information about the socio-economic background of clients; how clients' concerns might be resolvable through means other than legal remedies; how to read and interpret the behaviour of clients; and professional approaches to all parties present at clinics.	Successful applicants receive a full day of training in welfare rights law and PIP documentation from Leeds City Council.	Five compulsory sessions at the start of the academic year covering clinic processes, confidentiality, data protection, professional ethics, wellbeing and IT.	Training covers: ethics and conduct; client interviewing; practical legal research; drafting; group work; and file management.	Students are provided with six hours of training, split into three parts: • 'Interviewing and advising' (delivered on campus by two external solicitors from the Birmingham branch of a national firm) • 'Professional conduct and ethics', delivered by the LAC manager • 'Working at the LAC', including an overview of how the LAC works, the Student Volunteer Handbook, an overview of LawWorks and Intralinks (the cloud-based management system) and role play (interview practice).

	University of Leeds: Pop-up clinics	University of Leeds: Welfare rights project	Liverpool John Moores University: Drop-in clinics	University of Liverpool	University of Wolverhampton
How is advice provided?	Face-to-face by the practitioner; to clients who have been given an appointment. The students do not provide advice.	In person, on a one-to-one basis between the client and the student volunteer.	Face-to-face by the practitioner; to clients who turn up to the clinic on the day.	Either face-to-face or in writing depending on the module and service.	Advice is provided either face-to-face or written, both delivered by students and checked/amended or overseen by a supervisor.
What do students do?	Students work in pairs with one practitioner and one client, and take notes of the advice given. They have 48 hours to provide a concise set of notes to the law school: these are checked before being forwarded to the practitioner.	One-to-one support to applicants for PIP and ESA applications. Volunteers work with clients on a one-to-one basis, completing the applications with them. Supervisors are not present during those meetings, but are available if the volunteer requires support, and check all applications drafted by students.	Students work in pairs and take turns to sit in on a 20–30 minute advice session with a client, delivered by the solicitor. Students take notes.	Students research the law, manage files, draft letters of advice, interview clients, draft other documents and attend court hearings as McKenzie Friends.	Students work in pairs, and take initial enquiries from members of the public who visit the LAC. They also conduct fact-finding interviews, prepare research and deliver advice verbally under supervision, and also draft letters of advice, which are checked by a supervisor before being sent to the client.

	University of Leeds: Pop-up clinics	University of Leeds: Welfare rights project	Liverpool John Moores University: Drop-in clinics	University of Liverpool	University of Wolverhampton
How do clients know about the service?	Clients are referred to the clinic by the community organisation where the clinic is being hosted.	Clients are booked into the student-led appointments by Leeds City Council.	The clinic advertises in the local press and takes referrals from local third sector agencies.	There are a variety of ways. • Statelessness cases tend to be referred from immigration lawyers. • Family law advice clients are made aware of the service when they attend court. • The Alder Hey Children's Hospital assists with publicity for the service. • There is information on the website. • The clinic sends out flyers and leaflets to advice agencies such as CABx and law centres.	The LAC is in a prominent position in the City's Mander Shopping Centre, and the website provides a good overview of the service, along with an online enquiry form for members of the public to complete. No advertising is done routinely, but the clinic has occasional press coverage (for example, local radio). Referrals are also taken from Citizens Advice, Wolverhampton, Legal Companions (part of the CLOCK project) and other local agencies.
What records are retained?	A copy of the notes is retained by the practitioner; the law school and the community organisation (in the event the client returns and they need to know what the client has been advised previously).	All documentation is retained by Leeds City Council. Leeds City Council tracks the applications for all clients, including those supported by students during the application process, and the law school is notified of all outcomes.	Solicitors retain their own notes. The university retains the students' notes on file.	All clients have a case file and all handwritten and electronic notes are kept in the file. Students are taught to keep attendance notes and time-record their work. Files are kept and archived in accordance with regulatory obligations. There is an electronic case management system called Advice Pro.	All records are retained by the LAC manager, including student notes. Files are opened and closed as they would be in practice. External solicitors retain their own notes.

	University of Leeds: Pop-up clinics	University of Leeds: Welfare rights project	Liverpool John Moores University: Drop-in clinics	University of Liverpool	University of Wolverhampton
How is the clinic insured?	Insurance is either provided by the practitioner themselves (i.e. they come under their firm's usual indemnity insurance) or by LawWorks, with whom the law school has an arrangement.	No legal advice is given during this project.	Existing university insurance.	The law clinic has an independent insurance policy providing professional indemnity, which covers work undertaken by in-house lawyers and advice given by external lawyers who volunteer in the law clinic.	Insurance for the LAC is covered under the university policy.
For what period of the year does the clinic run?	All year round, with a reduced service over the summer period.	Term-time only.	October to May: term-time only.	October to May/June, term-time only.	The LAC is generally open from October to May, with a skeleton service until June.
Resourcing requirements?	These pro bono opportunities within the law school are supported by two members of staff within the School of Law: 1 full-time equivalent (FTE) Clinics Co-ordinator, and one member of staff whose Director of Community Engagement responsibilities equate to approximately 0.2FTE.		0.5FTE salary of in-house clinic coordinator. Approx £1,500 marketing budget. All other costs (stationery, travel) funded ad hoc by the School of Law.	The Liverpool Law Clinic represents a significant investment by the School of Law and Social Justice in terms of staffing, dedicated space and associated costs of IT and stationery. The clinic is staffed by six in-house lawyers (five full time, one 0.5) and two administrators employed by the university. First- and second-year students volunteer in the office to help with administration, such as answering phones and helping with the post.	0.5FTE salary of the LAC manager. Other costs are funded by the Law School, and the unit within the shopping mall is also covered by the Law School at a reduced rent.

Other models of clinical and public legal education

Further examples of broader clinical projects are discussed below to offer insights into other models of clinical services that can be developed.

Law Student Representation Project

The Law Student Representation Project, established in 2014, is a joint initiative between the City of Wolverhampton Council (Welfare Rights Service) and the University of Wolverhampton Law School.

The project provides much-needed First-tier Tribunal and Upper Tribunal appeals representation to vulnerable and disadvantaged people living in Wolverhampton who are in dispute with the Department for Work and Pensions over entitlements to disability benefits. It also undertakes appeals pertaining to benefit sanctions and the benefit rights of EEA nationals.

Students are trained and mentored by welfare rights officers within the Council's Welfare Rights Service. The training includes tribunal practice and procedure and observing at live appeal hearings. Students meet with appellants to gain instructions, study the appeal paperwork and draft written submissions. Students then attend and represent appellants at oral appeal hearings.

Wolverhampton is within the top 20 most deprived areas in the UK and in 2015 was ranked eighth for income deprivation and sixth for employment deprivation. The city's unemployment rate is 4.17 per cent (March 2016), which is higher than the average for the Black Country (2.9 per cent: January 2016) and significantly higher than the average for England (1.5 per cent: January 2016). There are high numbers of residents who are long-term unemployed and/or have health-related barriers to work.

The Law Student Representation Project benefits the community as a whole, both in terms of benefits to the students, and of course to the vulnerable people the service assists.

For those students who have gone on to undertake appeals, the project has provided experience in a 'real world' legal setting (where matters of evidence, facts and law are decisive) where there is a dispute between two parties. The project provides students with important experience and references for their CVs, helps them to develop their self-confidence and enables them to assist disadvantaged groups.

CLOCK

CLOCK (Community Legal Outreach Community Keele) was developed by Dr Jane Krishnadas at Keele University to assist unrepresented litigants by:

- identifying litigants who may qualify for legal aid and signposting them to a local law firm
- signposting litigants to a suitable pro bono/third sector service such as Citizens Advice or a university law clinic to obtain legal advice
- training students as 'Community Legal Companions' to assist litigants in person with form filling, or at court in line with the McKenzie Friend principles and on a non-fee charging basis.

Alongside the university, third sector agencies, court services and law firms collaborate to train students at the outset of their involvement in the scheme. CLOCK has won support from the Ministry of Justice and in April 2016 was Highly Commended for an Outstanding Contribution to Access to Justice by the Access to Justice Foundation at its annual awards ceremony.

The Support Through Court (STC) already operates in Liverpool Family & Civil Court, and with its kind support – and that of HHJ Margaret De Haas QC – a pilot ran during 2016–18 that involved Liverpool John Moores University (LJMU) students training and working alongside and under the supervision of the STC in court as an additional, complementary resource, with clinic students assisting in the signposting of clinic clients and other enquirers.

Being part of the scheme allows LJMU's Legal Advice Centre to provide a broader and more coordinated service for people in the Merseyside area, by signposting clients from the clinic to specific law firms or third sector agencies using a dedicated IT system and/or giving them assistance at court, while at the same time expanding the educational benefit for students by giving them court experience.

The scheme also helps dispel the myth that legal aid has been abolished completely, since the triaging system identifies 'red flags' that indicate the client may be eligible for legal aid and, via the online hub, links the enquirer with a law firm which can conduct the assessment. The publicity around the scheme also emphasises that legal aid is still available in some circumstances. The scheme's provision of an alternative to fee-charging McKenzie Friends is also aimed at assisting the most vulnerable litigants in person.[48]

Family Court Helpdesks

Both Liverpool Law Clinic and Greenwich Legal Advice Centre[49] run family law helpdesks aimed at supporting litigants in the Liverpool Family Court and

---

48 Further details of the scheme can be found at <https://www.keele.ac.uk/law/legaloutreachcollaboration/> accessed 16 August 2019 and <https://clock.uk.net/> accessed 16 August 2019.

49 Greenwich University Legal Advice Centre <https://www.gre.ac.uk/ach/study/law/legal-advice-centre> accessed September 2017.

the East London Family Court. The helpdesks aim to provide support at first hearings (FHDRA – first hearing and dispute resolution appointment) in child arrangement cases. Family courts tend to list these hearings on one or two days of the week as they need the presence of a CAFCASS (Children and Family Court Advisory and Support Service) officer at court.

The students in both courts work closely with the ushers on FHDRA days and speak to all litigants in person to see if they would like support. Students check that litigants understand the procedure involved in the hearing, and that all the correct forms have been filed. They attend the hearing with litigants as a McKenzie Friend, taking notes and helping the litigant remain calm and focused. Following the hearing, students make sure that litigants have a clear note of what needs to happen next (such as dates for filing statements) before they leave the court.[50] At Liverpool, the helpdesk offers a 20-minute appointment with a solicitor for legal advice before the hearing, while at Greenwich clients are referred to the Legal Advice Centre for advice following the hearing.

Both projects support between six and 10 clients a week due to the high number of litigants in person in child arrangement cases. Approximately 24 students a term are trained and take part. The majority of litigants have not had any legal advice before arriving at court for the first hearing and both helpdesks aim to reach some of the most vulnerable people in the court system by proactively working with the ushers and speaking to litigants at court.[51]

Setting up a court helpdesk is not difficult, but can take some perseverance and conviction. Some of the administrative burden of running a clinic that is hosted on campus is lifted as you do not need to advertise, look for clients or book appointments. However, you do need to take care that you are clear about the limits of the service offered and consider the practicalities of conflict checks and client care letters if you are regulated by the SRA[52] (for further details on this, see **Part 2.4**).

Some points to think about are set out below:

---

50   Sheffield Hallam University run a similar project for litigants in person in the small claims track of the County Court. Manchester University has an advice service based in the Civil and Family Court. This is an advice-only service; students do not go into court with litigants <https://www.law.manchester.ac.uk/legal-advice-centre/services/mflh/> accessed 16 August 2019. There are numerous other court schemes being run by university law clinics around the country.

51   The students from Greenwich can be seen talking about the project on two short films on YouTube <https://www.youtube.com/watch?v=G6Is29-oO3E> and <https://www.youtube.com/watch?v=SsLthh2zA6s> both accessed 16 August 2019.

52   The Law Society has issued a practice note: Court duty schemes in private law family cases <https://www.lawsociety.org.uk/support-services/advice/practice-notes/court-duty-scheme-for-private-law-family-clients/> accessed 16 August 2019.

- If you want to set up a court helpdesk, first of all you need to find out what services are already available in your local court.
- If the court already has a Support Through Court[53] find out if your students can volunteer with them, or if you can work in partnership with them in some way. Several law clinics have strong working partnerships with their local STC. If students volunteer through the STC this removes the burden and responsibility of supervision and training from the clinic staff.
- If there is no STC in your local court, consider whether your university will invest in a CLOCK scheme (see above).
- If you want to offer a more specialist service, find out who the manager of your local court is and approach them with a proposal to run a scheme. As with all pro bono services, make sure that you know what services are already running so that you are not competing with an established voluntary service, but are able to complement that service and provide something extra.
- Allow plenty of time to set up the scheme. Ask to go into the court and observe the way it works, as each court does things slightly differently.
- Pilot the scheme with a small number of students.

Have clear publicity and make sure the local legal profession know what you are doing and what the limits of your service are. Some advocates find McKenzie Friends controversial, often with good reason, so it is important that people know who you are and what you are trying to achieve.

A well-run court scheme is helpful to litigants as it removes some of the stress and anxiety of going to court, is helpful to the court as litigants in person are often more organised and better prepared with a student supporter, and the students can gain a huge amount in terms of personal confidence as well as learning about law and procedure.

Online/virtual clinics: Open Justice Law Clinic case study[54]

Technology is transforming the delivery of legal services and the administration of justice. Clinical legal education programmes can provide the opportunity to engage with these changes and develop pedagogical responses that can equip students to navigate a transformed legal landscape and provide new platforms to increase public access to legal advice and guidance. Original and

---

53   Personal Support Unit <https://www.thepsu.org/> accessed 16 August 2019.

54   This section was written by Francine Ryan and Hugh McFaul of the Open University and takes the form of a case study of the Open University's online clinic. For a more general consideration of virtual law clinics and associated issues see 'Lawyering in a digital age: reflections on starting up a virtual law clinic' by Ann Thanaraj and Michael Sales in Part 2 of this Handbook.

experimental models of clinical legal education are developing innovative ways in which to provide students with practical activities that teach the skills and competencies required to enable law students to respond creatively to the challenges and opportunities that technology can bring. The integration of technology into clinical programmes can provide students with a deeper understanding of the potential of technology to transform the legal process.

The Open University is the UK's largest provider of undergraduate legal education, teaching students from across the United Kingdom. Facilitating the participation of part time distance learning students in a meaningful clinical programme presented a range of logistical challenges. The solution chosen was to transfer the traditional face to face law clinic into a virtual setting. The Open Justice Law Clinic (http://law-school.open.ac.uk/open-justice/get-legal-advice) was opened in 2017. This virtual law clinic provides an industry-standard online platform which delivers legal services through a secure web portal in which communication with members of the public is encrypted and protected using a leading legal case management system.[55] This enables students to work virtually with clients to support them with their legal issues and provide the same professional standard of advice and guidance that is available in other face-to-face law clinics.

There are a number of reasons why other universities might consider developing a virtual law clinic:

Benefits for clients

- Anyone with an internet connection can access the clinic
- It is accessible for clients who cannot attend a face to face clinic because, for example, they have a disability, or live in a rural location
- It is preferable for clients who are familiar with online platforms and technology
- It is flexible; it allows clients to communicate with the clinic when it is most suitable and convenient to them.

Benefits for universities and students

- Cases can be accepted regardless of geographical distance
- It gives students the opportunity to collaborate on cases wherever they are located
- It facilitates the development of partnerships with external law firms irrespective of where they are based

---

55   The Open Justice Law Clinic uses Clio, a practice-based case management system, under the academic access programme: https://www.clio.com/uk/academic-access/ (accessed 22 Aug. 2019).

- It offers greater flexibility for supervising solicitors because they can participate remotely
- The absence of physical premises allows for lower running costs
- It opens up partnering opportunities with charities and organisations outside of the immediate locality
- It exposes students to emerging forms of legal practice
- Students have the opportunity to engage with technology and develop core competencies including online collaboration skills, gaining important employability and transferable skills.

Although there are many benefits to a virtual law clinic, it also has its limitations and it should not be seen as a replacement for all forms of face to face clinic. There are areas of law, and particular client groups, where a virtual law clinic would not be appropriate. Careful consideration should be given to the target client group and the areas of law likely to be most suitable for this type of clinic.

How to set up a virtual law clinic

Technology

Case management system – the clinic needs to procure a case management system to facilitate the case work and the interaction between the clients, students and supervisors. The software allows the clinic to manage the cases, contacts, calendars, documents, tasks, time recording and client communications via one platform. Storing all the case and contact information within the case management system enables the creation of documents prepared from templates. All documents are uploaded into the case management system; the clinic is paperless which makes information sharing easier and ensures that personal information is secure.

Text messaging – may be a useful method of sending reminders to clients about interviews, or outstanding information; there are a number of inexpensive providers including TextBurst, or FastSms.

Online meeting rooms – interviews are conducted virtually. The Open Justice Law Clinic uses Adobe Connect, but other clinics use different conferencing platforms such as Skype. If the interviews are recorded, they must be stored securely to ensure the clinic meets its obligations on confidentiality and data protection. Online meeting rooms are also used for supervision and firm meetings.

Computers/laptops/mobile devices – this will depend on the model the clinic adopts; students either use their own devices or they are provided by the clinic. If students are using their own laptops, strict rules are required to prohibit the storage of any clinic information or documents on a personal device.

Website – consideration needs to be given on how to attract clients into the clinic. The Open Justice Law Clinic generates enquiries via its website: clients complete an online form which is received and triaged via our clinic mailbox. Twitter and Facebook are effective ways of generating new enquiries, but often the internet is the last resort for some people looking for help so the cases can be complex.

Communication – casework discussion takes places via secure messaging within the case management system but general discussions about non-confidential clinic activities may occur in other ways, via university online forums, WhatsApp, Trello or Slack. Trello is a free way to manage projects and Slack is collaboration software; both have the potential to support online group work. Careful consideration should be given on how many tools are used by a clinic as there is a risk students will be overwhelmed by technology.

Customising the case management system

Template letters and documents can be created and uploaded into the system. Some case management systems work in conjunction with document storage systems and therefore a decision has to be made on where those documents are stored. The Open Justice Law Clinic customised its use of Clio so that all documents are created via templates and stored within the case management system to avoid the need for a separate document storage system. Students can be allocated into firms within the case management system and this enables the administrator to only allow the firm allocated to a case to access it. Students need very clear rules and guidance about confidentiality and data protection. As with other forms of clinic, it is advisable to ask students to sign an agreement, which specifies the requirements of the clinic.

Documents

A number of manuals are required to explain how the clinic operates. The Open Justice Law Clinic has student guides to Clio setting out how the clinic works, explaining how to log into Clio, navigating through the dashboard, matter screens and setting notifications. We advise students to work through the guide whilst having the Clio training site open so they can navigate the different screens and practise the tasks set out. Once they have worked through the general introduction to Clio, there is a second part of the Guide which explains the precise steps they need to go through for each case and how to carry out specific tasks. It is advisable to encourage students to use the guides in conjunction with the simulated case discussed below.

Training

Students require training on how to use a case management system, interviewing a client virtually and collaborating online with other students and supervisors. The Open Justice Law Clinic has two versions of Clio, a training and a live site. Students conduct a simulated case in the training site before moving into the live clinic. Students are provided with training sessions via Adobe Connect to cover all aspects of clinic work; confidentiality and data protection connected to the risks associated with technology are a significant feature.

Running a virtual law clinic

Clients

Clients access the case management system via a client portal. Clients benefit from having direct access to the case management system so they can send secure messages, upload documents and view correspondence from the clinic at any time. Clients are interviewed in an online meeting room so it is helpful to ask them to check prior to the meeting they can access the room or have a test call the day before to check everything is working. This also provides an opportunity to check the strength of the internet connection which may cause an issue if the client is an area where the connection is poor. A wired connection is better than wireless. It is good idea to suggest to clients that the interview should take somewhere private and quiet. The flexibility of being able to access an online meeting from a mobile device may encourage some clients to think that whilst they are driving or in a café are good places to conduct the meeting, so it is worth making it clear to clients in advance that they will need to be somewhere quiet, where they can give their full attention to the meeting. Providing clients with an information sheet is a good idea: it can offer guidance on how to access the case management system and the online meeting room.

Students

Online collaboration poses challenges for students and clients. Conducting an online meeting can be testing for students as they have to work harder to form a rapport, and it is important for them to slow down to allow time for the client to think and reflect. If the students are interviewing the client from different locations, it is essential that they have agreed each of their roles and the questions beforehand. Students require specific training and opportunities to practise interviewing before they enter a live clinic. A virtual law clinic is dependent on technology; it is important to build in sufficient time for students to become confident in using the various applications as well as learning the other skills required in clinic. It is essential that students receive training and that the clinic has robust procedures on confidentiality and data protection.

Supervisors

Supervisors need to be confident using the case management system and working collaboratively online to support students. A virtual environment can lead to task-related disputes escalating more quickly: it is important that supervisors know how to manage virtual teams. Supervisors need to encourage students to communicate regularly so any issues can be resolved quickly. Supervisors require training and guidance documents to support them in their role in the clinic.

Conclusion

Setting up and running a virtual law clinic is not without its challenges,[56] but virtual law clinics share many similarities with face-to-face clinics. Developing a virtual law clinic may not be appropriate for all law schools, but it may still be possible to incorporate technology into an existing clinic. A virtual law clinic can take many forms. One option a law school may want to explore is the possibility of developing one in partnership with a charity or free advice organisation.

Externships

Many law schools make arrangements with external organisations, such as third sector advice agencies, for their students to volunteer under the supervision of the external organisation's staff. Examples of the types of organisations that may be interested in hosting students on this basis include:

- Support Through Court
- local Citizens Advice
- local law centres
- the Free Representation Unit
- other small/local/independent advice services.

The role that students undertake in an externship arrangement and the amount of time that they commit to it will vary from project to project. For example, students might assist with a specific service being provided by the partner agency, such as a drop-in clinic or a telephone advice line. Or it might be agreed that students will commit a specified amount of time each week or month to help the agency with delivery of its day-to-day service.

As with the university-hosted clinics discussed earlier, the students' role might

---

56   F. Ryan 'A virtual law clinic: A realist evaluation of what works for whom, why, how and in what circumstances' (2019) The Law Teacher, <https://doi.org/10.1080/03069400.2019.1651550>.

involve provision of advice and/or undertaking casework and representation under supervision from a qualified professional. Alternatively, they might provide assistance to the qualified lawyer who is giving the advice by fielding initial enquiries, note-taking and so on.

Some universities may pay or make a donation to the external agencies for the supervision they provide to students. Other arrangements will have no direct cost implications for the university, particularly where student support provides a valuable resource and adds capacity for the agency.

The University of Birmingham has a number of externship arrangements in place, each of which adopts a slightly different model, depending upon the requirements of the partner organisation.

Support Through Court (STC)

Students are selected by STC following a written application and interview process. STC then trains the student volunteers, who agree to commit to a minimum of ten full days of volunteering over the course of the academic year. STC is responsible for supervising the students, who provide support and guidance to litigants in person, assist them with tasks such as filling in court forms and note-taking. The volunteer schedule is agreed directly between STC and the students.

Law Centre

Eight students per year are selected by the law school to assist the Law Centre with its weekly drop-in clinic during term-time. Students take initial details from clients that drop in to the clinic and take attendance notes of the advice given by the Law Centre staff. Training on professional conduct and client interviewing is provided by staff at the law school. The law school coordinates the rota of student volunteers, and the students are supervised by the Law Centre staff.

Birmingham People's Centre

Two students a year volunteer half a day each week during term-time (and more during holiday periods if they wish). Initial training on professional conduct, client interviewing and the basics of employment law is provided by staff at the law school. Ongoing training and supervision is provided by a solicitor employed by the People's Centre. Students field initial enquiries, provide advice under supervision and assist the supervising solicitor with casework.

Many of the considerations for setting up an externship arrangement will be the same as for a university-hosted clinic. It is important to follow your institution's own practices in relation to risk assessments. Training and supervision arrangements should be agreed with the partner organisation in advance and insurance arrangements should be checked to ensure students are covered. In some circumstances, a written agreement such as a memorandum of understanding, between the university and the external agency will be sensible in order to ensure all parties understand their respective roles and responsibilities.

Public legal education/Streetlaw

There are many different forms of public legal education (PLE). According to the Law Society, PLE can include:

- sessions or workshops in schools, youth groups, prisons and other venues
- information or resources about law-related issues
- awareness-raising campaigns
- mock trials and role-play exercises
- activities at community events.[57]

PLE is not legal advice. It is about enhancing people's general knowledge and understanding of the law, rather than answering specific individual legal queries. The emphasis in the UK on the important role that PLE can play has grown in recent years and, in 2018, 'A Ten Year Vision for Public Legal Education' was launched by the Solicitor General's Committee on Public Legal Education.[58]

Streetlaw (or Street Law) is the term commonly used to describe university PLE initiatives, in which law students go out into the community – usually via charities, community groups, schools and other organisations – and speak to people about what their legal rights and legal responsibilities are.

Typically, Streetlaw adopts an interactive methodology, which means that Streetlaw sessions are delivered in a way that actively engages the attendees in the topics covered.[59] By its very nature, Streetlaw is a versatile model and sessions can be designed to address the particular needs of the intended audience in terms of content, length, place, mode and style of delivery.

In order to give a sense of the diverse range of possibilities for Streetlaw

---

57   <https://www.lawsociety.org.uk/support-services/public-legal-education/> accessed 16 August 2019.

58   <https://www.lawworks.org.uk/sites/default/files/files/10YearVisionForPLE-web.pdf> accessed 16 August 2019.

59   See the resources at **note 4** for further details on the interactive approach to delivering Streetlaw sessions. **Part 6** also contains details of the annual UK and Ireland Streetlaw Best Practices Conference, which provides a forum for sharing Streetlaw methods and materials.

projects, below are three examples of projects which are, or have been, run by the University of Birmingham Law School:

- **Employment Tribunal Litigants in Person project**: Two fortnightly sessions delivered at the Employment Tribunal during term-time, which are aimed at litigants in person. The first session, 'An overview of the tribunal process', takes litigants step by step through the stages of a tribunal claim (such as a preliminary hearing, disclosure and so on). The second, 'What to expect at a final hearing' discusses issues such as the order in which a final hearing is likely to happen, the layout of the tribunal room, how to address the judge, etc.

- **Entrepreneurship and the Law**: A series of eight one-hour sessions delivered to year 12 pupils at a local secondary school on commercial law and entrepreneurship. Pupils are tasked with coming up with a business idea and then developing their business plan. Each week they are introduced to new legal issues they will need to consider and factor into their business plan, such as intellectual property law, finance and funding, employment law, etc. In the final session, pupils 'pitch' their idea to the law students and their business plan is put to the test in a *Dragons' Den*-style set up.

- **Homelessness project**: Law students delivered 20-minute sessions on areas of law that are of particular relevance to service users of a local homeless charity. Topics covered included domestic violence and housing rights, police stop-and-search powers and squatters' rights.

Streetlaw sessions are most effective when those designing and delivering them have an understanding of the interests, needs, prior knowledge and abilities of the people who will be attending the sessions. Therefore, university staff responsible for coordinating Streetlaw projects are advised to meet with representatives from the host organisations or community groups in advance of developing the sessions. In nearly all cases, it is possible for students to be involved in the design, as well as the delivery, of sessions.

Streetlaw requires students to practise a broad array of different legal and soft skills, including legal research, communication (speaking and listening), team-work and adaptability. Thought should be given as to how best to train students who will be delivering Streetlaw sessions. As is recommended in the section on training above, it is important to give students practical opportunities to practise the relevant skills and receive feedback.[60]

---

60   For helpful guidance on delivering Streetlaw training, see Seán Arthurs, Melinda Cooperman, Jessica Gallagher, Freda Grealy, John Lunney, Rob Marrs and Richard Roe (2017) 'From zero to 60: Building belief, capacity and community in Street Law instructors in one weekend' *International Journal of Clinical Legal Education* 4(2), 118–241.

Training may also need to address the limitations of Streetlaw, in order to ensure that students understand the distinction between information and advice, and do not inadvertently stray beyond the scope of the Streetlaw session into offering attendees advice on their individual situations.

Law schools will also need to have a system in place to check that the legal content of any sessions developed by students is accurate before they are delivered to members of the public. This may be done by a member of university staff or by an external lawyer acting in a voluntary capacity. Recommendations above in this **Part 1** regarding risk assessments, insurance, etc. should also be considered.

Research projects

Many university law clinics also engage in research projects on a pro bono basis. Often, these projects are carried out for non-governmental or not-for-profit organisations. The type of projects that might be carried out are many and varied. They might, for example, include researching the law on a specific issue in a number of jurisdictions and compiling a report; or researching and summarising the law in a particular area in order to inform the contents of a guidance note or webpage for service users of a charity. Universities are well placed to carry out such projects due to the research expertise and resources they have available.

Conclusion

There is no one right way to run a clinic. While the array of options on offer and factors to consider may be daunting to anyone new to CLE, it is a unique opportunity to combine the innovative education of students, essential free assistance to the public and the strategic aims of your institution. Once the regulatory and insurance positions have been clearly established, there is an enormous amount of creative space to craft a voluntary or credit-bearing offering that suits the needs of your students and civic community which will have a real impact on all stakeholders.

Any new clinician should also be encouraged to reach out to other clinics in their area or in the wider UK network via LawWorks and the Clinical Legal Education Organisation.[61] The clinic community in the UK is very active and vibrant and we regularly mentor each other either in establishing new clinics from scratch or expanding or improving existing services. Details of national and international networks are contained in **Part 6** of this Handbook.

---

61   <https://www.cleo-uk.org/> accessed 16 August 2019.

Part 2
Regulatory framework

Part 2.1
Regulation of solicitors and university law clinics[1]

*Linden Thomas**

The majority of people who run university pro bono programmes are solicitors. Therefore, this section sets out the regulatory framework that permits solicitors employed by universities to deliver legal services to the public.

As mentioned in the Introduction to this Handbook, at the time of writing the solicitors' profession is facing significant regulatory changes. On 25 November 2019 the Solicitors Regulation Authority (SRA) Standards and Regulations ('Standards')[2] will replace the 2011 SRA Handbook.[3] The SRA has promised guidance to accompany the new Standards. However, at the time of writing some of this is still to be published and the final version of the Standards is not yet available.[4] Readers are therefore encouraged to check the most recent version of the Standards and accompanying guidance on the SRA website in order to verify that the position set out in this Handbook remains correct.

Regulation of solicitors

The regulatory framework for the legal profession in England and Wales derives from the Legal Services Act 2007 (LSA). The LSA established the Legal Services Board (LSB), which has overarching responsibility for the regulation of legal services. There are ten separate bodies, known as 'approved regulators', which fall under the LSB's remit. The approved regulator for solicitors is the Law Society of England and Wales. However, as the LSA requires a separation between regulatory and representative functions, the SRA was established

---

1   Some of the content of this section was adapted from the following article: Linden Thomas, 'Law clinics in England and Wales: A regulatory black hole' (2017) *The Law Teacher*, early online publication   <https://www.tandfonline.com/doi/full/10.1080/03069400.2017.1322858> accessed 23 July 2019.

* Thank you to Patrick Reeve of MP Reeve Ltd (www.MPReeve.com) for his helpful comments on an early draft of this section.

2   SRA, Standards and Regulations (20 March 2019) <https://www.sra.org.uk/sra/policy/future/resources.page#resources> accessed 23 July 2019.

3   The SRA Handbook was introduced in 2011 and has been subject to a number of revisions; SRA, Handbook (6 December 2018, version 21) <https://www.sra.org.uk/handbook/> accessed 23 July 2019.

4   Guidance available to date can be accessed on the SRA website: <https://www.sra.org.uk/newregs/> accessed 26 July 2019.

in 2007 as an independent arm of the Law Society and is the independent regulator of solicitors and law firms.[5]

The SRA sets out the standards and requirements that it expects the community it regulates to achieve and observe. As explained above, the new Standards, which will come into effect on 25 November 2019 and replace the 2011 Handbook, introduce a number of significant changes to the ways in which solicitors are regulated. These include:

- the replacement of ten mandatory principles with seven, which are described by the SRA as 'the fundamental tenets of ethical behaviour that [they] expect all those [they] regulate to uphold'[6]
- the creation of two separate codes of conduct: one for firms and one for solicitors
- allowing solicitors to carry out 'non-reserved' legal work from within a business not regulated by a legal services regulator
- allowing solicitors to provide reserved legal services on a freelance basis, subject to certain conditions.

Reserved and non-reserved legal activities

Before commencing any explanation as to the legal services that a solicitor may or may not provide to members of the public, it is first necessary to understand that legal services can broadly be divided into two categories: reserved legal activities; and non-reserved legal activities. The way in which you choose to set up your clinic will probably depend upon the type of legal services you intend to offer and which of these categories they fall into.

There are also some limitations on solicitors providing legal services that include immigration work and financial services (including debt). These are addressed in **Parts 2.15** and **2.16**.

What are reserved legal activities?

The Legal Services Act 2007 (LSA) prescribes that certain legal activities are 'reserved'. Reserved legal activities can only be carried out by persons who are authorised to do so, or who are otherwise exempt.[7] Those activities that are reserved are listed at s 12(1) of the LSA:

---

5   LSA, s 30.
6   SRA Standards (**note 2**), 1.
7   LSA, s 13.

(a) the exercise of a right of audience;

(b) the conduct of litigation;

(c) reserved instrument activities (predominantly conveyancing activities);

(d) probate activities;

(e) notarial activities;

(f) the administration of oaths.

A description as to what constitutes each of these activities is contained in Schedule 2 of the LSA.

There are a number of activities falling within the above definition that could potentially be carried out by a university law clinic – conducting litigation and exercising rights of audience both being obvious examples.[8] These are considered in further detail below. However, it is a criminal offence to carry out a reserved legal activity without being either an authorised person or exempt; therefore, it is important for solicitors to understand whether the activity they propose to engage in is reserved or not.[9]

Conduct of litigation

'Conduct of litigation' is defined at Schedule 2 of the LSA as:

(a) the issuing of proceedings before any court in England and Wales,

(b) the commencement, prosecution and defence of such proceedings, and

(c) the performance of any ancillary functions in relation to such proceedings (such as entering appearances to actions).[10]

For these purposes, 'court' includes First-tier and Upper Tribunals.[11] It seems to be commonly accepted that it does not include the Employment Tribunal or First-tier (Social Entitlement Chamber), neither of which restrict rights of audience. Therefore, conducting litigation (or exercising rights of audience) in either of those tribunals would not amount to reserved activity.[12]

---

8   For example, the Student Law Office at Northumbria University offers representation in court hearings <https://www.northumbria.ac.uk/about-us/academic-departments/northumbria-law-school/study/student-law-office/contact-us/> accessed 23 July 2019, as does the University of Kent Law Clinic <https://blogs.kent.ac.uk/kentlawclinic/2019/02/28/law-clinic-helps-elderly-client-recover-15k-from-mobile-home-park/> accessed 23 July 2019.

9   LSA, s 14.

10   LSA, Schedule 2

11   LSA, s 207.

12   LawWorks, *Practice Guidance: In-house solicitors and pro bono: regulatory issues* (15 March

It is clear from the definition at Schedule 2 that in all other proceedings in courts where rights of audience are restricted, actions such as service of a claim form would amount to reserved activity. However, 'performance of any ancillary functions' has been interpreted narrowly by the courts. Therefore, actions such as engaging in general correspondence with an opposing party, drafting documents prior to proceedings being issued, giving legal advice in relation to matters in dispute and engaging in alternative dispute resolution (except where this has been ordered by the court) will not amount to 'performance of ancillary functions' and therefore will not be reserved activities.[13]

Exercising a right of audience

The LSA in Schedule 2 defines a 'right of audience' as 'the right to appear before and address a court, including the right to call and examine witnesses'. As the same definition of 'court' applies here, solicitors undertaking representation and advocacy in those exempted tribunals detailed above would be an unreserved activity. However, appearance in the County Court, for example, would be a reserved activity.

Solicitors should give careful consideration as to whether the work they propose to undertake is reserved and may wish to take a risk-averse approach where in doubt, given the criminal sanctions for conducting reserved activity when not permitted.

Carrying out non-reserved legal work

From 25 November 2019 a solicitor working for an organisation that is not regulated by the SRA (or by any other legal services regulator) is able to provide non-reserved legal services to the public on behalf of their employer.[14] It is anticipated that large commercial organisations such as banks, accountancy practices and supermarkets will seek to engage solicitors to work in this way,

2019) <https://www.lawworks.org.uk/solicitors-and-volunteers/resources/lawworks-practice-guidance-house-solicitors-and-pro-bono> accessed 23 July 2019.

13   Ibid. The LawWorks *Practice Guidance* offers some very helpful direction on the interpretation of 'conduct of litigation', citing relevant case law on this topic, including *Agassi v Robinson* [2006] 1 WLR 2126 and *Ellis v Ministry of Justice* [2018] EWCA Civ 2686.

14   Somewhat confusingly, this entitlement is not expressly set out in the new SRA Standards. Rather, the right to act in this way derives from the fact that the Standards do not contain any explicit prohibition against doing so. The Standards (**note 2**) place very few limitations on the way in which both reserved and non-reserved legal services can be provided, beyond those contained in statute. This is a significant move away from the previous regulatory provisions, which are set out later in this section for information. The SRA has produced a series of guidance notes for unregulated organisations providing legal services to the public, which are available at <https://www.sra.org.uk/newregs/> accessed 26 July 2019.

without the need for their organisation to be regulated in the same way as a law firm, which can be both onerous and costly.[15]

Solicitors employed by universities can also rely on this relaxation of the regulatory framework and are able to provide non-reserved legal services to the public on behalf of their institution. These services may be provided on a pro bono basis or for a fee.

It is important to bear in mind that although the university will not be regulated, the solicitors themselves are still regulated and are subject to those SRA Standards that apply to individual solicitors.[16] Solicitors employed in this way are required to explain to their clients the regulatory protection that is available to them.[17] They must also explain:

- the insurance arrangements that they have in place and make it clear that they are not covered by the SRA Minimum Terms and Conditions[18]
- that their clients will not be eligible to apply to the Solicitors Compensation Fund[19, 20]
- which activities will be carried out by them as a solicitor authorised by the SRA[21]
- that their employer is not SRA regulated.[22]

The SRA has produced a guidance note entitled 'SRA Standards and Regulations guidance for the not for profit sector', which contains a checklist of those matters that should be explained to clients in a client care letter before commencing work for the client, along with example wording.[23] The recommendations contained in that guidance note have been incorporated into the precedent client care letter in **Part 5.1.7** of this Handbook. For more information on client care letters, please refer to **Part 2.4: Client care and taking on new clients**.

---

15   Providing legal services from an unregulated entity will be an attractive option for many organisations as they will not be subject to a regulation fee, they will not be subject to the same insurance requirements and the organisation can operate without scrutiny from the SRA.

16   Set out in the SRA Standards, SRA Code of Conduct for Solicitors, RELs and RFLs (**note 2**).

17   Ibid, Standard 8.11.

18   SRA Transparency Rules, Rule 4.3(a) (contained within the SRA Standards (**note 2**)).

19   Ibid, Rule 4.3(b).

20   Rule 4.4 of the SRA Transparency Rules states that the requirements of Rule 4.3 do not apply to non-commercial bodies, which are defined an in the Glossary to the SRA Standards as bodies that are subject to the exemption at s 23(2) of the LSA. Some universities may therefore be exempt from these requirements, but may still wish to provide clients with the information in any event.

21   SRA Standards (**note 2**), Standard 8.10(a).

22   SRA Standards (**note 2**), Standard 8.10(b).

23   SRA, 'SRA Standards and Regulations guidance for the not for profit sector' (23 July 2019) <https://www.sra.org.uk/newregs/> accessed 26 July 2019.

Solicitors delivering legal services from a non-regulated entity are not permitted to hold client money, which may impact on the type of services a university clinic is able to offer.[24]

In summary, if none of the legal services offered by your clinic are reserved then you may provide them to members of the public on behalf of your university, as long as you fulfil the requirements for individual solicitors contained in the Standards and provide the requisite information to your clients prior to commencing work.

Carrying out reserved legal work

If any of the legal services provided to the public through the university's clinic are reserved activities, the clinic must either be authorised to provide such activities, or otherwise be exempt from authorisation.

With the implementation of the new Standards, the regulatory position set out by the SRA has been brought in line with the statutory position under the LSA. The LSA provides that reserved activity may be carried on by an employee who is an authorised person, **unless** the employee is providing the reserved activity to the public or a section of the public as part of the employer's business.[25] It does not matter whether the activity is being done with a view to profit or on a pro bono basis.[26]

This means that solicitors employed by organisations that are not regulated by the SRA can carry out reserved activities on behalf of their employer. For example, a solicitor employed by a university could engage in a reserved activity, such as litigation, when acting on behalf of the university. However, the same solicitor may not engage in any reserved activities on behalf of a member of the public in their capacity as an employee of the university where to do so forms part of the university's business. This is the case even where the services are being provided pro bono.

There is no definition in the LSA as to what amounts to part of an employer's business. However, guidance on the SRA website recommends that solicitors consider the following non-exhaustive list:

(a) whether your employer describes its business as including the relevant services

(b) how regularly it provides the services, the number of employees that do so and the overall proportion of time spent on providing them

24   SRA Standards (**note 2**), Standard 4.3.

25   LSA, s 15(4).

26   Ibid.

(c) the extent to which these services complement or enhance the business of your employer

(d) whether your employer provides management, training or supervision in relation to the provision of these services, or rewards you (directly or indirectly) for doing the work

(e) who provides the necessary indemnity insurance cover.[27]

Solicitors supervising in university law clinics will almost certainly find themselves providing relevant services to the public or a section of the public as part of their employer's business. There are a multiplicity of factors which are likely to lead to this conclusion, not least that law school clinics:

- tend to be funded by the university and are often housed in university premises

- are referenced by universities when marketing their courses to potential students and when promoting the university's public engagement work

- are commonly staffed by solicitors who have been recruited specifically for the purpose of providing legal services through the clinic

- are often covered by the university's own public indemnity insurance.[28]

Therefore, the requirement for authorisation or exemption will apply where reserved activities are to be provided.

When is a clinic exempt from authorisation?

The circumstances in which a clinic may be exempt from the requirement to be authorised to provide reserved legal activities are set out below.

Under the transitional provisions at s 23(2) of the LSA

Section 23(2) of the LSA permits not-for-profit bodies to 'carry on any activity which is a reserved legal activity' during a transitional period.[29] A not-for-profit body is defined as:

> ... a body which, by or by virtue of its constitution or any enactment–
>
> (a) is required (after payment of outgoings) to apply the whole

---

27   <https://www.sra.org.uk/solicitors/code-of-conduct/guidance/guidance/Does-my-employer-need-to-be-authorised-by-an-approved-regulator-.page> accessed 25 July 2019.

28   Thomas (**note 1**).

29   LSA, s 23. The transitional period was introduced on 1 January 2010. It can be brought to an end by the Lord Chancellor. At the time of writing the SRA website states that it is not aware of any plans to do so <https://www.sra.org.uk/solicitors/code-of-conduct/guidance/guidance/Does-my-employer-need-to-be-authorised-by-an-approved-regulator-.page> accessed 21 July 2019.

of its income, and any capital which it expends, for charitable or public purposes, and

(b) is prohibited from directly or indirectly distributing amongst its members any part of its assets (otherwise than for charitable or public purposes).[30]

As most universities are charities, they may fall within this definition and therefore continue to deliver reserved activities.[31] However, the position on this is perhaps not as clear cut as it may seem. In the 'SRA Standards and Regulations guidance for the not for profit sector' there is a case study which indicates that a university would not fall within the definition of a 'non-commercial body' under the LSA.[32] It is unfortunate that the SRA guidance on this point does not align with the statutory wording and does not offer further explanation.

In any event, if the transitional period is brought to an end, the not-for-profit body would need to become authorised.[33]

Universities seeking to rely on the exemption at s 23(2) should keep in mind that it expressly permits not-for-profit bodies to 'carry on' providing reserved activities. Again, there is arguably some lack of clarity here. If 'carry on' is interpreted as 'to continue' to do an activity, this would mean that any clinics delivering reserved activities for the first time since the transitional provision came into force on 1 January 2010 may not rely on the exemption.

However, ss 13, 14 and 15 of the LSA all use the term 'carry on' in the sense of 'engaging in' an activity rather than 'continuing to engage in' an activity you were previously undertaking, and would not make sense if they only applied to those who were engaged in reserved activity before the LSA came into force. Furthermore, the SRA guidance suggests all not-for-profit organisations and charities may rely on the exemption and makes no mention to the statutory reference to 'carry[ing] on'.[34]

SRA-regulated independent solicitors

Up to the introduction of the Standards in November 2019, solicitors practising alone have been required to have their practice authorised. The practice had to be a separate legal entity known as a sole practitioner firm. However,

---

30   LSA, s 207.

31   Most English universities are exempt charities under the Charities Act 1993 and are regulated by the Higher Education Funding Council for England (HEFCE).

32   SRA guidance for not for profits (**note 23**), 24.

33   LSA,s 106.

34   <https://www.sra.org.uk/solicitors/guidance/ethics-guidance/different-ways-working.page> accessed 23 July 2019.

following the introduction of the Standards it is possible for solicitors to offer some services without the practice itself being authorised or the need for the creation of a separate legal entity from which to provide those services.[35] In its guidance, the SRA refers to individuals delivering services in this manner as 'SRA-regulated independent solicitors',[36] although that term is not used or defined in the Standards.

The SRA guidance states that:

> We use the term independent solicitor to describe a self-employed solicitor who is:
>
> • practising on their own, and does not employ anyone else in connection with the services they provide
>
> • practising in their own name (rather than under a trading name or through a service company)
>
> • engaged directly by clients with fees payable directly to them without that practice being authorised.[37]

Where the independent solicitor's practice consists entirely of activities that are not reserved legal activities, no authorisation is required.[38] Where reserved legal activities are to be offered, it is still possible for the solicitor to provide these on their own account, without authorisation, as long as certain criteria are met.[39] For example, the solicitor must:

• have at least three years of post-qualification experience

• be self-employed and practising in their own name, and not through a trading name or service company

• not employ anyone in connection with services that they provide.[40]

Given that the vast majority of solicitors running university law clinics will be employed by the university and will provide their services on behalf of the university, they will not be trading on their own account as SRA-regulated independent solicitors and therefore will not be able to rely on this exemption. However, external solicitors employed in private practice or in-house at

---

35   'SRA Authorisation of Individuals Regulations', Regulation 10.2 (contained within the SRA Standards (note 2)).

36   <https://www.sra.org.uk/solicitors/guidance/ethics-guidance/Preparing-to-become-a-sole-practitioner-or-an-SRA-regulated-independent-solicitor.page> accessed 26 July 2019.

37   Ibid.

38   SRA Authorisation of Individuals Regulations, Regulation 10.2(a) (contained within the SRA Standards (note 2)).

39   Ibid, Regulation 10.2(b).

40   Ibid.

another organisation, wishing to practise as a volunteer with a university pro bono clinic, may be able to undertake both reserved and non-reserved activity, acting on their own account as an SRA-regulated independent solicitor, providing they comply with the requirements at Regulation 10.[41]

Schedule 3 of the LSA

There are further exemptions set out at Schedule 3 of the LSA. However, they are very specific and are unlikely to assist solicitors wishing to undertake reserved activities in university law clinics. For example, in relation to conduct of litigation, Schedule 3 provides that a person will be exempt if they are not authorised, but are granted a right to conduct litigation by the court in relation to those proceedings. It is unlikely to be viable to seek such permission in each piece of litigation that a clinic may take on.

If I am not exempt, how do I become authorised?

The SRA is able to authorise three different types of business:[42]

- **A sole practice:** This is where solicitor is practising on their own account, providing services in their own name, or a trading name. Solicitors working in universities will not be working for sole practices, as the services will be provided on behalf of the university.
- **A legal services body:**[43] This is a firm in which all of the managers and those who hold an interest in the business are lawyers. A legal services body might include a partnership, company or limited liability partnership. Again, universities will not fit into this definition.
- **A licensable body (commonly known as an alternative business structure (ABS)):** An ABS is an entity that provides legal services, and which is managed or owned and controlled by both lawyers and non-lawyers.[44] In order for the ABS to perform reserved legal activities, it must be licensed to do so by a regulator.[45] Given that law clinics tend to make up a very small part of a university's offering, it is unlikely to be feasible to turn the entire institution into

---

41   SRA Standards (**note 2**), Regulation 10. See also SRA guidance for not for profits (**note 23**), 23–24.

42   The following descriptions are abridged versions of the content of the SRA guidance on Firm authorisation <https://www.sra.org.uk/solicitors/guidance/ethics-guidance/Firm-authorisation.page> accessed 26 July 2019.

43   The Glossary to the Standards (**note 2**) states that 'legal services body' is given the same meaning as that given in s 9A of the Administration of Justice Act 1985.

44   LSA, s 72 sets out what makes a body licensable.

45   LSA, s 18.

an ABS. However, some universities have chosen to set up subsidiary companies from which to deliver their legal services to the public. See **Part 2.2** for more detail on the practicalities of setting up an ABS.

Where a clinic is authorised, it will be subject to the Code of Conduct for firms contained in the Standards.[46]

Our clinic does not do any reserved work. Is there any reason why we might want to seek authorisation anyway?

Even where your clinic does not undertake any reserved activities and therefore does not need to be authorised, you may still decide to seek authorisation. There are a number of reasons why this might be an attractive option. For example, authorised practices are able to offer clients greater protections, such as the requirement to have indemnity insurance that complies with the Minimum Terms and Conditions (see below) and the right of recourse to the Solicitors' Compensation Fund.

Reserved activities and external partnerships

Some clinicians may be keen to offer their students the opportunity to engage in reserved legal work, such as conducting litigation, but will have neither the resources nor the institutional backing to seek authorisation to do so through their university. In such cases, an alternative option is to adopt what is commonly referred to as an 'externship' arrangement, and partner with external organisations such as law centres, third-sector advice agencies and law firms that are authorised to carry out reserved activity and to arrange for students to undertake placements with them.[47] The duration of such placements can vary depending upon the external partner's needs and student capacity.

Further guidance on establishing an externship arrangement can be found in **Part 1** of this Handbook.

Using external solicitors as volunteers in a university-run clinic

Many university clinics rely on external solicitors to increase the capacity of their clinic by advising on client cases and/or supervising students in doing the same. The capacity in which the external solicitor is volunteering with the clinic and their eligibility to do so should be established at the outset. It is important to be clear on whose behalf the legal service is being provided. For example:

---

46   SRA Standards (**note 2**), SRA Authorisation of Firms Rules.

47   The pros and cons of arrangements of this type are explored in Thomas (**note 1**).

- Is the service being provided on behalf of the university, with the volunteer solicitor operating under the supervision of the solicitor employed by the university?
- Is the volunteer solicitor providing the service on behalf of their employer and, if so, is their employer an authorised firm or an unregulated organisation?
- Is the volunteer solicitor providing the service on their own behalf as a SRA-regulated independent solicitor?

It is important to be clear about these arrangements so that:

- appropriate supervision can be put in place, as required under the Code of Conduct for Solicitors (see below)
- it is clear whether the volunteer solicitor is permitted to undertake reserved activities
- accurate information can be given to the client as to the protections available to them
- it is clear whether appropriate insurance cover is in place and, if so, on whose insurance the volunteer will be relying.[48]

Universities may wish to consider entering into a written agreement with individual volunteers or –where the partnership is at an organisational level – with their employers, to address issues such as confidentiality, data sharing, quality of student supervision, insurance, etc.

Supervision of staff, professional and student volunteers in a university clinic

There are many different types of people who may be involved in the provision of legal services through a university law clinic. These can include:

- student volunteers
- staff employed by the university
- external lawyer volunteers.

Standard 3.5 of the SRA Code of Conduct for Solicitors states:

Where you supervise or manage others providing legal services:

(a) you remain accountable for the work carried out through them; and

(b) you effectively supervise work being done for clients.[49]

---

48   See SRA guidance for not for profits (**note 23**) 22–25.
49   SRA Standards (**note 2**), Standard 3.5.

Standard 3.6 goes on to provide that:

> You ensure that the individuals you manage are competent to
> carry out their role, and keep their professional knowledge
> and skills, as well as understanding of their legal, ethical and
> regulatory obligations, up to date.[50]

The SRA guidance for not for profits provides that the degree of supervision
and the proximity of the supervision will vary depending upon the type of work
being undertaken and the qualification, knowledge and experience of those
being supervised.[51] Therefore, student volunteers are likely to require much
closer supervision than an experienced external volunteer. Solicitors working
in university law clinics should be mindful of their obligations as supervisors
and ensure appropriate systems are in place to enable them to oversee work
being done for clients. They should also consider the training requirements of
those they are responsible for and ensure that these are met. See **Part 1** for
further guidance on training for students.

It is important to set out clearly in the client care letter the scope of the work
that the solicitor is responsible for before undertaking work on a matter.

Holding a practising certificate

Section 1 of the Solicitors Act 1974 states that you will not be 'qualified to act
as a solicitor' unless:

- you have been admitted as a solicitor
- your name is on the roll
- you have a valid practising certificate issued by the SRA.

Acting as a solicitor

Sections 20 and 21 of the Solicitors Act 1974 make it a criminal offence for a
person who is not qualified to act as a solicitor (for example, because they do
not have a valid practising certificate) to wilfully pretend to be so qualified or
to refer to themselves in any way that would imply that they are so qualified.[52]

Therefore, where an individual is described as a 'solicitor' they should either:

- hold a current practising certificate; or
- make it clear that they are not qualified to act as a solicitor because they

---

50   Ibid, Standard 3.6.

51   SRA Guidance for not for profits **(note 23)**, 19.

52   <https://www.sra.org.uk/solicitors/guidance/ethics-guidance/When-do-I-need-a-
practising-certificate-.page> accessed 26 July 2019.

do not have a valid practising certificate.[53]

Simply putting 'non-practising solicitor' at the end of your name or job title may not be sufficient to get around this requirement, as members of the public will not necessarily understand what is meant by that description.

Bear in mind that it may also be possible to impliedly hold yourself out as a solicitor through your actions, even where there is no reference to being a solicitor or legal practitioner in your job title. The only way to avoid any risk of this is to make it expressly clear that you are not qualified to act as a solicitor.[54]

Employed in connection with the provision of legal services

Under s 1A of the Solicitors Act 1974, you will be treated as 'acting as a solicitor' (and will therefore need to hold a practising certificate) if you are employed in connection with the provision of legal services by any of the following:

- a person who is qualified to act as a solicitor
- a partnership where at least one member is qualified to act as a solicitor
- a body recognised under s 9 of the Administration of Justice Act 1985
- any other authorised person entitled to provide reserved legal services; this would include a licensed body, or a body authorised by another approved regulator.

The SRA's guidance on this states that:

> If you come within section 1A, even if your job title has nothing in it to suggest you are a solicitor, your role does not involve dealing directly with clients, it is a role an unqualified person could do, or you are employed on a temporary or voluntary basis, you will still need to consider whether you require a practising certificate. The determining factor is whether you are employed in connection with the provision of legal services; if so, you are deemed to be practising as a solicitor and must therefore hold a practising certificate, regardless of whether you are held out as a solicitor.[55]

It is recommended that solicitors providing legal services on behalf of a university law clinic ought to have a current practising certificate in place unless absolutely satisfied that they are covered by one of the limited exemptions.

---

53   Ibid.

54   Ibid.

55   <https://www.sra.org.uk/solicitors/guidance/ethics-guidance/When-do-I-need-a-practising-certificate-.page>

Solicitors working in university law schools: position before 25 November 2019[56]

Up to and including 24 November 2019, a solicitor employed by a university to deliver, or supervise the delivery of, legal services to members of the public on behalf of the university, was likely to fall within the definition of an in-house solicitor under the Solicitors Practice Framework Rules.[57]

The Practice Framework Rules (PFRs) permitted an individual to practise as a solicitor:

> as the employee of another person, business or organisation, provided that you undertake work only for your employer, or as permitted by Rule 4 (In-house practice).[58]

It was the reference to 'Rule 4' of the PFRs (specifically, Rule 4.10) that enabled in-house solicitors to provide pro bono legal advice to a client other than their employer. However, this could only be done where the following conditions were met:

- the work was covered by professional indemnity insurance reasonably equivalent to that required by the SRA
- either: no fees were charged; or the only fees charged were those received from the opposing party by way of costs if the client was successful and all costs were paid to charity
- the solicitor did not undertake any reserved legal activities, unless the provision of relevant services to the public or a section of the public (with or without a view to profit) was not part of their employer's business.[59]

Each of these requirements is addressed in turn below.

Professional indemnity insurance reasonably equivalent to that required by the SRA

Solicitors working in private practice were required to obtain insurance that complied with Minimum Terms and Conditions (MTCs).[60] As set out above, Rule 4.10 made it clear that in-house solicitors wishing to do pro bono must do so under 'reasonably equivalent' terms to the MTCs.[61] However, the SRA did not

---

56   Further details on the position prior to 25 November 2019 can be found in Thomas (**note 1**).

57   The Practice Framework Rules are part of the SRA Handbook 2011 (**note 3**).

58   Practice Framework Rules, Rule 1.1(e).

59   Ibid.

60   The MTCs are set out in the SRA Indemnity Insurance Rules, Appendix 1 to the 2011 SRA Handbook (from 25 November 2019 they are contained in the new Standards (**note 2**)).

61   Practice Framework Rules (n 57).

provide any guidance as to how 'reasonably equivalent' ought to be interpreted, or as to what a reasonably equivalent insurance policy might include.

Universities contemplating whether they have insurance that satisfies this test should have taken into account factors such as the overall indemnity cover provided by university insurers for any single event and the risk and value of cases being taken on by the clinic. Further guidance on ensuring your clinic has appropriate insurance in place both up to and after 25 November 2019 is set out at **Part 2.3**.

Charging fees

The proviso that fees must not be charged was likely to be overcome easily for most university law clinics, given that nearly all provide their services on a pro bono basis.

Undertaking reserved legal activities

As is the case from 25 November 2019, a law clinic either needed to be authorised or exempt in order to provide legal services that include reserved legal activities. If the services provided were limited to non-reserved activities, then no authorisation or exemption was required and solicitors could act for members of the public under the provisions of PFR 4.10.

Part 2.2
Establishing a law clinic as an alternative business structure[1]

Nick Johnson

In view of the potential restrictions that could arise if the transitional provisions under s 23(2) of the Legal Services Act 2007 (LSA) are not extended indefinitely,[2] and for further reasons suggested below, the option of applying for an alternative business structure (ABS) licence has been pursued by some law schools, in order to ensure that their activity is sustainable in the light of any regulatory change. Providing such activity stays within the limits of any charitable objects of the university or any of its subsidiary bodies, the ABS licence also enables clinics to charge for certain services.

Universities that are considering applying for an ABS licence will need to address the following issues:

- **Which regulator should be approached?**

  This is very much a decision for the law school/university concerned. Licences are granted by a range of regulators, including the Solicitors Regulation Authority (SRA), the Bar Standards Board (BSB) and the Chartered Institute of Legal Executives (CILEx). References to processes here are based on seeking a licence from the SRA. This is likely to be the regulator of choice for many university clinics, as it is likely to fit most closely with the professional profile of the clinic staff and with the likely career destinations of the largest proportion of the university's students.

- **Which legal entity should hold the licence?**

  The licence is granted to a specific legal entity. Given that the licence is granted on the basis of the identity of certain managers, it may not be practicable for the licence to be granted to a university as this could entail investigation into the personal circumstances of many senior figures within the institution and potentially the governing body. It is likely to be more appropriate to grant the licence to a separate legal entity (such as a charitable company limited by guarantee). Specific employees of the university can then be appointed as directors and managers of that entity. This model is not unusual in higher education.

---

1 The material in the section is based on material delivered in conference papers given in Manchester in January 2017 and in Tel Aviv in December 2017.

2 See **Part 2.1** for more detail on this.

Most UK universities run subsidiary companies, often to perform specific functions, and such entities may themselves be subsequently sold off.

- **Identify the compliance officers**

  All practising entities are required to identify a Head of Legal Practice[3] and a Head of Financial Affairs,[4] commonly referred to as Compliance Officers for Legal Practice (COLPs) and Financial Affairs (COFAs). These persons should be sufficiently senior to enable them to carry out their role. Both persons must be suitably qualified (in the case of the COLP, legally qualified) as they have a crucial role in reporting potential regulatory infringements. It is incumbent on both officers to report all infringements to the regulator (in contrast to the more limited responsibility of a traditional firm to report material breaches[5]).

- **Identify appropriate managers**

  In addition to the COLP and the COFA, it is necessary to identify those people who will act as managers of the entity. The regulator will undertake character and suitability checks on all managers. It is important to ensure that such people are sufficiently senior within the organisation to ensure that they can make representations to the appropriate people within the university (e.g. Estates and Directors of Finance) if university policy or activity conflicts with the requirements of the licensed entity.

- **Insurance**

  Many university law clinics rely on the insurance of their institution rather than carrying specific professional indemnity. Where the legal services are provided through an ABS it will be necessary to ensure appropriate insurance is in place to cover legal services provided through that entity. Unless a waiver is obtained, this will probably need to be specific insurance approved by the relevant regulatory body.[6] Rather than relying on existing university insurance, which is unlikely to meet regulatory requirements, it is likely a separate policy which satisfies the Minimum Terms and Conditions will be required.[7] More detailed guidance on insurance can be found in **Part 2.3** of this Handbook.

- **Policies**

  The process of obtaining the licence requires scrutiny of the practice's

---

3   LSA, Schedule 11, Part 2, para 11.

4   Ibid, para 13.

5   Ibid, ss 91 and 93.

6   Ibid, Schedule 11, Part 3, para 13.

7   For SRA minimum terms see <https://www.sra.org.uk/solicitors/handbook/indemnityins/appendix-1/content.page> accessed 24 July 2019.

policies and processes. These might include, for example, processes for holding client money, payment of interest, complaints, and equality and diversity policies. It is important that these are properly established and made available as required as part of the process of granting the licence.

- **Status of students**

  Given the more formal arrangements for engaging students through an ABS, it is necessary to clarify their status as persons within the practice. It may be necessary to prepare a formal agreement that students are required to sign, in which it is made clear on recruitment to the clinic that students may be subject to disciplinary action by the regulator, even when unqualified, for failing to observe key obligations.[8] The regulator may raise the following concerns during the application process:

  – the high ratio of qualified to unqualified staff: such concerns can be allayed by outlining specific arrangements for supervision and training

  – the processes by which students can be disciplined for infringements: these can include using the university's own Student Disciplinary processes if needs be.

- **Relationships with third parties**

  It will be necessary to review arrangements with third party organisations, law firms and referral agencies to ensure that these are acceptable to the regulatory authority granting the licence. In some cases it may be necessary to draw up memoranda of understanding to ensure that issues such as terms of referral and insurance arrangements are clearly set out. Note that this is good practice when working with third parties in any clinic setting, even where the clinic is not an ABS.

  It will also be necessary to agree a series of agreements between the ABS and the university on such issues as data sharing, occupation of premises, rights of access and provision of finance and HR functions. To the extent that staff are employed by the university rather than the entity which holds the licence, it may be that they will need to be formally seconded by the university to the subsidiary entity – the ABS licence holder – to ensure sufficient control of them by the regulated ABS entity.

- **Establish compliance review procedures**

  Taking on an ABS licence will almost certainly require a review of management compliance procedures. For example, the ABS will need

---

8   See **Part 2.10** for points to be mindful of when requiring international students to sign up to contracts regarding their participation in a law clinic.

to have registers of interests, conflicts and complaints; a system of file review; and clear policies on such matters as money laundering, client interest and data protection.

Regular compliance review meetings should be instigated, at which complaints, concerns about potential breaches of practice rules and 'near misses' can be discussed. Universities might consider engagement of students in the practice committee structure. Again, many of the above ought to be considered good practice, even where a clinic is not an ABS.

Advantages and disadvantages of applying for ABS status

As the above suggests, the process of applying for the ABS licence is rigorous. Those universities that have been through the process report that they generally found the regulator willing to engage in discussions over aspects of clinic practice which are unusual (e.g. the use of student volunteers). This enables an applicant to review and tighten up procedures and particularly to address its relationship with the university.

It will be necessary to undertake a full policy review and clarify aspects of practice to obtain the licence. These discussions will assist in ensuring that both the clinic and the university are clear about what is required to maintain the licence.

It is also necessary to develop clear processes around the issue of reporting to the regulator. This needs to provide clarity about reporting matters of professional concern and clear routes for staff to be able to report concerns.

The establishment of a separate legal entity to hold the licence will require you to address the issue of who the managers and directors of the subsidiary should be. It will be necessary to obtain support from senior staff in the university to guarantee the clinic has sufficient influence within the institution to ensure that action is taken to preserve the licence and that nothing is done which jeopardises it. This also provides a vehicle with which a clinic can engage and contract with outside organisations and maintain a degree of autonomy within the university structure. It also ensures clarity so that, for example, issues such as Freedom of Information Act requests, which might be used by other parties, can be dealt with by the practice rather than the university.

The existence of a separate entity arguably provides greater clarity for those lawyers operating within the practice as to where regulatory responsibility lies.

Note that the process of obtaining the licence can be long and relatively expensive. It is likely that the university will wish to appoint external lawyers to provide support, although many consultants are able to provide similar services. Ultimately, much of the work to obtain the licence will need to be undertaken by law school and university staff, which will involve a considerable investment of staff time. Application processes are generally relatively straightforward, although the regulator will require information about the managers and their backgrounds. There will also be some increased costs, most notably insurance: this will be an additional overhead where the regulator requires professional indemnity insurance that meets its minimum requirements. The application costs vary depending on the regulator, but may be substantial.

One potential benefit of holding a licence is that a clinic will be able to charge for services, subject to it remaining within its charitable objectives. However, it is questionable whether or not sufficient money can be earned to recoup fees spent and this issue will need careful consideration, both as to the financial benefit and whether or not such a focus detracts from the social justice mission of a clinic.

Any arrangements for billing and holding client money will require engagement with the university finance department, and conflicts can arise between the rules relating to the handling of client money and university standing financial procedures. The practice will need to have clear agreed protocols with those administering its accounts, in particular an understanding of the need for client confidentiality, as well as an understanding of the regulator's accounting rules.

Reporting and recording requirements will entail some additional burden but also provide a clear incentive to ensure that responsibility for regulatory issues is clearly allocated and dealt with within the practice.

A further potential benefit of obtaining the licence is to enable the law school to more clearly articulate a clinic's strategy. This in part stems from an original idea behind ABSs, which was to look at different ways of providing access to justice and to see if outside investment – or, indeed, other professional expertise – would be able to deliver access to justice more effectively.

One specific model which has been identified is that of a 'teaching law firm', an idea that clearly mirrors the medical model which is often invoked for law school clinics. However, a university's position as an educational organisation can enable the practice to focus, in part, on the provision of public legal education and to look at addressing the justice gap through educational means – part of the 'alternative business' that runs alongside the main legal practice.

Further, such alternative businesses can also investigate and evaluate, as a research objective, new methods of delivering access to justice, in keeping with the university's research function. The model that this perhaps most closely resembles is the American Bar Association's establishment of an Access to Justice Innovation Centre.[9] Establishing a clinic as a separate legal entity and obtaining the licence can provide a platform to seek to develop and evaluate access to justice issues, in keeping with the key strategic objectives of many universities. However, whether developing or articulating such a mission requires the expense and time of establishing an ABS will be a matter for each clinic to decide itself on the merits.

9   <https://www.americanbar.org/groups/legal_aid_indigent_defendants/initiatives/resource_center_for_access_to_justice.html> accessed 24 July 2019.

Part 2.3
Insurance

LawWorks

Arranging professional indemnity (PI) insurance is an important requirement for a law clinic to consider. All clinics should be insured against the risk of liability in respect of providing legal advice, assistance and/or representation given to clients. Under the Solicitors Regulation Authority (SRA) rules, clinics must ensure that insurance cover is in place which meets the regulatory minimums. Cover should explicitly extend to students and supervisors.

Prior to 25 November 2019, the minimum sum insured for any one claim had to be £2 million,[1] in order to ensure compliance with the Minimum Terms and Conditions (MTCs) set out in the SRA's Solicitors Indemnity Insurance Rules (SIIR) for 'qualifying insurance'.

However, from 25 November 2019 the requirements were modified when the SRA's Handbook reforms were introduced. Under the SRA'S changes to the Code of Conduct for Solicitors, solicitors practising in a 'non-commercial body' must ensure that the body takes out and maintains indemnity insurance that provides 'adequate and appropriate' cover in respect of the legal services provided.[2] The meaning of 'adequate and appropriate' is discussed further below.

There are different options of how to secure insurance cover depending on the type of clinic you decide to operate and what structure it follows.

Student-led clinics

Where advice is researched, written and delivered by students working or volunteering under supervision from someone else:

- **Where supervision is 'internal' to the university (e.g. by an academic or practitioner within the law school and employed by the university):**
    - Insurance under the university's existing policy may be sufficient: you must notify the insurance provider of the activities being conducted at the clinic.

1   This is equivalent to firms that are required to take out and maintain professional indemnity insurance (PII) of at least £2 million for any one claim, or £3 million in the case of a limited liability firm   <https://www.sra.org.uk/solicitors/code-of-conduct/guidance/guidance/Professional-Indemnity-Insurance-cover.page> accessed 31 July 2019.

2   SRA, *Standards and Regulations* (20 March 2019) <https://www.sra.org.uk/sra/policy/future/resources.page#resources> accessed 23 July 2019.

- A separate insurance policy for the clinic may be necessary: you will need to arrange and pay for a separate policy to cover the work of the clinic only.
- **Where supervision is 'external' to the university (e.g. by a solicitor from a local law firm):**
  - Cover could be provided by extending the existing university policy to include 'external' supervisors, e.g. lawyers from local law firms.
  - Coverage could be provided by the law firm's insurance provider, with agreement and confirmation from the parties.
- **Where an advice agency hosts the clinic (supervision is either internal or external to the university):**
  - It may be possible to rely on an insurance policy held by a partner organisation, where an advice agency is involved in the delivery of the clinic, subject to their agreement and confirmation that the activity is covered by the policy.

Solicitor-led clinics

Where advice is given directly from solicitor to client, but where the law school facilitates the clinic service and students provide administrative support and/ or are shadowing the solicitor giving the advice:

- The solicitor might be employed by the university or by an external law firm and assisting with the clinic in a voluntary capacity:
  - Coverage may be provided by a volunteer lawyer's firm's insurance (where applicable): it would be advisable to confirm that the policy extends to pro bono work.
  - The university insurance policy may be extended to cover any written work provided by the students and/or solicitor employed by the university to the client on the clinic headed paper. Otherwise, any written notes are provided to the client on law firm headed paper and covered by law firm insurance.

Under SRA rules all solicitors providing advice must be covered by 'qualifying' professional indemnity insurance, unless a waiver from these requirements has been given by the SRA. The same applies for RELs and RFLs (Registered European Lawyers and Registered Foreign Lawyers) undertaking pro bono work in clinics.

Qualifying insurance is cover that complies with the SRA's Indemnity Insurance Rules; further information can be found here: www.sra.org.uk/solicitors/ handbook/indemnityins/.[3]

---

3   This link may change following the introduction of the SRA *Standards and Regulations* (**note 2**).

LawWorks waiver and insurance

LawWorks has obtained an SRA waiver that can be applicable to clinics which are part of the LawWorks Clinics Network; this document waives the requirement to follow the Solicitors Indemnity Insurance Rules (SIIR) and instead requires the clinic to only have 'adequate and appropriate' insurance.

This reflects the SRA's new language to describe the insurance requirement for not-for-profit bodies, namely that insurance cover should be 'adequate and appropriate'. Previously, the requirement had been to secure insurance that would be 'reasonably equivalent' to the MTCs of the SIIR.

Unfortunately, the SRA has not provided a definition or produced guidance to assist clinics in interpreting the phrase 'adequate and appropriate'. The phrase is clearly intended to enable clinics to move away from the minimum monetary amounts contained in the MTCs (i.e. £2 million).

LawWorks understands that the SRA's new language, while not changing the underlying requirement to have insurance cover in place, is intended to encourage clinics towards a more realistic assessment of the likely claims that might actually be brought against them. In order to determine what might be an adequate and appropriate cover, it will be necessary to look at the potential risks to clients if things go wrong and ensure there is sufficient cover for this. This will depend on the service you provide and the risk profile of your organisation, and the key to the assessment will be to ensure that clients are protected.

It is not possible in the context of this section to be more specific, and in time we expect the SRA to issue further guidance. If you are at all unsure whether your insurance cover is compliant, you should contact the SRA helpline directly (call 0370 606 2577 or email professional.ethics@sra.org.uk), and seek confirmation in writing. Another source of help is the Law Society's Practice Advice Service on 020 7320 5675/practiceadvice@lawsociety.org.uk.

Also waived are certain of the other outcomes set out in the SRA Code of Conduct relating to written prior notification to clients of a complaint procedure; complaint handling and advice as to the overall costs of a client's matter. It does, however, impose conditions related to each of these subjects. All solicitor volunteers must be provided with a copy of the waiver. The current waiver expires on 14 January 2022.

Further information about the LawWorks waiver from the SRA can be found at: www.lawworks.org.uk/solicitors-and-volunteers/resources/sra-professional-indemnity-insurance-rules-waiver

LawWorks insurance

LawWorks has in place a policy of insurance which, at LawWorks' discretion, may be extended to clinics and volunteers undertaking pro bono work on behalf of clinics registered with the Clinics Network. This policy has recently been revised to include cover for in-house lawyers and/or law firms working on pro bono projects.[4]

While the policy is not generally used for clinic work or appropriate for a law school clinic, it may be made available to clinics in exceptional circumstances – for example, to cover an in-house member team who would not ordinarily have an existing PI policy in place. LawWorks regards its insurance offer as a 'safety net' policy, so the cover provided will only extend to circumstances where no other PI insurance is available. For example, the PI insurance scheme will not apply if a clinic is undertaking pro bono legal work through a law centre and the law centre's PI insurance provides coverage.

Coverage of clinics is not automatic and must be agreed by LawWorks. Prior to approaching LawWorks to discuss this possibility, clinics should investigate alternative options. To be considered for coverage under the LawWorks policy, a clinic must complete an application form (available from LawWorks) accepting the terms and conditions, and a clinic will not be covered unless express confirmation from LawWorks is given in writing.

More information on LawWorks insurance can obtained from clinics@ lawworks.org.uk.

Immigration work

For organisations undertaking immigration work, the Office of the Immigration Services Commissioner (OISC) expects organisation-wide PI insurance to cover the provision of advice and for the limit of indemnity to be above £250,000.

Insurance advice

To assist with finding a new insurance policy or for advice, please refer to the website of the British Institute of Insurance Brokers (BIBA).[5] Information provided to insurers must be clear and comprehensive so that insurers understand the full extent of any liability they are covering.

---

4   <https://www.lawworks.org.uk/solicitors-and-volunteers/get-involved/house/lawworks-pro-bono-professional-indemnity-insurance> accessed 31 July 2019.

5   <https://www.biba.org.uk/find-insurance/> accessed 31 July 2019.

Clinics should bear in mind that insurers and brokers may not have experience of the work of pro bono clinics; consequently, they need to ensure that insurers understand the nature of the work being undertaken and by whom. Failure to explain the activities of clinics effectively to insurers could, in certain circumstances, render such cover void.

Other insurances to consider

Apart from professional indemnity cover, it is also important to ensure that other relevant insurances, such as public liability cover, are in place.

Part 2.4
Client care and taking on new clients

Lee Hansen*

In this section we highlight steps that should be taken at or prior to a first client interview, including conflict screening. We also look at client care, which is about 'providing a proper standard of service, which takes into account the individual needs and circumstances of each client'.[1] This includes consideration of the information given to a client prior to giving advice or taking on a case.

Having clearly defined procedures for client intake will place your service on the best footing for the initial client interview and beyond; it will also provide reassurance to your students (whatever their level of experience) and should help to ensure that any lawyers involved in supervising client work will be compliant with the requirements placed on them by their regulators.

This section sets out a number of points to consider; however, the particular requirements that apply to your clinic may vary depending on how the service is regulated. The Solicitors Regulation Authority's (SRA's) requirements will be relevant to many clinics, as the majority are staffed by practising solicitors. Therefore, reference is made in this section to the SRA's rules on conduct.[2] **Part 2.18** sets out some provisions that apply specifically to barristers. The particular approach taken may also be influenced by other factors including your institution's policies and procedures (e.g. in the area of data protection) and any requirements laid down by your insurer.

Intake guidelines

As a matter of good practice, clinics should develop written guidelines setting out the areas of law in which advice, casework or representation is available. These should be accessible to all volunteers and staff of the clinic, and for new clinic participants training on these should be a part of their induction. The

---

*   Thank you to Nick Johnson and Elizabeth Fisher-Frank for helpful comments on drafts of this section.

1   SRA Handbook 2011 (version 21), Chapter 1: Client care <https://www.sra.org.uk/solicitors/handbook/code/part2/rule1/content.page> accessed 31 July 2019.

2   On 25 November 2019 the new SRA Standards and Regulations came into force, which include a new SRA Code of Conduct for Solicitors, Registered European Lawyers and Registered Foreign Lawyers (SRA Code for Solicitors) and a separate SRA Code of Conduct for Firms (SRA Code for Firms) <https://www.sra.org.uk/sra/policy/future/resources.page#resources> accessed 23 July 2019. In this section reference will be made to both the previous Code (**note 1**) and the new SRA Code for Solicitors.

guidelines should also set out any criteria that apply to potential clients, for example an income limit or other financial requirements.

It may be that your clinic does not take on certain types of matters for regulatory reasons, for example immigration, consumer credit or reserved activities may be excluded from your service.[3] Such areas where assistance cannot be provided should be set out clearly in the guidelines.

Client information, instructions and documents

Naturally clinics will need to receive and record certain client information. They will need information to conduct conflict checks, as noted below. It is important to ensure that client contact information is completely and accurately recorded. Even if your service is providing one-off advice you will need to have contact details so that you are able to contact the client to correct any errors in the unlikely event that an inaccuracy in the advice is discovered.[4]

A preferred method of communication may also be noted, for example email, and special procedures for contact may be needed and recorded, for example in cases of domestic violence where the client specifically does not want an advice letter sent to their home address or does not want you to contact them via a landline.

Advisers will also need to take down a full and clear record of the client's instructions. These can be confirmed in the advice letter or in a written record filled out at the conclusion of the interview.

The clinic will often take copies of client documents in order to properly advise the client. Unless the clinic has secure storage facilities for deeds, etc. it is important to retain copies and not to take the originals.

Conflict screening

The 2011 SRA Code of Conduct defined conflict of interests as:

> … any situation where:
>
> (i) you owe separate duties to act in the best interests of two or more clients in relation to the same or related matters, and those duties conflict, or there is a significant risk that those duties may conflict (a 'client conflict'); or

---

3   See **Parts 2.15, 2.16, 2.1** and **2.18** for more detail on these restrictions.

4   In this regard you should consider your obligations to keep data accurate and up to date.

(ii) your duty to act in the best interests of any client in relation to a matter conflicts, or there is a significant risk that it may conflict, with your own interests in relation to that or a related matter (an 'own interest conflict').[5]

Under the SRA Glossary, which accompanies the new SRA Standards and Regulations, separate definitions provide that:

- a **conflict of interest** 'means a situation where your separate duties to act in the best interests of two or more clients in relation to the same or a related matters conflict'
- an **own interest conflict** 'means any situation where your duty to act in the best interests of any client in relation to a matter conflicts, or there is a significant risk that it may conflict, with your own interests in relation to that or a related matter'.[6]

This section will focus on client conflicts in particular. However, solicitors should also keep in mind that they must not act where there is a conflict, or a significant risk of conflict, between them and their client. For example, an own interest conflict might arise if a potential client is seeking advice about a complaint they have against a company in which the supervising solicitor holds shares. Students should also be trained to look out for situations in which they might find themselves with an own interest conflict.[7]

Client conflicts

When taking on a new client a clinic should undertake conflict checks to ensure that there are no actual or potential conflicts of interest with a current or former client. The duty to avoid conflicts is a matter of professional conduct for solicitors and barristers. It is an approach that is 'known about and adopted by others providing legal advice',[8] and should be followed as a matter of good practice.

---

5   SRA Handbook 2011 (**note 1**), Glossary.

6   SRA Standards and Regulations (**note 2**), Glossary.

7   There is another category of conflicts known as **commercial conflicts**: in these cases a lawyer, a firm or a clinic may not be legally prevented from acting but may decline from doing so for some commercial reason. For discussion of commercial conflicts as they apply to a pro bono practice, and for strategies to overcome and manage these, see Law Society Pro bono manual, pp. 80–81, available at <https://www.lawsociety.org.uk/support-services/practice-management/pro-bono/pro-bono-manual/> accessed 12 April 2019.

8   Elaine Heslop, Giving legal advice: An adviser's handbook (Legal Action Group, 2014, 2nd edn), p. 50.

Particular areas in which a university should not act include where the other party is a student, staff member of the university or if the complaint is against the university. It will therefore be necessary to ensure as a part of the intake procedure that checks are made that others involved are not university students or staff.

In order to conduct a conflict check you will need the full name of the opposing party. Additional information may also assist for the purposes of conducting the check, for example date of birth and address. This is particularly handy when checking against common names like 'John Smith'. Any current or previous aliases of the client or opposing party should also be taken and checked.

You will also need to conduct a check using your prospective client's name. A current or former client may have listed them as an opposing party, and your system for checks or your database should reveal this. An electronic case management system is not essential, but can be an efficient way to conduct conflict checks and allow for potential conflict issues to be flagged.

Where the clinic works with external volunteer solicitors or barristers there will often be a need to share details of potential clients with them so that they can carry out their own conflict check. In some cases this may make it more complex to utilise the services of pro bono solicitors in drop-in clinics.[9] Therefore, pro bono lawyers may be better suited to an appointment-based rather than drop-in-based clinic where conflict checks can be carried out in advance. In accordance with data protection requirements you should ensure that prospective clients have consented to their data being shared in this way.

A conflict check should be performed prior to providing any legal advice or assistance to a client. As a practical matter you will want to ascertain whether or not there is a conflict at the earliest possible juncture to avoid any inconvenience to the client. For example, it would be regrettable if a straightforward conflict was discovered at an interview where the client had been waiting for their appointment for some time.

Your advice and case recording procedures should clearly indicate that a conflict check has been performed, against which individuals (e.g. client and opposing party), the date that it was undertaken, by whom and the outcome of the check, i.e. usually that there is 'no conflict'. A form can be designed to allow for this to be recorded quickly (see example below).

Figure 1: Recording a conflict check

Conflict check

Client's name checked: Yes [ ] No [ ]

Opposing parties' name(s) checked: Yes [ ] No [ ]

Is there a conflict or potential conflict?   Yes [ ] No [ ]

Conflict check done by _____ [*insert name here*]

Date _____ [*insert date that conflict check is performed*]

In the sphere of free legal advice, conflicts of interest pose a particular problem. That is, declining to provide a service to a prospective client in order to maintain professional obligations, may have the result that an impecunious client may be unable to find alternative sources of assistance. Conflicts of interest can in this sense create a barrier to accessing justice.[10] In view of this and the need to promote access to justice, consideration should be given as to whether any exceptions to the conflict rules apply.[11] There is a narrow exception in the SRA Code requiring written consent and a substantial common interest by both parties.[12]

A related principle that arises when considering conflicts is the duty of confidentiality owed to one's clients. As this has the potential to conflict with one's duty to disclose material information to a current client it is often considered together with conflicts issues. Chapter 4 of the SRA Code deals with the need to maintain confidentiality in these circumstances, while reconciling this with the duty of disclosure.[13] This may require a practitioner to cease to act.

One potential solution in these circumstances is to set up an information barrier in order to separate lawyers, staff, records and management acting

10   Some regulators in the USA have provided an exception for not-for-profit legal services providing limited legal services. For example, Rule 6.5 in the American Bar Association's Model Rules of Professional Conduct provides an exception to the conflict rule if a lawyer without knowing of a conflict 'under the auspices of a program sponsored by a nonprofit organization or court, provides short-term limited legal services to a client without expectation by either the lawyer or the client that the lawyer will provide continuing representation'. There is no such equivalent in England and Wales.

11   The Legal Services Act 2007 (LSA), s 1(c) lists improving access to justice as one of the regulatory objectives of the Act.

12   SRA Code for Solicitors (**note 2**), para 6.2; previously SRA Code (**note 1**), outcomes 3.6 and 3.7.

13   SRA Code for Solicitors (**note 2**), paras 6.3–6.5.

for or with either client. University law clinics are usually modest and discrete operations taking place within larger institutions and so it may not be feasible to separate out operations in this way.

A further solution if conflicts arise would be to come to a referral arrangement with other local or like services, which would need to be done with informed client consent.[14]

Client identification

Linked to the issue of conflicts is the question of identification. In order to accurately conduct conflict checks we might either take a client at face value when they provide their details, or we might take further steps to positively identify that our clients are who they say they are, for example by requiring them to produce photographic identification. This latter approach is the most prudent and is supported by para 8.1 of the new SRA Code for Solicitors which provides that 'You identify who you are acting for in relation to any matter'.[15]

Requiring clients to provide identification will also protect your clinic against persons seeking to establish a false identify or operating under a false identity for fraudulent purposes.[16]

Requesting client identification will also help you to comply with your anti-money laundering obligations.[17]

Time limits

It is certainly the case that any applicable time limits or limitation periods should be confirmed when advice is provided. Even prior to advice, when enquiries are received and before accepting instructions to act, clinic volunteers and staff should assess whether or not there are approaching time limits and inform prospective clients of the potential impact of missing a time limit. It would not only be regrettable if a time limit were to expire while a client was waiting for their first appointment, or following an interview if the time limit were to pass while they were waiting for their advice; it is likely that the clinic or its staff could face accusations of negligence if the matter has not been addressed.

14   See **Part 2.6: Signposting and referrals** for more information on this.

15   Further guidance on this can be found in the 'SRA Standards and Regulations guidance for the not for profit sector' (23 July 2019) <https://www.sra.org.uk/newregs/> accessed 26 July 2019.

16   Law Society, 'Mortgage fraud' <https://www.lawsociety.org.uk/support-services/advice/practice-notes/mortgage-fraud/> accessed 21 April 2019.

17   See **Part 2.5: Anti-money laundering** for further details.

Relevant staff and volunteers should have access to a table of limitation dates so that pending time limits may be readily calculated. Care should be taken with particularly brief limitation periods (for example in public law or employment matters). What may seem on its face as a non-urgent enquiry may actually be quite urgent when regard is had to a pending limitation date, so it is advisable to have incoming queries reviewed by experienced staff to check for this.[18]

Clinics taking forward ongoing matters will need systems in place to flag relevant limitation dates as well as other critical milestones (e.g. filing dates, court dates). A valuable skill in this regard involves being able to calculate a particular limitation date, although this cannot always be done with precision.

Staff and volunteers' knowledge of time limits should also include an awareness that in some circumstances time limits may be extended. This depends on the particular area of law, and some time limits are not able to be extended. Therefore, that a time limit has passed prior to the client approaching your service will not necessarily negate the value of advice.

Client care

Client care includes consideration of the information provided to a client prior to the provision of legal services. The particular requirements that apply will depend upon the regulatory status of the clinic and those operating under its auspices (for example if the clinic employs practising solicitors). The necessary disclosures are often done in the form of a client care letter but may be done in other formats, for example a client information sheet.[19]

Although many of the matters requiring disclosure do not need to be communicated in writing, it may be easier to demonstrate compliance – as well as being more useful for a client – if the information is provided in writing. You could consider streamlining this process, for example by including information on the clinic website and building this into scripts that advisers, students or administrative staff use leading up to or at the client interview.

---

18   LawWorks provides a table of limitation dates at <https://www.lawworks.org.uk/solicitors-and-volunteers/resources/table-limitation-dates> which is available to LawWorks clinics – accessed 31 July 2019.

19   The Law Society has issued a detailed practice note on client care letters: <https://www.lawsociety.org.uk/support-services/advice/practice-notes/client-care-letters/> accessed 31 July 2019. Sample client care letters can also be found in **Part 5.1.7** of this Handbook.

Client disclosure: Key areas for attention

Data protection

Under the Data Protection Act 2018 it is necessary to explain to your client why you wish to obtain any personal data, for what purposes and that you will treat it confidentially. For further detailed guidance, see **Part 2.14: Data security**.

Complaints policy

Your clinic should have a policy in place to address client complaints.[20] Having a clearly accessible complaints policy will give clients the opportunity to raise any concerns and thereby help to avoid matters escalating unnecessarily. It will also help you to identify any areas where your systems or processes could be adjusted to better meet the needs of your clients.

You could also provide avenues to clients to provide feedback (including compliments) about the services received; this is an excellent way to capture evidence of the value of your service to the community it serves.[21]

You should provide details in writing at or before an initial interview of where or how the client can access your complaints policy.[22] You should also provide details of how to complain to the Legal Ombudsman, including timeframes and contact details.[23]

Free services and costs

The SRA Handbook deals with disclosure of fees.[24] Most university clinics offer a free service, and in this case it is advisable that they clearly state that the service being offered is for free. Regulated fee-charging clinics will have more detailed disclosure requirements.

Even if a service is offered for free there may be some costs associated with a client pursuing a course of action. For example, there may be a risk to the client of receiving an adverse costs order if they are or will be engaged in litigation. There may be other costs associated with the client's case such as court fees,

---

20   A sample complaints procedure can be found in **Part 5.2.5** of this Handbook.

21   Members of LawWorks have access to a sample compliments and complaints policy available online at <https://www.lawworks.org.uk/solicitors-and-volunteers/resources/clinics-compliments-and-complaints> accessed 13 April 2019.

22   SRA Code for Solicitors (**note 2**), para 8.3(a) and (b); previously SRA Code (**note 1**), O(1.9).

23   Ibid, para 8.3(c); previously SRA Code (**note 1**), O(1.10).

24   See, for example, SRA Code for Solicitors (**note 2**), para 8.7; previously SRA Code, IB(1.13; 1.14; 1.16).

expert and witness fees. The client should, at the outset, and if the case is ongoing then as the matter progresses, 'receive the best possible information… about the likely overall cost of their matter'.[25]

The client should also receive information about any public funding that may be available for their matter.[26] In addition, other available sources of funding for the client's matter should be disclosed, including legal expenses, insurance or funding that is available through a trade union.[27]

Regulated status and insurance

Where the service is regulated or provided by regulated persons, the SRA Code provides that you are required to disclose whether and how the service is regulated,[28] and there are also requirements for disclosure relating to insurance arrangements.[29]

The EU Provision of Services Regulations 2009 provides additional disclosure requirements in relation to compulsory insurance cover (in addition to a range of additional matters).[30] These apply to services that are defined in reg 2(1) as 'self-employed economic activity normally provided for remuneration'. The vast majority of university law clinics operate on a pro bono basis and therefore fall outside of the scope of the regulations. If any aspect of your clinic does operate on a remunerated basis then refer to the Law Society practice note for guidance on implementing the regulations in your clinic.[31]

SRA waivers

Where there is an SRA waiver in place the waiver itself may be a source of further disclosure requirements. For example, LawWorks obtained a waiver from the

---

25   SRA Code for Solicitors (**note 2**), para 8.7; previously SRA Code (**note 1**), O(1.13).

26   SRA Code (**note 1**), IB(1.16) (current as at the time of writing). The Law Society publishes a useful resource 'Legal aid guide for pro bono clinics' <https://www.lawsociety.org.uk/support-services/advice/articles/legal-aid-guide-for-pro-bono-clinics/>. This includes practical guidance on what is in scope; financial eligibility; exceptional case funding; how to find a provider; and handy checklists on scope and financial eligibility (on pp. 12–14).

27   SRA Code (**note 1**), IB(1.16). For a useful checklist setting out details of various funding options that may exist, see the Law Society's Pro bono manual, Chapter 28: Other funding options checklist, available at <https://www.lawsociety.org.uk/support-services/practice-management/pro-bono/pro-bono-manual/> accessed 13 April 2019.

28   SRA Code for Solicitors (**note 2**), para 8.10; previously SRA Code (**note 1**), O(1.7).

29   See **Part 2.3: Insurance** for more detail.

30   The Law Society provides detailed guidance on the application of the regulations to solicitors in private practice <https://www.lawsociety.org.uk/support-services/advice/practice-notes/provision-of-services-regulations-2009/> accessed 21 April 2019.

31   Ibid.

SRA for clinics registered to its network. This requires clinics that rely on the waiver and that are not covered by qualifying insurance to disclose to clients in writing that the 'Solicitors Regulation Authority's compulsory insurance scheme will not apply and appropriate information as to the arrangements in place for indemnity insurance cover'.[32]

A waiver may also waive the need for compliance with certain disclosure requirements.[33]

Service level agreement

A client care agreement, albeit one which is shorter than that used by full service law firms, should set out the service levels that you agree with your client.[34] For example, if your clinic provides written advice following an initial fact-finding interview you may set out in writing prior to the initial interview the clinic's commitment as to the period of time by which an advice letter will be provided.

Contact details

A client care agreement should set out contact details of the person directly handling the matter, their status (as applicable) and any other person responsible for the matter.[35]

Limiting or defining the scope of your assistance

You may confirm in writing the agreed action or next steps arising from an initial consultation.

Whatever the scope of the assistance provided at your clinic – whether it is an advice-only service, providing one-off advice or ongoing casework – the clinic should clearly define the scope of its assistance in writing. This can help manage the client's expectations about the level of assistance that the clinic has agreed to provide. Any extension to the agreed assistance should be confirmed

---

32   SRA Professional Indemnity Insurance Rules Waiver for LawWorks Clinics <https://www.lawworks.org.uk/solicitors-and-volunteers/resources/sra-professional-indemnity-insurance-rules-waiver> accessed 21 April 2019.

33   For example, the LawWorks waiver (**note 32**) waives the SRA Code 'relating to written prior notification to clients of a complaint procedure; complaint handling and advice as to overall costs of the client's matter. It does, however, impose conditions related to each of these subjects'.

34   SRA Code (**note 1**), IB(1.1) (current as at the time of writing). This indicative behaviour is not directly replicated in the new SRA Code for Solicitors, but will remain good practice.

35   SRA Code (**note 1**), IB(1.3) (current as at the time of writing). This indicative behaviour is not directly replicated in the new SRA Code for Solicitors, but will remain good practice.

in writing.

Termination of the agreement

In the usual course of things your assistance with a matter will conclude at the point when the clinic has completed the service that has been agreed, for example, following a fact-finding interview it has provided the requested advice. For ongoing work or even one-off advice you may wish to set out the circumstances in which you will terminate the agreement. Reasons for terminating the agreement might include losing contact with the client or a breakdown in confidence between the clinic and the client. The position under the SRA Code is that 'when deciding whether to act, or terminate your instructions, you comply with the law and the Code'.[36]

Summary

In summary:

- Clinics should adopt practices and procedures to ensure clients receive a proper standard of service.
- While the position of a clinic will depend on its particular regulatory status and that of its employees and volunteers, the following factors should be considered as a matter of good practice:
  - Having intake guidelines that clearly set out your service's remit.
  - Having procedures for the capture of essential information (such as contact details), and relevant documents and instructions.
  - Having a system for conflict screening and recording the outcome of conflict checks.
  - Having a system for establishing a client's identity for the purpose of conflict screening and to avoid identity fraud.
  - Closely monitoring time limits or limitation periods, including those applicable to prospective clients enquiring with the service or who have been offered an appointment.
- There are a number of matters that, depending on the regulatory position, may or must be disclosed to clients. These include data protection requirements, a complaints policy, that the service is free, and its regulated status.

---

36   SRA Code (**note 1**), O(1.3) (current as at the time of writing). This outcome is not replicated in the new SRA Code for Solicitors, but will remain good practice.

Part 2.5
Anti-money laundering

Christopher Simmonds

Introduction

Money laundering is often seen as something that stems from high-level crime. The mind conjures up images akin to those from *Goodfellas* and other similar movies with mobsters sitting around tables in diners and restaurants owned and operated by large-scale organised crime syndicates, in order to make it appear as though money obtained through criminal activities has come from legitimate sources.

But while such an image has a basis in fact, money laundering occurs across a spectrum of criminal activity. No doubt organised crime continues to form a part of the overall landscape, but even what we consider to be lower value crimes can result in money laundering. This can cover a wide range of offences, including relatively small-scale drug dealing, theft, benefit fraud, etc.

The legal sector has long been a target for people seeking to legitimise the source of funds. The policy paper *National risk assessment of money laundering and terrorist financing 2017* assessed there to be a high risk associated with the abuse of legal services in money laundering, although the risk associated with the abuse of legal services in order to facilitate terrorist financing is low.[1] Perhaps more worrying is that while the 2015 *National risk assessment* assumed that the majority of money laundering in the legal sector involved complicit legal professionals,[2] more recent work suggests that the majority of money laundering occurs due to wilfully blind or negligent professionals.[3]

The potential role of law clinics in facilitating money laundering will vary depending on the nature of the clinic and the range of services that the clinic offers. This section will help you to:

1   HM Treasury and Home Office, *National risk assessment of money laundering and terrorist financing 2017* (October 2017), para 7.3 <https://www.gov.uk/government/publications/national-risk-assessment-of-money-laundering-and-terrorist-financing-2017> accessed 16 August 2018.

2   HM Treasury and Home Office, *UK national risk assessment of money laundering and terrorist financing 2015* (October 2015), para 6.69 <https://www.gov.uk/government/publications/uk-national-risk-assessment-of-money-laundering-and-terrorist-financing> accessed 16 August 2018.

3   HM Treasury and Home Office (**note 1**), para 7.2.

- understand your legal obligations
- assess how much of a risk your clinic poses in light of the activities it undertakes
- implement such precautions as are needed to demonstrate that you are meeting best practice within the sector.

It is necessary at this stage to include a caveat on the contents of this section. The recommendations that are made are just that – recommendations. For some clinics the scope of their activities will mean that their legal obligations do not require them to undertake all of the recommended actions.

Similarly, given the ambiguity of elements of the legal framework, certain elements may or may not apply to clinics, and in such cases the recommendations work on the basis that they **do** apply.

You should therefore read this section as a best practice guide and, in particular, clinics should remember the need for a risk-based approach to anti-money laundering. Each clinic is individual and what is put in place should reflect the nature of the clinic's work and its client base.

The guidance contained in this section should be read in conjunction with the Legal Sector Affinity Group's *Anti-money laundering: Guidance for the legal sector 2018*, which has been approved by HM Treasury.[4]

Your legal obligations

Three key pieces of legislation constitute the framework for anti-money laundering activity within England and Wales. These are:

- the Proceeds of Crime Act 2002 (POCA)
- the Terrorism Act 2000 (TACT)
- the Money Laundering, Terrorist Financing and Transfer of Funds (Information on the Payer) Regulations 2017 (the Regulations).

The POCA and TACT create a series of offences that relate to money laundering and terrorist financing. These are broken down into two categories:

- offences that can be committed by any person
- offences that can only be committed by a person working within the 'regulated sector'.

---

4   Legal Sector Affinity Group, *Anti-money laundering: Guidance for the legal sector* (March 2018) <https://www.lawsociety.org.uk/policy-campaigns/articles/anti-money-laundering-guidance> accessed 16 August 2018.

In turn, the Regulations set out certain administrative requirements that must be undertaken by those who fall within the scope of the Regulations.

It is perhaps more useful to consider the legislative framework in these terms, rather than by listing the provisions that are contained within each of the three key pieces of legislation.

Offences that may be committed by any person

The POCA (as amended) creates a number of money laundering offences that can be committed by any person, including:

- concealing criminal property (s 327)
- entering into, or becoming concerned in, an arrangement knowing or suspecting that it facilitates the acquisition, retention, use or control of criminal property by or on behalf of another person (s 328)
- the acquisition, use or possession of criminal property (s 329).

For the purposes of the POCA, criminal property includes money, all forms of property whether real or personal, heritable or moveable, and things in action and other intangible or incorporeal property that constitute a person's benefit from any conduct that constitutes an offence in the UK. It is irrelevant who carried out the conduct or who benefited from it (s 326).

Similarly, the TACT introduces a range of offences that can again be committed by any person, including:

- fundraising for the purposes of terrorism (s 15)[5]
- use of money or property for the purposes of terrorism, or possessing money or property with the intention, or with reasonable cause to suspect that it might be used for the purposes of terrorism (s 16)
- arranging for money or property to be available to another knowing, or having reasonable cause to suspect that it may be used for the purposes of terrorism (s 17)
- facilitating the retention or control of terrorist property by concealment, removal from the jurisdiction, transfer to nominees, or in any other way (s 18).

The TACT also contains a general obligation that where a person believes or suspects that one of the offences listed above have been committed, and that belief is based on information which has come into their possession in the

---

5   The offence is committed if a person receives money or property, or provides or invites another person to provide money or property, knowing or having reasonable cause to suspect that it might be used for the purposes of terrorism.

course of a trade, profession or business, or in the course of their employment, then there is a duty to disclose that information to the police. If they fail to do so then they commit a criminal offence (s 19).

While both the POCA and TACT contain further offences, those listed above are the most relevant to the work of a law clinic within a university. As such, it is essential to ensure that procedures are in place to ensure that offences are not committed through the work of the clinic.

Offences within the regulated sector

The POCA and TACT also contain offences that can only be committed within the 'regulated sector'. These primarily relate to a failure to notify authorities of potential criminal activity under the Acts, and tipping off persons suspected of committing offences.[6] In each case, the offences are only triggered if an offence is suspected because of information that has come into a person's possession in the course of a business that is within the 'regulated sector'.

These offences may not be relevant to all clinics, but in determining whether you are working within the regulated sector it is first necessary to bear in mind the employer.

Many clinic staff are not employed directly by the law clinic as it is not a legal entity in its own right. Instead, their employer is the university, and it is therefore necessary to consider the activities of the university as a whole when determining whether we are within the regulated sector. For some, they will be employed directly by the clinic, for example where the clinic has been established as an alternative business structure (ABS).

The meaning of 'regulated sector' is identical in both the POCA (see Schedule 9) and TACT (see Schedule 3A). There are 21 separate categories of work that are considered to fall within the regulated sector, and the vast majority of those categories will not cover the work of either the law clinic or, for that matter, the university. Perhaps the key provision is Part 1, Paragraph 1(n) (of both Acts), namely:

> (n) the participation in financial or real property transactions concerning –
>
> (i) the buying and selling of real property (or, in Scotland, heritable property) or business entities;
>
> (ii) the managing of client money, securities or other assets;
>
> (iii) the opening or management of bank, savings or securities accounts;

6   See, for example, TACT, s 21A and POCA, ss 330 and 333A.

(iv) the organisation of contributions necessary for the creation, operation or management of companies; or

(v) the creation, operation or management of trusts, companies or similar structures,

by a firm or sole practitioner who by way of business provides legal or notarial services to other persons.

Clearly some clinics will not be involved in any of the activities listed and therefore the other elements of the definition will be of no concern. There are clinics, however, that provide advice to start-up businesses and may offer advice on the creation of a company structure. Similarly, in some civil actions (such as criminal injuries compensation cases) it may be necessary to advise on the creation of a personal injury trust or similar.

For those clinics we come to the grey area, mentioned in the introduction to this section, namely: are we covered by this definition?

For example:

- Are we participating in a financial transaction in circumstances where we have no client account and do not handle money for and on behalf of the client? There is no definition of 'financial transaction' provided in the legislation.

- Are we acting as a firm or sole practitioner? For those clinics that have set themselves up as an ABS, this is perhaps an easier question to answer. They will be regulated by the Solicitors Regulatory Authority and will be an entity in their own right and are therefore likely to fall within the definition.[7]

But what of those clinics that still fall within the remit of the university?

Guidance suggests that the definition excludes in-house solicitors, which will include solicitors working within most university law clinics.[8] However, unlike the majority of in-house solicitors we are not solely advising our employer. We also advise members of the public. Some clinics also use external lawyers volunteering on a pro bono basis. So does this change the position?

There is no simple answer. Each clinic must consider its own position in forming a conclusion. That said, it is perhaps best to err on the side of caution. While the guidance issued has a statutory basis and has been approved by HM Treasury, the position remains ambiguous. It is therefore recommended to assume that if you are participating in any of the listed activities, then it is best to ensure that you have policies and procedures in place to ensure compliance. These are considered in more detail later in this section.

---

7   See **Part 2.2** for further information about alternative business structures.

8   Legal Sector Affinity Group (**note 4**), p. 16.

Application of the Regulations

The application of the Regulations is almost identical to the definition of the regulated sector contained within the POCA and TACT, and therefore if a clinic considers that it falls within that definition then it is likely that the provisions of the Regulations will also be relevant.

Again, there is some conflict here between the stated purpose of the Regulations and the guidance that has been issued to the legal profession. For example, in the anti-money laundering guidance issued by the Legal Sector Affinity Group, it states that HM Treasury has confirmed that it would not generally consider the following to constitute participation in a financial transaction:

- payment on account of costs to a legal professional or payment of a legal professional's bill
- provision of legal advice
- participation in litigation or a form of alternative dispute resolution
- will-writing, although you should consider whether any accompanying taxation advice is covered
- work funded by the Legal Services Commission.[9]

Later in the guidance, however, sham litigation is considered to be a risk area that should be considered[10] and so it would appear that the conduct of litigation would be very relevant, particularly where litigation would result in the transfer of funds from one party to another, for example in the case of a breach of contract claim against a small business.

It is perhaps telling that the phrasing of the above would not **ordinarily** be considered to constitute participation in a financial transaction. This in turn suggests that there may be circumstances in which those activities could fall within the definition of a financial transaction, and it is therefore likely best to err on the side of caution.

Implementing control measures

In the following section, we will consider what steps clinics need to take to ensure compliance with their legal obligations. As has been mentioned above, as a bare minimum clinics should ensure that they are not committing offences under the POCA and TACT. Where, however, the clinic is also carrying out work that could be considered to fall within the scope of the regulated sector and the Regulations, there are additional steps that must be undertaken.

---

9   Ibid, p. 17.

10   Ibid, pp. 24 and 25.

A risk-based approach

For clinics whose work does fall within the scope of the Regulations and which are therefore within the regulated sector, there is a legal requirement that they carry out a risk assessment in order to identify the areas where the business is at risk of being used for the purposes of money laundering and/or terrorist financing, and to implement control measures to reduce the risks facing them.[11]

However, for all clinics, conducting a risk assessment reduces the potential liability of the clinic. Even for clinics that do not consider themselves to fall within the scope of the Regulations, a risk assessment can achieve the following:

- Identify areas where the clinic's work may be targeted for the purposes of money laundering and implement control measures in order to avoid criminal liability under the POCA and TACT.
- Ensure that defences available under the POCA and TACT are available in the event that the clinic's work is used for the purposes of money laundering or terrorist financing.
- Record the reasons why the clinic would not fall within the scope of the Regulations in order to demonstrate that the clinic has considered its legal responsibilities in full.

In order to carry out an appropriate risk assessment, you should consider the risk profile of the work that you are engaged in, including:

- your customers
- the countries or geographical areas within which your business operates
- your products or services
- your transactions
- your delivery channels.[12]

The above risks should be considered in light of the additional guidance set out in the Legal Sector Affinity Group's guidance. The points that are considered of greatest relevance in the clinical setting are summarised below, but you should refer to the guidance in order to satisfy yourself that your clinic faces no other risks.

Key risks

While some of the risks highlighted in the guidance seem to be of little relevance to clinics (for example, working for politically exposed persons) others are of

11   Money Laundering, Terrorist Financing and Transfer of Funds (Information on the Payer) Regulations 2017, reg 18.

12   Ibid, reg 18.

more relevance, including:

1. high turnover of clients and relatively short-lived cases
2. acting for clients without meeting them (for example, through Skype clinics, written instructions etc.)
3. clients with high cash turnover businesses
4. creation of trusts, companies and charities
5. sham litigation.

In the case of points 1 and 2 above, the nature of clinics can make it difficult to properly establish the identity of our client base.

In terms of point 3, where clinics act for small businesses those may be retail start-ups where the vast majority of transactions will be cash. It may be that the clinic will act for small businesses defending breach of contract claims, where again there is a high cash turnover. It may even be that the businesses we are pursuing for clients in consumer claims have a high cash turnover. In such cases, the risk of sham litigation is high (see below).

For those clinics that are engaged in small business work, criminals can use trust and company structures in order to retain control of criminal assets and create difficulties for law enforcement agencies investigating possible offences. In respect of point 4, clinics should therefore be wary of receiving instructions for carrying out the routine steps involved in forming an entity without advice on the appropriateness of the structure.[13]

In terms of point 5, sham litigation occurs where the nature of the dispute has been fabricated in order to disguise the transfer of assets obtained through criminal activity. This is perhaps one of the greatest risks faced by clinics. Key warnings would be where a client is ready to settle too easily, for example where a claimant is willing to settle far below the value of the claim, or a defendant is willing to settle for too high an amount. Similarly, it could occur where a defendant to a claim offers to settle where the prospects of success for the claimant were low.

All of these factors should be taken into account when implementing control measures.

---

13   Legal Sector Affinity Group (**note 4**), p. 25.

Control measures

Because the nature of the work that we carry out in clinics is generally lower risk than would be the case in private practice, the risks that we face can be dealt with through relatively easy measures, namely by ensuring that we carry out appropriate customer due diligence that is proportionate to the nature of the work that we are doing.

The risks outlined above would ordinarily be reduced to acceptable levels by ensuring that we carry out sufficient checks to satisfy ourselves as to the identity of the client and, importantly, any other parties to the case.

Customer due diligence

Taking steps to identify the client can help to significantly reduce the risk of money laundering. Customer due diligence (CDD) should not be seen as just a 'tick-box exercise', and should take place at the start of the contractual relationship with the client.

Where possible, original documents are the best way of ensuring that CDD is properly carried out, although this may be easier in the case of an individual as opposed to a business or trust.

Documents such as a passport, national identity card, driving licence, etc. bearing the photograph of the client, together with some other official document confirming the client's name and address, are ideal ways of ensuring the identity of the client.

In some cases, it may be that the client uses different names for some reason or another. In such a case, it will be necessary to satisfy yourself that the client is who they claim to be, such as by obtaining alternative documentary verification.

In the case of a company or trust, if it is well established then lesser steps can be taken. In the case of a registered company, a search of Companies House to establish the name, registered address and company directors may suffice. In the case of an unincorporated business, sole trader or partnership, checking trade directories, establishing the identity of the owner or instructing person, etc. in the same way as an individual client may be sufficient.

If the client does not have suitable identification then it is necessary to consider the risk posed. If the subject matter of the dispute would not involve a financial transaction (for example, a complaint to a local authority) then the risk of money laundering is low. Similarly, even if the transaction is financial, if the other side is well established (such as a local authority, NHS Trust or national company) then again the risks of money laundering are low.

It is important to document the steps that have been taken in the CDD process for the client file and this will help to demonstrate compliance with the legal provisions.

For further details on client care and procedures when taking on new clients, see **Part 2.4**.

Policies and procedures

Documenting your risk assessment and control measures in appropriate policies and procedures will help to ensure compliance with the legislation and will reduce the risk of an offence being committed. In university-based law clinics, it is essential to draw students' attention to the policies.

Simply having a policy or procedure may not be enough, though. As with health and safety considerations, it is also essential to demonstrate that you are complying with your own policies and procedures. This will include training staff and students on the relevant policies and procedures and documenting that you have done so. You may want to consider asking students in particular to confirm that they have read and understood their obligations under the policy before they undertake work in the clinic.

Additional requirements under the Regulations

For organisations that are within scope of the Regulations, there is also a requirement to have a Money Laundering Reporting Officer. This person is responsible for determining whether the circumstances of a case require reporting to the National Crime Agency. They should be of sufficient seniority to make the decision as to whether a report is necessary and, if so, to take such steps as they consider appropriate in order to ensure an adequate report is made.

Summary

- All clinics should ensure that they do not commit an offence under the POCA and/or TACT.
- In order to do so, a risk assessment should be carried out to identify the risk profile of the clinic and any control measures that have been implemented to reduce the risk.
- In the event that a clinic does not consider that it falls within the scope of the regulated sector and the Regulations, it should document the reasons for this within the risk assessment.
- Clinics should ensure that they implement appropriate CDD policies and procedures and train staff and students on them.
- If the clinic is subject to the Regulations, then the clinic should appoint a Money Laundering Reporting Officer.

Part 2.6
Signposting and referrals

*Lee Hansen**

Advice services undertake signposting and referral, indicating alternative sources of assistance where they are unable to help a client who has approached them for advice. This is of particular significance to law school clinics due to the nature and timing of the service provided, with many clinics closing outside of term-time.

In the 2015–16 *LawWorks Clinics Network Report* it was reported that 16,471 enquiries were received by law school clinics.[1] Of all these enquiries, law school clinics were able to deliver advice in 46 per cent of cases. The clinics were able to provide information, signposting or referrals in response to 38 per cent of enquiries. This left 16 per cent of enquirers who were unable to receive any information, signposting or referral from the law school clinics.[2]

There are a variety of reasons why your service may not be able to provide advice, and therefore the appropriate response to a client's enquiry is signposting to other sources of assistance or referral.[3]

For example:

- closure outside of term-time
- the enquiry is outside the subject area advised on by the clinic
- the client falls outside the target area (e.g. household income exceeds the clinic's thresholds or they are located outside of the clinic's geographical catchment area)
- conflict of interest
- lack of capacity or competency in the relevant area
- the complexity or urgency of the client's enquiry is not suitable for the clinic to assist with
- the clinic provides an information, signposting and referral service rather than advice

---

* Thank you to Linden Thomas and Lucy Davies for helpful comments on drafts of this section.

1   *LawWorks Clinics Network Report April 2015–March 2016*, p. 17 <https://www.lawworks. org.uk/sites/default/files/LawWorks%20Clinics%20Network%20Report%202015-16.pdf> accessed 21 April 2019.

2   Ibid, p. 17.

3   Advice UK, *Key steps to effective signposting and referral*, p. 2 <http://asauk.org.uk/wp-content/uploads/2013/09/Referral-Networks-key-steps-to-effective-signposting-and-referrals. pdf> accessed 21 April 2019.

- the advice sought falls within an area the clinic is not authorised to advise on (for example, debt or immigration advice).

It is important to have a system in place to promote effective signposting and referrals in these cases to help prevent referral fatigue and deliver access to justice.

What is signposting and referral?

In England and Wales, it is important to understand the two terms that are used in this context and the difference between the two.

A commonly accepted definition of signposting is set out below:

> Signposting takes place before a centre has started in depth work with a client about a query. It normally takes place when the client first visits a centre with a new problem. It describes the process of giving a client the details of other organisations that will be able to help them.[4]

Referral involves more active involvement in the process of directing a client to another organisation. It may involve contacting the other organisation with the client's consent to confirm that the other organisation is able to accept the referral and to provide any required information, again with client consent:

> There are two key differences with referral: firstly, with referral an agency is more likely to have started work on a client's case. Secondly, the agency will make contact with the referral agency directly on behalf of the client.[5]

In individual cases those working and volunteering in clinics will be faced with the decision of whether to provide more straightforward signposting information or a more active referral. The principles set out later in this section will assist with this.

Referral roundabout

The 'referral roundabout' refers figuratively to the problem of enquirers or prospective clients being bounced from service to service without being able to gain the help they need. The problem arises in a context in which there are limited sources of free or low-cost help and/or there is a lack of information available on potential sources of help.

4 *LawWorks Clinics Network Report* (**note 1**).
5 Ibid, p. 2.

This is linked to the problem of referral fatigue, which has been described as follows:

> Choices of sources of help can be unpromising, and where people are forced to look elsewhere they can suffer referral fatigue, getting lost in the system.[6]

This longstanding problem has been exacerbated in the context of legal aid cuts and cuts to local authority funding, resulting in an advice sector that is under considerable strain.

Set out below are some of the potential impacts of referral fatigue:

- a client may give up seeking help if referrals or signposting do not result in them receiving relevant advice
- a client may become disillusioned with the legal system if they are given referrals or signposting information that does not lead anywhere
- ineffective signposting and referral can waste time. If the client's case involves time limits for taking action, then seeking help at a 'dead-end' referral may cause problems for resolving the legal issue in the required time
- it is undesirable for a client to have to repeat their story to strangers time and again; this is particularly problematic where the subject matter involves something that is traumatic or sensitive
- providing an ineffective referral may deter clients from seeking help from your service again or recommending it to others in need.

Key principles of effective signposting and referral

What follows are the key principles of effective signposting and referral, aimed at helping clients to avoid the referral roundabout and to find a more direct path to an appropriate source of advice and assistance. All volunteers and staff who interface with the public should be aware of these principles. Several of them are good practice and will apply to all client interaction, not only in preliminary dealings and when considering signposting and referral. They are derived and adapted from *Getting off the referral roundabout: Effective legal referral*: a video and workbook developed by Kingsford Legal Centre, an Australian Student Law Clinic and Law Centre.[7]

---

6   Pascoe Pleasence and Nigel Balmer, *How people resolve 'legal' problems*, p. 1 <https:// research.legalservicesboard.org.uk/wp-content/media/How-People-Resolve-Legal-Problems. pdf> accessed 21 April 2019.

7   The film is available on YouTube at <https://youtu.be/FD_6NaKEUP0>; the workbook is available at <https://www.klc.unsw.edu.au/sites/klc.unsw.edu.au/files/doc/Referral_ Roundabout.pdf> both accessed 21 April 2019.

1. Value and respect the client
2. Effective and appropriate communication
3. Identify the needs of the client
4. Know your own service
5. Know the legal system
6. Know service providers
7. Meet the client's needs
8. Prepare the client for interview

1. Value and respect the client

A professional relationship that is founded on value and respect for the client can help us to effectively assess clients' needs and therefore best direct them to an appropriate source of assistance. We can show that we value and respect clients by:[8]

- being sensitive to the particular needs of the client
- not being judgemental and approaching the problems that they present objectively
- demonstrating patience and empathy
- demonstrating a commitment to confidentiality.

Case study

Angel has been referred to your clinic by the law school's administrative team. She has a debt problem, which unfortunately falls outside of the type of cases that your clinic can take on.

Angel arrives at the reception desk that you are staffing. Instead of simply telling Angel that you can't help, consider which sources of assistance might be available for her. These could be online, telephone or face-to-face services. There may be local or national services available.

Depending on the type of debt problem it is also worth exploring whether legal aid is available.

---

8   *Getting off the referral roundabout: Effective legal referral* (Kingsford Legal Centre 2006), p. 5   <https://www.klc.unsw.edu.au/sites/klc.unsw.edu.au/files/doc/Referral_Roundabout.pdf> accessed 21 April 2019.

2. Effective and appropriate communication

Effective and appropriate communication helps clinic staff and students to assess clients' (or potential clients') needs. For example, active listening and relevant questioning techniques can be used to clarify and confirm the person's requirements.[9] This can be done in the first encounter with a potential client, whether by telephone or in person.

Clarity in communication is also important when describing 'the purpose and limits of the services provided by your own agency'.[10] Consider how you and your clinic staff and volunteers can ensure this in your clinic marketing materials, as well as in face-to-face encounters and when handling telephone enquiries.

We should adjust our communication to meet our clients' needs – using plain English 'appropriate to the client's level of education without being condescending'.[11] We should avoid jargon and, where we need to use technical legal expressions, do so with appropriate explanation. For example, your clinic might not undertake any contentious work. A client will not necessarily understand what is meant by that term. It will therefore be clearer to explain to the client that your clinic is not able to assist with any matters that are being dealt with by the courts.

It is also important to be aware of a range of factors that can impact upon communication, 'things such as cultural, lingual or language differences, education and literacy levels, disabilities and mental illness to name just a few' and to tailor your communication appropriately.[12]

3. Identify the needs of the client

This step is concerned with identifying the information, signposting and referral needs of the client. This will involve 'identifying both the legal and non-legal issues and the urgency or otherwise of each one'.[13] You will also need to have some regard to how complex the client's issues are, as this will help you to understand whether generalist or specialist support may be required.

In identifying the needs of a client:

1. Some information will be needed on the substance of the legal help required.

---

9   Ibid, p. 6.
10   Ibid.
11   Ibid.
12   Ibid.
13   Ibid, p. 7.

2. The stage that any dispute is at will also be relevant.

3. The capability of the client themselves to act or access other services will also be relevant.

With regard to points 1 and 2 above there is no need for you to take full details of a client's case in order to identify their needs, and in fact it would not be appropriate to do so where you are not able to offer the client advice. However, it is, for example, unlikely to be enough just to know that a client has a dispute with their employer. Instead, you will want to know broadly what type of dispute it is (e.g. has the client been dismissed? Do they think they have been discriminated against?) and what stage the dispute is at (for example, has the client already brought a claim? Or did the issue only arise yesterday?). This will enable you to direct the client to the most appropriate alternative source of support. If the dispute has only just arisen then signposting to an initial advice service might be appropriate. Whereas, if the client is in the middle of ongoing ligation, a referral to a firm of solicitors or local law centre might be the best course of action.

With regard to point 3 above, you may need to consider whether the client has any vulnerabilities that could be a barrier to them accessing other advice or support. There may also be particular communication needs, for example where the client has limited English, a cognitive disability or low levels of literacy.[14] There may be emotional blocks to clients taking action or other support needs, for example due to mental health issues. Or there may be digital barriers to access if a client does not have access to email or the internet. Finally, the client may have geographical access issues, for example if they are situated in an area with no local or nearby advice organisations, if they do not drive and/or if there are poor local transport links.

4. Know your own service

It is important for staff and students to know about their own clinic, the services it provides and any limits in place for that service, so that they can then accurately provide this information to potential clients and other stakeholders that might refer or signpost clients to you.[15] It is a waste of everyone's time if a client is booked in for an advice appointment with a clinic only to find out that their query falls outside an area of law that the clinic can assist with. Other important information to know includes the level of service available (e.g. advice only or representation) and timescales over which advice may be provided.

---

14   Ibid.

15   Ibid, p. 8.

5. Know the legal system

Clinic participants may have varying knowledge of the legal system depending on their level of experience. Student volunteers may well have very little experience. However, there is a certain basic knowledge of the law and the legal system that anyone involved in providing signposting information or referrals in the clinic should possess.[16]

Some areas worthy of particular attention include:

- that there are different areas of law, e.g. employment, criminal and family law
- that it is not always obvious that a problem may have a legal aspect to it, e.g. welfare benefits or consumer issues
- the range of different courts and tribunals
- an awareness of alternative dispute resolution, e.g. that referral to a mediation service might be an option
- an awareness of limitation dates (so that clients can be made aware that they may need to seek advice quickly).

Note that the above should not be used as a basis on which to give clients advice, where a clinic has determined that it is not able to do so. However, they are often essential pieces of information in order to be able to direct a client to the most appropriate alternative service.

6. Know service providers

Once students and staff of the clinic understand the client's support needs and have ascertained that their own service is unable to assist, the next important step is to select appropriate organisations that may be able to assist the client.[17] This requires knowledge of alternative potential service providers and should extend to those that can help with both the legal and non-legal issues that have been identified.

Various techniques can be used to acquire and consolidate such knowledge. For example:

- Participation in formal and informal networks, particularly those of relevance to the local community or to relevant communities of interest. These might include local law society committees or networks, local advice agency networks, etc.

16   Ibid, p. 9.
17   Ibid, p. 12.

- Use appropriate tools and resources, such as referral databases and guides. Some examples of referral databases and online guides and search forms include:
  - The LawWorks Signposting & Referral Index, which is available to members of the LawWorks Clinics Network: <https://www.lawworks.org.uk/solicitors-and-volunteers/resources/signposting-referral-index>
  - The Law Society's Find a Solicitor website: <http://solicitors.lawsociety.org.uk>
  - The UK government's Find a Legal Aid Adviser or Family Mediator website: <https://find-legal-advice.justice.gov.uk/>
  - The OISC Adviser Finder to find registered immigration advisers: <https://home.oisc.gov.uk/adviser_finder/finder.aspx>.

By knowing the level of service provided by other agencies, clinics are also able to manage client expectations about the service they may receive if they are signposted or referred to them.

It is important to have an understanding of the following details of other agencies:

- Which services are provided and by what method. For example, are they telephone-based services, drop-in or appointment services?
- Any geographical catchment or other eligibility criteria (such as an income limit, age requirements (e.g. youth support, pensioner services), veterans, specific health/mental health eligibility requirements).
- Accurate contact details (e.g. phone numbers, street address, email address and opening hours).
- For legal services, the areas of law they cover.
- Whether the service is free or if there are any fees.
- Whether there is any access to interpreter services and whether access to interpreters is free.
- Disability access.
- Whether services are by referral from other providers only or whether clients can access the service directly. Sometimes there may be different contact details provided for the public and some services are only available by referral from other organisations, not individuals.

7. Meeting the client's needs

This step is about ensuring that the services to which you are referring the client match the needs of the client, and that the method of referral (signposting or referral) is appropriate to the client's needs.[18]

As is noted in the referral roundabout handbook:

> Clients have a wide range of needs and capabilities. You should take these into account when making a referral. For example, you may contact a service on behalf of a distressed client to explain the situation and make an appointment. Some clients, on the other hand, may need minimal assistance, and simply providing them with the relevant details of a service is appropriate. What you do will also vary depending upon the referral policies of the service you are making the referral to.[19]

A number of steps can help to ensure that the signposting or referral is done in a way which best meets the client's needs:

- Make sure that information provided to clients is accurate and current, including whether there are limitations on the services being referred/signposted to.
- Be realistic in describing what assistance the client will receive from the service to which they are being referred. For example:
  - 'there may be a waiting list'
  - 'it's an advice-only service'.
- Use interpreter services where necessary.
- Sometimes more than one signposting or referral option should be identified and offered to a client.
- You might invite the client to come back to you for further guidance if the signposting or referral is unsuccessful.

8. Prepare the client for the interview

Finally, whether signposting or referring to a lawyer or alternative advice service or offering a client an appointment with your own clinic, there is information that you can provide to help them prepare for the interview. If there are particular communication needs, for example the need for an interpreter, you should make arrangements for this.

Avoid creating any unrealistic expectations about what a lawyer may be able to achieve for the client. If you are able to indicate how long the client will have with the lawyer this will help them plan to make the best use of their time. Finally, help the client identify the relevant documentation to bring along with

---

18   Ibid, p. 13.
19   Ibid.

them. There is a helpful list on the LawWorks website of documents a client should bring along to an interview.[20]

Referral systems

There are various ways for you to record the details that your clinic holds about organisations to signpost or refer clients to. It may be a paper-based list or you may use an electronic referral system containing a list of organisations, the services they provide and their contact details, etc. This could range from an Excel spreadsheet to an online database.

You may wish to design your own online database, and this is something that could be done in collaboration with other local service providers.[21]

Some existing online referral systems include:

- NellBooker: <https://www.nellbooker.net>
- Refernet: <https://www.refernet.co.uk>
- CLOCK: <https://clock.uk.net>

However, for more basic systems you could build a referral list using an Excel spreadsheet or a printed manual. Students can also be involved in building and maintaining your referral list. For example, students who have a good knowledge and involvement in local community organisations will be well placed to contribute.

If using a printed manual, you could include pockets in which to slide relevant pamphlets and updates. Naturally, it is important to ensure that any system you use is kept up to date so that you can continue to provide appropriate referrals.

Referrals under the SRA Standards and Regulations

The new SRA Standards and Regulations came into force on 25 November 2019 and replaced the 2011 SRA Handbook. Therefore, clinics making referrals should be mindful of paragraph 5 of the new Standards, which sets out how

---

20 See <https://www.lawworks.org.uk/sites/default/files/files/List%20of%20 Documents%20for%20Clinics.pdf> accessed 20 July 2019.

21 For example, Peterborough Citizens Advice manage an online local referral network that is comprised of local advice providers. Client details are able to be shared instantaneously and a decision made as to whether to accept the referral immediately. See Citizens Advice, *The referral gap: How stronger referrals between free guidance and paid for advice can help people manage their money*, p. 14 <https://www.citizensadvice.org.uk/Global/CitizensAdvice/Debt%20and%20 Money%20Publications/ReferralGap.pdf> accessed 21 April 2019.

referrals must be dealt with and what information must be shared with the client.[22]

As with the previous Handbook, the Standards are particularly concerned with situations in which either referring party will derive a financial benefit. It will remain the case that payments for introductions should not be made in certain circumstances, such as where clients are subject to criminal proceedings.

Paragraph 5.3 of the new Standards makes it clear that in all cases, a client must only be referred, recommended or introduced to a separate business where the client has given their informed consent to the same. Therefore, where making referrals to another organisation, it would be good practice to keep a record of the client's consent for you to do so.

Summary

By their often seasonal nature, law clinics may often respond to a high proportion of enquiries by providing a referral or signposting information. It is important to have effective systems in place in order to avoid sending clients on the referral roundabout and in order to avoid the problem of referral fatigue.

There are certain key principles of effective referral that all persons interfacing with the public should know about. These are:

1. Value and respect the client
2. Effective and appropriate communication
3. Identify the needs of the client
4. Know your own service
5. Know the legal system
6. Know service providers
7. Meet the client's needs
8. Prepare the client for interview

You can develop your referral system online or on paper. Online options present you with a particular opportunity to collaborate with local networks.

Finally, the SRA Handbook and LASPO have particular outcomes, requirements and prohibitions relating to referrals; these tend to be circumstances where an introduction is made pursuant to some financial arrangement.

---

22   SRA, *Standards and Regulations* (20 March 2019) <https://www.sra.org.uk/sra/policy/future/resources.page#resources> accessed 23 July 2019.

Part 2.7
Quality assurance: Advice standards

Tony Martin

Introduction

In the late 1990s, the then Legal Aid Board created the Legal Aid Franchise Quality Assurance Standard (LAFQAS). To a large extent, this was driven by the agenda of value for money for taxpayers in public expenditure. LAFQAS followed the introduction of franchising in 1993.[1] By 2003 LAFQAS had been replaced by the Specialist Quality Mark (SQM). Holding the LAFQAS and then the SQM was a requirement for all legal aid contract holders.

The Law Society's rival quality mark, Lexcel, was developed from the Law Society's practice management standards, which were awarded as a result of membership of specialist panels. Introduced in 1998, initial take-up was slow. By 2004 Lexcel had been awarded to only 265 private practices, 113 local authorities and three in-house/commercial departments.[2] Three years later, however, the promoting of Lexcel had led to it being awarded to 700 practices, including over 100 local authority legal departments.[3] By the tender round in 2011, legal aid suppliers could hold either the SQM standard or Lexcel; this remains the case today.[4]

The Legal Services Commission (LSC) also developed the General Help Quality Mark (later known as the Advice Quality Standard (AQS)), which was devised as a funding mechanism for the now severely reduced legal aid funding and was a complementary standard to the SQM. On 1 April 2013, the LSC was replaced by the Legal Aid Agency, an executive agency of the Ministry of Justice, and the ownership of the AQS was transferred to the Advice Services Alliance.[5]

In 2014 the Low Commission reviewed the quality standards in the not-for-profit sector.[6] Currently, over 700 separate local advice services across England

---

1   University of Strathclyde, *Monitoring quality to raise standards of legal practice within the legal aid system in the UK* (2014).

2   'Promoting Lexcel' *Law Society Gazette* (5 January 2004).

3   'Risk management at core of revised Lexcel standard' *Law Society Gazette* (20 July 2007).

4   <https://www.gov.uk/guidance/legal-aid-agency-quality-standards> accessed 14 November 2018.

5   <http://advicequalitystandard.org.uk/about-the-aqs/ownership-aqs/> accessed 14 November 2018.

6   <https://www.lag.org.uk/about-us/policy/the-low-commission-200551>

and Wales hold the AQS,[7] while over 1,700 solicitors' firms, in-house legal departments and law centres are Lexcel accredited. These range from sole practitioners to multi-partner firms, local government legal departments to the Government Legal Service. Practices are spread across the regions.

Absent are the largest city firms, with the notable exception of Mishcon de Reya LLP and Slater and Gordon.[8] It has been suggested that the Lexcel standard is not as relevant to city law firms that have already established their reputation for high-quality work. City firms 'perceived Lexcel to be more relevant to firms at the smaller end of the profession' in order that individual firms could signal the firm's quality to clients less accustomed to purchasing legal services.[9]

In September 2018 there were 10,456 solicitor practices, recognised bodies and alternative business structures regulated by the Solicitors Regulation Authority (SRA) in England and Wales.[10] It can be estimated that around 16 per cent of those are therefore accredited with Lexcel. Therefore, it is a reasonable prospect that law students are heading for practice in an accredited organisation.

In addition to organisations being accredited, the Law Society also has an accreditation scheme for individual solicitors specialising in certain areas of law:

- Children law
- Clinical negligence
- Conveyancing quality scheme
- Criminal litigation
- Family law
- Family mediation
- Immigration and asylum
- Immigration law advanced
- Mental capacity (welfare)
- Mental health
- Personal injury

---

7   <http://advicequalitystandard.org.uk/about-the-aqs/> accessed 14 November 2018.

8   Lexcel Accredited Practice List 2017.

9   'Benchmarking the supply of legal services by city law firms' prepared for the Legal Service Board by Charles River Associates (August 2011) <https://www.legalservicesboard.org.uk/news_publications/latest_news/pdf/benchmarking_city_law_firms_final_report_v3.pdf> accessed 19 August 2019.

10   <https://www.sra.org.uk/sra/how-we-work/reports/data/solicitor_firms.page> accessed 14 November 2018.

- Wills and inheritance

While the requirements vary according to specialism, the process focuses on the need to demonstrate expertise in the particular practice area.

Need for quality assurance

That a measure of quality assurance is required in law school pro bono clinics is beyond doubt. For example, the Joint Pro Bono Protocol states that 'pro bono legal work should always be done to a high standard'.[11] Furthermore, the Legal Services Board states that:

> By improving the information available on the quality of legal services we anticipate that providers will be encouraged to focus on the areas of their work in need of improvement and consumers will be able to more easily identify the outcomes they can expect.[12]

The SRA also imposes requirements to ensure the quality of advice. For example, Standard 3.2 of the Code of Conduct for Solicitors, RELs and RFLs in the SRA's 2019 Standards and Regulations provides that solicitors must ensure that the service they 'provide to clients is competent and delivered in a timely manner'.[13]

However, it is important to remember that while quality standards can measure the extent to which a clinic complies with written procedures and certain minimum standards, they do not measure the quality of either the advice or of the learning experience for any law student involved in the delivery of advice.

In recognition of this, the Advice Services Alliance, owners of the Advice Quality Standard, are piloting a peer review process, via an online platform, so that external experienced reviewers will review a sample of case files to ensure that the advice given is competent and reflects current best practice.[14]

---

11   The Protocol was developed under the auspices of the Attorney General's Pro Bono Coordinating Committee and has been endorsed by the Law Society of England and Wales, Bar Council of England and Wales and Chartered Institute of Legal Executives: <https://www.lawsociety.org.uk/Support-services/Practice-management/Pro-bono/The-pro-bono-protocol/> accessed 14 November 2018.

12   Legal Services Board, *Approaches to quality: Summary of responses to consultation and LSB response* (September 2012) <https://www.legalservicesboard.org.uk/Projects/developing_regulatory_standards/pdf/20120913_summary_responses_recd_lsb_response_approaches_quality_final.pdf> accessed 14 November 2018.

13   SRA, *Standards and Regulations*, Code of Conduct for Solicitors, RELs and RFLs (20 March 2019) <https://www.sra.org.uk/sra/policy/future/resources.page#resources> accessed 23 July 2019.

14   <http://advicequalitystandard.org.uk/2019/01/prop-pilot-testing-expressions-of-interest/> accessed 13 February 2019.

Clinics and advice quality standards

There are a number of things that clinic managers must consider when deciding whether to apply for a quality standard:

- The potential impact, if any, on:
  - student involvement
  - client confidence
  - involvement of external supervisors (solicitors and barristers)
  - funding arrangements and applications.
- The benefits of an external audit process.
- The cost to the clinic (some guidance is given below but in all cases a quote should be obtained as there are many variables).
- The degree of changes that may be required to obtain the accreditation.

Advice standards options for clinics

There are three 'advice standards' options that may be available to clinics.

- Specialist Quality Mark (SQM)
- Lexcel
- Advice Quality Standard.

The pro and cons of each are considered below.

Specialist Quality Mark (SQM)

Pros:

- The SQM was introduced in 2002 as a quality management system for legal aid providers.
- It aims to enable legal services providers/organisations to demonstrate that they are well managed, provide good levels of client care and have systems in place to ensure delivery of good quality advice.
- The SQM is owned by the Legal Aid Agency, but contracted to Recognising Excellence Ltd.

Cons:

- The SQM is more relevant to legal aid contract holders than university pro bono clinics.
- Many legal aid suppliers have moved from the SQM to Lexcel.[15]

---

15   In *Legal Action* (June 2012) p. 44, Vicky Ling, one of the authors of the Legal Aid Handbook,

- In the view of the Low Commission: 'Unfortunately, it has never been fundamentally reviewed and it has become out of date. There is no longer any active development of the standard by the Legal Aid Agency.'[16]

Information on the numbers of organisations holding the SQM is not readily available, nor is the cost information.

Lexcel

Pros:

- Lexcel is widely acknowledged as an industry standard. The Law Society's view is that: 'Lexcel is the Law Society's legal practice quality mark for excellence in legal practice management and client care. It provides a flexible, supportive management framework to help practices and in-house legal departments develop consistent operational efficiencies and client services, manage risk effectively, reduce costs and promote profitability. It is the most appropriate Standard for the legal profession as it was written by solicitors for solicitors.'[17]

- Given that it is widely adopted, it is likely that a student subsequently qualifying in private practice, in house or in a law centre will work within an organisation holding Lexcel, so it can be seen as good preparation for professional practice.

Cons:

To use Lexcel a clinic must be either:

- a law practice in the form of a partnership, limited liability partnership, sole practitioner, incorporated law firm or alternative business structure (ABS) authorised and regulated by the SRA,

or

- an in-house legal department: including those in corporations, public sector, law centres, not-for-profit and government organisations.

---

reported that a significant number of legal aid practitioners are working towards Lexcel. Although figures are hard to come by, DG Legal, another of the leading legal aid consultants, argue that Lexcel has gained significantly in popularity over the past few years and this can be attributed to the synergy between Lexcel and key elements of the SRA Handbook; a higher number of insurers may be willing to insure a practice that is Lexcel accredited and there is improved marketability and competitive advantage gained as a result of achieving Lexcel.

16   'Report of the Low Commission on the future of advice and legal support: Annex 8' (January 2014) <https://www.lag.org.uk/about-us/policy/the-low-commission-200551> accessed 14 November 2018.

17   <https://www.lawsociety.org.uk/support-services/accreditation/lexcel/> accessed 14 November 2018.

While Lexcel is designed for any legal practice – regardless of the size or type of work undertaken from private practices in England and Wales and international markets, to not-for-profit organisations and in-house teams in organisations and local authorities – the entity applying for it must be an SRA-regulated entity. While solicitors employed by universities to supervise student law clinics are practising in-house, most clinics are a very small part of the university and may not meet the management requirements of Lexcel. Nonetheless, the standards, which in many ways overlap with the SRA Standards and Regulations, provide a useful framework for the organisation of clinics.

The costs of Lexcel include an annual assessment fee and a registration fee. The annual assessment is based on a daily rate of between £600 and £800 (as at July 2019). The number of days needed to carry out the assessment will depend on the size of the organisation and the number of practice areas, but for most clinics it is likely to be between one and three days. The registration fee is based on the number of fee earners, with two to 15 fee earners being £225 plus VAT (as at July 2019).[18]

Advice Quality Standard (AQS)

Pros:

- The AQS is the quality mark for organisations that provide advice to the public on social welfare issues.
- The AQS claims that it 'is an independently assessed quality mark that, when awarded, demonstrates a well-managed service. It has been developed specifically to assure quality legal service provision and will identify you to clients, funders, and other agencies who refer to you'.[19]
- The AQS is owned by the Advice Services Alliance (ASA), a nationally recognised body supporting advice services nationwide.
- Over 700 advice providers hold the AQS, from national bodies like Citizens Advice to local advice centres.
- There is an emphasis on continuous improvement.

Cons:

- The AQS is not as widely recognised as Lexcel.
- The AQS is not the standard used by most solicitors and is aimed predominantly at the advice sector.
- The clinic concerned must fit within the social welfare criteria (which

---

18   <https://www.lawsociety.org.uk/support-services/accreditation/lexcel/lexcel-fees/> accessed 3 July 2019.

19   <http://advicequalitystandard.org.uk/> accessed 13 February 2019.

does not include advice on family law or commercial law advice to small businesses, for example).

While the AQS is owned by the Advice Services Alliance, the assessment process is independently managed by Recognising Excellence.[20]

The costs of the AQS is a registration fee of £175 (discounted by £100 if an application for assessment is made within three months of registering), an initial (one-off) desktop audit fee (£475) and a biennial audit fee dependent on the number of staff. For four to 15 staff, the cost is £1,250. These are for the level two audit only (see below).

As with Lexcel, the AQS provides a useful framework for the organisation of clinics, client care and the delivery of advice.[21] On balance, the AQS is likely to be the most accessible and relevant starting point for many law clinics. This has also been recognised by LawWorks, who have promoted the AQS to clinics registered with its network.[22]

Audit process: A case study

This section draws on the experience of one student legal advice clinic (BPP University Law School's Legal Advice Clinic) undergoing the AQS audit.

The AQS recognises three levels of client-based work:

- the Information Service
- the Advice Level
- the Advice with Casework Level.

The Information Service covers:

- providing general information, e.g. leaflets or an information kiosk provided in a reception or waiting area. Clients select the information they want themselves and there is no direct guidance by a receptionist or other staff member
- signposting, e.g. providing factual information about the role of another organisation or how to find or contact that organisation
- assisting clients to find information that relates to their enquiry, e.g. providing clients with leaflets, website addresses or other details which

---

20   <https://www.recognisingexcellence.co.uk/> accessed 13 February 2019.

21   <http://advicequalitystandard.org.uk/about-the-aqs/content/> accessed 13 February 2019.

22   <https://www.lawworks.org.uk/solicitors-and-volunteers/training-and-events/quality-standards-and-accreditation-clinics-webinar> accessed 13 February 2019.

will help them contact other organisations, such as the Department for Work and Pensions (DWP).

The Advice Level covers:

- diagnosing clients' problems
- giving information and explaining options
- identifying further action the client can take
- giving basic assistance, e.g. filling in basic forms, contacting third parties to seek information.

This will generally be done in one interview, although there may be some follow-up work. The client then retains responsibility for further action.

The Advice with Casework Level covers the above plus:

- the service may also be providing a casework service, i.e. taking action on behalf of clients in order to move the case on. This may include negotiation and advocacy on the client's behalf to third parties on the telephone, by letter or face to face. By definition, most cases will involve follow-up work with the service provider retaining responsibility for this.

There is also a separate Telephone Service audit where advice is provided by this method.

The service is then judged against various standards within the framework. It would be a long process to set out the framework in full here, and anyone considering applying for the AQS (or indeed for any quality standard) needs to read the framework carefully.[23] In general terms, however, this requires a clinic to have policies and procedures that comply with the framework and to demonstrate adherence to those policies and procedures. The form of client consent is likely to need amending, to allow for the auditor's access.

The desktop audit considers the policies and procedures required for first applications. This is followed by the onsite audit, which involves the inspection of files, interviews with staff and student volunteers and looking further into any issues arising under the desktop audit. Client consent is needed for the inspection of their files, which can be incorporated into the standard consent forms used with clients. If there are corrections needed from either the desktop or onsite audit then 28 days are allowed to comply. Once awarded, there is a requirement for re-auditing every two years.

There is a clear benefit to having an external auditor look at your policies and

---

23   <https://www.recognisingexcellence.co.uk/media/1039/aqs-v2-final.pdf>   accessed   19 August 2018.

procedures and the extent to which you adhere to them. BPP's experience was that the audit made clinic staff look critically at the clinic's policies and procedures and how far BPP's practice mirrored those policies and procedures. The process ensured that staff gained a fresh perspective on file reviews and overall it was a positive learning process.

The award of the AQS has allowed BPP to demonstrate externally (to clients, partner agencies, etc.) our commitment to quality. Within the university itself, the award of the AQS raised the profile of the clinic. In addition, there were many positives in the report of the auditor, which provided staff and students with welcome feedback and encouragement.

Part 2.8
Quality assurance: Higher education and clinical legal education

Nick Johnson

For those who run clinics in higher education where the clinic's activities are part of the curriculum, the issue of quality assurance is one that, at some stage, will have to be faced, especially when developing a new module or programme of study.

Each higher education provider has a primary responsibility for ensuring that its programmes offer a high quality of education; that students achieve required standards; and that assessments are appropriate, rigorous and fair. Despite the existence of common principles of higher education quality assurance, each individual institution will have its own processes that will need to be followed. For this reason, the comments in this section are of necessity general. The first port of call for those seeking to introduce or further develop clinical programmes will be their own faculty or university quality assurance department.

Quality assurance processes are often seen by academic staff as opaque and confusing, especially when enthusiasm for the subject area being taught is far greater (as would be expected) than enthusiasm for quality processes. Those administering quality assurance processes and providing guidance may seem remote from the day-to-day activity of academic staff. However, engagement with the quality framework in an institution is necessary and, in many cases, highly beneficial when establishing and developing clinical programmes. Often, through engagement with such processes the clear educational benefits of clinical legal education can be clearly demonstrated.

This section highlights some of the key issues associated with validating, reviewing and developing a clinical module or course. Assessment is clearly a key focus of the quality assurance process and although this section highlights some issues associated with assessment, this is dealt with in detail in **Part 3** of this Handbook and you should refer to that section when considering some of the issues referred to here.

Quality assurance framework in the UK

The framework for quality assurance for UK universities is set out by the Quality Assurance Agency (QAA) which, by agreement with the statutory higher education regulator, the Office for Students, is responsible for providing guidance to higher education providers on ensuring the quality of provision.[1] This is done principally through the UK Quality Code for Higher Education. The provisions the Code, which covers 12 specified areas of quality assurance, will in practice be largely incorporated into local institutional policies which will have been developed to ensure compliance with the Code.

For those developing clinical programmes and modules, therefore, many institutional policies will already give guidance to ensure that modules developed fit within the QAA Code. For those wishing to look in more depth at the Code, of particular relevance are those areas that relate to course design, assessment, learning and teaching, partnerships and work-based learning.[2]

The QAA also produces Subject Benchmark Statements, which set out the nature of study and the academic standards expected of graduates in specific subject areas, outlining what graduates in a particular subject might reasonably be expected to know, do and understand at the end of their programme of study. The Law Subject Benchmark Statement[3] provides extensive guidance, which is discussed further below. For those whose clinical programmes seek to cover some of the learning outcomes of vocational courses (such as the Legal Practice Course skills), the written standards for particular courses also give guidance on the levels of competence expected.

It is beyond the scope of this section to discuss in detail the quality assurance framework for higher education and for specific professional qualifications.[4] However, clinical programmes often present particular issues that will need consideration when either validating, reviewing or engaging in the assessment of the quality of any programme offered. The purpose of this section is therefore to consider the issues that apply specifically to clinical programmes and to address some of the quality assurance issues which are raised by faculty, university and external assessors when establishing and running clinical programmes. It will be seen that established clinical practice, including much of that outlined in this book, reflects good quality assurance practice in general, supporting the assertion of many clinicians that law clinics are a potent and high-quality educational experience.

Clinical modules will often differ in the style of teaching and assessment from other law school modules, particularly those that are more likely to focus on

1   Higher Education and Research Act 2017, ss 23–25.

2   <https://www.qaa.ac.uk/quality-code> accessed 1 August 2019.

3   <https://www.qaa.ac.uk/docs/qaa/subject-benchmark-statements/sbs-law-15. pdf?sfvrsn=ff99f781_10> accessed 19 July 2019.

4   For a more detailed discussion of this and many issues arising, see Roger Ellis and Elaine Hogard (eds), *Handbook of quality assurance for university teaching* (Routledge, 2018).

specific legal content. While clinical modules may have a focus on a particular area of law, teaching and assessment methods commonly used on, for example, core modules are unlikely to be suited to clinical modules.[5] Further, particularly in those modules that involve 'live client' work, concerns may be raised that students will have very different learning experiences, depending on the clients they see and the area of law they deal with. It is a good idea to address such issues at the outset of a review or validation process.

Specific quality assurance issues in clinical legal education

Designing and developing modules

Learning outcomes

When developing a clinical module, the first step ideally is to specify learning outcomes (LOs). It is easy to assume that skills development will be the primary focus of any clinic module and suggest learning outcomes based on these. While skills development is a key part of many clinic modules, a law clinic is a powerful teaching and learning tool for such topics as legal ethics, law and society issues, and principles and practice of the justice system, as well as potentially providing a grounding in a subject area (e.g. housing, family or even commercial law).

Examples of typical learning outcomes are set out in the sample module specifications set out in **Part 5.4** of this Handbook. Defining LOs at the start of the development (or, indeed, the review) of a module provides clear focus for the module and gives a clear steer on the best method of assessing students. It also addresses some of the issues associated with consistency of experience, which are often raised when introducing or reviewing clinic programmes.

Assessment methods

The QAA guidance provides that assessment should be:

- reliable, consistent, fair and valid
- inclusive and equitable
- explicit and transparent.[6]

Assessment and feedback are to be 'purposeful and support(s) the learning

---

5   See **Part 3**.

6   <https://www.qaa.ac.uk/en/quality-code/advice-and-guidance/assessment> accessed 1 August 2019.

process' and students to be supported and prepared for assessment.[7] Assessment should also encourage 'academic integrity'.[8]

The requirement that assessment should be consistent can present difficulty for those running live client modules. The claim is often made that inevitable differences in student experience when dealing with live clients, mean that assessment will not be fair: for example, one student or group has a particularly interesting case or another has a challenging and difficult to handle client.

This does present a challenge. QAA standards clearly require students to be provided with an '... *equivalent* high-quality learning experience', although differences in experience will undoubtedly arise in other modules, for example dissertation and research modules.[9]

To some extent, the requirement is countered by the fact that the same standards require providers to ensure that the learning environment is 'accessible, relevant and engaging to all students' and 'encourages and enables students to take an active role in their studies'.[10] Many clinicians would argue that the experiences they enable clearly do both these things, even if this may come at the perceived expense of 'equivalence'.

As well as ensuring that assessment processes are robust, with clear marking criteria and moderation processes, it is most important to ensure that the assessment method clearly aligns with the identified LOs. It is unlikely to be appropriate, for example, to assess an LO that seeks to develop a student's capacity to reflect on their performance by simply assessing performance in a particular skill such as legal writing or interviewing. Other methods, such as viva or a reflective journal, will be more appropriate. A variety of assessment methods, even if a module only has a single point of assessment, will be best if the LOs are widely drawn.

Quality assurance processes will rightly require formative assessment and feedback opportunities to be included and identified in course design. A law clinic is usually rich in opportunities to provide students with feedback but consideration should be given to how this may be recorded and evidenced. Consideration should be given to what opportunities there are for formative feedback during and at the end of a module. Feedback is clearly an integral part of reflective learning and, given the bond between clinical legal education and

---

7   Ibid.

8   Ibid.

9   <https://www.qaa.ac.uk/quality-code/advice-and-guidance/learning-and-teaching> accessed 1 August 2019.

10   <https://www.qaa.ac.uk/docs/qaa/quality-code/qc-a-g-learning-and-teaching. pdf?sfvrsn=1f2ac181_6> accessed 1 August 2019.

reflective learning,[11] course design should highlight the occasions when formal feedback is given to provide students with the essential material to reflect on.

Finally, student feedback is an essential part of the quality assurance process. Many clinics, as well as having centrally gathered feedback from students provided by their university, will often as a matter of course seek more specific written feedback on students' learning and working experience. This represents a valuable source of information not just as to the quality of supervision and experience in a clinical module but also, if carefully constructed, gives an indication of whether or not the learning experience of students reflects the intended LOs.

Contact hours

Given the relationship between academic credit and notional study hours, many institutions will require a clear breakdown of hours devoted to particular activities when validating a course or module. This will entail identifying not just the numbers of large and small group sessions (lectures, seminars and tutorials) but also any supervision sessions.

Identifying contact hours is clearly essential for timetabling. However, given that staff:student ratios are normally lower in a law clinic than in traditional seminars, and the numbers of lectures and seminars may well be fewer, particularly in live client modules, this may present a problem when validating courses. Given the 'workshop' nature of clinic activity, formal contact time with clinic staff is often less than on modules with a more standard format. With university management being increasingly concerned about the effect of reducing contact hours on Key Information Set (KIS) data, those developing clinic courses may well find themselves urged to fit clinic modules into the same format as other more content-based modules.

As well as being inappropriate for clinic modules, such an approach presents a significant risk of undermining students' learning experience. Clinic participation often results in students committing time in excess of that normally required by a credit-bearing module because they are highly motivated. This will not necessarily be reflected in comparison between the numbers of timetabled sessions with other modules. Therefore, unless a realistic element of time allocation is built into clinic modules to ensure students' actual workload in the clinic is properly reflected, and excessive dependence on the traditional lecture/seminar format avoided, there is a danger that students' learning experience both in clinic and in other modules will be adversely affected.

---

11   See **Part 3** of this Handbook on assessment and **Part 4** on research and clinical legal education.

Conduct of live client work and work-based learning requirements

To some extent, whether undertaken with an external organisation or via an in-house clinic, most clinic work in university law schools can be described as work-based learning, whether or not the learning outcomes relate to specific employability objectives. The QAA Code indicates that work-based learning should:

- consist of structured opportunities for learning
- be achieved through 'authentic activity'
- be supervised.[12]

The QAA Code also indicates that work-based learning opportunities should 'enable students to apply and integrate areas of subject and professional knowledge, skills and behaviours'.[13]

As other contributions to this Handbook suggest,[14] structured learning through following clinic processes and supervision are clear attributes of clinics and their work. When seeking validation it is possible to stress the way in which clinical modules meet standards for work-based learning.

Further, the way in which work-based learning will often be seen as a way of integrating and synthesising knowledge, skills and behaviours suggests that clinical modules are more appropriate in the latter stages of an undergraduate or postgraduate course, which are likely to have higher level learning outcomes.

Partnership working

Part 1 of this Handbook discussed examples of partnership working, where clinical legal education experience is provided by an external agency. The QAA directs higher education providers to consider any specific issues in relation to the workplace environment and deal with them appropriately. In most cases, a formal agreement between the workplace and the institution should be in place to outline the responsibilities of each partner. Similarly, students engaged in external placements should have some formal agreement that governs their work and responsibilities at the host organisation.

The Code states that such placements should be delivered 'through a meaningful partnership between students, employers and the education organisation' and that those involved 'understand and respect' their respective roles.[15] As suggested, appropriate training and support needs to be provided for students

---

12 <http://www.qaa.ac.uk/docs/qaa/quality-code/advice-and-guidance-work-based-learning. pdf?sfvrsn=f625c181_2> accessed 1 August 2019.

13 Ibid.

14 See **Part 3** of this Handbook.

15 See **note 12**.

going into an external organisation, and responsibility for this identified. Opportunities should be 'inclusive, safe and supported' and 'designed, monitored, evaluated and reviewed' in partnership.[16]

Notably, the Code states that 'feedback from internal and external stakeholders' should be used to inform course content.[17] Working with external agencies does provide an opportunity for a teaching team to use feedback from partner organisations to develop and enhance materials when reflecting and reviewing a module.

Subject Benchmark for Law

As indicated above, part of the QAA framework includes the provision of 'subject benchmarks', which provide non-prescriptive guidance for those delivering courses in subject areas. The Subject Benchmark for Law was last updated in 2015.[18] It provides extensive guidance on both the attributes that a law graduate can be expected to have at the end of a programme of study in law, and methods of teaching, learning and assessment.

A detailed consideration of the Subject Benchmark is beyond the scope of this section. Further, the Subject Benchmark applies across a whole course or programme of study so not every item will need to be addressed within a single module. However, it is recommended that those developing and promoting clinical programmes consult and use it when developing programmes of study. In many senses, it provides a wide and varied set of attributes for a student and a diverse range of teaching and assessment methods, many of which are reflected in clinical programmes (such as the ability to gain an awareness of the principles and values of law and justice and the use of a variety of methods of delivering the curriculum). The use of the statement provides potentially significant support to anyone seeking to establish clinical modules within their law school, as it supports the type of engaged learning with which clinical legal education is associated.

---

16   Ibid.

17   Ibid.

18   <https://www.qaa.ac.uk/docs/qaa/subject-benchmark-statements/sbs-law-15. pdf?sfvrsn=ff99f781_8> accessed 1 August 2019.

Part 2.9
Clinical legal education as solicitor qualifying work experience

Victoria Roper, Rachel Dunn and Vinny Kennedy

Introduction

The Solicitors Regulation Authority (SRA) is intending to introduce a new qualification regime for solicitors. During the relevant consultation process, there was strong support for retaining the requirement for solicitors to undertake a period of legal work experience before qualification.[1] The SRA has, accordingly, decided to keep a two-year work experience requirement, which will in future be known as qualifying work experience (QWE).

At the time of writing, it is anticipated that QWE will replace the current 'period of recognised training system' in September 2021.[2] When the new system is introduced, a broader range of work experience will potentially be able to qualify as QWE. There will also be more flexibility about when such QWE can be undertaken and scope to satisfy the requirement within up to four different firms, educational institutions or other organisations. This means that, in future, clinical legal education (CLE) work undertaken by students at university/within a student law clinic could 'count' towards QWE. Universities and law clinics will not be mandated to offer QWE, but may choose to do so if they wish. The SRA hopes that the changes will promote access to and diversity within the profession.

In this section we will discuss the background and detail of the SRA's plans, and analyse the practical considerations clinicians will need to take into account should they decide to confirm CLE as QWE. The arguments for and against offering CLE as QWE, and how employers might perceive solicitors with such experience, are outside the scope of this section, but such issues are explored in our 2018 *Law Teacher* article, 'Clinical legal education as qualifying work experience for solicitors'.[3]

---

1   SRA, 'A new route to qualification: The Solicitors Qualifying Examination (SQE): Summary of responses and our decision on next steps' (April 2017), p. 9 <https://www.sra.org.uk/globalassets/documents/sra/consultations/sqe-summary-responses.pdf> accessed 1 January 2019.

2   The exact implementation date is yet to be confirmed.

3   Rachel Dunn, Victoria Roper and Vinny Kennedy, 'Clinical legal education as qualifying work experience for solicitors' (2018) 52 *Law Teacher* 439–52.

SRA's proposals in relation to qualifying work experience

How will QWE be different to the current regime?

The SRA has published Draft SRA Authorisation of Individuals Regulations (as amended) (the Draft Regulations) setting out its proposals in relation to QWE.[4] Note that references in this section are to the latest version of the Draft Regulations available at the time of writing, and readers should check the final implemented version to ensure compliance, as there may be further changes.

The Draft Regulations provide that:

> 2.1 Qualifying work experience must:
>
> (a) comprise experience of providing legal services which provides [the candidate] with the opportunity to develop the prescribed competences for solicitors;
>
> (b) be of a duration of a total of at least two years' full time or equivalent; and
>
> (c) be carried out under an arrangement or employment with no more than four separate firms, educational institutions or other organisations.[5]

The new system is much more flexible than the current regime, and will allow a candidate with a portfolio of work experience gained at a number of different firms, educational institutions or organisations to meet the QWE requirement, provided that their work experience adds up to at least two years' full time equivalent (and provided it is confirmed in accordance with the Draft Regulations – discussed further below). 'Educational institution' is currently undefined in the Draft Regulations but it seems clear that the SRA intends this to include universities.

It appears the SRA will adopt a fairly light-touch approach to the regulation of QWE and does not intend to be as prescriptive as it is under the current regime. The SRA's justification for this is that the SQE Stage 2 Examinations (which are expected to be taken at the end of the QWE) will test a candidate's competence to practise and therefore heavier oversight is unnecessary.[6]

---

4   SRA, 'Draft SRA Authorisation of Individuals Regulations [20XX] (Post Consultation)' (November 2017) 1 <https://www.sra.org.uk/globalassets/documents/sra/consultations/draft-sqe-reg-board.pdf> accessed 1 January 2019.

5   Ibid.

6   SRA, 'A new route to qualification: The Solicitors Qualifying Examination (SQE)' (October 2016), pp. 21–22 <https://www.sra.org.uk/globalassets/documents/sra/consultations/solicitors-qualifying-examination-2-consultation.pdf> accessed 3 January 2019.

The current system and the new system of QWE are compared in **Table 1** below.

Table 1: Current and proposed regimes compared

Requirement	Current period of recognised training regime	Proposed QWE regime from September 2021
Length of work experience?	Normally not less than two years if undertaken full time or pro-rata if part time.	At least two years' full time or equivalent. Could be satisfied working on a full-time or part-time basis.
Ability to obtain work experience with different firms or organisations?	Sometimes training is undertaken at more than one organisation but the majority undertake a two-year training contract with one law firm/ organisation immediately before qualification.	Candidates will be able to obtain their QWE with up to four firms, institutions or organisations. Note: the SRA is not intending to prescribe any minimum length of time for work experience placements/CLE experience, etc. The key thing is that the candidate's total work experience must add up to two years' full time or equivalent. The SRA is keen to emphasise this as a benefit of the new system. This is expressly provided for under the Draft Regulations.
Method of satisfying work experience requirement?	Majority undertake a two-year full-time, paid training contract with a law firm (or other organisation) immediately before qualification, although other routes are available.	The SRA envisages many firms will still want to offer a two-year block training contract. However, a significant number of candidates are likely to want to take advantage of the increased flexibility, satisfying their QWE requirement through voluntary or paid placements, paralegal work and CLE (or a combination of these). Solicitor apprenticeships may grow in popularity.
Requirements for the type of experience that must be gained?	At least three distinct areas of English and Welsh law and practice.	None specified.

| When is work experience completed? | Usually after the academic stage (which includes a law degree or post-graduate conversion course and the Legal Practice Course (LPC)) but before qualification. Usual for this to be completed by working full time in one block before qualification. | Any point before qualification. Recommended that QWE is undertaken after SQE Stage 1 and before SQE Stage 2 but this will not be mandatory. No requirement for work experience to be completed in a 'block' after the LPC – could be gained at different times with different firms/organisations. |

What type of work experience will be allowed to constitute QWE?

The Draft Regulations do not prescribe the type of work experience that can contribute to the QWE. Rather, they state that QWE must comprise of experience of providing legal services which provides the candidate with the opportunity to develop some or all of the prescribed competences for solicitors (discussed further below).[7]

The SRA has said that:

> periods of work experience acquired under a formal training contract, through working in a student law clinic, as an apprentice or a paralegal, or through a placement as part of a sandwich degree could all contribute to [the QWE] requirement.[8]

The Draft Regulations make reference to QWE comprising experience of 'providing legal services', which may indicate that purely simulated work will not count, although the position is not particularly clear.

Clinical legal education as qualifying work experience

What type of CLE will be allowed to constitute QWE?

Universities should note that the SRA has indicated that multiple clinical experiences undertaken with the same institution will only count as one 'arrangement', although this is not stated in the Draft Regulations themselves. It appears that the SRA is not proposing to impose a minimum time period for

7   SRA (**note 4**), Regulation 2.3(b).
8   SRA (**note 6**), p. 21.

any QWE arrangement, including CLE.[9]

Universities employ various forms and models of CLE. Therefore, the first question clinicians are likely to ask is: what type of CLE can constitute QWE? The SRA has said that 'clinical legal education and working pro bono or in student law clinics' could count as QWE.[10] The difficulty, of course, is that these terms have no legal or universally agreed definitions and are open to interpretation. Nor are 'CLE' or 'law clinics' expressly referenced or defined in the Draft Regulations. The key question clinicians must ask themselves, just as any other provider of QWE will have to do, is whether students are given the opportunity to develop all or some of the solicitor competences.

In March 2015, the SRA published a competence statement for solicitors. This defines the standards for practice as a solicitor and therefore the knowledge and competences that aspiring solicitors need to demonstrate in order to qualify.[11] The statement consists of three parts:

- a statement of solicitor competence
- the threshold standard
- a statement of legal knowledge.[12]

It is the statement of solicitor competence that is particularly relevant for QWE, and clinicians should consider the competences stated therein and whether students are given the opportunity to develop some or all of them. What is meant by 'some' of the competences is not defined.

The SRA has made it absolutely clear within the Draft Regulations that all that is being confirmed is that the opportunity for development has been provided;[13] law clinics will not be required to confirm the student is competent (this being tested at SQE Stage 2). The SRA has highlighted that the new regime will allow individuals to obtain QWE with more than one organisation, so that they develop different competences at different times and places.[14]

The responsibility to ensure that a candidate has undertaken sufficient QWE prior to sitting SQE Stage 2 firmly rests with the candidate, and not upon those who provide confirmation. Universities may need to make this clear to

---

9   SRA (**note 1**), pp. 9–10.

10   See, for example, ibid.

11   SRA, 'Statement of solicitor competence' (11 March 2015) <https://www.sra.org.uk/solicitors/competence-statement.page> accessed 1 January 2019.

12   Ibid.

13   SRA (**note 4**), Regulation 2.1(a).

14   SRA, 'A new route to qualification: New regulations consultation response' (November 2017) 12 <https://www.sra.org.uk/globalassets/documents/sra/consultations/sqe3-response-regulations.pdf> accessed 3 January 2019.

their students. Universities may also take a view that it is only worth offering QWE if students are given the opportunity to develop a reasonable number of competences.

At Northumbria University, where we work, we have undertaken an exercise whereby we have mapped the activities students undertake in our in-house clinic, the Student Law Office, on to the competences in the statement of solicitor competence (see **Table 2** below). We are confident that the Student Law Office gives students the opportunity to develop most of the competences.

The opportunity to develop the competences is what is key rather than the type or model of CLE concerned, although the form and model may have an impact on the practicalities of supervision and confirmation (discussed further below). This will particularly be the case where the CLE or pro bono work is undertaken by a student on a voluntary, extra-curricular basis. In such circumstances it is likely that the student will have had the opportunity to develop competences, and therefore the Regulations regarding confirmation (referred to below) could still apply to such experience.

However, there will be no formal method of assessing the work undertaken by the student. This may create difficulties upon confirmation whereby the solicitor may not feel there is sufficient evidence to make the required confirmation. Universities may therefore conclude that for CLE and pro bono work undertaken on a voluntary basis, no confirmation will be available. As suggested previously, this will need to be clearly communicated to students. Nevertheless, you are welcome to use **Table 2** below as the basis for your institution's own mapping exercise if you so wish.

Table 2: Northumbria's Student Law Office mapped to the statement of solicitor competence[15]

Competency	Competency description	Mapping to activities in Student Law Office	Mapping to assessment criteria[16]
A1	Act honestly and with integrity, in accordance with legal and regulatory requirements and the SRA Handbook and Code of Conduct ...	Students are regularly exposed to ethical dilemmas and the Code of Conduct is regularly discussed. They must abide by the Solicitors Code of Conduct and the Principles at all times.	Understanding of client care and professional conduct.
A2[17]	Maintain the level of competence and legal knowledge needed to practise effectively, taking into account changes in their role and/or practice context and developments in the law ...	Students are required to assess their own strengths and weaknesses. They have the opportunity to learn from their supervisor and others.	Students are partly assessed by way of reflective presentation.
A3	Work within the limits of their competence and the supervision which they need ...	While autonomy is encouraged, all students learn to recognise when to seek advice from their supervisor. They are encouraged to openly address mistakes.	Understanding of client care and professional conduct.
A4	Draw on a sufficient detailed knowledge and understanding of their field(s) of work and role in order to practise effectively ...	All students are required to identify and apply legal principles to factual issues taking into account the client's commercial or personal circumstances.	Knowledge and understanding of the law/legal practice.

15   The table is best read alongside the whole of the statement of solicitor competence, including the behavioural characteristics.

16   A student's practical work is assessed against 10 assessment criteria (Northumbria University, Student Law Office Assessment Guide 2018/2019).

17   Note that the behavioural characteristics for A2 place emphasis on taking responsibility for one's learning, reflecting from practice and learning from other people.

Competency	Competency description	Mapping to activities in Student Law Office	Mapping to assessment criteria[16]
A5	Apply understanding, critical thinking and analysis to solve problems ...	All students are required to evaluate key issues and risks, identify knowledge gaps and make reasoned judgements.	Knowledge and understanding of the law/legal practice. Case management and strategising.
B1	Obtain relevant facts ...	All students are required to undertake fact-finding interviews and to review documentation. They must recognise when additional information is required.	Case management and strategising.
B2	Undertake legal research ...	All students are required to produce research reports. These form the basis for any advice provided.	Strength of research skills.
B3	Develop and advise on relevant options, strategies and solutions ...	All students are encouraged to consider a client's individual circumstances and are required to cover the advantages and disadvantages of different options where relevant.	Case management and strategising.
B4	Draft documents which are legally effective and accurately reflect the client's instructions ...	Many students have the opportunity to draft legal document(s).	Strength of written communication skills.
B5	Undertake effective spoken and written advocacy ...	Some students have the opportunity to undertake spoken and/or written advocacy. Not all matters are contentious, though.	Strength of written communication skills. Strength of oral communication skills.
B6	Negotiate solutions to clients' issues ...	Some students have the opportunity to present/respond to options for compromise.	Case management and strategising.

Competency	Competency description	Mapping to activities in Student Law Office	Mapping to assessment criteria[16]
B7	Plan, manage and progress legal cases and transactions ...	Students usually have the opportunity to progress a case from start to file closure. All students are exposed to office procedure and are required to 'progress' their case(s).	Autonomy and efficiency. Case management and strategising. Understanding of client care and professional conduct.
C1	Communicate clearly and effectively, orally and in writing ...	All students are required to communicate orally and in writing with at least their client. Students may also need to communicate with third parties, the court, etc.	Strength of written communication skills. Strength of oral communication skills.
C2	Establish and maintain effective and professional relations with clients ...	All students are required to treat clients with courtesy and respect.	Understanding of client care and professional conduct.
C3	Establish and maintain effective and professional relations with other people ...	Students must work with a partner and must keep their partner/supervisor updated.	Teamwork skills and contribution to group meetings.
D1	Initiate, plan, prioritise and manage work activities and projects to ensure that they are completed efficiently, on time and to an appropriate standard, both in relation to their own work and work that they lead or supervise ...	All students must manage their clinic work (which may involve multiple cases) with their other studies and often part-time work.	Organisation: time and file management.
D2	Keep, use and maintain accurate, complete and clear records ...	Students are required to maintain a client file and make attendance notes of meetings and telephone calls. Students undertake file reviews throughout the academic year to ensure that such records are up to date.	Organisation: time and file management.

Competency	Competency description	Mapping to activities in Student Law Office	Mapping to assessment criteria[16]
D3[18]	Apply good business practice ...	Students do not bill clients as all work is free, but some students may deal with disbursements. Students are required to time record. Students usually develop an understanding of the context in which legal clinics operate and their role in it.	Organisation: time and file management. Students are encouraged to explore wider issues relating to the legal profession.

Practicalities

In this section, we will consider the key practicalities that law schools will need to consider if they are to offer clinical legal education as qualifying work experience: supervisory and confirmation arrangements, and how to calculate the period of QWE gained.

Supervisory and confirmation arrangements

The Draft Regulations provide that candidates must arrange for each firm, organisation or institution in which they have undertaken their QWE to provide a 'confirmation' in a prescribed form. In this section we will therefore explain:

- who can provide this confirmation and the implications for CLE specifically
- the matters that must be confirmed
- the implications for supervision in clinics.

Who can provide the required confirmation?

Regulation 2.2[19] states that only the following people can provide the required confirmation of QWE:

> 2.2   [...]
> (a) the organisation's COLP [Compliance Officer for Legal Practice];

---

18   This is perhaps one of the most difficult competences to map on to a law clinic. The behavioural characteristics place emphasis on a number of things that clinic students will not normally be exposed to, e.g. applying the rules of professional conduct to accounting and financial matters.

19   SRA (**note 4**), pp. 1–2.

(b) a solicitor working within the organisation; or

(c) if neither (a) or (b) are applicable, a solicitor working outside of the organisation who has direct experience of [the candidate's] work and who has, in order to be so satisfied:

> (i) undertaken a review of the work [the candidate] has done during the relevant period of work experience, which may include review of a training diary or portfolio of work; and

> (ii) received feedback from the person or persons supervising [the candidate's] work.

Anyone providing the required confirmation will need to have taken sufficient steps to satisfy themselves as to the matters they are confirming (discussed further below). It is worth highlighting that the definition of a solicitor will include those who are on the roll, but do not have a current practising certificate, something that has been subject to some criticism.[20]

Who gives the confirmation statement will likely depend on the supervisory model of the CLE in question. Few law clinics will have a COLP, but many will employ an internal supervisory model with solicitors in the clinic acting in a supervisory role.[21]

Where the internal supervisory model is adopted, confirmation provided by the solicitor with supervisory responsibilities for that particular student will satisfy the provisions within Draft Regulation 2.2(b), as specified above. Alternatively, if there is a solicitor with overall supervisory responsibility for the running of the clinic, they could provide confirmation for all students as this would provide consistency. Either would satisfy Draft Regulation 2.2(b), although the supervisor with overall responsibility would need to satisfy themselves as to the matters they are certifying (which makes this the less efficient model involving additional work over and above the time spent on supervision by the supervisor).

If clinics employ a non-solicitor supervisory model they should still be able to provide a QWE confirmation. The solicitor providing the confirmation need only be working within the 'organisation' and therefore they do not have to have direct responsibility for supervising students within the legal clinic. Provided someone in the organisation is a solicitor and can provide the required confirmation, this should satisfy Regulation 2.2(b). The solicitor would need to satisfy themselves as to the matters they are certifying.

Universities that offer a model of CLE where students are supervised by external solicitors should be covered by Regulation 2.2(c). However, prior to suggesting

---

20   SRA (note 14), p. 14.

21   Rachel Dunn, Victoria Roper and Vinny Kennedy (note 3), p. 449.

that such experience could be confirmed as QWE the law school will have to first agree, ideally contractually, with the external legal services provider that such confirmation can and will be provided. The law school should consider how it will protect itself/its students so as to ensure confirmation is provided in accordance with the Draft Regulations. Clarity should be sought as regards exactly who has agreed to provide the confirmation, and that they have agreed to review the candidate's work/receive feedback from the person supervising the work (where relevant). It should also be clear what would happen in the case where the relationship between the legal services provider and the law school (or individual student) were to cease. Again, ideally this is likely to involve contractual obligations.

Regulation 2.2(c) appears to be drafted widely enough that a university that offers CLE which does not involve a solicitor in any capacity (internal or external) and does not otherwise employ a solicitor could still provide confirmation of QWE if it could persuade an external solicitor to review the student's work, obtain feedback and give the required confirmation. It is suggested that most solicitors would be reluctant to do so, although perhaps the institution's external lawyers might be willing to undertake this role to further cement the client/law firm relationship.[22]

Matters that must be confirmed

The Draft Regulations specify the matters which have to be confirmed; and that prior to providing such confirmation, the person must take sufficient steps to satisfy themselves as to those matters. The matters which the persons specified in Draft Regulation 2.2(a)–(c) have to confirm are as follows:

> 2.3[23]   [...]
>
> (a) details of the period of work experience carried out;
>
> (b) that it provided [the candidate] with the opportunity to develop some or all of the prescribed competences for solicitors; and
>
> (c) that no issues arose during the period of work experience that raise a question as to [the candidate's] character and suitability to be admitted as a solicitor, or if such confirmation cannot be given, then details of any such issues.

Where the person providing the required confirmation has also supervised the CLE experience, proving the required confirmation may be a relatively straightforward process that does not necessitate a lot of extra work (although see comments below in relation to calculating the period of work experience).

---

22   Ibid, p. 450. See also discussion in SRA (**note 14**), p. 13.
23   SRA (**note 4**), p. 2.

However, any model which requires a person other than the CLE supervisor to provide the confirmation will involve additional work over and above that required for supervisory purposes. The solicitor giving the confirmation will need to satisfy themselves as to the matters they are confirming in relation to that particular student. It is suggested this would likely involve, whether or not the solicitor was external or internal, undertaking a review of the work the student has done (such as a review of a training diary or portfolio of work) and receiving feedback from the person or persons who supervised the student's work (i.e. the things specified in Draft Regulation 2.2(c)). It appears that the SRA does intend to issue some further guidance on this point in due course.[24]

Implications for supervision in clinic

In contrast to supervision of a traditional training contract, the SRA does not specify in the Draft Regulations who can provide supervision of an individual undertaking QWE. While it seems possible that anyone can provide QWE supervision, a solicitor must provide the actual confirmation, and this may impact in practice on who supervises. Some solicitors who provide confirmation may be happy not to have been involved in supervision and to base their confirmation on a review of the student's work. Others might want to have been involved, at least to a certain extent, in supervision so as to ensure that they can confidently confirm whether or not the experience provided the candidate with an opportunity to develop some or all of the solicitor competences.

It is clear that the SRA has provided a great amount of discretion to supervisors of work experience in terms of:

- who can actually supervise
- the type and number of competences that the individual has the opportunity to develop
- the type of work undertaken.

This flexibility is useful for universities as they employ a wide range of supervisory models and differ greatly in terms of type and breadth of the work undertaken.

Calculating the period of QWE gained

As referred to previously, Draft Regulation 2.1 states that a candidate's QWE must amount to at least two years' full-time equivalent. There is no real guidance on how exactly to calculate an individual's QWE, but the period of time to be credited as QWE will need to be decided by the institution providing

24   SRA (**note 14**), p. 14.

it (i.e. the person giving confirmation), rather than the SRA.

The SRA has also commented that it expects:

> candidates and firms to take a common sense approach to deciding how long the period of QWE should be if the candidate has to take any extended time off, for example, through illness.[25]

This issue may not be subject to further regulation, as the SRA says it will not be possible to draft regulations that will cover every individual situation, and decisions should be made on each candidate's circumstances.[26]

There are a number of potential issues with calculating the period of QWE for CLE that will be discussed in this section (over and above the current lack of guidance regarding calculation). Where possible, we will suggest solutions to such issues or highlight alternative areas for further consideration.

Issue 1: Calculating the period of QWE when CLE is part time/ad hoc

The new model lends itself very well to law firms, where trainees and paralegals will work a set amount of hours per week, making it easier to confirm that they have had the opportunity to develop the solicitor competences over a period of two years. This becomes more difficult with CLE, however, which is usually undertaken on a part-time basis. Consideration will need to be given as to how much full-time equivalent the part-time work equates to.

Some CLE is timetabled, where students are required to attend and are expected to undertake additional work outside of these timetabled sessions. For others, such as at Northumbria Law School's Student Law Office, attendance is not timetabled and arrangements are made directly between the supervisor and students. For others yet still, students undertake CLE on a voluntary basis and as such attendance is sporadic and not monitored. Therefore, students do not work a set amount of hours or days and the full-time equivalent is harder to calculate and monitor.

The statements made by the SRA indicate that those who provide confirmation in relation to CLE will need to provide confirmation of the period of QWE based on the work **actually** undertaken by the student. This means that they will not be able to estimate the amount of time the student has worked on cases, nor will they be able to take an average based on the notional learning hours of the module/average time spent per week.

For example, at Northumbria Law School, we expect students in the Student Law Office to dedicate an average of 12.5 hours per week, over the 20 weeks the module runs, i.e. 250 hours in total. However, we would not be able to confirm

---

25   Ibid.

26   Ibid.

that each student who completed the Student Law Office had undertaken 250 hours as the standard number of hours allocated to QWE. We would need to consider how many hours each individual student has **actually** worked.

Issue 2: Monitoring attendance and absence

We believe providers will need to credit QWE based on the amount of time an individual spends working in their particular firm or institution. If it is literally just a case of adding up the hours a student has worked, then presumably a student cannot be credited any hours where they have missed a session, even for legitimate reasons such as sickness. If a student is ill or is absent for other reasons, it still does not appear that this missed time can count towards QWE.

For training contracts under the current system, the SRA is clear that matters relating to holiday and sickness leave should be agreed between the trainee and employer within the terms and conditions of employment.[27] The terms and conditions of employment are likely to be compliant with the Equality Act 2010, in particular with regards to making reasonable adjustments.[28] Universities will therefore need to ensure that any policy adopted is compliant with the current legislation on disability.

Student law clinics may or may not currently track attendance, illness and absence, and the real challenge will be in terms of calculating exactly how many hours individual students have worked (as referred to above). Keeping track of attendance and hours may be easier for smaller legal clinics, supervised by a small number of people. For larger legal clinics, this may be more challenging. Potential methods to monitoring attendance are discussed below as part of the solutions to these issues.

Issue 3: Over-inflation of hours worked

Where reliance is placed on students to keep accurate records – for example, attendance outside of timetabled hours, hours undertaken on a voluntary basis or hours spent completing a task – students may be inclined to work too many hours in clinic to obtain more QWE. This could lead to over-inflation of the hours worked or it could have a detrimental impact on their other studies.

Issue 4: Relationship between a university and a law student is not an employer/employee relationship like that of a law firm and a trainee

Policies regarding sickness and absence are usually contained within an employment handbook and form part of an employee's contract of employment. Absence without good reason may result in a loss of wages, the employee being

---

27 SRA, 'FAQs for trainees: Period of recognised training' <https://www.sra.org.uk/trainees/resources/faqs-trainees.page> accessed 12 March 2019.

28 Equality Act 2010, s 20.

disciplined and, in the worst-case scenario, dismissal.

However, CLE students are not employees, and the main sanction for non-attendance in assessed CLE settings is normally a lower mark (or in particularly bad cases, failure of the module). There may be no repercussions for failing to attend voluntary CLE a student has signed up for. The repercussions for non-attendance in clinic are not as serious as those an employee would face in practice. Also, our experience is that non-attendance rates due to sickness or for other reasons in clinic are higher than one generally encounters in private practice on the part of fee earners. These things mean it is reasonable to expect that there may be more issues with non-attendance in a clinical setting than at a law firm.

Solutions and further considerations

In light of the above issues, the following are suggestions of possible solutions or areas to which further consideration would need to be given.

- Individual attendance, including hours worked, will need to be monitored and recorded by the institution/organisation offering CLE rather than the onus being placed on students – this may necessitate a change in policy/procedure. Although such records may not need to be as detailed as records kept by an employer, it will still be an additional administrative burden on the institution/organisation.

- Taking each student's attendance and monitoring time spent on CLE can be done in a couple of different ways, but each could be problematic. The two potential ways we have considered are:

  - Student time recording: We already ask our students in the Student Law Office to time record all of their activities, and we could base their period of QWE on this. However, as referred to above, there is a risk students may exaggerate time spent, although this may be partly addressed by having a policy whereby there is a maximum period of time that can be confirmed. Students sometimes also forget to time record, so supervisors may have to 'police' time recording more regularly. Alternatively, it will need to be made clear to students that where they have failed to time record in the proper manner, they will not be credited with time retrospectively.

  - Swipe card monitoring: For legal clinics that have a designated space, student card swiping could monitor attendance when a student enters and leaves the space. We currently have a swipe card system in the Student Law Office, although it is used to restrict access to clinic students rather than to monitor hours worked. This would lessen the administrative task of supervisors keeping track of each individual student. However, this method may not be that reliable, as students may enter the space but not actually conduct any work that would count towards their QWE.

- Legal clinics may want to have a policy in place that details the minimum/ maximum amount of time they are prepared to confirm so as to avoid over-inflation of hours recorded by students.

- The solicitor who directly supervises the student may wish to have some oversight on the monitoring of attendance and hours worked, perhaps checking time has not been claimed for periods of absence, etc. (which will also need to be recorded) and ensuring that the amount of time is not disproportionate to the amount of work produced. Alternatively, if the solicitor overseeing the legal clinic is confirming the work for every student, they will need to trust that each individual supervisor has been monitoring attendance adequately, to ensure they are not crediting hours of QWE that have not actually been attained. Monitoring attendance becomes crucial here.

- Clear, robust polices will need to be in place that detail how time is calculated and the circumstances that would impact upon this, such as sickness and absence. In particular, policies will need to set out expectations from students and how non-attendance/lack of work will impact on both their grade and period of QWE confirmed. Equality Act considerations may also need to be borne in mind with regard to the formulation of policy.

- Irrespective of the approach taken by the institution/organisation to monitoring attendance and hours worked, this will need to be clearly communicated to students.

- General Data Protection Regulation considerations will need to be taken into account with regards to the storage and retention of student data. Such matters are outside the scope of this section but are dealt with in **Part 2.14** of this Handbook.

Summary

While a number of matters relating to QWE remain unclear, this section is intended to provide practical support and guidance to those who may be considering the possibility of offering CLE as QWE. We are working with the Clinical Legal Education Organisation (CLEO),[29] which has set up a working group to consider the issues raised by the SRA's proposals. This group will consider the practicalities of legal clinics using CLE as QWE and intends on

---

29   See **Part 6** for more information about CLEO.

providing best practice guidance, once it has consulted with members. This section is designed to encourage debate and the development of such best practice and we are happy to receive any comments or suggestions.

In review:

- From September 2021 CLE may be able to count towards a candidate's two-year QWE requirement.
- Universities/law clinics will not be mandated to offer CLE as QWE, but may do so if they wish, provided they comply with the SRA's Regulations (currently in draft form).
- The Draft Regulations do not prescribe types of work experience/CLE that can and cannot count, but place emphasis on work experience giving students the opportunity to develop some or all of the solicitor competences.
- Conducting a mapping exercise similar to that in **Table 2** above may be able to assist with evaluating whether the CLE in question gives students the ability to develop some or all of the competences.
- What is meant by 'some of the competences' is not defined, so QWE providers will need to decide for themselves whether they think the CLE in question covers enough of the competences to warrant confirming it as QWE.
- Certain information about the QWE would need to be confirmed to the SRA. The confirmation arrangements within the Draft Regulations are widely drafted and appear to be compatible with a wide range of supervisory models – both internal and external.
- Working out what period of QWE can be credited for CLE is likely to be tricky, and thought needs to be given to developing clear policies and procedures regarding monitoring attendance and hours that can be consistently implemented.

Key considerations checklist

- Will students have the opportunity to develop 'all or some of the solicitor competences'?
- Who will provide confirmation?
- How will you calculate the period of QWE gained? Consider:
  - How you will convert part-time work to full-time equivalency
  - How you will monitor individual student hours, attendance and absence.

- What additional policies and procedures would need to be implemented to ensure consistency and protection for both legal clinics and students?
- How will these policies/procedures be clearly communicated to students and all staff?
- Do arrangements with any external law firms (if any) need to be reviewed and amended?

Part 2.10
International student participation in law clinics: immigration issues

LawWorks

Introduction

This section deals with the immigration rules applicable to foreign students volunteering in law clinics, both university-led and other clinics.

In practice the immigration issue for all clinics is whether immigration checks must be or ought ideally to be carried out and, if so, when to undertake immigration checks and how to go about those checks. Additionally, there may be limitations on the number of hours that students are permitted to work in clinics.

For the purpose of this section it is assumed that foreign student volunteers are present in England and Wales either as EEA/Switzerland nationals or under the Tier 4 (General) student category, i.e. students coming to the UK for post-16 education. For university-led clinics it is assumed that the university is also the Tier 4 sponsor. Different rules and practices may be applicable for students present in the jurisdiction under a different tier, or where a Tier 4 sponsor is not the university at which the student is currently enrolled.[1]

This section reflects the law and guidance as of summer 2019, and provides policy guidance if you are a student coming to the UK under Tier 4 of the points-based system, and should be read alongside the Immigration Rules (Part 3: Students). These can be found on the Home Office pages at the GOV. UK website.[2] Immigration rules and Home Office guidance is subject to change, and this section is not a substitute for legal advice.

Volunteer, worker or employee?

Illegal working rules generally apply to the employment or engagement of individuals as workers under a contract of service (employment) or other

---

1   Home Office, *Tier 4 of the points-based system – Policy guidance* (2 August 2019) <https://www.gov.uk/government/publications/guidance-on-application-for-uk-visa-as-tier-4-student> accessed October 2019.

2   A collection of the current Immigration Rules <https://www.gov.uk/government/collections/immigration-rules> accessed April 2019.

contract (worker) and **not** to volunteers.

Whether foreign students engaged by clinics are volunteers or employees (or unpaid workers) will depend on all of the circumstances, including the terms (whether express or implied, written or oral) of their engagement. As a result the role of a volunteer may in practice give rise to employment or worker status; hence, in some circumstances it may be advisable for organisations to comply with illegal working rules when taking on volunteers.

If you are in any doubt as to whether your clinic volunteers are employees or workers then you should carry out right-to-work checks as a precaution, or seek legal advice.

Volunteers

Who is a volunteer?

The essential quality of volunteering is a freedom to choose whether or not to work, or, put another way, an ability to come and go as you please. This means that a contract of employment between clinics and volunteers must not exist. This would not, however, preclude an agreement being in place, for example because a clinic wished to outline its guideline voluntary working hours; however, any such agreement should be expressed as no more than a reasonable expectation.

The Home Office's Tier 4 policy guidance makes it clear that Tier 4 students can volunteer and explains how the Home Office differentiates between 'voluntary work' and 'volunteering'.[3] For example, volunteers do not have a contract and are not paid, though reasonable travel and living costs can be reimbursed. Volunteers usually assist a charity, voluntary organisation or public sector organisation. In this context it is also important to consider the distinction between volunteering and 'voluntary worker' under the illegal working rules (see **What is voluntary work?** below).

If clinics are concerned that volunteer roles may give rise to an employment, worker or 'voluntary worker' status they should undertake immigration checks as outlined later in this section. In addition, clinics will need to ensure that any such work complies with all relevant limitations, for example in terms of permitted number of hours.

Volunteer agreements

As a matter of good practice clinics are recommended to ensure that volunteer agreements are in place (examples of which are contained in **Part 5.1** of this

3   Home Office (**note 1**), paras 229–30.

Handbook). However, if volunteer agreements are used, they should avoid the use of contractual language and the creation of mutual obligations, which could be regarded as creating contractually binding obligations between the parties.

The agreement may:

- include a reference to any training necessary for the volunteer role
- include a reference to a supervisor for the volunteer, with regular supervision meetings
- treat volunteers in line with its equal opportunities policy
- reimburse out-of-pocket expenses where there are receipts or similar evidence of cost to the volunteer
- provide insurance cover for the volunteer
- implement good health and safety practice.

All work should be expressed as voluntary. A volunteer agreement usually provides that both parties may end the agreement at any time with no notice period or threat of breach of contract. In practice, as most clinics require students to make a specific commitment, it may be difficult to satisfy this requirement.

A volunteer agreement should set out the organisation's expenses policy in relation to volunteers. Where there is a genuine expense payment incurred as part of voluntary work, the volunteer should be reimbursed those costs provided that they are actually, and reasonably, incurred. Expenses claims should be supported by evidence (receipts, tickets, etc.).

Expenses may include:

- travel
- meals taken while volunteering
- postage and telephone costs
- care of dependants while volunteering
- the cost of protective clothing or special equipment necessary for the role.

Employees

Who is an employee?

Certain circumstances can give rise to employment relationships between foreign student volunteers and clinics. A contract of employment exists if the following four conditions are fulfilled:

- the individual undertakes to provide their own work and skill in the performance of some service in return for remuneration
- in performing that service, the individual is subject to a sufficient degree of control by the other party
- there is mutual obligation between the parties, which means:
    - an obligation on the individual to do work that is offered by the other party
    - an obligation on the other party to pay the individual (whether or not work is provided), and in some cases an obligation also to provide work
- the other provisions of the contract are consistent with it being a contract of employment.

Voluntary work

What is voluntary work?

The illegal working rules make a distinction between volunteering and 'voluntary work' (unpaid). Volunteering is **un**restricted; 'voluntary work' is unpaid work that is restricted in the same way as employment or other types of work as set out in this section.

Tier 4 (General) students can do 'voluntary work' **only** if permitted to work under the terms of their visa, but any such 'voluntary work' must not exceed the number of hours permitted during term-time. For example, if you are permitted under your visa to work for 20 hours during term-time and you have paid work of 15 hours a week during term-time, then you cannot do more than five hours' voluntary work per week.

'Voluntary work' is not a separate category recognised in employment law, in which an absence of an obligation to pay for work done would clearly be a significant factor in determining an individual's status. As a result, in practice it is possible that the range of relationships captured by the illegal working rules is wider than simple employment law definitions. Therefore, in order to avoid any voluntary arrangement giving rise to the status of 'voluntary work', clinics are advised to focus on the characteristics of volunteers set out elsewhere in this section to ensure that they are demonstrably present in any volunteering role.

Factors that may be taken into account when considering whether it is voluntary work or volunteering are:

- 'Voluntary workers' will usually have contractual obligations to perform the work (e.g. to attend at particular times and carry out specific tasks) with the employer being contractually required to provide the work.

- Students who are 'volunteering' do not have a contract; they must not be substituting for an employee or receiving payment in kind as unpaid work, although a non-binding volunteer agreement including reimbursement of out-of-pocket expenses is acceptable and good practice (see above).

University clinics

Depending on the particular circumstances, it may be advisable for some university-led clinics to comply with illegal working rules when taking on student volunteers (not least, as the administrative burden may for many be minimal).

The features of university clinics that could conceivably give rise to a **risk** that the relationship would be treated as one of employment, worker or 'voluntary work[er]' include:

- Once recruited as a student clinic volunteer, an obligation (whether express or implied, written or oral) to work regularly at clinics, i.e. volunteer students who are not free to 'come and go as they please'.
- Assessment of students' clinic work and/or integration of clinic work into a course of study, for example where students undertake work placements that are integral and related to the course and are assessed as part of the course (see **Work placements** below).
- The contractual relationship between universities and students – many universities have now introduced 'model contracts', following a recent review by the Competition and Markets Authority.[4] Most university-student contracts will not give rise to any employment rights or obligations, but additional course-specific agreements could be added or appended, for example assessed clinic activity (again see **Work placements** below).
- Clinics that charge in respect of some of their services (this is unlikely to be a consideration in practice for most clinics).

As a Tier 4 sponsor, universities are required to ensure that all students requiring a visa have valid immigration permission to study. Consequently, depending on the particular circumstances – including clinics' corporate status and any procedures to ensure compliance – clinics may be in a position to adopt a zero-risk approach to interpreting the illegal working rules without taking on significant additional administrative burdens; those checks having

---

4   <https://www.universitiesuk.ac.uk/policy-and-analysis/reports/Documents/2018/briefing-student-contracts.pdf> accessed April 2019.

already been undertaken (and subject to ongoing monitoring) by the wider organisation within which the clinic sits. In such circumstances, clinics should also ensure that any work complies with any relevant limitations, for example in terms of the permitted number of work hours.

Other partnering agencies and non-university clinics

Subject to limited exceptions, many non-university clinics may avoid the need to undertake immigration checks altogether, **provided** they ensure that the relationship between the clinic and volunteer does not give rise to employment, worker or 'voluntary work[er]' status, for example by ensuring that in practice volunteers can 'come and go as they please', subject to any reasonable expectation that might be included in the volunteer agreement (see above).

Should non-university clinics determine that there is a risk that a volunteer role gives rise to employment, worker or 'voluntary work[er]' status, illegal working checks should be undertaken in respect of **all** student volunteers in order to verify their status, regardless of what students claim to be their status. In such circumstances, clinics should also ensure that any work is compliant with any relevant limitations, for example in terms of permitted number of hours.

Work placements

Should university clinics be concerned that volunteering arrangements give rise to employment, worker or 'voluntary work[er]' status, it may be possible to satisfy the requirements of the rules concerning work placements (which are generally permitted), subject to limited restrictions.

Work placements are intended to enable the student to gain specific experience of working in the field for which they are studying. Tier 4 students are allowed to undertake work placements where they are integral and related to the course and are assessed as part of the course. Clearly, students' work, whether in the capacity as employees or otherwise engaged by clinics is, subject to the particular circumstances, capable of coming within the definition of 'work placement'. Clinical legal education course providers will need to ensure that they structure their courses accordingly, but a work placement scheme can be run by the sponsor institution or a partner body. Universities running clinics in which students participate on an extra-curricular basis will not be able to satisfy the definition of a 'work placement'.

The main advantages of work placements are:

- a formalised arrangement so as to manage any risk that the illegal working rules are breached
- to ensure that the requisite number of hours, both in terms of a particular course of study and the immigration rules, are satisfied. Whether this is a factor will depend on an individual student's permitted Tier 4 (Student) working hours as well as the length of a course of study and the type of course (see below). In some cases a greater number of hours might be permitted under the work placement rules as compared with the maximum hours permitted by the Tier 4 (Student) restrictions.

Activity as part of a course-related work placement is restricted to no more than one-third of the total length of the course undertaken in the UK, unless:

- the student is following a course at degree level or above and is sponsored by a Higher Education Institution (HEI) or by an overseas HEI to undertake a short-term Study Abroad Programme in the UK, in which case the work placement is restricted to no more than 50 per cent of 33 per cent of the total length of the course, depending on the course/ sponsor[5]
- there is a statutory requirement for the course to include a specific period of work placement that exceeds this limit.

Tier 4 education sponsors should provide clinics with letters confirming that the work placement forms an integral part of the course and does not, by itself or in combination with other periods of work placement, breach the above restrictions. The letter should also include the terms and conditions of the work placement, including the work that the student will be expected to do, and how and when they will be assessed.

While student employees are undertaking work placements as required by their course, this period of placement is not included within the period of term-time employment permitted by their immigration conditions (which may include limitation on working hours). A student could therefore undertake a work placement while also undertaking other part-time work, as the work placement is part of the course.

Clearly, university clinics will need to undertake illegal working checks, as outlined above and below, in circumstances where students enter into work placements in university clinics, with checks having already been undertaken by the university prior to students entering on to courses.

---

5   Home Office (**note 1**), para 210.

Clinics that are unsure as to whether students are engaged under a work placement for the purpose of the rules should seek legal advice as to the particular arrangement. Non-university clinics that receive requests to host university students under work placement schemes will need to undertake illegal working checks.

Immigration rules

Individuals from the European Economic Area (EEA) and Switzerland are generally permitted to come to the UK and work as volunteers, although the position may change depending on the position with the UK leaving the European Union. Additionally, Tier 4 (General) students (i.e. non-EEA and Switzerland) are generally able to **volunteer** at clinics without restriction. However, clinics that engage volunteers in circumstances where the relationship could give rise to employment, worker or 'voluntary work[er]' status should consider the applicable immigration rules. The immigration rules applicable to foreign student volunteers are different depending on their nationality.

EEA (and Swiss) students

EEA students are those students from the following countries:

Austria, Belgium, Bulgaria, Croatia, Republic of Cyprus, Czech Republic, Denmark, Estonia, Finland, France, Germany, Greece, Hungary, Iceland, Ireland, Italy, Latvia, Liechtenstein, Lithuania, Luxembourg, Malta, Netherlands, Norway, Poland, Portugal, Romania, Slovakia, Slovenia, Spain, Sweden (and the United Kingdom).

EEA nationals have the right to work in the UK. At the time of writing, there are no restrictions on EEA students volunteering in law clinics.

Swiss nationals have the same rights as EEA nationals since June 2002, under the Agreement on Free Movement of Persons between the EC and the Swiss Confederation. This is reflected in the Immigration (EEA) Regulations 2016, which include Switzerland within the definition of an EEA state.

Non-EEA

Students granted permission to be in the UK as Tier 4 (General) students and who are permitted to work will have an endorsement in their passport or biometric residence permit that states they are permitted to work and the number of hours of work allowed during term-time, e.g. 10 hours or 20 hours in a week, considered to be Monday to Sunday. If this information is not set out in these documents, the student does not have the right to work. Students who have the right to work are permitted to work full-time during vacations.

Short-term students are not permitted to work, either in the term-time or the vacation, nor undertake a work placement.

Croatian nationals

Croatian nationals have not been subject to worker restrictions and no longer require worker authorisation from the Home Office since 1 July 2018. Croatian nationals may now demonstrate their right to work in the same way as any other EEA national.

Employer's obligation to prevent illegal working

It is unlawful to employ someone who does not have the right to reside and the appropriate right to work in the UK or who is working in breach of their conditions of stay.[6] Clinics engaging volunteers as employees, workers or as 'voluntary work[ers]' should conduct a right-to-work check on **all** students in order to verify their status and avoid any sanction for breach.[7]

To comply with their obligation to prevent illegal working, an employer must:

- carry out right-to-work checks on all prospective employees before the employment starts
- conduct follow-up checks on employees who have a time-limited permission to live and work in the UK, or require a document to evidence their right as in the case of non EEA family members of EEA nationals, or an application pending
- keep records of all the checks carried out
- not employ anyone it knows or has reasonable cause to believe is an illegal worker.

The consequences of a breach of the immigration rules are:

- a civil penalty may be imposed if an employer employs someone without the right to undertake the work for which they are employed. The maximum civil penalty is £20,000 for each individual who does not have

6   The source of the rules on the duties and process of employers to prevent illegal working and the checks, obligations and sanctions imposed are found under the Immigration, Asylum and Nationality Act 2006 as extended by the Immigration Act 2014.

7   Note that, as outlined earlier in this section, this duty does not apply where the students are volunteers and not employees, workers or 'voluntary work[ers]'.

the right to work. A civil penalty may also impact on the institution/employer's sponsorship license

- a criminal offence will be committed if an employer knew or had 'reasonable cause to believe' that the employee did not have the appropriate immigration status.

Defences

Clinics will **not** have an excuse if:

- no prescribed right-to-work check has been undertaken **before** employment commenced
- a document has been accepted that clearly does not belong to the holder
- documentation clearly shows the person does not have the right to work/stay in the UK and/or do the job in question
- the endorsement demonstrating work entitlement or the biometric residence permit has expired
- someone is employed in circumstances where clinics know they are not allowed to work in the UK, regardless of whether checks have been carried out
- the statutory excuse has expired
- a 'reasonably' apparent forgery has not been detected.

Immigration checks

The Home Office guidance sets out three basic steps to conducting a right-to-work check.

1. Obtain original versions of one or more 'acceptable documents':

- A passport, national identity card, Immigration Status Document, Registration Certificate or Document Certifying Permanent Residence, current Biometric Immigration Document, Permanent Residence Card issued by the Home Office, a birth certificate combined with a National Insurance number (see Home Office guidance).

2. Check the document's validity in the presence of the holder. Check:

- the documents are genuine and belong to the person presenting them
- photographs/appearance and dates of birth are consistent across documents

- expiry dates for permission to be in the UK have not passed
- the reasons for any difference in names across documents
- any work restrictions to determine what type of work they are allowed to do.

3. Make and retain a copy and record the date the check was made.

- Ensure it is a clear copy in a form that cannot be altered.
- Copies should be kept securely for the duration of any employment period and for two years afterwards; the copy must then be securely destroyed.

There is an online right-to-work check service at www.gov.uk/view-right-to-work; however, it will not be possible to conduct an online check in all circumstances, as not all individuals will have an immigration status that can be checked online. The online right-to-work checking service sets out what information you will need, but if an online check is not possible you should conduct a manual check. Currently, the online checking service only supports checks in respect of those who hold:

- a Biometric Residence Permit
- a Biometric Residence Card
- status issued under the EU Settlement Scheme.

For a more comprehensive step-by-step guide as to how to undertake right-to-work checks, including which documents are acceptable, please consult the latest Home Office guidance.

Please note that the Home Office regularly updates its guidance. As at the time of writing, the latest Home Office guidance is at:

https://assets.publishing.service.gov.uk/government/uploads/system/uploads/attachment_data/file/773780/An_employer_s_guide_to_right_to_work_checks_-_January_2019.pdf

See also *Tier 4 of the points-based system – Policy guidance*:

https://www.gov.uk/government/publications/guidance-on-application-for-uk-visa-as-tier-4-student

Part 2.11
Digital security

Christopher Simmonds

This section discusses the issues associated with digital data security and storage of information in a clinic. It is accompanied by a case study in **Part 2.12** on Intralinks, a cloud-based system used by BPP University's clinic to manage client data, which is made available by LawWorks to clinics in its network.

Introduction

This section considers the responsibilities that are imposed on clinics to ensure that the data we hold in relation to clients, students and staff is handled securely and lawfully.

The section will consider the legal and regulatory obligations, before going on to consider some of the issues that clinics face in the management of data.

Legal and regulatory obligations

When considering what steps to take in order to ensure the integrity of your digital files, it is essential to consider the legal framework that applies in order to assess what steps are necessary and proportionate to take. There are also a number of regulatory requirements that should be taken into account, particularly by clinics carrying out reserved legal activities.[1] As with so many things, digital security in a clinic involves an element of risk assessment, a consideration of the likelihood of a breach, coupled with the severity of the repercussions should a breach occur. Understanding your legal obligations will help to inform that risk assessment.

Legislative framework

General Data Protection Regulation

The General Data Protection Regulation[2] (GDPR) and the Data Protection Act 2018 (DPA) are substantial, and a detailed discussion of their provisions is beyond the scope of this section. However, the overarching role of the GDPR is

---

1   For the definition of 'reserved legal activities', please refer to Legal Services Act 2007, s 12.
2   Regulation (EU) 2016/679.

to regulate the way in which entities process personal data. For the purposes of the GDPR, personal data is defined as any information that relates to an identified or identifiable natural person, and an identifiable natural person is defined as:

> one who can be identified, directly or indirectly, in particular by reference to an identifier such as a name, an identification number, location data, an online identifier or to one or more factors specific to the physical, physiological, genetic, mental, economic, cultural or social identity of that natural person.[3]

It is therefore likely that a substantial amount of the electronic data held by law clinics will fall within the scope of the GDPR and DPA, as it will likely contain personal data in relation to clients, students and/or staff.

As a result, it is important to ensure that information which is held digitally complies with the requirements of the GDPR. The GDPR sets out a number of principles that underpin the processing of any personal data ('the GDPR Principles'), namely that any processing of the data should be:

- lawful and fair[4]
- for purposes that are specified, explicit and legitimate[5]
- adequate, relevant and not excessive[6]
- accurate and up to date[7]
- time-limited (i.e. the data is not kept for longer than is necessary)[8]
- done in a secure manner.[9]

Processing of personal data should also only take place if at least one of the following criteria is met:

> (a) the data subject has given consent to the processing of their personal data for one or more specific purposes;

> (b) processing is necessary for the performance of a contract to which the data subject is a party or in order to take steps at the request of the data subject prior to entering into a contract;

> (c) processing is necessary for compliance with a legal obligation

---

3   Ibid, Article 4(1).
4   DPA, s 35(1).
5   Ibid, s 36(1).
6   Ibid, s 37.
7   Ibid, s 38(1).
8   Ibid, s 39(1).
9   Ibid, s 40.

to which the controller is subject;

(d) processing is necessary in order to protect the vital interests of the data subject or of another natural person;

(e) processing is necessary for the performance of a task carried out in the public interest or in the exercise of official authority vested in the controller;

(f) processing is necessary for the purposes of the legitimate interests pursued by the controller or by a third party, except where such interests are overridden by the interests or fundamental rights and freedoms of the data subject which require protection of personal data, in particular where the data subject is a child.[10]

The GDPR also recognises that certain categories of data are worthy of special protection in light of the fact that the misuse of such data would conflict with a person's fundamental rights. These categories of data are referred to as 'special category data' and are defined as data relating to:

- racial or ethnic origin
- political opinions
- religious or philosophical beliefs
- trade union membership
- sex
- sexual orientation
- genetics
- biometrics (where used for ID purposes).[11]

The default position is that the processing of such data is prohibited unless one of ten criteria[12] are met, namely:

- The data subject has given explicit consent to the processing of the personal data for one or more specified purposes.
- Processing is necessary for the purposes of carrying out the obligations and exercising specific rights of the controller of the data subject in the field of employment and social security and social protection law.
- Processing is necessary to protect the vital interests of the data subject or of another natural person where the data subject is physically or

---

10   GDPR (**note 2**), Article 6.

11   Ibid, Article 9(1).

12   Ibid, Article 9(2)(a)–(j). The criteria listed here have been summarised. If your clinic is processing special category data then you should refer to the GDPR for the full criteria.

legally incapable of giving consent.

- Processing is carried out in the course of its legitimate activities with appropriate safeguards by a foundation, association or any other not-for-profit body with a political, philosophical, religious or trade union aim and on condition that the processing relates solely to the members or former members of the body or to persons who have regular contact with it in connection with its purposes and that the personal data are not disclosed outside that body without the consent of the data subjects.

- Processing relates to personal data which are manifestly made public by the data subject.

- Processing is necessary for the establishment, exercise or defence of legal claims or whenever courts are acting in their judicial capacity.

- Processing is necessary for reasons of substantial public interest.

- Processing is necessary for the purposes of preventive or occupational medicine for the assessment of the working capacity of the employee, medical diagnosis, the provision of health or social care or treatment or the management of health or social care systems and services.

- Processing is necessary for reasons of public interest in the area of public health.

- Processing is necessary for archiving purposes in the public interest, scientific or historical research purposes or statistical purposes.

It should be noted that a personal data breach could result in a penalty of up to €10,000,000 or 2 per cent of the organisation's total worldwide turnover of the preceding financial year, whichever is the higher.[13]

A breach that concerns the processing of special category data is treated particularly seriously given the potential impact on a person's fundamental rights. Such a breach can attract a fine of up to €20,000,000 or 4 per cent of the organisation's total worldwide turnover for the preceding financial year.

A number of factors will be taken into account when considering whether a penalty should be imposed and, if so, the extent of any penalty. These factors include, but are not limited to:

- the severity of the breach
- any steps taken to mitigate the damage to data subjects
- the categories of personal data affected.[14]

---

13   Ibid, Article 83(4).
14   Ibid, Article 83(2).

Professional negligence

In addition to our legislative obligations, we also have a duty of care to our clients. They are entrusting us with their personal data and with information that, if it came into the public domain, has the potential to cause them harm.

The test for professional negligence requires a claimant to establish that the defendant acted in a way that no other reasonable member of the profession would have acted. In order to prevent claims for professional conduct arising from data breaches, it is therefore essential to take into account industry best practice when implementing data security measures.

Regulatory framework

SRA Standards and Regulations: Code of Conduct for Solicitors, RELs and RFLs

In addition to the legislative framework, there are clear regulatory requirements to ensure that confidentiality is maintained and that client information is secure. Key provisions contained within the SRA Code of Conduct[15] include:

- 6.3: [a solicitor must] keep the affairs of current and former clients confidential unless disclosure is required or permitted by law or the client consents
- 7.1: [a solicitor must] keep up to date with and follow the law and regulation governing the way [they] work.

Silver linings: Cloud computing, law firms and risk

Although now somewhat out of date, most notably in light of the introduction of the GDPR, *Silver linings: Cloud computing, law firms and risk*[16] remains the only guidance issued by the SRA on issues surrounding data security and, in particular, in relation to the growing use of cloud storage.

While the guidance needs to be read in the context of the GDPR, much of it remains relevant and the considerations that need to be taken into account remain the same.

In addition to the points addressed above in terms of the SRA requirements, the guidance also highlights the need to ensure that the SRA is able to access

---

15   SRA, *Standards and Regulations*, SRA Code of Conduct for Solicitors, RELs and RFLs (20 March 2019)   <https://www.sra.org.uk/solicitors/standards-regulations/code-conduct-solicitors/> accessed 23 July 2019.

16   SRA, *Silver linings: Cloud computing, law firms and risk* (November 2013) <https://www.sra. org.uk/risk/resources/cloud-computing-law-firms-risk.page> accessed 29 March 2019.

information in the event that it is required to intervene in the practice.[17] It also highlights some of the discrepancies in the way in which personal data is protected in different jurisdictions, particularly raising the example of the USA and the lack of protection for personal information in American law.

Implementing data security

Taking the legal framework set out above, it is therefore possible to identify a number of key factors that data security measures need to achieve, namely:

- Client data must be kept securely and in a manner that prevents accidental or deliberate processing that goes beyond that which the client has explicitly agreed to.
- When processing data, steps must be taken to ensure that data is not accidentally or deliberately released into the public domain.
- Industry best practice should be followed wherever possible.
- Any data storage should be implemented in such a way that it can be provided to regulatory bodies if required.

When considering data security arrangements for your clinic, it is a good idea to engage with university IT security teams. They can be asked to do due diligence on any software you are contemplating using in the clinic and may also be able to recommend improvements to clinic procedures and processes in order to maximise data security.

The remainder of this section sets out the considerations that you should take into account when protecting the electronic data that your clinic holds. For a further consideration of electronic data storage and transfer solutions, associated compliance issues and a discussion of some of the software available on the market that may be suitable for use in clinics, see **Part 2.13**.

Local or cloud storage?

When considering the steps that you need to take in respect of data security, the first step is to identify where files are currently being stored. While this may seem to be obvious, in the context of university-based law clinics the physical location of computer storage is not necessarily obvious.

Many universities allow staff and students to save work to a dedicated drive. Unlike the ordinary C:\ drive, which is located on the hard drive of the computer, laptop or tablet, this drive is located and managed centrally. This allows the IT service to monitor and address any issues that might arise.

17   This requirement is contained in the SRA Code of Conduct for Solicitors (**note 15**), 7.4(b).

In some cases, the drive will be hosted on servers owned by the university and that are physically located within the university itself. Increasingly, though, universities are using third party storage arrangements, including cloud storage such as Microsoft OneDrive or Azure, Google Drive, etc. in order to reduce the costs associated with hosting a physical server.

Local storage

Where the files are stored on campus, on servers owned and maintained by the organisation, then the points to consider are perhaps more straightforward.

Ensuring that your data is held securely is the main consideration. However, universities are large organisations and tend to invest heavily in their information technology infrastructure, including security features such as firewalls and anti-virus software. Their systems are therefore relatively secure and are likely more secure than those of many small law firms that have significantly less IT support.

Internal security should also be considered. It is good practice to make arrangements with the university's IT team to limit access to drives containing clinic documentation to a prescribed list of individuals working or volunteering with the clinic. Where a staff member moves to another role or a student's time with the clinic comes to an end, their access should be removed. The university's IT team can also be asked to give written confirmation that they will not access the contents of servers on which clinic documentation is stored without prior consent of specified staff members working in the clinic or senior managers within the law school.

Ensuring the continuation of data in the event of an emergency should also be considered. While the move to the paperless office is something that the legal profession has aspired to for a number of years, most of us still retain both paper and digital records. If both are stored in the same location, however, with servers and paper records in the same building, then the risk of loss is higher. For example, in the event of a fire in the building, both digital and paper records could be lost. Keeping digital and paper records in different locations, or at least backing up digital records to an alternative server, can help to ensure integrity of the data in the longer term.

Cloud storage

Cloud storage is becoming increasingly more popular, both personally and for organisations. It reduces the costs of maintaining hardware and often has added benefits, such as access to the most up-to-date software packages, for example the latest version of Microsoft Office in the case of OneDrive.

However, the use of cloud storage can still present some issues for clinics.

The first issue is access. One of the benefits to cloud storage is that it is accessible anywhere. For many of us, cloud storage has become our go-to due to the fact that it means we can work on documents in the office, at home and even when travelling abroad for work with equal facility, and without having to worry about whether we have the most up-to-date version. For clinic work, though, allowing access to documents off site can cause issues.

Under the provisions outlined above, we have a duty to ensure our client's privacy and to ensure that their case remains confidential, but limiting access to cloud folders can be problematic. Students are often living in shared accommodation. Accessing client's documents or even information from home poses significant risks both in terms of the GDPR but also in terms of professional obligations.

Another issue with cloud computing is the location of the servers. As highlighted above, the protection of personal data is stronger in some countries than in others. With cloud storage, the information is still on a physical server somewhere in the world. In order to comply with the GDPR it is necessary to take steps to ensure that the server location is somewhere where there is sufficient respect for personal data (the EU, for example).

Third party software

Third party software can also pose certain challenges for clinic work. Again, this arises from the fact that often software is procured by the university rather than the clinic staff and so the full nature of the software may not be known. It is essential to perform due diligence on any software that is proposed to be used in the clinic, in order to establish whether it is fit for purpose and will meet the requisite security standards.

End User Licence Agreements (EULAs)

As we move increasingly towards a society driven by big data, more and more of the software that we use is capturing the information that we enter into it in order to understand more about us. This can be for a range of reasons, whether it is for research, in order to more effectively target marketing, or just to improve the product for those using it.

It is therefore essential to understand the terms of the end user licence agreement (EULA) to understand what information is being collected and what it is being used for. This can be especially important in relation to case management software or software that is being used for processing the client's information, such as scanning software.

Storage locations

As with cloud storage of documents, software can also be web hosted with data inputted being stored on the cloud. The location and protections afforded to that software are therefore equally important.

Email, document transfer and document encryption

The transfer of documents can also raise specific issues in relation to digital security. Email in particular raises certain risks. The autofill function on email software can lead to emails being sent to the wrong recipient. In the majority of cases, errors are easy to rectify with little impact, but there is always a possibility that an email may be misdirected to someone with knowledge of the case.

As a result, it is important to consider whether steps should be taken to ensure the secure transmission of the data. Document encryption software can be expensive and will likely need to be approved by the university's IT services. Implementing such software should therefore be considered in terms of the risk of documents going astray and the impact that such a breach would have. One solution may be Intralinks VIA, which is the subject of a case study in **Part 2.12**.

An alternative to consider is agreeing standard passwords with clients at the outset of a case. Password-protecting documents with a password set by the client would minimise the risk of information becoming publicly accessible, and most word processing packages have the option to password-protect documents.

Similarly, transferring documents in other ways should also be considered. Where clinics assess the work of students, it may be necessary to provide external examiners with portfolios of work. Secure transfer by courier is expensive but prevents future difficulties. Alternatively, secure USB sticks are now available with a significant amount of storage and high-level encryption.

Conclusion

As with so much of the work that we do in clinic, digital security is a matter of risk assessment. It is important to assess the likelihood of a breach in conjunction with the severity of a breach in order to determine what steps it is reasonable to take to protect the client's personal data.

Simple steps, such as checking the location of cloud storage servers, can prevent significant issues in the long term.

Further, making sure that central university services understand the role of the clinic and the work that it does will mean that they are able to provide much more tailored advice on the systems that you are using and will allow them to react more quickly and effectively to any issues that arise.

Part 2.12
Document management case study:
Intralinks VIA

Tony Martin

Intralinks VIA is an external document management system, which student pro bono clinics can obtain free of charge through LawWorks. It can be used as an electronic file management system, thus eliminating the need for paper files. It should be noted, however, that it is **not** a complete file management system and in particular does **not** operate as a database and cannot be used for potential conflict of interest checks.

Intralinks is owned by Synchronoss Technologies, a US company, but the data entered in Europe is stored within Europe. It is compliant with both the General Data Protection Regulation 2018 and with Solicitors Regulation Authority requirements. It is used by many large solicitors' firms when acting on mergers and acquisitions.

Intralinks' own description is that it is the 'secure enterprise platform for simple file sync and share, collaborative team workspaces, large-scale virtual data rooms and structured workflows'.[1] The company claims a 20-year track record of enabling high-stakes transactions and business collaborations, and also claims that the system has been used by more than three million professionals.

Intralinks allows documents to be accessed on any computer or tablet anywhere. This is both the key benefit and the risk.

Intralinks permits the creation of folders and sub-folders and allows access to be given at three levels:

- **Viewer**: can only see documents.
- **Editor**: can download and upload documents and change documents.
- **Owner**: effectively an administrator in that they can do everything an Editor can do, but also control who has access. They can also create other Owners.

When a person is added to an Intralinks folder (or sub-folder), they receive an email requiring them to complete a registration form, which requires them to complete the following fields:

- first name

---

1   <https://www.intralinks.com/content/secure-collaboration> accessed 20 August 2019.

- last name
- password
- phone number
- security question (for password recovery).

In a clinic setting the typical use of Intralinks for file management purposes might be:

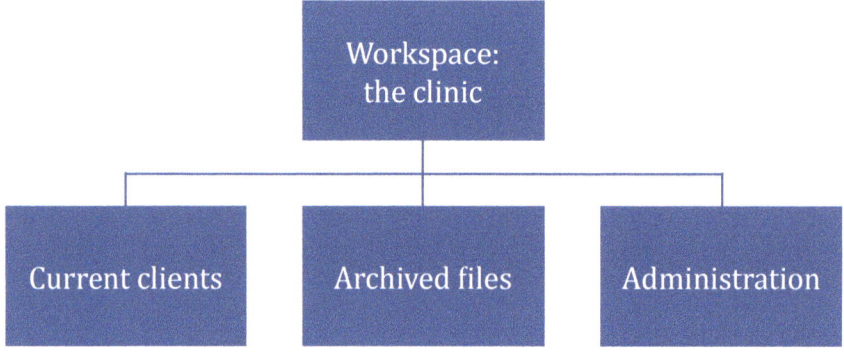

Within 'Current clients' each client would have a file with a series of sub-folders, for example:

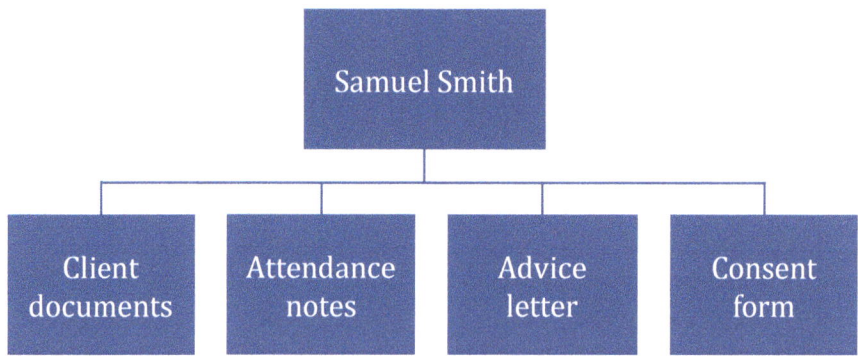

The file model is customisable with the ability to keep adding further sub-folders as required. An Owner can determine who is given access to each file or sub-folder. So, for example:

- students working on a particular client matter can be given Editor access to the entire Administration folder but only to the specific client that they are working on

- an external supervisor can be given Editor access to the client's folder of the case they are supervising
- a client can be given Editor access only to the Client documents sub-folder of their client file, thus allowing them to upload their own documents
- where a client requests a copy of their file, they can be given Viewer access to their file.

In this way all participants are able to access and, in a controlled way, add to the client file.

Security

In order to maintain client security the following factors need to be considered:

- Owner(s) should be staff members of the institution that runs the clinic.
- In case of the incapacity of an Owner, it is prudent to have a minimum of two Owners.
- Access should only be given to those who have a legitimate reason for needing access. In granting access, the Owner should grant access only to the folder or sub-folder needed and to only allow the level of access (Viewer or Editor) the individual requires.
- Anyone granted access to a client folder or sub-folder must have agreed to (and be bound by) the clinic's client confidentiality policy.
- As soon as practical after the conclusion of the case, access to a client folder or sub-folder should be removed for everyone except the Owner(s). This should be a part of the file archiving regime.
- Everyone accessing client folders or sub-folders must consider the environment in which they are working and whether their screen is visible to other people. Particular care should be taken with shared computers.
- Where confidential documents are downloaded from Intralinks, the user must delete these from both their computer drive and from the recycle bin, once they are no longer needed.
- Restrictions could be put in place to require that Intralinks is only accessed on university network computers in order to ensure any downloaded documents are not on personal devices.
- When confidential documents are printed, they must be disposed of using a secure waste disposal system, which will usually require the documents to be brought into the clinic for disposal.

- While Editors (and Owners) have the ability to delete documents from Intralinks, deleted documents are always recoverable by an Owner. In addition, Intralinks records the identity, date and time that anyone accesses a folder or sub-folder.

Part 2.13
Lawyering in a digital age: Reflections on starting up a virtual law clinic

Ann Thanaraj and Michael Sales

In this section, Ann Thanaraj and Michael Sales share their experience and reflections on setting up and running a virtual law clinic (VLC). The section should be read in conjunction with **Part 2.11: Digital security and the Online/Virtual clinics: Open Justice Law Clinic case study in Part 1.**

Legal practice and the legal profession are undergoing a vast change and as those who are responsible for the education of the future generation of lawyers, we need to make a fair prediction of the sorts of knowledge and skills necessary for new lawyers to be successful based on the emerging technology and trends, especially in the practice and delivery of legal services.[1] At the outset it must be stated that the preparation of students in this regard is disruptive and fluid as the landscape changes at an exponential pace. Knowledge of this area among academics in professional legal education appears to be developing, with examples of communities of practice growing in this area of legal education.[2]

Having written about the emerging trends in the delivery of online legal services, we hope to encourage and inform law schools to consider changes to their curriculums that are necessary to make them fit for purpose. Building upon a practice report titled 'Lawyering in a digital age: a practice report on the design of a virtual law clinic at Cumbria' in 2015, and offering a digitally transformative strategy towards a 'digital lawyering' curriculum in 'Making a case for a digital lawyering curriculum in legal education' in 2017, here we will share our reflections on the design of a VLC and suggest topics for

---

1   Law Society, *The future of legal services* (January 2016) <https://www.lawsociety.org.uk/support-services/research-trends/the-future-of-legal-services/> accessed 16 August 2019; Research in this field includes the Society for Computers and Law's (SCL's) Tech Law, which is an exciting new initiative designed to gauge the tech law sector, and define and understand the booming and ever-expanding sector in which we all work; and Ann Thanaraj and Craig Laverick's BILETA funded project on 'Exploring and understanding the evolving technological trends in legal practice in order to identify and address any gaps in legal education', which is researching the use of technology in legal education and practice. It explores how law schools are addressing the increasing needs and expectations of legal practice in supporting and preparing students for 'digital lawyering'. The primary research activity will involve gathering and analysing data from interviews with law firms and organisations in England and Wales.

2   How are law schools preparing students for the technologically advancing future of work? The 'Lawyering in a digital age: Equipping students for the technologically advancing practice of law' conference aims to discuss and shape the direction of legal education both here in England and Wales and globally: <https://www.digitallawconference.uk/> accessed 16 August 2019.

consideration that may become a useful theoretical framework for a module on future lawyering, with the aim to equip and empower our future lawyers with the skills for the future workplace.

This work is framed around the role of law schools in addressing the emerging trends in the profession. The virtual law clinic (VLC) has been designed to enhance and digitally transform legal education for students, and is also used as a tool for training through a tripartite system of student-academic-legal professional. The entire process is recorded and archived for feedback, reflection and evaluation to help turn the experiences gained into actual learning and development. The VLC is a form of technology-enhanced clinical legal education that facilitates the integration of practical and lawyering skills with professional values through the process of internalisation to develop a sense of professional identity.

The VLC, supported by a curriculum on technology, together make up the digital lawyering framework. It is a theoretical framework that enables students to develop their awareness of law in a deep and active learning context supported with feedback, while developing judgement skills, professional responsibility and professional identity and values of working online through the examination of one's own personal epistemology by way of constructive reflection.

The VLC has also developed opportunities for international and intercultural experience.[3] Within this framework, reflection is a crucial component of conceptualising the learning. Research on the benefits of learning using the VLC, including areas for improvement in the construction and pedagogic design of the VLC, is continuous and ongoing to ensure that the framework meets the objectives of equipping students with the knowledge, awareness, skills and attributes for legal practice.[4]

In developing legal education to meet the emerging trends in practice, specific to digital lawyering, the 'digital lawyering' framework aims to contribute

---

3   A Thanaraj, 'Internationalizing education: Evaluating the growth of intercultural communication and competency in students through an international negotiation project using an online law clinic' (2015) *Journal of Pedagogic Development*, available at: <http://insight.cumbria.ac.uk/id/eprint/2490/> accessed 16 August 2019.

4   Research on some of the benefits of the VLC training initiative and curriculum can be seen in: A Thanaraj, 'Identifying students' perspectives on skills and attributes gained from working in a virtual law clinic to create an impact on "the whole lawyer": A grounded theory study' (2017) *US-China Law Review*; A Thanaraj, 'Understanding how a law clinic can contribute towards students' development of professional responsibility' (2016) *International Journal of Clinical Legal Education*, available at: <https://www.northumbriajournals.co.uk/index.php/ijcle/article/view/521> accessed 16 August 2019. Research on some of the areas for improvement in the design and learning construct embedded into the VLC can be seen in: A Thanaraj, 'Evaluating the potential of virtual simulations to facilitate professional learning in law: A literature review (2016) *World Journal of Education*, available at: <https://www.sciedu.ca/journal/index.php/wje/article/view/10607> accessed 16 August 2019.

to students' awareness and understanding of the extent of professional competencies required of a lawyer in a digital legal practice, recognising an awareness of the current trends in the delivery of legal services and knowledge of new technologies required to meet those demands. This also goes to address the need to raise awareness of the effects of modern technology on society and creating an understanding of the digital literacy within society, and how individuals must adapt to the needs of different groups in order to promote an inclusive attitude.

Through this work, it is intended for students to explore the uses of technology in law, such as for client interviewing, negotiating and managing a case, including time keeping, collaborative learning through communication, interactions, advising clients and dealing with all aspects of a case.

It is expected that students will gain an awareness and skills from using technology and understanding the risks of using technology for legal practice, and of safety, privacy, appropriateness and ethical issues posed by the use of technology in practice. This helps students acquire the skills they need to contribute successfully to the professions. As such, the VLC integrates theory and practice by combining academic inquiry with actual experience and constructive reflection, with the aim of increasing knowledge, developing skills, clarifying values and developing students' capacity to contribute to the changing legal practice.

Setting up and design principles of VLCs

A VLC is a secure, encrypted online portal created to deliver professional legal services, advice and practice between a lawyer and a client; an undertaking that is bound by all the usual professional responsibilities, standards and ethics of a lawyer, and one that takes place in an authenticated, private and secure platform which complies with the relevant electronics, technical and data security standards. This undertaking or practice is what Ann has termed in her research papers as 'digital lawyering'. In legal education, digital lawyering needs to be accompanied by a solid interdisciplinary curriculum that raises awareness, knowledge and skills required for the understanding of theoretical manifestations of digital practice and the necessary aptitude of a professionally responsible lawyer for the purpose of collaborating, advising clients, undertaking dispute resolution and other forms of legal transactions.

The practice of digital lawyering is a relatively new concept, both in terms of its adoption by the profession and in its definition, although the use of technology to enhance legal practice and process is not a new initiative. The digital and IT resource list in **Part 5.5.6** of this Handbook offers a wealth of examples of creative uses of technology in legal practice.

In England and Wales, the introduction of the Legal Services Act 2007 (LSA 2007) sought to change the legal landscape, making the legal services market more commercially focused, innovative in its services and delivery and allowing a more diverse market for consumers. The Act created an opportunity for lawyers and non-lawyers to work together to deliver legal services through alternative business structures, supported with a flexible approach to how legal services are being offered to clients; and through this to offer greater access to justice for clients who may not be able to afford legal help or may not have accessibility geographically or physically to a law clinic.

The distinction as to whether an online portal is used as a space for retrieving legal advice or accessing templates for an individual's own use[5] – or if it is an online portal where a lawyer is involved in handling a legal matter – is vital. Different professional conduct and ethical implications may arise when conducting digital lawyering as opposed to using online tools to seek a solution to a legal problem. Further, there are no bespoke guidelines or professional body requirements in England and Wales on the features and functionalities that should be present in a virtual law clinic.

In setting up a VLC, designers will need to be mindful of a number of key factors, such as:

- the type of intended legal practice, the architecture of the practice in relation to its unique aspects, typical problems which are raised and the typical needs of a client
- the technology chosen to enable an online service, including the sorts of services on offer and the affordances/limitations of the chosen technologies
- integration of the technology with other systems and processes in the firm/clinic, ensuring a seamless experience for all users
- accessibility and inclusivity functionalities in the technology including seamless and responsive use across the various interfaces (mobile, tablets, PCs)
- privacy, encryption and data security features in the chosen technologies and infrastructures that combine the technologies for the intended experience and use
- intended user interface and structure of the client journey
- step by step navigation
- the desired client experience.

---

5   These are information-rich websites that offer templates of documents such as wills and contracts. Legal Zoom is an example of this.

We advocate that regardless of the technology and features chosen, the key purpose of a virtual law clinic is its ability to deliver legal services online to clients through the secure client portal with safe and secure handling of client information, maintaining confidentiality and minimising the risks of privacy and security breach.[6]

Out-of-the box, the cloud-based solutions

Microsoft Teams is a cloud-based solution that provides a range of tools suitable for the deployment of VLCs. Private groups can be set up within a team site for lawyer/client communications, with tools including real-time video conferencing, live chat and document management with version control.

The simple learning curve for non-technical users makes Teams a particularly attractive option as a platform for VLCs. Aside from the user-friendly user interface, those administering a VLC can deploy an AI-driven 'help bot' to provide answers to frequently asked questions, such as 'How do I message a user?' or 'How do I upload a document?' and receive a near-instantaneous response.

Using the @User notation on the discussion board within a Teams site can be used to send notifications to users about an update to a topic or a change to a document.

Another cloud-hosted option for building a VLC is **Slack**. Although less feature-complete than Teams in its out-of-the box state, Slack has many apps available to transform it into a VLC solution, including support for video conferencing, integration with a document storage/sharing platform such as Google Drive, OneDrive or Dropbox, and the ability to provide notifications and workflow.

Slack largely works in a similar way to Microsoft Teams and provides a private channel for lawyer/client communications, enabling them to discuss a case, share and collaborate on documents and be notified of updates within Slack or via email.

Organisations that are not comfortable cloud-hosting their VLC may prefer an on-premises solution. One particular example of a mature, self-hosted collaboration platform is **RocketChat**, which like cloud-hosted offerings provides tools for video conferencing, file sharing and live chat within private channels.

---

6   A case study of a law clinic run by the Open University, which delivers its services exclusively online, can be found in **Part 1** of this Handbook. **Part 2** also contains further guidance on IT security and other regulatory and compliance issues that may be relevant to establishing an online clinic.

All of the platforms listed above are GDPR-compliant and their creators are committed to ensuring that their customers are aware of their GDPR obligations. Other platforms are, of course, available.

Bespoke creation

The VLC we designed has evolved over several years, drawing upon feedback from users, law firms and students, and empirical research on the sorts of learning and experience students are developing from using the VLC as a training tool. Over the years, we have developed some key functions and embedded these into the online portal.

These include:

- all activities relating to the client and legal matter being undertaken via the encrypted and secure portal, rather than through various different pieces of technologies outside the intended portal
- an enhanced client retrieval system, including search functionality of all documents and correspondence in relation to a matter, which the client can track and view
- document automation through template searches and downloads
- intuitive legal forms for clients to complete, including informative educational video tutorials on various aspects of areas of legal services on offer (not legal advice but information on rights and practical tips)
- video and audio-conferencing facilities to enable online dispute resolution
- archiving, recorded transcription of communication, recorded video conferencing for interviews, negotiations and general e-meetings, including relevant permissions written in a user-friendly manner setting out the purpose and use of recordings (which are all purely for student feedback, evaluation and improved learning through reflection)
- online discussion threads with clients and others in the firm
- automated checks on confidentiality, conflict of interest, privacy and security
- integrated project management tools with calendar and time recording to help meet deadlines and keep tasks flowing and updated
- notification alerts to clients on updates made to their case file, alerting them to emails, status updates, to pay invoices or respond to requests for information or documents.

From our experience of designing a VLC and undertaking annual updates on the platform, you may want to consider the following points if you are thinking of creating a bespoke VLC:

- Identify a clear purpose for creating and setting up a VLC for education and training of law students, such as:
  - instigating a small but powerful initiative towards digital transformation of legal education for learning and training purposes
  - taking an integrated ecosystem approach to learning, teaching and assessment of practical legal skills to deliver an outstanding learning experience
  - designing meaningful learning activities via the VLC to position students' learning for future-readiness by emboldening them with the knowledge and skills needed to thrive in a technologically-mediated world of work
  - developing staff to deliver cutting-edge educational practices that are recognised as being at the forefront of the sector by drawing upon emerging technologies and pedagogic practices across the education, legal and professional sectors.
- Consider whether the VLC supplements existing clinical experience and/or offers alternative access to legal support. To do this, it is important to:
  - address client needs due to flexibility and wider reach of services
  - be clear on issues of jurisdiction, and any limitations on the service that can be provided
  - be mindful of the appropriateness of using a VLC when dealing with sensitive areas of the law and consider accessibility issues.
- Once a clear purpose is established, consider the required features and functionality of the VLC:
  - What do you want the VLC to be capable of doing/achieving?
  - What do you want to do on a VLC platform?
  - What sort of user experience would you like your clients to have?
  - What sorts of user interface will deliver the intended user experience?
  - How will clients be supported on the use of different features and functionalities to navigate through the platform?
  - How will a client be on-boarded to the VLC process of service delivery, including being fully aware of how expectations will be managed, communications, turnaround times, billing and fees (where applicable), clear lines of terms of engagement, liability, complaints and remedies?
  - In an unbundled service model, responsibilities and accountabilities are key factors that need precision and clarity, such as what part of

the work is handled by a third-party and what the implications are.[7]

– To what extent does your design brief for the VLC take a privacy-by-design approach, including compliance with data security regulations and best practice and compliance with platform regulations and best practice?[8]

– What sorts of work from on-boarding to completion of legal matters become automated? This may include elements of document automation, jurisdictional checks and conflict of interest checks.

– If tasks or checks are automated, how is accuracy determined? To what extent should the lawyer check the accuracy of the automated outputs?[9]

• Understanding of effective delivery of online service:

– Does the client portal offer accessible and meaningful navigation and user support?

– To what extent do the technologies used afford an effective method or tool for activities such as client interviewing, negotiating and managing a case – including time keeping, scheduling, etc.?

– To what extent do the technologies offer encrypted and embedded security features – handling, sharing and safe storage of data, safety and privacy – and enable appropriate use of technology practices?[10]

---

7   SCL, 'The future of outsourcing' <https://www.scl.org/articles/10286-the-future-of-outsourcing> accessed 16 August 2019.

8   SCL, 'Protecting privacy in a world of big data: The role of enhanced accountability' <https://www.scl.org/articles/3651-protecting-privacy-in-a-world-of-big-data-the-role-of-enhanced-accountability> accessed 16 August 2019; SCL, 'Managing data breaches – Notification and risk management' <https://www.scl.org/articles/10324-managing-data-breaches-notification-and-risk-management> accessed 16 August 2019; SCL, 'Data security and the challenges for the modern law firm' <https://www.scl.org/blog/10174-data-security-and-the-challenges-for-the-modern-law-firm> accessed 16 August 2019; SCL, 'Data protection: Controllers, processors, contracts, liability – the ICO Draft Guidance' <https://www.scl.org/articles/10017-data-protection-controllers-processors-contracts-liability-the-ico-draft-guidance> accessed 16 August 2019.

9   SCL, 'Trust me, I'm a computer' <https://www.scl.org/articles/3835-trust-me-i-m-a-computer> accessed 16 August 2019; SCL, 'Artificial intelligence: Who's to blame?' <https://www.scl.org/articles/10277-artificial-intelligence-who-s-to-blame> accessed 16 August 2019; H Surden, 'Machine learning and law' (2014) *Washington Law Review* pp. 89–95 <https://www.law.uw.edu/wlr/print-edition/print-edition/vol-89/1/machine-learning-and-law> accessed 16 August 2019; J O McGinnis and R Pearce, 'The great disruption: How machine intelligence will transform the role of lawyers in the delivery of legal services' (2014) *Fordham Law Review* Vol. 82, pp. 3041–66 <https://ir.lawnet.fordham.edu/cgi/viewcontent.cgi?article=5007&context=flr> accessed 16 August 2019.

10   SCL, 'The Network and Information Security Directive ("Cybersecurity" Directive)' <https://www.scl.org/articles/3591-the-network-and-information-security-directive-cybersecurity-directive> accessed 16 August 2019; SCL, 'EU Network and Information Security Directive' <https://www.scl.org/articles/3224-eu-network-and-information-security-directive>   accessed 16 August 2019.

- Can users of the platform use the features and functionalities of the platform to its fullest affordances?
- To what extent are those using technology or working in a VLC emboldened with digital literacy and knowledge, including the need to adapt one's practice for an inclusive client base?
- To what extent are those using technology or working in a VLC digitally empowered through the time and training to reflect and refine on their experience of working collaboratively online and building relationships online?
- Can individuals in the VLC interpret, understand and apply the Code of Conduct and Professional Standards statements to establish a client-lawyer relationship online?
- To what extent do the online system and processes and the technology lend themselves to safe handling of data?
- Is continuing professional development (CPD) made available and encouraged around the skills, knowledge and aptitude necessary for a competent digital professional to represent a client in a manner that is consistent with the rules of the profession?

Regulation and compliance of VLCs

The practice of law, online dispute resolution and the establishment of online courts is on the increase within the jurisdiction of England and Wales. The House of Lords recently published a set of recommendations on the regulation of the internet, in particular whether online platforms have sufficient accountability and transparency.[11] A paper co-authored with colleagues from Northumbria University's Northumbria Internet and Society Research Interest Group (NINSO) sought to explore whether adequate processes are in place to moderate content effectively, proposing a number of mechanisms to improve regulations, including effective user education. This research also identified the power imbalance between the platform and the user, as well as the insufficiency of an approach to compliance centred on long and opaque terms and conditions that may be difficult to understand and interpret meaningfully.[12] The research took an evidence-based and holistic approach to a multidisciplinary challenge

11   House of Lords Select Committee on Communications, *Regulating in a digital world* (2019) <publications.parliament.uk/pa/ld201719/ldselect/ldcomuni/299/299.pdf> accessed 16 August 2019.

12   Guido Noto La Diega, Claire Bessant, Ann Thanaraj, Cameron Giles, Hanna Kreitem and Rachel Allsopp, 'The internet: to regulate or not to regulate? Submission to House of Lords Select Committee on Communications' inquiry' (2018) <http://insight.cumbria.ac.uk/id/eprint/3836/> accessed 16 August 2019.

that will inform the Digital Authority, a new body whose creation has been commendably recommended by the House of Lords. Similarly, the guidance for the safe and ethical digital practice of law from our professional regulators has yet to shape the nature of digital legal practice.

In 'Making a case for a digital lawyering framework',[13] Ann explores various examples of how technology is being used to aid and supply legal services, in its delivery, productivity and creativity. In England and Wales, the delivery of legal services – whether in a bricks-and-mortar law firm or on a virtual law firm platform – adhere to the same professional and ethical regulations and compliance requirements as set out by the Solicitors Regulation Authority (SRA) and Bar Standards Board, and rightly so. We advocate that with virtual law practice, there needs to be some further monitoring, additional guidelines and regulations from our regulators on safe, secure and ethical practices to help lawyers and clients address the challenges that come with professional online practice.

Our work on the VLC is guided by the best practice[14] and guidelines on professional and ethical practice set out by the American Bar Association (ABA). Students undertaking this work will become familiar with ABA's advisory recommendations, which set guidelines and minimum requirements for delivery of legal services online.[15] The Law Society or the Bar Council are yet to develop any specific guidance in this area. Therefore, these are helpful threshold requirements and starting points to identify safe and ethical practices and compliance with existing professional rules.

Cloud computing considerations

Software-as-a-Service (SaaS) is a cloud-based software delivery model that enables the VLC application to be hosted by a secure, scalable third-party provider.

Considerable cost savings can be made by using a SaaS platform, as there is no requirement for internal hosting equipment (servers, storage or software licensing), which also translates into reduced IT staff expenditure. SaaS cloud

---

13   A Thanaraj, 'Making the case for a digital lawyering framework in legal education' (2017) *International Review of Law*, Volume 2017, Issue 3 <https://www.qscience.com/content/journals/10.5339/irl.2017.17> accessed 16 August 2019.

14   Thomson Reuters, 'OWN IT: How to start a law firm in the virtual law office era' <https://store.legal.thomsonreuters.com/law-products/news-views/small-law-firm/how-to-start-a-law-firm/virtual-law-office> accessed 16 August 2019.

15   SRA, 'The changing legal services market' <https://www.sra.org.uk/globalassets/risk/resources/changing-legal-services-market.pdf?version=4a1ad4> accessed 16 August 2019; American Bar Association eLawyering Task Force, 'Suggested minimum requirements for law firms delivering legal services online'.

hosting providers manage operating system security updates, infrastructure upgrades and offer robust, fully-tested data backup and recovery procedures.

Cloud providers offer flexible provisioning of server resources, allowing an application to scale up in terms of usage without the risk of performance bottlenecks. With early generation cloud platforms this incurred some downtime; however, modern cloud administration tools enable server memory, storage allowances and network bandwidth to be exponentially increased on-the-fly.

Larger cloud providers – including Amazon, DigitalOcean and Linode – have data centres in multiple locations across the globe, ensuring customers are able to select a location that is covered by the relevant data protection laws. This extends to backups that are kept within the same region, although at different sites, in order to provide redundancy in the case of a catastrophic failure of a particular data centre.

As a minimum, all cloud hosts support the installation of a secure SSL certificate and encrypted data transfer. Full disk encryption is also an option for highly sensitive applications.

Drawing upon the expertise of Dr De Silva's work as Chair of the Law Society's Technology and Law Reference Group and as a member of the EU Commission's Expert Group on Cloud Computing and Technology,[16] we have developed a set of principles of which to be mindful when handling cloud computing.

While it offers a broad range of advantages, especially in cost reduction and storage space for data, risks to data handling and storage is high as third-party providers are involved. As such, the handling of confidential information in all lawyer-client dealings could be breached without strict safeguards. A combination of our data laws, security laws and lawyers' Code of Conduct could help manage such practice.[17]

When working with cloud computing service providers, we would advise clinics/firms to undertake due diligence over their cloud service provider for risks and compliance. The following factors should be taken into consideration:

- The service level agreement (SLA) will need to state explicitly that data is secured and handled in a responsible and ethical manner. If the software provider is working with a third-party hosting company it is important for the law firm to review the contract between these two companies.

16   CMS Digitalbytes <https://cms.digitalbytes.law/u/102eoji/sam-de-silva> accessed 16 August 2019.

17   S De Silva, 'Fine or cloudy weather ahead? Cloud computing for law firms' (August 2017) The Law Society <https://www.lawsociety.org.uk/news/blog/fine-or-cloudy-weather-ahead-cloud-computing-for-law-firms/> accessed 16 August 2019.

The agreement should outline the data handling, locality, security and backup procedures used for the law clinic data. This should be in line with data protection legislation and ethical practice of the jurisdiction in which the firm/clinic is operating from.

- There should be defined clauses in a SLA regarding the exporting and transfer of law clinic data, allowing the data owner to migrate to an alternative cloud host or obtain data for internal audit purposes or requests initiated by the authorities or regulators.

- Data should be available upon lawful request for access to data by foreign law enforcement agencies.[18]

- Confidentiality agreements may be required for those who have responsibility handling confidential law clinic data.

- Ensure compliance with the General Data Protection Regulation (GDPR), EU Data Protection Directive (95/46/EC) and the international information security standard ISO 27001, which is a framework of policies and process that sets out information risk management handling.

- Maintenance to the server platform and any handling of law clinic data should only be carried out with prior permission from the data owner.

- There is the right to sue the cloud provider for damages or terminate the contract for breaches typically around data storage, handling, retrieval.

Professional and academic development

In designing the functions of the VLC and in developing training and curriculum for students as support in the VLC module, we focused on:

- a curriculum that underpins knowledge and understanding of legal ethics and professional conduct rules, the interpretation of confidentiality and professional representation in online legal services

- a continual and robust programme of user development on information technology governance, security and protection, including a set of clear principles dictating codes of conduct when working online

- both a theoretical and practical understanding of SLAs, which covers the roles and responsibilities of software and cloud providers, negotiating of

18   Law Society, 'GDPR in practice: Cross-border data flows and Brexit' (December 2018) <https://www.lawsociety.org.uk/support-services/practice-management/advice-and-guidance-on-gdpr-compliance/gdpr-in-practice-cross-border-data-flows-and-brexit/> accessed 16 August 2019; Law Society, 'GDPR in practice: Legal professional privilege and client confidentiality' (December 2018) <https://www.lawsociety.org.uk/support-services/practice-management/advice-and-guidance-on-gdpr-compliance/gdpr-in-practice-lpp-and-client-confidentiality/> accessed 16 August 2019.

the management of the infrastructure and ethical handling and security of data

- understanding the operations and limitations of the types of technology used in the VLC
- ensuring that the mechanisms created in the VLC effectively undertake conflict of interest checks
- as online representation is borderless, being absolutely clear about jurisdictional restrictions and applicable governing law
- understanding when and to whom legal services should not be offered via a VLC
- understanding technology and the security risks
- clarity and distinguishing between legal websites and VLCs
- learning how to create a good online client experience for clients, including building a strong and trustworthy lawyer-client relationship online
- understanding user experience and user design architecture in creating a VLC
- awareness of alternative forms of technology-driven legal service delivery and keeping updated with best practice for the use of these delivery models, with a focus on the legal ethics of online delivery of legal services
- useful understanding of benefits and risks of automated document and service agreements, including any predictive technology
- learning how to work collaboratively in a team online, including multidisciplinary teams of experts
- being knowledgeable about perceived barriers to online legal service because of accessibility issues, lack of digital skills from potential clients and the impact of technology on access to the legal system, and consequently knowing when it is appropriate to use a VLC
- the evolving future of the work landscape and the skillset needed for a professional world mediated by technology, including new careers in law.

Further resources

Technological advancements in law clinics is a fast-developing area. As technology evolves and becomes capable of minimising many of our administrative burdens, there is a need to keep constantly updated on new developments. At the same time, there is a question to ask about the direction of the legal profession and practice, which is becoming mediated by technology. 'Lawyering in a digital age',[19] is an international initiative that brings together a global audience to shape the direction of legal education fit for a digital age. The annual conference brings a globally connected set of speakers to shape conversations around how we are preparing students for practising and studying law in a digital age.

For further examples of the sorts of readings that could be helpful in understanding digital transformation of the legal profession, see **Part 5.5.6** of this Handbook.

---

19   'Lawyering in a digital age: Equipping students for the technologically advancing practice of law' conference <https://www.digitallawconference.uk/> accessed 16 August 2019.

Part 2.14
Data security

Linden Thomas

A summary of the legislative and regulatory framework that governs data security is contained in **Part 2.11: Digital security** and is therefore not repeated here. That section focused particularly on data security in the context of the use of digital technology in law clinics. This section deals with more general considerations that clinicians should take into account in order to ensure that legal and regulatory obligations relating to data protection are met.[1]

Who is responsible for data protection compliance within the clinic?

It is a good idea to designate a member of staff within the clinic to have responsibility for ensuring compliance with data protection requirements and for monitoring this on an ongoing basis. This role might include:

- ensuring that necessary policies and processes are in place and are regularly maintained and updated
- monitoring the clinic's compliance with those policies and processes
- being a first port of call for any data protection-related queries
- making sure that training materials are up to date and that new staff, students and volunteers receive training on data protection before undertaking any client work
- being a point of liaison with others in the university with responsibility for data protection (see below).

What institutional policies and processes are in place and what support is available?

Universities process a significant amount of personal data and will therefore have policies and processes that govern how data should be handled and how any breaches ought to be dealt with.

Clinicians are advised to make contact with the individuals and/or teams in your own institutions that have responsibility for data compliance, in order

---

1   Data protection is a complex and convoluted area of law and therefore the following is intended to be high-level guidance only. Clinicians are encouraged to seek expert guidance where specific queries regarding compliance arise.

to ensure that any processes implemented in the clinic are consistent with the university's governing policies. Indeed, there may be a stipulation contained in your university's policies that require you to seek their guidance. In any event, such colleagues can be a valuable source of help and support when seeking to navigate the complex legal and regulatory requirements involved in handling personal data.

What data is your clinic storing, handling and/or processing?

In order to ensure that you are processing data in a lawful manner, it is necessary to have a clear idea as to what data your clinic is handling. This can be achieved by carrying out an audit of the personal data the clinic holds in relation to students, clients, potential clients and others. Where a number of staff are involved in the operation of the clinic they should be asked to feed into the audit, in order to ensure that all categories of data are captured.

Depending on the way your clinic is set up, it may be helpful to consider the data handled in relation to each different project or area of activity. For example, if students apply to volunteer with your clinic, you might handle the following student data as part of the application process:

- name
- university email address
- mobile number
- details given on the application form regarding past experience, suitability for the role, etc.

If the student's application is successful, the clinic might then hold the following information for the duration of their time as a volunteer:

- name
- contact details (phone number/email address).

In relation to an in-house live client clinic, the following personal data might be held about clients:

- personal client data (including sensitive data), for example:
  - name
  - address
  - contact details
  - potentially race, gender, religion, etc.
  - potentially details regarding health, if relevant to query
  - personal legal issues (family law, employment, etc.)

- personal data (names, etc.) of other parties involved in the client's query.

For each set of data, consider the following:

- Precisely what data is held?
- Why does the clinic process that data?
- Is it necessary to process that data and, if so, why?
- How long is it necessary to retain the data? (This is considered in more detail below.)
- Who is the data shared with?
- Is the clinic allowed to hold the data?
- Is the clinic the data controller or processer?
- How is the data held/processed?[2]

A template data audit is contained in **Part 5.5.5** of this Handbook. The outcome of the audit should be considered carefully. You may find, for example, that the clinic is collecting data that is not required. In such cases, processes can be streamlined to remove any unnecessary questions from client questionnaires, etc. It is good practice to review and update the audit on a regular basis in order to ensure that any changes or developments in terms of data collection are considered, for example where a new project is established.

Obligations under the General Data Protection Regulation[3] vary, depending on whether you are a data controller, joint controller or processor. There is a checklist available on the Information Commissioner's Office (ICO) website that gives an indication as to which category you are likely to be in.[4] Most clinics will be data controllers as they determine the purpose and means of processing the personal data that they hold.

Do you have a 'lawful basis' for processing the data you hold?

As outlined in **Part 2.11: Digital security**, data must only be processed where there is a lawful basis for doing so. There are six available lawful bases. In most cases, data processed by a clinic will be done on the basis that the data subject

---

2   Several of these questions are based on recommendations contained in LawWorks, *General data protection regulation toolkit* (Revision 2, 25 May 2018) p. 3 <https://www.lawworks.org.uk/solicitors-and-volunteers/resources/general-data-protection-regulation-toolkit-gdpr> accessed 22 August 2019.

3   Regulation (EU) 2016/679.

4   <https://ico.org.uk/for-organisations/guide-to-data-protection/guide-to-the-general-data-protection-regulation-gdpr/key-definitions/controllers-and-processors/> accessed 22 August 2019.

(i.e. the client or student) has given their express consent.[5] Thought should be given as to how consent is obtained.

For example, clinics should consider:

- How can you ensure that the client's consent is informed? It needs to be made clear to the client what they are consenting to.
- What information do you need to tell the client in order that they can give informed consent? Consider what you will do with the client's data as part of the service you provide: who will it be shared with and how? For example, if you will share any of the client's data with a third party, such as an external law firm that will provide volunteer lawyers to supervise, the client should be informed of this and their consent should be sought before the data is shared.
- How will you evidence that consent has been given? Often this will be through a written agreement (usually a client information agreement or similar). However, there may be times when clients give their consent verbally, for example when giving initial details of their query over the telephone for conflict checking purposes. Consider what information will need to be given to the client at this point, how it will be conveyed to them and how you can record their verbal consent to proceed (i.e. in a telephone attendance note).
- What information might you need to give students before they begin working in the clinic about how their data will be used? Does your student volunteer agreement need updating to make this clear and to seek their consent?

The Information Commissioner's Office (ICO) has useful guidance, which offers good practice on obtaining consent.[6]

Do you have a privacy notice?

Law clinics must provide clients with privacy information at the time their personal data is collected from them. Where personal data is obtained from another source, it must be provided within a reasonable period and no later than one month after obtaining the data.

The ICO guidance contains a checklist, outlining the information that ought to be provided. It includes the following:

- the name and contact details of your organisation

---

5   Note the further guidance in **Part 2.11: Digital security** on special category data.

6   <https://ico.org.uk/for-organisations/guide-to-data-protection/guide-to-the-general-data-protection-regulation-gdpr/lawful-basis-for-processing/consent/> accessed 22 August 2019.

- the name and contact details of your representative (if applicable)
- the contact details of your data protection officer (if applicable)
- the purposes of the processing
- the lawful basis for the processing
- the legitimate interests for the processing (if applicable)
- the categories of personal data obtained (if the personal data is not obtained from the individual it relates to)
- the recipients or categories of recipients of the personal data
- the details of transfers of the personal data to any third countries or international organisations (if applicable)
- the retention periods for the personal data
- the rights available to individuals in respect of the processing
- the right to withdraw consent (if applicable)
- the right to lodge a complaint with a supervisory authority
- the source of the personal data (if the personal data is not obtained from the individual it relates to)
- the details of whether individuals are under a statutory or contractual obligation to provide the personal data (if applicable, and if the personal data is collected from the individual it relates to)
- the details of the existence of automated decision-making, including profiling (if applicable).[7]

The information must be provided in a manner that is concise and easy to understand, so care needs to be taken when drafting to ensure it is written in an accessible style. Typically, this information will be contained in a privacy notice, which should be linked on the clinic's website and in any marketing materials. Clinics may also include the information in, or appended to, the client care letter. Two examples of a privacy notice are included in **Parts 5.2.2** and **5.2.3** of this Handbook; however, your university may have its own template for privacy notices that your clinic may be required to follow.

The precise content of privacy notices will vary between clinics, and will depend upon the service being provided and the way that data is handled by each clinic. The data audit recommended above should be used to inform the content of the privacy notice.

---

7   <https://ico.org.uk/for-organisations/guide-to-data-protection/guide-to-the-general-data-protection-regulation-gdpr/individual-rights/right-to-be-informed/> accessed 22 August 2019.

Do you have appropriate data processing and/or data protection arrangements in place with partners and service providers?

The ICO guidance states that:

> accountability is one of the data protection principles – it makes you responsible for complying with the GDPR and says that you must be able to demonstrate your compliance.[8]

One example of accountability that the guidance cites is having written contracts in place with organisations that process personal data on your behalf. Therefore, where your clinic engages any other individual or organisation to process data on its behalf (for example, to store data or delete it) they would be a data processor and a written agreement should be put in place to confirm what type of personal data is being processed, the duration of the processing, the purpose of the processing and so on.[9] The ICO guidance gives examples of the kinds of clauses that any such agreement should include.[10]

What measures are in place to keep personal data secure?

Give careful consideration to the measures employed in the clinic to keep data secure. Digital security considerations are addressed in **Part 2.11: Digital security** and **Part 2.13: Lawyering in a digital age: Reflections on starting up a virtual law clinic**. However, thought should also be given to storage and transmission of hardcopy documents that contain personal data. For example, how can you ensure that access to hardcopy documents is limited to only those with authority to view them? Lockable rooms and filing cabinets are essential.

Also, what rules and processes can you put in place to avoid hardcopy documents being lost or stolen? This will be of particular concern where clinics take place off campus and must be transported from one location to another.

How do those studying, working and volunteering in your clinic know what their obligations are?

It is essential that all those who work, study and volunteer with the clinic understand their duties and obligations to keep data secure. Data security

---

8   <https://ico.org.uk/for-organisations/guide-to-data-protection/guide-to-the-general-data-protection-regulation-gdpr/accountability-and-governance/> accessed 22 August 2019.

9   <https://ico.org.uk/for-organisations/guide-to-data-protection/guide-to-the-general-data-protection-regulation-gdpr/accountability-and-governance/contracts/> accessed 22 August 2019.

10   Ibid.

should therefore be factored into training sessions for new staff and students. Records should be kept of who has undertaken the training and has received copies of the relevant policies. It would be good practice to seek written confirmation that policies have been read and understood. Again, a clause to that effect could be included in student volunteer agreements.

Consider also how external volunteers will be made aware of their obligations and the university's processes. Volunteer agreements and volunteer handbooks could both assist with this.

How long are you keeping personal data for?

Personal data must not be kept for longer than it is needed.[11] There is no 'one size fits all': the timescale will vary depending on the data concerned. For example, personal data relating to students applying to volunteer with the clinic will be needed for a much shorter period of time than details of clients advised by the clinic.

When considering retention periods, there will be a number of factors to consider, such as:

- the limitation periods of any potential claims arising out of advice given by the clinic; and
- the data needed to carry out conflict checks, in order to meet the ongoing obligation not to act where there is a conflict of interest.

The clinic should adopt a data retention policy detailing the length of time different types of records will be retained for. Processes should be put in place to ensure data is deleted upon the expiry of retention periods.

Do you know what you need to do if there is a data breach?

According to the ICO:

> there will be a personal data breach whenever any personal data is lost, destroyed, corrupted or disclosed; if someone accesses the data or passes it on without proper authorisation; or if the data is made unavailable, for example, when it has been encrypted by ransomware, or accidentally lost or destroyed.[12]

Clinics should have clear processes in place dictating what should happen in

11   <https://ico.org.uk/for-organisations/guide-to-data-protection/guide-to-the-general-data-protection-regulation-gdpr/principles/storage-limitation/> accessed 22 August 2019.

12   <https://ico.org.uk/for-organisations/guide-to-data-protection/guide-to-the-general-data-protection-regulation-gdpr/personal-data-breaches/> accessed 22 August 2019.

the event of an actual or potential data breach. Clinic participants should be trained to recognise where a breach may have occurred and should be clear as to who this should be reported to and the timescales for doing so.

It is important that staff and students understand their obligation to report breaches and near misses. It would be sensible to nominate a member of staff within the clinic to whom reports should be made in the first instance. This person can then determine whether the issue needs to be escalated further within the university. The university will have protocols in place which will dictate this.

It is likely that any breach will need to be reported to the university's designated Data Protection Officer, who will then take a view as to whether it needs to be reported to the ICO. Not all breaches must be reported to the ICO, and will depend upon the likelihood and severity of the resulting risk to people's rights and freedoms.[13] Where this risk to rights and freedoms is likely, the ICO must be notified. Even where the duty to notify the ICO does not arise, the decision not to report should be documented, along with the rationale behind the decision.

Where the duty to report arises, the data breach must be reported without undue delay and, in any event, not later than 72 hours after becoming aware of it. It is therefore important that the matter is escalated through the appropriate internal channels within the university as quickly as possible once a breach is made known.[14] Consideration will also need to be given as to whether the individuals whose data has been compromised ought to be notified.[15]

Even where no report is made to the ICO and/or data subjects are not notified, any breaches or near misses should be recorded, along with details of actions taken to avoid similar issues arising in the future.

Further resources

As outlined above, this section is intended to give an overview of some of the key considerations that you will need to take into account when contemplating data security in law clinics. For those wishing to learn more, there are a wealth of additional useful resources available on data protection and GDPR compliance. In particular, the ICO guidance referenced frequently through this section provides a detailed but accessible starting point.[16]

13   Ibid.

14   The consequences for failure to notify can be significant and can result in a significant fine of up to €10 million or 2 per cent of your global turnover.

15   See **note 12**.

16   <https://ico.org.uk/for-organisations/guide-to-data-protection/guide-to-the-general-data-protection-regulation-gdpr/> accessed 22 August 2019.

Part 2.15
Provision of immigration advice and services by university law clinics

Frances Ridout

Office of Immigration Services Commissioner

The Office of the Immigration Services Commissioner (OISC)[1] is the statutory regulator of immigration advice and services in the UK. The OISC was established by Part 5 of the Immigration and Asylum Act 1999[2] in response to growing concerns that vulnerable migrants, in particular asylum seekers, were falling prey to unqualified and unregulated immigration advice providers (often for extortionate fees). Even within the charitable sector, well-meaning but incorrect advice was provided, which could be devastating to an individual's long-term prospects.

The ethos underpinning the regulator's work fits squarely with the ethos of most, if not all, university clinics: that access to justice means that people receive advice that is of a sound and proper quality. The OISC has been in operation for the last 17 years and at the time of writing regulates approximately 3,000 advisers operating in 1,500 registered organisations.

Who needs to be OISC-registered?

Any person providing immigration advice and services in the UK who is not already regulated by a designated qualifying regulator (DQR)[3] and thus a 'qualified person' under the Act, must be regulated by the OISC in order to provide immigration advice and services. Immigration advice and services relate to an application to the UK authorities for any type of leave to enter or remain (including asylum and immigration bail work), applications for British nationality and citizenship and admission to or residence in the UK under EU law.

---

1   <https://www.gov.uk/government/organisations/office-of-the-immigration-services-commissioner> accessed 24 April 2019.

2   <https://www.legislation.gov.uk/ukpga/1999/33/section/83> accessed 24 April 2019.

3   Designated qualifying regulators include the General Council of the Bar, Law Society of England and Wales, Chartered Institute of Legal Executives, Faculty of Advocates, Law Society of Scotland, General Council of the Bar of Northern Ireland and Law Society of Northern Ireland.

It is important to note that it is the entity which the OISC registers and then, through the entity, the OISC also regulates the immigration advisers who provide the advice and services. To provide immigration advice and services while not regulated is a criminal offence.[4] The OISC investigates and prosecutes those who operate when not authorised to do so.

The statute

Whether individuals working within certain bodies are in fact regulated by a DQR can be a complex issue. Solicitors working in law firms and barristers in chambers are likely to be fully regulated by their respective regulatory bodies; further, they are normally permitted to supervise non-legally qualified staff and volunteers to also provide immigration advice and services acting on behalf of the regulated organisation. Outside of law firms and chambers, however, the situation becomes less clear.

Solicitors working in practices that are set up as an alternative business structure[5] and authorised to operate by a DQR can also supervise non-legally qualified staff and volunteers, and these individuals do not need to be regulated by the OISC.

However, practising solicitors working in law centres and certain charitable organisations that have been permitted to employ solicitors to provide advice and services to the public are permitted to provide immigration advice themselves, but are not (in England and Wales) permitted to supervise others in doing so.[6]

This means that while practising solicitors in these settings may be regulated by the Solicitors Regulatory Authority (SRA), or barristers regulated by the Bar Standards Board (BSB), other staff providing immigration advice and services must be regulated by the OISC. This therefore applies to students working and volunteering with such organisations as part of their clinical legal education programme (whether under the supervision of employed and qualified clinicians or volunteer barristers or solicitors).

---

4   Immigration and Asylum Act 1999, s 91(1) <https://www.legislation.gov.uk/ukpga/1999/33/section/91> accessed 24 April 2019.

5   See **Part 2.2** for guidance on alternative business structures.

6   Further guidance on the position under the SRA Standards and Regulations which came into force on 25 November 2019 can be found in SRA, 'SRA Standards and Regulations guidance for the not for profit sector' (23 July 2019) <https://www.sra.org.uk/newregs/> accessed 26 July 2019.

What does this mean for university law clinics?

What does this mean for law clinics operating in the UK that provide immigration advice and services to the public? Those operating in England and Wales will need to consider carefully how they deliver their advice and services.

Where the services are provided entirely through a practising solicitor (even one employed by the university rather than a law firm), with all advice and any representations made to the UK immigration authorities' being made in the solicitor's name, then it is likely they will not need to be regulated by the OISC. This is the case even if students assist in the research or gathering of information that supports a particular application.

However, if advice and services are provided in the name of the law clinic or university (or in the name of the solicitor but on the headed paper of the law clinic or university), then the law clinic or university as an entity – and any non-solicitor staff and volunteers (including student volunteers) – will need to apply to the OISC for regulation.

Law clinics operating in Northern Ireland and Scotland should confirm with their respective regulators if they regulate students who provide immigration advice and services in the name of the law clinic.

Reality of registering a law clinic

There is no doubt that the regulatory position of university law clinics for delivering advice in this area has been a confused picture for some time. Some clinics have tentatively and nervously reached out to the OISC to try and resolve the regulation of work already being undertaken.[7] Far from reprimanding these clinics, the OISC is keen to work with clinicians to support them through the regulatory maze, and find a flexible approach where good work can continue. All indications are that the OISC will continue with this approach.

Step 1: Registering the clinic

University law clinics wanting to give immigration advice should first start by registering the clinic as an OISC-approved body to provide legal advice

---

7   The Queen Mary Legal Advice Centre being a pilot regulated university law clinic with the OISC <https://www.lac.qmul.ac.uk/advice/immigration-law/> accessed 24 April 2019. The pilot programme is outlined in F Ridout, D Gilchrist and J Dunn, 'Immigration university clinics and regulation: A working case study' (2018) *International Journal of Clinical Legal Education* 25(3), 135–49 <https://www.northumbriajournals.co.uk/index.php/ijcle/article/view/770> accessed 24 April 2019.

by submitting the relevant form.[8] This should be done regardless of whether the clinic is a separate legal entity or part of the university. The form is primarily designed for independent advice organisations, meaning some of the information requested is more difficult for law clinics to provide (for example accounts). However, the OISC is amenable to discuss such issues and often takes a flexible approach to the evidence submitted. It is likely that the OISC will want to do an audit as part of this registration process. Further details on the audit process are provided later in this section.

If a clinic has volunteer lawyers (or indeed employed barristers or solicitors) who give or supervise immigration legal advice at the clinic, they will need to be listed in this form. It is only necessary to list those providing immigration advice. The registration is updated each year, meaning that if this list changes, alterations can be made to the information quite easily.

Clinic supervisors (whether lawyers employed by the clinic/university or external barristers or solicitors who are volunteering) often need to change at short notice. If as a clinic you are able to show that you have adequate handbooks and processes in place, which ensure a consistency of service at times when another volunteer lawyer steps in to cover for a registered volunteer lawyer, the OISC is content.

Step 2: Authorising the student advisers

The turnover of students involved in clinics (whether immigration or otherwise) is inevitably high. Further, the academic year is very short, meaning that the moment students start in September/October they need to be in a position to immediately start in the clinic in order to complete a sufficient number of cases and have a meaningful educational experience.

Applications for new student advisers are twofold. Firstly, students need to complete an OISC 'New adviser application and competence statement'.[9] This relatively straightforward form can be completed within 20 minutes or so by the student with guidance from a member of staff. Again, the OISC takes a pragmatic position when the form asks for applicants to list all jobs and work experience. Clinics may wish to speak with the OISC before registering students, to get a flavour of the flexibility in this form.

Secondly, applicants need to have a suitable Disclosure and Barring Service

---

8   <https://www.gov.uk/government/publications/oisc-application-for-regulation-of-a-new-legal-entity> accessed 24 April 2019.

9   <https://www.gov.uk/government/publications/new-adviser-application-and-competence-statement> accessed 24 April 2019.

(DBS) check.[10] Depending on the university, it may be that a central Widening Participation team is able to assist with this. The cost of a DBS check is dependent on whether the activity is voluntary or not. If a student is working on an unpaid basis in a clinic the application will be free. If this is not the case then the basic check (the level required by the OISC) is £25. An enhanced check is £44. There is no discount for universities.

To qualify for a free-of-charge check volunteers must not:

- benefit financially from the position
- receive payment (except expenses)
- be on a work placement
- be in a trainee position or undertaking a course of study that will lead to a full-time role or qualification.[11]

DBS forms are lengthy and can be complex (especially for international students). Submitting these forms and sending them in with copies of appropriate documents can be a very lengthy and drawn out task. The OISC is amenable to clinics submitting new registration forms without the DBS checks and then submitting these at a later date when the certificate has been processed. The OISC is also flexible in allowing those advisers to volunteer in the clinic while the registration and DBS checks are being processed. Clinics might find it useful to try and have a clinician able to complete the DBS forms for submission rather than relying on a different university department.

Being registered as Level 1 advisers[12] with permission by the OISC to provide Immigration Advice and Services up to Level 2 under supervision will be sufficient for most clinics to undertake advice work. Students can advise on work one level above that in which they are registered. Level 1 work is advice and assistance, Level 2 is case work and Level 3 is advocacy and representation. Within each of these levels there are three categories of work:

- Immigration (applications for variation of entry clearance or leave to enter or remain in the UK; unlawful entry; nationality and citizenships; and admission, residence in and citizenship of EU members states);
- Asylum and Protection; and
- Judicial Review Case Management.

---

10 <https://www.gov.uk/government/organisations/disclosure-and-barring-service> accessed 24 April 2019.

11 <https://www.gov.uk/government/publications/disclosure-application-process-for-volunteers/disclosure-application-process-for-volunteers> accessed 24 April 2019.

12 <https://www.gov.uk/government/publications/competence-oisc-guidance-2012> accessed 23 November 2018.

If clinics want to offer advocacy in immigration matters this would be Level 3 work and therefore students would need to gain authorisation at Level 2 (which requires an additional application procedure). For a full list of areas that are permitted at each level please view the Guidance on Competence (2017).[13]

Advisers seeking authorisation with the OISC normally undertake a written competence assessment. For Level 1 registration, OISC takes a pragmatic view of students in clinics who are undertaking a law degree, and therefore normally do not require a test if there are sufficient arrangements in place for training and developing knowledge. The Guidance on Competence[14] lists areas of knowledge, and skills and attributes.

- Knowledge includes: identifying that a client is subject to immigration control, applicable categories, relevant forms and time limits, requirements of the immigration rules and cases, and operational guidance.
- Skills and aptitudes include: the ability to draft letters, and demonstrate interpersonal skills, support vulnerable clients, gather evidence, identify appropriate resources, follow good practice, appreciate urgency and keep good records.

For Level 2 and 3 registration, this involves a written exam paper taken under exam conditions at an OISC test centre. Any adviser authorised by the OISC may apply through the registered organisation to take assessments at higher levels. There is no cost to the individual or organisation to make such an application. Law clinics might therefore consider whether they wish to make such applications for students where they feel the student has gained sufficient knowledge and experience and is interested in gaining a higher level of authorisation.

It is very important to note that students are only authorised to give legal advice at the clinic that has applied for their authorisation because it is the clinic itself which is registered, then the adviser through the clinic. Therefore, this is not transferable to another organisation or clinic. This will need to be stressed to students.

Given the short period of time that students volunteer with a clinic there may be no obvious benefit for the students undertaking examinations for the higher levels. If they undertake clinic work and therefore obtain the experience to do the examination, by the time the assessment is complete they are likely to be moving on from the clinic. Having said this, students may feel that it is a good qualification to gain.

---

13   <https://assets.publishing.service.gov.uk/government/uploads/system/uploads/attachment_data/file/604807/OISC_GoC_2017.pdf> accessed 24 April 2019.

14   See **note 12**.

What happens at an audit?

The OISC considers the clinic premises, handbooks, procedures and client file format to check that everything is to standard. The initial audit is a lengthier process (typically one day), but following this the audits are likely to decrease in length (typically half a day) and frequency depending on the size of the clinic. This is, of course, subject to a complaint being made or a problem being identified. The clinic will usually be asked for a list of cases in advance of the audit.

Teaching ethics through immigration regulation

There is no doubt that the regulation of law clinics is complex[15] and has not been fully resolved. This niche area can feel unnecessarily bureaucratic, especially having to gain authorisation for each student within the clinic.

However, there are benefits. It is a great way to teach students about regulation and ethics. Linking ethics to regulation can often feel very abstract for students, and the immigration clinic context can be an effective way of practically tethering the two together. It is also an excellent mechanism to teach social justice, as the regulation is in place to protect vulnerable members of the public who have historically been exploited by some sections of the legal profession. It ensures students are exposed to and can reflect on certain realities when entering the legal profession; that not all barristers and solicitors act with integrity and to the highest standards of client care at all times.

The opportunities for teaching ethics that arise from working closely with a regulator are both obvious and subtle. The obvious professional ethics principles to discuss with students include: upholding the rule of law and the proper administration of justice,[16] delivering a competent standard of work[17]

---

15   Linden Thomas 'Law clinics in England and Wales: A regulatory black hole' (2017) *The Law Teacher*, 51:4,469–85 <https://doi.org/10.1080/03069400.2017.1322858>.

16   SRA, Standards and Regulations (20 March 2019), Principle 1 <https://www.sra.org.uk/sra/policy/future/resources.page#resources> accessed 23 July 2019 (previously SRA, Principle 1 <https://www.sra.org.uk/solicitors/standards-regulations/principles/> accessed 24 April 2019); and the Bar Standards Board Core Duty 1 <https://www.barstandardsboard.org.uk/uploads/assets/7679cfab-8237-451e-8fefd8bdd68edf90/bsbhandbookversion40.pdf> accessed 24 April 2019.

17   SRA, Standards and Regulations (20 March 2019), SRA Code of Conduct for Solicitors, RELs and RFLs, para 3 <https://www.sra.org.uk/sra/policy/future/resources.page#resources> accessed 23 July 2019 (previously SRA, Principle 5 <https://www.sra.org.uk/solicitors/standards-regulations/code-conduct-solicitors/ > accessed 24 April 2019; and the Bar Standards Board Core Duty 7 <https://www.barstandardsboard.org.uk/uploads/assets/7679cfab-8237-451e-8fefd8bdd68edf90/bsbhandbookversion40.pdf> accessed 24 April 2019.

and acting with integrity,[18] etc.

However, there is a wealth of learning to be had in situations where clients come to clinics having previously received bad legal advice. For example, is there a duty for the clinic to inform the client that they could make a complaint to the OISC or elsewhere? Is there actually a duty on an OISC-regulated clinic to make an anonymous complaint itself? How does a clinic uphold confidentiality in these circumstances? Is making a complaint against the wishes of a client acting in their best interests?

We are all well aware of the rich and diverse range of ethical issues that clinical legal education already produces. Students rarely fully appreciate the complexities of complying with a regulator, especially when they feel a long way off practising under the remit of the SRA or the BSB. Engaging with the OISC alongside legal education can be an effective tool to practically demonstrate the need for regulatory compliance.

Clinics work hard to ensure that some of the most vulnerable in society are respected and not taken advantage of, while simultaneously teaching students good practice. Both these principles underpin the work of the OISC, which aims to support the provision of good quality (usually free) legal advice that clinics provide to this vulnerable group in society.

While there is undoubtedly some bureaucracy involved in the OISC registration process it is clear that the OISC does not wish to create barriers to innovative programmes such as those designed by university law clinics. The OISC recognises that such programmes not only provide a much needed service to local communities but also lay the groundwork for competent and ethical immigration advisers of the future.

As more clinics start to register with the OISC it will in all likelihood be necessary for the OISC to consider how to make the application process more efficient, especially when the student advisers usually only need to be registered for a short period of time. This may, of course, lead to changes in the individual adviser authorisation process. However, for the moment the statute remains in force and an involved two-stage registration process continues, which considers both the acceptable legitimacy and standard of the clinic itself (how it operates and is managed), and the fitness and competence of the student advisers within the clinic.

---

18   SRA (**note 16**), Principle 5 (previously SRA, Principle 2 <https://www.sra.org.uk/solicitors/handbook/handbookprinciples/part2/content.page> accessed 24 April 2019; and the Bar Standards Board Core Duty 3 <https://www.barstandardsboard.org.uk/uploads/assets/7679cfab-8237-451e-8fefd8bdd68edf90/bsbhandbookversion40.pdf> accessed 24 April 2019.

Useful contact information

Should you be concerned that your law clinic may need to be regulated by the OISC, please contact the Voluntary Sector Support Group at the OISC (VSS@ oisc.gov.uk). You can email the group with details of how your clinic operates and it will confirm whether or not you need to be regulated.

The Voluntary Sector Support Group at the OISC also has a dedicated section on its website that provides advice about regulation specifically for the voluntary and community sectors which may be helpful to consult. This can be found at <https://www.gov.uk/government/publications/guidance-for-the-community-and-voluntary-sector>.

Summary

- Most clinics wishing to give immigration advice and services will need to be registered with the OISC.
- Each individual adviser within the clinic will also need to be registered with the OISC. Their registration is linked to the clinic and is not transferable.
- Registered students within a registered clinic can advise under supervision to one level above that which they are registered.

Part 2.16
Provision of debt advice by university law clinics

*Lee Hansen**

There are significant regulatory barriers to university law clinics undertaking debt advice. This is an unsatisfactory state of affairs, as university clinics are well placed to provide assistance in this area of significant unmet need.

Unmanageable debt is a problem that may cluster, occurring together with other legal problems including those concerning benefits, housing, employment and relationship issues.[1] This means that clients may present to university law clinics with multiple issues alongside their debt problem. There is strong evidence of a link between unmanageable debt and poor mental health,[2] so the recent creation of barriers to people seeking legal help in this area is particularly troubling.

In this section we set out the regulatory arrangements that may prevent clinics from assisting clients in these cases and explore some of the potential workarounds.

Regulated activities and the general prohibition on giving debt advice

Section 19 of the Financial Services and Markets Act 2000 (FSMA) sets out a general prohibition on carrying on a regulated activity unless a person is authorised or exempt from this requirement ('the general prohibition').

A regulated activity includes:

- debt counselling
- debt adjusting
- debt collecting
- debt administration
- credit broking

---

* Thank you to Linden Thomas and Andrea Fejos for helpful comments on drafts of this section.

1 Citizens Advice, *A debt effect? How is unmanageable debt related to other problems in people's lives?* <https://www.citizensadvice.org.uk/Global/CitizensAdvice/Debt%20and%20Money%20 Publications/The%20Debt%20Effect.pdf> accessed 19 April 2019.

2 Ibid, p. 21.

- credit information services.

Contravention of the general prohibition is an offence and renders a person liable on conviction to up to two years' imprisonment or a fine or both.[3]

University law clinics should ensure that appropriate systems and controls are in place, including adequate supervision, to avoid any contravention of the general prohibition by the institution, its staff, students and volunteers.

Debt counselling

Debt counselling is a regulated activity. It includes 'giving advice to a borrower about the liquidation of a debt due under a credit agreement'.[4]

Credit agreement is defined as:

> an agreement between an individual or relevant recipient of credit ('A') and any other person ('B') under which B provides A with credit of any amount.[5]

The Financial Conduct Authority (FCA) has stated that the expression *liquidation of a debt* has a wide meaning, including:

- paying off the debt in full and in time;
- agreeing a rescheduling or a temporary halt to paying off the debt;
- the debtor being released from the debt;
- agreeing a reduced repayment amount (including the creditor agreeing to accept token repayments);
- a third party taking over the debtor's obligation to discharge the debt;
- discharging the debt or making it irrecoverable through personal insolvency procedures such as bankruptcy, a voluntary arrangement or a debt relief order.[6]

---

3   FSMA, ss 20 and 23. There is a summary offence variant with a penalty of up to six months' imprisonment or a fine or both: s 23(1).

4   Financial Services and Markets Act 2000 (Regulated Activities) Order 2001 (as amended), Art 39E(1) ('Regulated Activities Order'). It also includes at (2) giving advice to a hirer about the liquidation of a debt under a consumer hire agreement.

5   Regulated Activities Order, Art 60B.

6   FCA, *The Perimeter Guidance Manual* (PERG), Chapter 17: Consumer credit debt counselling, Q3.1 <https://www.handbook.fca.org.uk/handbook/PERG.pdf> accessed 21 April 2019.

The FCA has stated that in order to fall within the ambit of debt counselling 'advice must relate to a particular debt and debtor'.[7] Therefore, advice given to the public will not come within the scope of this activity as it does not relate to 'a' debt.[8] Accordingly, public legal education (PLE) such as Streetlaw sessions conducted by a university law clinic on consumer credit and debt issues or the preparation of written PLE materials are unlikely to be a regulated activity if they are undertaken for a sufficiently broad audience.

The FCA also distinguishes between regulated advice and the provision of information,[9] noting that:

> simply giving balanced and neutral information without making any comment or value judgement on its relevance to decisions which a debtor may make is not advice.[10]

However, an express or implied recommendation as to a course of action that might be adopted will render such a communication 'advice'. This means that it is possible for clinics which are not authorised to undertake debt counselling to provide 'information-only' services in which no advice or recommendations are actually given. However, it would be crucial to ensure that these services are closely supervised to ensure that inadvertent advice is not given.

The FCA notes that the 'range of activities covered by debt counselling is wide'.[11] Examples of advice that are likely to be debt counselling according to the FCA include budgetary advice,[12] as well as statements such as:

- 'I recommend you enter into a debt management plan'[13]
- 'I recommend you prioritise the repayment of your electricity bill over all other debts.'[14]

Debt adjusting

Debt adjusting is a regulated activity. It includes negotiating, with a lender on behalf of a borrower, terms for the discharge of a debt due under a credit

---

7   Ibid, Q2.1, para (2).
8   Ibid, 17.4, Q4.1.
9   Ibid, Q5.3.
10   Ibid.
11   Ibid, Q5.4.
12   Ibid, Q7.1, example (16).
13   Ibid, example (1).
14   Ibid, example (14).

agreement.[15] An example of how this might arise in a clinic setting is as follows:

> if a Clinic client's lender were contacted by the Clinic advisor to discuss or negotiate the restructuring of that borrower's debt on behalf of the Clinic client.[16]

This is an area to take note of for clinics that undertake negotiation with other parties on behalf of clients.

Debt collecting

Debt collecting is a regulated activity, which includes 'taking steps to procure the payment of a debt due under a credit agreement ...'[17] LawWorks has provided the following example of how a clinic may be taken as undertaking such an activity:

> Debt collecting could be carried out if a Clinic client lends money to a third party borrower, for example, a friend, relative or business associate etc, and that third party falls into arrears or default or otherwise and refuses to pay it back and then the Clinic advisor assists the Clinic client to take steps to recover that debt.[18]

Debt administration

Debt administration is a regulated activity. It includes performing duties under a credit agreement on behalf of a lender.[19] It has been noted that undertaking debt collecting as described in the example above may also involve debt administration.[20]

---

15   It also includes for a debt due under a consumer hire agreement, negotiating with an owner on behalf of the hirer. Under the Regulated Activities Order, Art 39D(1)(c) and (2)(c) also included is any similar activity concerning the liquidation of a debt under a credit agreement of a consumer hire agreement.

16   LawWorks, *Briefing for Bill Team at DWP and HM Treasury* (December 2017), para 3.7(b) <https://www.lawworks.org.uk/sites/default/files/files/Financial%20Guidance%20Bill%20Briefing.pdf> accessed 21 April 2019.

17   Regulated Activities Order, Art 39F(1); see also Art 36H(1), (3) and (4) on agreements and (2) on consumer hire agreements.

18   LawWorks (**note 16**), para 3.7(c).

19   Regulated Activities Order, Art 39G(a); see also Art 36H(1), (3) and (4) on agreements and (2) on consumer hire agreements.

20   LawWorks (**note 16**), para 3.7(d).

Credit broking

Credit broking is a regulated activity. It extends to a range of activities including the introduction of individuals to credit providers.[21] An example might include:

> if a borrower were introduced to a third party such as a bank, pay day lender or broker, in order to (e.g.) refinance an existing loan.[22]

This is an area to take note of when considering the clinic's signposting and referral practices.[23]

Credit information services

The provision of credit information services is a regulated activity. Credit information services include 'undertaking a specified kind of activity' or giving advice on taking steps to undertake a specified kind of activity.

The specified activities are set out at Art 89A of the Regulated Activities Order. They are:

> (a) ascertaining whether a credit information agency holds information relevant to the financial standing of an individual or relevant recipient of credit;
>
> (b) ascertaining the contents of such information;
>
> (c) securing the correction of, the omission of anything from, or the making of any other kind of modification of, such information;
>
> (d) securing that a credit information agency which holds such information–
>
> (i) stops holding the information, or
>
> (ii) does not provide it to any other person.

An example of a clinic undertaking this regulated activity would arise if the clinic was:

> to ascertain whether a credit information agency held information relevant to the financial standing of an individual or relevant recipient of credit.[24]

---

21   Regulated Activities Order, Art 36A.

22   LawWorks (**note 16**), para 3.7(e).

23   For more on this topic, see **Part 2.6: Signposting and referrals**.

24   LawWorks (**note 16**), para 3.7(f).

Authorisation and the 2014 changes

In order for a clinic to undertake any of the above regulated activities either it would need to be authorised or an exemption would need to apply.

In April 2014, responsibility for regulatory oversight of consumer credit and debt advice moved from the abolished Office of Fair Trading (OFT) to the FCA. Under the OFT, a group licence had been issued to the Law Society and administered by the SRA. The licence authorised solicitors to provide advice on debt and consumer credit.

However, upon the change in regulatory oversight, the group licence issued to the Law Society was removed and solicitors providing debt advice at university clinics were no longer authorised to do so. LawWorks advised 'all clinics not otherwise covered by FCA limited permission authorisation to stop advising in all areas of consumer credit and debt from the 1 April 2014'.[25]

The regulations implementing these changes included grandfathering permission for certain not-for profit organisations under an existing group licence to continue offering debt adjusting, debt counselling and credit information services.[26] Such organisations – which include Citizens Advice, the Law Centres Network and Advice UK – do not require authorisation in order to continue to offer these services.

However, most university law clinics are not covered by these grandfathering provisions. University law clinics might consider working in partnership with the above types of organisations; this could be in areas including the development of public legal education sessions or on law reform projects.

A university law clinic might also consider applying for authorisation from the FCA. It should be cautioned that applying and maintaining authorisation would be an undertaking of significant regulatory complexity. LawWorks has described the practical considerations for pro bono clinics seeking authorisation in the following terms:

> [A]pplying for FCA authorisation is a long, expensive and generally difficult process. Preparing an application takes a considerable amount of time. This is because of the need to submit a complete application form, to ensure systems are in place to comply with the FCA Handbook, determine the minimum regulatory financial

---

25   LawWorks, *Briefing Sheet: Consumer Credit and Debt Advice* <https://www.lawworks.org.uk/sites/default/files/files/LWBriefing-RegulationofConsumerCreditandDebtAdvice.pdf> accessed 21 April 2019.

26   Financial Services and Markets Act 2000 (Regulated Activities) (Amendment) (No. 2) Order 2013, Art 60.

requirements, prepare a business plan setting out the planned activities, budget and resources. Once an application is submitted, the FCA can also take up to six months to decide whether to grant authorisation. Also, applying for FCA authorisation is expensive. The fees charged by the FCA for granting permissions vary. As an estimate the application fee for a consumer credit permission ranges between £600 and £15,000. The actual fee would depend on the level of complexity of the permission(s) required (from straightforward credit broking to complex debt counselling) and the firm's consumer credit income. Legal costs would also run to approximately £60,000 and then there is the cost of maintaining the licence.[27]

Impact of these changes

These changes came about in a context in which there had already been significant cuts to the availability of legal aid in debt matters following the enactment of the Legal Aid, Sentencing and Punishment of Offenders Act 2012 (LASPO). **Table 1** below represents the decline in legal aid matter starts since LASPO was implemented in 2013.[28]

Table 1: Decline in legal aid debt matter starts since LASPO

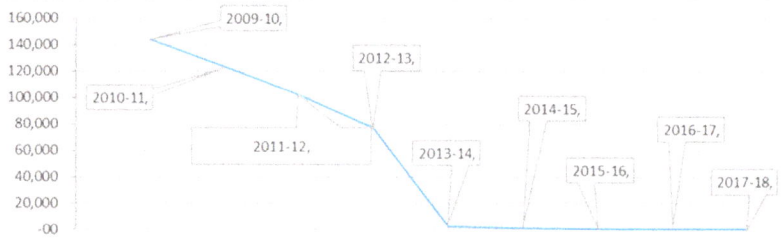

In 2015, LawWorks wrote about the impact of the changes to the regulation of debt advice on clinics in their network (which includes law school clinics, as well as other types of pro bono clinics):

> Prior to the 1 April 2014, 78 of LawWorks registered clinics provided consumer credit under the Law Society's Group licence. In the period April 2013 to March 2014, 29,279 people accessed

27   LawWorks (**note 16**) para 7.1.

28   *Legal Aid Statistics: April to June 2018,* Table 5.1 <https://www.gov.uk/government/statistics/legal-aid-statistics-april-to-june-2018> accessed 20 July 2019.

the LawWorks Clinics Network and debt advice constituted 7% of all advice delivered. The clients accessing clinic services are some of the most vulnerable members of society: 75% of clinic clients earn below the Joseph Rowntree Foundation's socially acceptable minimum standard of income.

As a result of the removal of the group licensing regime, LawWorks clinics not covered by limited permission (to our knowledge 61 clinics in our network that previously offered pro bono debt advice services are not covered by limited permission) have had to suspend all debt advices services, thereby leaving many vulnerable clients across the country without any options for accessing free legal advice for debt matters. Those clinics covered by limited permission authorisation (for example those hosted at a Citizens Advice Bureaux) are seeing an increased demand for debt advice in their already oversubscribed services.[29]

Exemptions

University law clinics might consider whether an exemption from the general prohibition applies that would enable them to undertake a regulated activity such as debt counselling. An exemption applies to members of a profession,[30] undertaking professional services whereby a regulated activity is incidental to the provision of those professional services.[31]

LawWorks has reported that:

The FCA have stated that it is open to firms to provide pro bono legal advice (including debt advice) provided that – the debt advice (as regulated activity) is incidental to (i.e. arises out of or is complimentary to) the professional services offered to clients, and the firm is a member of a Designated Professional Body (DPB) which has rules approved by the FCA under Part 20 FSMA in respect of consumer credit.[32]

The SRA is a designated professional body. It has set out rules for firms carrying out financial services under this exemption.[33]

---

29   LawWorks (**note 25**) p. 3.

30   It extends to those who are controlled or managed by members of a profession.

31   FSMA, Part 20.

32   LawWorks (**note 25**), p. 4.

33   SRA Financial Services (Conduct of Business) Rules 2001; SRA Financial Services (Scope) Rules 2001. The new SRA Standards and Regulations came into force on 25 November 2019 and replaced the Rules with new Financial Services (Conduct of Business) and (Scope) Rules. See SRA

In light of the exemption, consideration may be given as to whether in-house solicitors employed within university law clinics or pro bono solicitors volunteering for such clinics might be able to undertake an exempt activity. This appears to be excluded as the business rules highlighted above are expressed so as to apply to authorised bodies and recognised sole practitioners.

The introduction to the SRA Financial Services (Conduct of Business) Rules and SRA Financial Services (Scope) Rules which came into force on 25 November 2019 state that 'These rules do not apply to solicitors, RELs or RFLs practising outside firms authorised by us'. This would likely exclude pro bono solicitors from carrying out these activities in pro bono sessions of a university law clinic. With regard to the situation of an alternative business structure (ABS), the SRA has stated that they would be able to operate pursuant to this exemption.[34] The new rules do not appear to modify this position.

The possibility of utilising the exemption also raises the question of what activities may or may not be incidental in this context. Certainly, it is no longer possible to provide a regulated consumer credit activity to a client in isolation, as was the case under the group licensing regime.[35] Some gloss is given on what is meant by the term *incidental* in s 332 of the FSMA which deals with the rules that must be set out by a DPB:

> Rules made in compliance with subsection (3) must be designed to secure that, in providing a particular professional service to a particular client, the member carries on only regulated activities which arise out of, or are complementary to, the provision by him of that service to that client.[36]

However, as a result of uncertainty as to what is and what is not 'incidental to professional service', LawWorks has noted that despite the FCA's confirmation that solicitors can rely on Part 20 exemptions:

> ... solicitors have taken a prudent approach on extending these exemptions to pro bono work at clinics as they are unsure whether advice delivered at clinics is in fact 'complimentary to the professional services offered to clients...' Solicitors would need further clarification that the exemptions covered extend to issues incidental to the particular service provided to clinic/pro bono clients. Solicitors are taking a cautious approach preferring

Standards and Regulations (SRA, published 7 February 2019, updated 20 March 2019).

34   SRA, *The architecture of change – Part 2: The new SRA Handbook – feedback and further consultation,* para 127 <https://www.sra.org.uk/sra/consultations/OFR-handbook-October.page> accessed 21 April 2019.

35   LawWorks (**note 16**), para 6.3.

36   FSMA, s 332(4).

to not take on any cases in this area given the ambiguities in the legislation and in light of the fact that to carry out consumer credit activities without the relevant permission or authorisation is a breach of FCA regulation and a criminal offence under section 23(1A) FSMA.[37]

University law clinics that are not regulated by the SRA could consider under the current regulatory arrangements opportunities for student involvement and collaboration on pro bono projects with solicitors' firms. If the advice is provided through the firm, and student involvement is controlled or managed by the firm, then the firm may be able to rely upon the exemption detailed above.

Signposting information for debt advice

Legal aid is still available for debt advice if a person's home is at risk. Individuals in this situation should be signposted to Civil Legal Advice:

- <https://www.gov.uk/civil-legal-advice>

  Telephone: 0345 345 4 345

In all other cases, debt assistance will be out of scope. An application to the 'safety net' legal aid regime for exceptional case funding (ECF) may be considered; however, note that the Lord Chancellors' guidance on the availability of ECF in debt matters indicates that this may be somewhat limited:

It will only be in those circumstances where enforcement proceedings are considered to be part of the same proceedings for the purposes of Article 6(1) ECHR18 that an obligation to provide legal aid may potentially arise.[38]

For information on making an application for legal aid under the ECF scheme see <https://publiclawproject.org.uk/what-we-do/current-projects-and-activities/legal-aid/exceptional-funding-project/>.

Other national services that may be able to assist with debt advice and information include:

- Money Advice Service:

  <https://www.moneyadviceservice.org.uk/en>

---

37   LawWorks (**note 25**), p. 6.

38   *Lord Chancellor's Exceptional Funding Guidance (Non-Inquests)*, para 50 <https://assets. publishing.service.gov.uk/government/uploads/system/uploads/attachment_data/file/477317/ legal-aid-chancellor-non-inquests.pdf> accessed 21 April 18.

0800 138 7777

- National Debt Line:

  <https://www.nationaldebtline.org>

  0808 808 4000

- StepChange:

  <https://www.stepchange.org>

  0800 138 1111

Summary

In conclusion there are significant regulatory barriers to university law clinics undertaking debt advice.

However, there are avenues or workarounds that might be explored by university law clinics to help address this area of significant unmet legal need. This includes the development of:

- public legal education/Street Law projects
- law reform projects
- information-only services, which are closely supervised to ensure that inadvertent advice is not given
- student involvement in projects that are covered by the grandfathering provisions, such as projects with law centres, Citizens Advice or Advice UK organisations
- student involvement if law firms undertake pro bono projects, including debt advice, where this meets the requirement of being incidental to the professional service offered by the firm.

Part 2.17
Legal professional privilege

Vivien Cochrane and Will Hayes

One of the fundamental differences between seeking advice from a lawyer and any other type of professional adviser is the protection afforded to communications between a lawyer and a client that may reveal the advice sought or provided, or preparations for litigation. This principle is known as legal professional privilege (LPP).

LPP is essentially a special type of confidentiality; but, unlike the professional duty of confidentiality required by the Solicitors Regulation Authority (SRA) and Bar Standards Board (BSB) – which can be overridden in certain circumstances – lawyers and their clients cannot be compelled to disclose material that is covered by LPP, even during the course of a police investigation or in court proceedings.

There are two types of LPP:

- legal advice privilege
- litigation privilege.

Definitions of each type of privilege are set out in detail below.

Legal advice privilege

Legal advice privilege applies to the information provided by a client to a lawyer in order to seek legal advice, and to the advice given by a lawyer to their client.

For example, a client may seek advice after having been involved in a road traffic incident in which someone was seriously injured. If the client failed to stop at the time of the accident they may believe the police to be looking for them. The instructions that the client provides to the lawyer may be useful evidence to the police. However, the communications between the lawyer and client are privileged; the police cannot compel the lawyer or the client to disclose what was said during their meetings.

This type of LPP only covers communications between a client and their lawyer, and will not therefore apply to conversations between a lawyer and a third party, such as a friend or family member who might attend with the client at a meeting. Extra care should be taken to explain these parameters to the client.

Legal advice privilege checklist

- **There must be a communication**: a letter, email or text message is a communication, and a note of a conversation is evidence of a communication so would also be covered by privilege. Certain documents generated as part of the advice sought or given, or that reveal the content of the advice sought or given, may also be privileged, such as a draft contract, which may include commentary from a lawyer, or may from its amendments betray the content of the advice given.

- **The communication must be confidential**: this generally is a question of fact; if the conversation is between the lawyer and client only, it will almost certainly be confidential. However, a presentation to a group of young people regarding their rights if they are stopped by the police would not be confidential advice, and therefore would not be privileged.

- **Between a client and a lawyer**: only the communications between the client and the lawyer acting in their professional capacity are privileged, not between the client and other people, or the lawyer and a third party, even if they are about the case or the advice.

- **Status of the adviser**: privilege attaches to advice given by a qualified lawyer. However, advice given by advisers who are not legally qualified is privileged so long as they are properly supervised by a lawyer acting in their professional capacity. It would therefore extend to students giving advice in a law clinic under the supervision of a qualified lawyer. The advice given will be that of the firm, department or clinic, rather than that of the individual themselves.

- **For the purpose of seeking or providing legal advice**: the content of the communication must relate to legal advice. General social chat or discussions regarding costs or fees between lawyers and clients is unlikely to be privileged.

Litigation privilege

The main difference between litigation privilege and legal advice privilege is that litigation privilege can also cover communications between a lawyer and a third party, such as a witness, and can also cover communications between the client and a third party. As with legal advice privilege, the protection afforded to these communications is absolute and disclosure cannot be compelled.

There is an important requirement for litigation privilege, which is that the dominant purpose of the communication must be for use in connection with actual or reasonably contemplated litigation. For example, if the client is considering taking action against their employer for unfair dismissal and their lawyer takes a statement from an ex-colleague, intending to rely upon it during the proceedings that will follow, the communications between the lawyer and the witness – and potentially the client and the witness – will be covered by litigation privilege.

As with legal advice privilege, litigation privilege applies to all types of communication.

Litigation privilege checklist

- **The requirements for confidentiality and the definition of communication** are the same as for advice privilege above.

- **Litigation must be in progress or reasonably in contemplation**: criminal proceedings (post-charge) are litigation, as is any matter before a court or tribunal. Reasonable contemplation that the police may investigate at a later stage is unlikely to amount to reasonable contemplation of litigation. The proceedings must also be adversarial, not investigative or inquisitorial; a public inquiry is therefore not litigation.

- **The communication must have been made for the dominant purpose of conducting that litigation**: a lawyer may communicate with a third party for a number of reasons. For example, they may seek a report from an expert in order to assess liability for an accident, and also to establish the cause and remediate any problems. The report will only be privileged if the dominant purpose in obtaining it was to obtain legal advice in relation to, or aid in the conduct of, the litigation.

Implications for practice

Given the definitions set out above, almost all files held by a lawyer will contain a mixture of confidential client information and privileged information. During the course of everyday practice there is no need to draw any distinction between the two, or make any special provision for privileged material. In all likelihood, the distinction will only become important if the issue of compelled disclosure to a third party arises.

If students wish to refer to cases in which they have provided advice as part of an academic assignment or reflective portfolio they should ensure that all details which could identify the client, including details that could lead to jigsaw identification, are removed.

For example, saying 'the client was the head teacher at a large local secondary school who required advice about separating from his partner' could lead to identification of the individual in question, so references to the client's profession and location should also be removed.

As long as confidentiality is maintained, referring to the nature of advice provided and the circumstances should not amount to a waiver of privilege.

Compelled disclosure

If a legitimate request is made by a third party to access a client's files, the first port of call is well established: the client's consent to disclose the material must be requested. For example, the police may seek access to a file in the event of a criminal investigation, or a local authority could seek access to a file in the event of care proceedings relating to vulnerable children.

If the client consents to the disclosure and this consent is evidenced in writing, then the disclosure can be made, but the client should be advised as to the potential implications of waiving privilege in relation to the requesting party. Once the disclosure is made, the material may be deemed to have lost confidentiality and therefore privilege could be deemed to have been waived in its entirety. The consequences will depend on the exact nature of the material, the request and the status of the client, and it would be wise to seek legal advice before agreeing to make any disclosure of this sort, regardless of the client's willingness to consent.

In the event that the client does not consent, but the request is in the form of a court order, or other statutory obligation, it will be necessary to notify the requesting party that the items required may contain material subject to LPP, and that disclosure can only be made in respect of the non-LPP material. There are a range of potential responses that may arise depending on the nature of this request and the party making it. It may be necessary to seek legal advice to ensure that the adviser is properly able to resist disclosure in order to protect the client's privilege, as failure to do so could have regulatory consequences.

Loss or waiver of privilege

A more routine practical consideration is the need to advise clients of the risks of waiver of privilege. It is often the case that a client will bring a friend or family member to a consultation with a lawyer. This arises in particular for children and vulnerable adults who may be accompanied by a parent, social worker or other professional involved in their care.

Regardless of the status or qualification held by the accompanying party, conversations with third parties are not covered by LPP (unless they can fit the criteria for claiming litigation privilege as set out above) and therefore what the third party does with the information is outside of the client's and lawyer's control. It is extremely important that the adviser explains this to the client, and offers the client the opportunity to consult the adviser without the third party present. If a client is insistent that they wish to seek or obtain legal advice in the presence of a third party then a careful note of their wishes, and their signed authority to do so, should be obtained and retained on their file.

If a client proceeds on this basis they will have waived privilege in respect of that third party, but they will not have waived privileged entirely. However, one risk is that if the third party was to become a party to the proceedings (such as a friend who then became a co-accused in a criminal case) they could, should it assist, rely on the privileged information as part of their case. Another, more common risk is that the third party shares the information more widely; and the privileged information then falls into the hands of an opposing party who can use it to their advantage.

Similarly, written communications to clients, such as letters and emails, ought to be marked 'confidential and subject to legal professional privilege', ideally in their subject line, to ensure that inadvertent access or waiver is avoided as far as possible.

In reality, issues relating to the law of privilege ought not to arise on a regular basis. It is, however, important to be aware that this is a particularly complex area of the law, and that deliberate or inadvertent waiver could have potentially serious implications for both the client and the lawyer. Compelled disclosure should always raise a red flag of suspicion and, if necessary, regulatory or legal advice should be sought before disclosing any potentially privileged material to a third party.

Part 2.18
Regulation of barristers and university law clinics

Frances Ridout

University law clinics and clinical legal education (CLE) initiatives can, and regularly are, run by a multitude of individuals. Where they employ qualified practitioners, they tend to be solicitors. However, this does not mean that barristers cannot or should not work in university law clinics, either as clinicians employed by the university, or as volunteers giving pro bono legal services outside their usual working day to clients and/or voluntarily supervising students in the provision of legal services. The Bar can provide an important and valuable perspective to the oversight, education and management of CLE and should not be overlooked as a valuable resource for clinics.

The Bar Standards Board (BSB) is responsible for the regulation of barristers and publishes a Handbook that sets out the standards for barristers and regulated BSB entities.[1] The BSB Handbook is regularly updated and available online. It is highly unusual for a university law clinic to be a regulated entity by the BSB, so this section will concentrate on the regulation of the individual barristers working within university law clinics – both in an employed and voluntary capacity.

The BSB is also responsible for the education and training of barristers. This section will not address the specific routes to qualifying as a barrister or indeed the changes from 1 April 2019 in the qualification process.[2] It will instead look at the regulation of already qualified barristers employed and volunteering within university law clinics.

Registered and practising barristers

After a Qualifying Law Degree (or post-graduate alternative) the training route for a barrister comprises of the following steps:

- the Bar Professional Training Course

---

1   Bar Standards Board Handbook (April 2019, 4th edn: updated in July 2019) <https://www.barstandardsboard.org.uk/media/1993311/bsb_handbook_version_4.1.pdf> accessed 16 July 2019.

2   Future Bar Training <https://www.barstandardsboard.org.uk/qualifying-as-a-barrister/future-requirements/> accessed on 16 July 2019.

- training requirements through an Inn of Court
- call to the Bar at an Inn of Court and becoming a non-practising barrister
- first six months of pupillage (non-practising)
- provisional authorisation to practise being issued
- second six months of pupillage (practising under supervision)
- full authorisation to practise at the end of the second six months of pupillage.

As set out above, barristers are officially bestowed with the title of 'barrister' when they are 'called to the Bar',[3] which typically happens at the end of a postgraduate course, the Bar Professional Training Course. This ceremony must take place before a practising certificate can be awarded at the end of the first six-month period of pupillage (work-based training). A full practising certificate cannot be awarded until the 12-month pupillage is completed.

For numerous reasons (not least the limited number of pupillages available), barristers tend to fall into one of two categories: practising barristers and non-practising or unregistered barristers. Those who are practising/registered are permitted to do reserved legal activity,[4] and are subject to safeguards such as training, insurance, stricter regulation by the BSB and potential routes of complaint by clients.

Once all the training requirements are completed (including the 12-month pupillage), a barrister must apply and pay for an annual practising certificate if they wish to continue to 'practise'.[5] If the certificate is awarded they will then be part of an online register of practising barristers that can be searched by the public.[6] This is known as 'Authorisation to Practice' and includes a practising certificate fee based on earnings.[7] When applying, there is an optional Bar representation fee that supports various welfare-related projects for barristers. A discount is available if someone is out of work for an extended period of time, for example due to maternity leave.

---

3   By one of four Inns of Court: Middle Temple, Inner Temple, Gray's Inn or Lincoln's Inn.

4   These are: the exercise of rights of audience, the conduct of litigation, reserved instrument activities, probate activities, notarial activities (although no barrister practising or unregistered may do this) and the administration of oaths. Further information on reserved activities can be found in **Part 2.1: Regulation of solicitors and university law clinics**.

5   By 31 March each year.

6   The Barristers' Register <https://www.barstandardsboard.org.uk/regulatory-requirements/the-barristers'-register/> accessed 16 July 2019.

7   The fees based on annual earnings as of 2019/20 are: £0–30,000 (£100); £30,001–60,000 (£246); £60,001–90,000 (£494); £90,001–150,000 (£899). For full details see <https://www.barstandardsboard.org.uk/regulatory-requirements/for-barristers/practising-certificate/201920-practising-certificate-fee-for-the-employed-bar/> accessed 16 July 2019.

Reserved legal activity can only be conducted by practising barristers and includes the exercise of rights of audience, the conduct of litigation,[8] reserved instrument activities, probate activities and the administration of oaths. Barristers employed full time in law clinics who either supervise students undertaking reserved legal activities[9] or provide these services themselves will need an employed (rather than self-employed) practising certificate. It is a criminal offence for a barrister to carry out reserved legal activity without a practising certificate.[10] A barrister may also face potential sanctions from the BSB (such as suspension).

There are many university law clinics that do not conduct any reserved legal activity but do undertake legal activity such as:

> (i) the provision of legal advice or assistance in connection with the application of the law or with any form of resolution of legal dispute; [and]
>
> (ii) the provision of representation in connection with any matter concerning the application of the law or any form of resolution of legal disputes.[11]

Where barristers employed by a clinic undertake legal activity but not reserved legal activity they are not required to hold a practising certificate, meaning they can be unregistered (see below for further information on unregistered barristers).

As part of the practising certificate renewal process a barrister will have to confirm that they have completed the required continuing professional development (CPD) (see later in this section),[12] and that they have a suitable level of insurance.[13] Self-employed barristers must have in place an individual insurance policy and confirm this is the case during the practising certificate renewal process. Barristers employed within clinics may be able to rely on the clinic's insurance policy, which does not need to be submitted to the BSB.

> Where you are working in an authorised (non-BSB) body, the rule does not require you to have your own insurance if you provide legal services only to your employer. If you supply legal services

---

8   With the correct qualification (see **Public access and litigation work** below).

9   Legal Services Act 2007 (LSA), s 12(1) <http://www.legislation.gov.uk/ukpga/2007/29/section/12> accessed 16 July 2019.

10   Ibid, s 14 <https://www.legislation.gov.uk/ukpga/2007/29/section/14> accessed 16 July 2019.

11   Ibid, s 12(3) <https://www.legislation.gov.uk/ukpga/2007/29/section/12> accessed 16 July 2019.

12   BSB Handbook (**note 1**), Part 4, Rule Q133 and Rule Q134 at p. 152.

13   Ibid, Part 2, Rule C76 at p. 55.

to other people (to the extent permitted by the Scope of Practice and Authorisation and Licensing Rules set out at Section S.B you should consider whether you need insurance yourself having regard to the arrangements made by your employer for ensuring against claims made in respect of your services. If your employer already has adequate insurance for this purpose, you need not take out any insurance on your own. You should ensure that your employer's policy covers you, for example, for any pro-bono work you may do.[14]

When registering a practising certificate, barristers are required to list the area of law they practise in. For many clinicians this may span a large range of work. The BSB have included a 'General' category which clinicians may find useful.

All barristers must inform the BSB as soon as reasonably practicable (in any event within 28 days) if anything in their practising certificate application changes.[15]

It is also important to note that where a clinic is reliant on 'outsourcing of work' to a third party (perhaps where volunteer supervisors supervise legal work done by students), the outsourcing does not alter a barrister's obligations to their client.[16] This includes when the legal advice is outsourced, or indeed any other aspect such as administration. For example, the barrister will still need to ensure that the Core Duties are being complied with, such as that the person doing the legal work is acting with honesty and integrity towards the client. If a volunteer barrister outsources a supervisory role to their pupil there is not the same obligation on the barrister, as their pupil is a registered individual who takes on their own obligations to the client.

Unregistered barristers (barristers who do not hold a practising certificate)

The term non-practising barrister is not used any more (it being thought to cause confusion with non-practising/unregistered barristers who are still working in a legal capacity, albeit not as a practising barrister).

All unregistered barristers are still considered to be part of the profession and are expected to conduct themselves in an appropriate manner. They continue

---

14 BSB Handbook (**note 1**), Part 2, Guidance C116 at p. 56.

15 Practising Certificate Rules, C5. Rule S69 at p. 110 <https://www.barstandardsboard.org.uk/media/1979519/practising_certificate_rules_jan_19.pdf> accessed 16 July 2019.

16 BSB Handbook (**note 1**), Part 2, Rule C86 at p. 58.

to be subject to the Core Duties and Conduct Rules.[17] It is very important that they do not mislead anyone about their status. It is a criminal offence for a barrister without a practising certificate to provide legal services that are reserved activities.[18]

There are also strict rules on not 'holding yourself out' to be a barrister unless you have a practising certificate.[19] This is particularly so in the situation where there is the supply of legal services to the public (even if not reserved legal activities).

Therefore, if there is a member of a clinic who is an unregistered barrister they would fall foul of this rule if they were to use the term 'barrister' to describe themselves in an email signature or on a business card in the course of their work in the clinic.[20] Using the term separately to the supply of legal services would not be a problem (for example, if a member of staff just held a teaching post). The most important point is that an unregistered barrister should not 'mislead'.[21]

Other unreserved legal services can be provided, including: sitting in a judicial (or similar) capacity; lecturing or teaching; editing law books and publications; media/press communications; giving advice free to a friend or relative; or acting as unpaid or honorary legal adviser to any charitable institution, and (if a barrister is a non-executive director of a company or a trustee) giving the benefit of experience to that organisation.

Immigration advice is not a reserved legal activity, but is regulated by the Office of the Immigration Services Commissioner (OISC). This means that unregistered barristers will need to be regulated by the OISC to provide advice in immigration. Practising barristers are exempt from such regulation. Please see the **Part 2.15** for further detail on providing immigration services.

Unregistered barristers are still subject to all ten of the Core Duties listed in the BSB Handbook.[22] In addition, as per Part 2, rule C1.2.b:

---

17   Ibid, Part 2, D4 from p. 80 (for the specific section on unregistered barristers).

18   LSA, s 12 <https://www.legislation.gov.uk/ukpga/2007/29/section/12> accessed 16 July 2019.

19   BSB, 'Unregistered barristers (barristers without practising certificates) – Supplying legal services and holding out' (November 2017), section 4 at p. 3
<https://www.barstandardsboard.org.uk/media/1787993/guidance_for_unregistered_barristers_barristers_without_practising_certificates__-_supplying_legal_services_and_holding_out__november_2017_.pdf> accessed 16 July 2019.

20   Ibid, at p. 3.

21   BSB Handbook (**note 1**), Part 2, Rule C19 at p. 36.

22   Ibid, Part 2, Rule C1.1 at p. 21.

Rules rC3.5, rC4, rC8, rC16, rC19 and rC64 to rC70 (and associated guidance to those rules) and the guidance on Core Duties also apply to unregistered barristers. If an unregistered barrister practises as a barrister as set out in rS9 then those rules which apply to practising barristers shall also apply.

In relation to legal services, unregistered barristers are still subject to Rules C144[23] and C145[24] regarding the notification of your status to clients. Part 2, D.4, Rule C144 of the BSB Handbook stipulates that if you are a non-registered barrister providing legal services to any inexperienced client then before doing so you must tell them a number of things. These include:

- that you are not acting as a barrister
- you are not subject to certain parts of the Code of Conduct
- the BSB will only consider complaints about you relating to the Core Duties
- you are not covered by professional indemnity insurance
- how a complaint can be made against you
- there is a risk that they will not be able to rely on legal professional privilege.

An unregistered barrister needs to obtain written confirmation from a client that this has been explained. There is a useful template provided by the BSB to notify clients of a barrister's non-registered status (so as to comply with Rule C144).[25]

However, if this legal advice is being provided by an unregistered barrister at a Legal Advice Centre (as described below) then Rule C144 does not apply.[26] Therefore, clinics who charge or operate in any type of commercial capacity need to be aware that there may be a duty to notify clients of services provided by any unregistered barrister, but other university law clinics are likely to be exempt from this requirement.

Universities/law clinics employing barristers

The majority of practising barristers are self-employed practitioners working from a set of chambers or similar organisation. However, an increasing number of barristers are now undertaking employed roles – including full- or part-time

23   Ibid, Part 2 at p. 80.
24   Ibid, Part 2 at p. 81.
25   BSB (note 19), p. 11.
26   BSB Handbook (note 1), Part 2, Rule D.4, rC145 at p. 81.

employment in universities and university law clinics. This trend is likely to continue.

A *Legal Advice Centre* is defined in the BSB Handbook[27] as:

> ... a centre operated by a charitable or similar non-commercial organisation at which legal services are habitually provided to members of the public without charge (or for a nominal charge) to the client and:

> which employs or has the services of one or more solicitors conducting work pursuant to rule 4.16 of the SRA Practice Framework Rules 2011; or

> which has been and remains designated by the Bar Standards Board as suitable for the employment or attendance of barristers subject to such conditions as may be imposed by the Bar Standards Board in relation to insurance or any other matter whatsoever.

At the time of writing, Rule 4.16 of the SRA Practice Framework Rules 2011 sets out four criteria that allow those employed by a law centre or advice service operated by charitable or similar non-commercial organisation to give advice to the public. These criteria are:

- the body is independent, without a funding agent having a majority representation in the management of the service
- any fees earned are paid to the service
- the organisation is not described as a law centre unless it is a member of the Law Centres Federation
- legal advice is covered by legal indemnity cover at the organisation reasonably equivalent to that required by the SRA.[28]

Therefore, if clinics wish to use the services of barristers (on a voluntary or employed basis), but do not have a solicitor working in the team (on a voluntary or employed basis), they will need to consult the BSB to seek permission for the organisation to be deemed suitable for attendance by barristers.

An employed practising barrister (working in a non-authorised body, such as a university) is able to provide advice through student law clinics, subject to the following limitation outlined in the Handbook.[29]

---

27 BSB Handbook (**note 1**), Part 6, Definition 111 at p. 246.

28 <https://www.sra.org.uk/solicitors/handbook/introAuthPrac/practising/> accessed 16 July 2019. Note that in November 2019 the SRA introduced new Standards and Regulations that have replaced the SRA Handbook and removed the Practice Framework Rules. It is likely that this BSB provision will change to reflect these developments.

29 BSB Handbook (**note 1**), Part 3, B7, Rule S39 at p. 102.

Subject to s. 15(4) of the Legal Services Act 2007,[30] you may only supply legal services to the following persons:

[...]

8. if you are employed by or at a Legal Advice Centre, clients of the Legal Advice Centre;

9. if you supply legal services free of charge, members of the public ...[31]

Legal services are defined in the Handbook as:

include[ing] legal advice representation and drafting or settling any statement of case witness statement affidavit or other legal document ...[32]

Volunteer barristers at university law clinics

Barristers may volunteer in the supervision of students and/or to give legal advice themselves at a university law clinic, provided the clinic meets the definition of a *Legal Advice Centre* as specified in the Handbook and outlined above.

You may supply legal services at a Legal Advice Centre on a voluntary or part time basis and, if you do so, you will be treated for the purposes of this Handbook as if you were employed by the Legal Advice Centre.[33]

There are three conditions to the rule outlined above.

- Barristers must not receive either directly or indirectly any fee or reward for the supply of any legal services to any client of the Legal Advice Centre (except where a salary is paid by the Legal Advice Centre).
- Barristers must ensure that any fees in respect of legal services supplied by them to any client of the Legal Advice Centre accrue and are paid to the Legal Advice Centre, or to the Access to Justice Foundation, or other such charity as prescribed by order made by the Lord Chancellor under s 194(8) of the LSA 2007.

---

30   'P does not carry on an activity ("the relevant activity") which is a reserved legal activity by virtue of E carrying it on in E's capacity as an employee of P, unless the provision of relevant services to the public or a section of the public (with or without a view to profit) is part of P's business.' (P= person employing and E = employee.)

31   BSB Handbook (**note 1**), Part 3, B7, Rule S39 at p. 102.

32   Ibid, Part 6, definition 113 at p. 246.

33   Ibid, Part 3, B9, Rule S41 at p. 104.

- Barristers must not have any financial interest in the Legal Advice Centre.[34]

For the most part these criteria will not be problematic for practising barristers who want to volunteer at student law clinics. They may therefore complete both reserved legal activity and other legal activity subject to the criteria above. If a clinic charges fees to the client, or does not have a solicitor conducting work at the clinic (or is exempt by the BSB from this requirement) then there may be some restrictions.

When barristers register for their practising certificates, they are asked to estimate how many days pro bono work they have completed in the last 12 months. The pop-up box defines 'pro bono' as:

> ... providing legal advice or representation to those within England & Wales for free to a person who cannot afford their fees or is ineligible for legal aid. International pro bono encompasses both legal assistance to those overseas and rule of law support.

There are no compulsory pro bono hours for barristers. That this criteria appears on the renewal form, as well as being a monitoring process, may be an indication that the BSB wants to encourage barristers to voluntarily participate in pro bono activities.

Core Duties

The Core Duties are the ten fundamental principles that underpin the framework for the regulation of barristers.[35] The Handbook also lists outcomes (what it aims to achieve), rules (mandatory processes to be followed) and guidance that assists in the interpretation of the rules and Core Duties. The content of the Handbook regulates all practising and non-practising barristers, and first six pupils.

The ten Core Duties are listed as follows (with Core Duty 1 overruling all others):

CD1   You must observe your duty to the court in the administration of justice.

CD2   You must act in the best interests of each client.

CD3   You must act with honesty, and with integrity.

CD4   You must maintain your independence.

CD5   You must not behave in a way which is likely to diminish

---

34   Ibid, Part 3, B9, Rule S42 at p. 104.

35   Ibid, Part 2, B at p. 22.

CD6   the trust and confidence which the public places in you or in the profession.

CD6   You must keep the affairs of each client confidential.

CD7   You must provide a competent standard of work and service to each client.

CD8   You must not discriminate unlawfully against any person.

CD9   You must be open and co-operative with your regulators.

CD10   You must take reasonable steps to manage your practice, or carry out your role within your practice, competently and in such a way as to achieve compliance with your legal and regulatory obligations.

These echo the spirit (and in some cases the drafting) of the Principles produced by the SRA.[36] Most do not cause any obvious conflicts with clinical work. But there are a few points of interest.

- A duty to act in the best interests of clients includes consideration of whether a client would be better served by using a service outside of a university law clinic, perhaps a firm with a legal aid contract or a service that is able to deliver advice more efficiently than a student law clinic. It is advisable to be aware of other local services, firms with legal aid contracts and the current threshold and areas of law falling within the scope of legal aid, and to signpost clients to these services where appropriate.

- Barristers working at university law clinics must be independent. This means prioritising independence above other pressures from universities or educational establishments. For example, if a case is more complex than a university law clinic can undertake, pressures from the university should not encourage a barrister to accept the case. Equally, pressures to involve students in cases should not mean that a client receives a less competent standard of care than they should have. Most clinicians will be subject in some form to the UK Professional Standards Framework as managed by the Higher Education Academy, which echoes many of the traits outlined above, in particular a commitment to professional values.[37]

36   SRA, Standards and Regulations (20 March 2019), Principles <https://www.sra.org.uk/sra/policy/future/resources.page#resources> accessed 23 July 2019 (previously contained in the SRA Handbook <https://www.sra.org.uk/solicitors/handbook/> accessed 16 July 2019.

37   *The UK Professional Standards Framework for teaching and supporting learning in higher education* (2011) <https://www.heacademy.ac.uk/system/files/downloads/UK%20

- Keeping the affairs of each client confidential seems simple. Fundamentally, the role of clinical legal education requires discussion of cases among student cohorts and using the cases as educational tools. Provided you have informed your client at the outset that this is the position and have not misled their understanding of how you will use their information and personal details, this is not a problem. It does, however, feed into the wider point of how important it is for clinics to have robust client engagement letters, and confidentiality policies and practices for students. Barristers will need to be mindful of the fact that students may have differing levels of commitment to confidentiality. If clinics are working with volunteer supervising lawyers or other organisations, they will need to consider whether professional codes of conduct already bind the third party to an appropriate level of confidentiality (e.g. solicitors under the SRA) or whether a separate confidentiality agreement is necessary.

- There is a requirement to provide a competent standard of work to clients. Most clinics provide highly competent work as there are so many checks and safeguards in their processes. However, this is a timely reminder that there is a regulatory duty on barristers to ensure that clients get a competent standard of service at all times.

- Not discriminating unlawfully against any person is a Core Duty. Clinics and universities are likely to have many policies in place to promote equality and diversity, but there are some issues that are specific to clinics. For example, many clinics have set criteria outlining the grounds they use to select clients. These are often advertised on clinic websites. Clinics need to be aware of potential conflicts of interest and have proper safeguards in place to deal with these from the outset, including re-directing clients to other services in a timely manner if appropriate.[38] For example, clinics must be mindful of the health and safety of their students and not expose them to cases or clients that are too complex or difficult. If a potential client has a severe mental health illness, then the competencies and safety of the students may need to be considered alongside the duty not to discriminate.

'Cab-rank' rule

The cab-rank rule is a rule designed to stop barristers picking and choosing the cases they want to do based on inappropriate (or even unlawful) criteria, such as the type of client, individual characteristics of the client, the likelihood of success of the case, the guilt or innocence of the client, the nature of the case, etc.

The three circumstances in which barristers must accept instructions (subject to more obvious safeguards like appropriate level of experience, seniority, field of practice, etc.) are where:

- a self-employed barrister is instructed by a professional client, e.g. a solicitor or other instructing body such as a local council
- a barrister who is an authorised individual is working within a BSB-regulated entity (which most clinics will not be)
- there is a BSB-regulated entity and the body/person instructing the case seeks the services of a named authorised individual (e.g. a named barrister) working for that entity.[39]

The majority of barristers working or volunteering at university law clinics will not fall into these categories as they are unlikely to be either self-employed or working for a BSB entity. In any event, the BSB Handbook does stipulate that the 'cab-rank' rule does not apply in certain situations. However, university law clinics do not seem to wholly fit within the scope of these exceptions. Exception 8 is the closest:

> you have not been offered a proper fee for your services (except that you shall not be entitled to refuse to accept instructions on this ground if you have not made or responded to any fee proposal within a reasonable time after receiving the instructions).[40]

However, if you are advertising yourself as a free law clinic, the requirement of a proper fee for services is not applicable.

Even if the cab-rank rule does not apply to a barrister working or volunteering for your clinic, the BSB Handbook is clear that there must be no discrimination in your approach to clients[41] and that you must not mislead clients in any way about the service you are offering. To uphold best practice it is advisable to ensure that the university law clinic has clear and precise guidance on the basis on which it accepts and refuses different cases.

Continuing professional development

When a registered barrister renews their practising certificate in March each year they will be asked to declare that they have completed the required

39   Ibid, Part 2, Rule C29 at p. 44.
40   Ibid, Part 2, Rule C30, at p. 45.
41   Ibid, Core Duty 8, Part 2, B at p. 22.

continuing professional development (CPD) for the previous year (ending in the preceding December). CPD is the profession's way of ensuring that barristers continue to meet the standards of the Professional Statement (knowledge and skills expected of a practising barrister).

From 1 January 2017, CPD changed, removing the need to undertake specified hours and accredited courses. Barristers are now required to continue to undertake CPD and keep a log, and must now create a CPD plan that includes objectives, activities and reflection on the overall process.[42] The New Practitioner Programme outlines the rules for barristers who are in the first three years of practice.[43] For those who have been practising over three years, the Established Practitioner Programme applies. This programme offers a wider range of activities and more discretion to the barrister.

There are four components to CPD compliance for barristers:

- **Reviewing**: setting learning objectives. These could be around legal knowledge and skills, advocacy, practice management (including management of employees, working environments and mental health concerns), working with clients and others (communicating, advising, understanding procedures), ethics professionalism and judgement (GDPR, conflicts of interest, confidentiality, money laundering, etc.).

- **Recording**: recording the activities that meet the specified learning objective. You should keep a written record of the CPD activities that you have undertaken over the past three years. The record should include: title, date, type of CPD activity, CPD provider, learning objectives, reflection, etc.). Barristers are encouraged to keep evidence of CPD activity.

- **Reflecting**: a written reflection which demonstrates how learning is embedded into regular practice. This should also be kept for three years.

- **Reporting**: declaring CPD when renewing your practising certificate. If checked[44] the BSB will review the relevance of the CPD activities and consider your experience in relation to the CPD you undertook in the previous year. For example, does this build on your CPD from the previous year? Is the CPD at the correct standard to assist your development?

The guidance[45] usefully gives a non-exhaustive list of activities that might

---

42 A template log can be found at <https://www.barstandardsboard.org.uk/regulatory-requirements/for-barristers/continuing-professional-development-from-1-january-2017/> accessed 16 July 2019.

43 Including nine hours of advocacy and three hours of ethics.

44 The BSB undertakes spot checks of barristers.

45 BSB, *Continuing professional development (CPD): Guidance for barristers*, para 37 at p. 19 <https://www.barstandardsboard.org.uk/media/1800835/cpd_guidance_for_barristers.pdf>

constitute CPD. These include: face-to-face training courses (including university ones), online courses, podcasts, conferences, reading or research, authorship or editing of published works (such as exam papers or consultations/law reform proposals, professional blogs, etc.), presenting at seminars, teaching relevant legal courses on LLBs, MMLs, GDL, LPC, BPTC, etc.

There is also a non-exhaustive list of things that do not count: updating social media or following others on social media, work or research 'completed as part of routine practice, including pro bono or volunteer legal case work'.[46]

Most clinicians will find that they can easily satisfy the CPD requirements through training and events on offer. Completing the written record might be the more onerous task. If barristers who teach in clinic are relying on teaching as part of their CPD, it is important to show how this is developing the barrister as a practitioner, rather than focusing on the effect of the teaching on the student.

Public access and litigation work

Public access is a term used to describe when a client can seek and receive the services of a barrister directly, rather than needing to go through a solicitor. To undertake public access work barristers must have a full practising certificate, have undertaken public access training and be registered as a public access practitioner.[47] Once completed, barristers may apply for an extension to their practising certificate to undertake litigation.[48] If a barrister has fewer than three years' qualification there are additional supervisory requirements.[49]

Litigation is when a lawyer instigates legal proceedings against another party and conducts the proceedings. This is different from conducting advocacy. Advocacy gives a voice to a particular client and champions their cause.[50] If a barrister wants to undertake litigation work, they must undertake additional training to apply for an extension to their practising certificate to conduct litigation.[51]

---

accessed 16 July 2019.

46   Ibid, para 38 at p. 19.

47   BSB Handbook (**note 1**), Part 2, D.2, Rule C119 at p. 74.

48   BSB, 'Authorisation to Conduct Litigation' <https://www.barstandardsboard.org.uk/regulatory-requirements/for-barristers/authorisation-to-conduct-litigation/> accessed 16 July 2019.

49   BSB Handbook (**note 1**), Part 2, D.2, Rule C121 at p. 74.

50   Definitions of reserved activities can be found at Schedule 2 of the LSA. They are also explored further in **Part 2.1: Regulation of solicitors and university law clinics**.

51   BSB Handbook (**note 1**), Part 3, C1, Rule S47 at p. 107.

There are three requirements in order for an application to conduct litigation to be granted. The barrister must:

- be over three years standing (or under if they are practising in a chambers or office where a specifically qualified person[52] is ready to guide them)
- have relevant administrative systems in place
- have procedural knowledge to enable them to conduct litigation competently.

Having a barrister who is able to undertake public access work and litigation may be an attractive option for student law clinics, especially if there are students interested in learning about the full case process, including trial strategy and advocacy. This would circumvent the need to ensure that there is a practising solicitor who is able to undertake litigation, or having to ask the client to self-represent for certain aspects of casework.

Complaints against registered and unregistered barristers

The BSB handles complaints about barristers. Unregistered barristers may still face a complaint and be investigated; barristers who do not hold practising certificates (including first six pupils) are permitted to provide free legal advice to clients of a legal advice centre, providing they do not hold themselves out as barristers and do not undertake or offer to undertake any reserved legal services.[53]

Clinicians who are barristers (especially those who are practising) are encouraged to look at the monthly regulatory updates to ensure that they do not miss an update to how they are regulated.[54]

Reporting misconduct

The BSB Handbook places a duty on barristers to report serious misconduct by others:

---

52   Ibid, Part 3, B2, Rule S22.3.a at p. 96.

53   BSB (**note 19**) at para 8.5.

54   As published on the BSB website <https://www.barstandardsboard.org.uk/regulatory-requirements/regulatory-update-2019/> accessed 16 July 2019.

Subject to your duty to keep the affairs of each client confidential and subject also to Rules rC67 and rC68, you must report to the Bar Standards Board if you have reasonable grounds to believe that there has been serious misconduct by a barrister or registered European lawyer, a BSB entity, manager of a BSB entity or an authorised (non-BSB) individual who is working as a manager or an employee of a BSB entity.[55]

It is not unusual for free clinics to come into contact with dissatisfied (and often vulnerable) clients who have previously received poor legal advice. As such it is important for barristers working in clinics to remember their duty to report serious misconduct.

It is also important to note that the BSB has the power to inspect any premises that a barrister works at and/or provides legal services from.[56]

Summary

- There is no requirement stipulating that a university law clinic should or should not employ a barrister.
- If there are employed barristers within university law clinics they may be registered or unregistered. This will determine the type of work they are able to undertake and the regulation that they are subject to.
- Registered or unregistered barristers are able to undertake voluntary work at university law clinics.

---

55   BSB Handbook (**note 1**), Part 2, Rule C66 at p. 49.

56   Ibid, Part 2, Rule C70 at p. 51.

Part 3
Assessment in clinics: Principles, practice and progress

Part 3
Assessment in clinics: Principles, practice and progress

Richard Grimes and Beverley Rizzotto

Introduction

Academics and students spend considerable amounts of their time undergoing various forms of assessment, be it revising for exams, marking scripts or otherwise producing evidence of performance and achievement.

Not all clinics are, of course, assessed.[1] This section, however, is aimed at those lecturers and institutions developing clinics that form part of the curriculum, or those delivering extra-curricular clinics, who want to maximise opportunities for learning and reflection even where participation in a clinic is not assessed summatively.

Given that assessment is time-consuming, resource-intensive and brings with it significant pressure – even stress – we need to be sure, as participants in the process, that what we are doing has an identifiable rationale and value.

Before looking at the detail of assessment in a clinical legal education (CLE) context, let us raise some fundamental questions:

- What do we mean by assessment?
- Why do we assess in any given circumstance?
- When is it appropriate to assess?
- In what form might and should assessment take place?

We will deal with each question in turn and then look at assessment in the clinic.

Finally, it is worth raising the point that those assessing students' performances in clinical work are sometimes subject to the criticism that the nature of assessment in this context is overly subjective and possibly inconsistent. Working in close proximity with clinic students does mean that the 'teacher', first, has a high degree of interaction with the student and, second, this regular contact understandably rubs off on the student. It raises the question of whose work is being assessed – the student's or the teacher's?

---

1   See **Part 1** for a discussion on the many different models of clinic.

Also, if students are working in teams or 'firms' within the clinic, they may be putting in – to a greater or lesser extent – collective effort. How is this taken into account in assessment?[2]

We acknowledge that these issues are problematic, but would ask:

- Why shouldn't a student benefit from the advice and guidance of their teacher?
- Isn't all assessment ultimately a subjective exercise, mitigated only by a careful and robust adherence to assessment regimes and a system of moderation and independent[3] review?

Ensuring that learning outcomes are specific and measurable and that assessment tools accurately capture the extent to which students achieve these outcomes should minimise any difficulties presented by experiential learning.

Meaning of assessment

In common parlance, *assessment* can be taken to mean a process of evaluation.[4] In universities and colleges this is normally considered to be focused on the measurement of student performance. We suggest – particularly in the context of assessment for learning (see below) – that assessment can be much more: incorporating reflection on the form and content of the curriculum, on teacher/learner perceptions of the educational process and on the efficacy of the module or programme, particularly if it involves a live client dimension.

We wish to add one other consideration encapsulated by the saying 'less can be more'. The temptation in many law schools is to teach as much as possible in what is often an overcrowded and content-driven curriculum. This stress on volume and substance is normally reflected in a raft of learning outcomes (LOs), each of which, if their inclusion is to be justified, needs to be capable of measurement in terms of the extent of student attainment.[5]

Careful consideration needs to be given to what the LOs cover, whether this is essential in the context of the wider curriculum and whether the assessment

---

2   For more on the existing literature exploring these issues, see Tribe Mkwebu's literature review in **Part 4**.

3   Often through external examining.

4   For a discussion on what *assessment* means in the light of traditional and more contemporary approaches to the subject, see P Griffin (ed), *Assessment for teaching* (Cambridge University Press, 2014).

5   Linking outcomes and assessment modes and enhanced learning is sometimes referred to as 'constructive alignment': see J Biggs, 'Enhancing teaching through constructive alignment' (1996) *Higher Education* 32(3), 347.

of each LO is, in fact, measurable, specifically related to the individual LO concerned, achievable given the context and timeframe and appropriate to the level of study.[6]

Further, assessment is often categorised as either summative or formative.[7] The former is concerned with a definitive statement of performance at a defined moment (such as an examination result), whereas the latter is intended to support the learning process, often being accompanied by detailed feedback.

While we recognise that the distinction between these types of assessment is clear and widely practised, there is no reason why assessment should not contain both summative and formative elements, and indeed every reason why this might be highly appropriate.[8] Unless the form of assessment is designed to endorse competence (the legal equivalent of the driving test) we suggest that every effort should be made to have a formative element in all assessment – whether or not the student is being summatively assessed. In other words, students' work should, ideally, be linked to feedback to enable the students to reflect on the quality of their efforts and how to improve in future.

The starting point in all assessment has to be with the LOs. What are the outcomes that the module/programme is designed to achieve? These may focus on doctrinal principles, on legal and related skills and/or on professional responsibility and wider ethical considerations.

The LOs may be a combination of knowledge, skills and values depending on desired outcomes. For example, on an undergraduate law degree the emphasis, understandably, could be focused on developing doctrinal understanding. On a vocational course undertaken by aspirant legal professionals, the focus may be more on skills and professional practice considerations. Some argue (and we agree) that ethical issues are pervasive to all legal study and a clinical (or other) module and degree programme must take this into account in setting relevant outcomes.[9]

6   One device for ensuring that outcomes are effectively linked to assessment is in the use of the management tool often referred to by the acronym SMART: specific, measurable, achievable, realistic and timely. See G Doran, 'There's a SMART way to write management's goals and objectives' (1981) *Management Review* 70(11), 35.

7   For a discussion of both summative and formative assessment and the relationship between them, see K Sambell, L McDowell and C Montgomery, *Assessment for learning in higher education* (Routledge, 2013), and in particular pp. 32–48.

8   For a further discussion of this, see R Grimes and J Gibbons, 'Assessing experiential learning – us, them and the others' (2016*) International Journal of Clinical Legal Education* 23(1), 107.

9   See in particular D Nicolson, *Teaching and learning legal ethics: What, how and why?*, in R Grimes, *Rethinking legal education under the civil and common law: A roadmap for constructive change* (Routledge, 2017).

Why we assess

There may be a wide range of externally imposed reasons for assessment, many of which appear – in practice at least – to relate to defined outputs, such as university performance league tables, inter-student rankings and assessing competency for the purpose of a professional qualification.

We suggest that for educators and students the first initial objective of assessment should be to support the educational process or, in other words, focusing on *assessment for learning*.[10] Second, albeit importantly and unavoidably, assessment can, and often must, serve additional purposes including the supply of evidence for a variety of purposes and, of course, the marking and grading of students.

When to assess

If assessment is to aid learning then the timing of assessment is highly significant. A very common assessment regime – whether it is of student performance or academic input – is for the evaluation to take place at the end of the period of relevant delivery. This might typically be at the end of the term or semester following the student's completion of the module in question.

We suggest that while it may be logical and/or required by university regulations to place the entire assessment requirement at the end of the relevant period of study, to do so misses learning and revision opportunities. Thought should therefore be given to introducing formative (and possibly summative) assessment components at different points of a programme so that you can monitor the progress of the student and the teacher/module/ programme and build on the lessons learnt. The term *continuous assessment* is sometimes used to describe this process, although we prefer the expression *regular and frequent assessment*, as this is more reflective of how assessment is actually delivered, especially in a clinical setting.

A model for evaluation that has staggered assessment – a mix of the formative and summative (together and, if necessary, separately) – offered at different points during a course of study has the potential to capture the maximum learning opportunity and the means by which to assess relative progress, be that the progress of the students or the teaching/module/programme.

Outlines for clinical modules are contained in **Part 5.4** of this Handbook as examples of how such an assessment regime might be designed and delivered.

---

10   For a practical but thorough guide to this, see P Black, C Harrison, C Lee, B Marshall and D Wiliam, *Assessment for learning: Putting it into practice* (Open University Press, 2004).

The models suggested are simply examples of what can be done and are intended to be neither prescriptive nor exhaustive.

What and how to assess: the options for the clinic

What to assess clearly depends on the overall programme aims and learning outcomes for specific modules. **Part 5.4** of this Handbook contains sample outline clinical modules. You will need to think about the assessment criteria (applicable regardless of the mode of assessment) and the grade descriptors against which the relative quality of student work can be judged. These descriptors may, of course, be institutionally set and required.

Given all of the above considerations, what are the assessment options for a clinical module?

In principle any of the following assessment methods could be used to assess either student and/or teacher/module/programme performance. The relative advantages and challenges associated with each are noted briefly. The options are not mutually exclusive and a combination of two or more may be appropriate depending on LOs set and university/regulator practices and requirements.

Let us first consider the assessment of a student's academic performance.

Written examination

This may be seen or unseen, open or closed (in terms of materials allowed to be used in the exam), take home or conducted in a university setting and under exam conditions. For assessing clinical work the written examination is perhaps the least appropriate, although it can be used to assess LOs, as for any other module. The reason for this is that the interactive and reflective nature of clinical legal education and the stress on assessment for learning opens up the opportunity for models of assessment that build on knowledge and understanding.

Written examinations also traditionally take place at the end of a module which, referring to the point made above, deprives the student of the chance to test their learning part-way through a module, and of the space to further develop their studies through involvement in the latter stages of the module.

That said, the attraction of the written examination is that it can be set, sat and marked in a relatively short-time and fits in with much of the rest of the taught programme. It is, of course, possible to introduce a formative element to examinations through the use of practice or mock exams, and the use of previous exam papers for the students to practise and receive feedback on.

Multiple choice tests (MCTs)

This means of assessment appears to be increasingly favoured at the vocational stage of legal education.[11] MCTs have a 'right' or preferred option in terms of answer. While this may be objectionable to many (on the basis that there is often no 'correct' answer), MCTs can be a very effective and resource-economical tool for assessment, particularly when delivered and assessed by computer and online. In the context of clinic they could, for example, be used as part of an induction programme to check whether a student understands fundamental principles, such as client confidentiality or conflicts of interest.

At York Law School a package was developed to assess such issues and used as a pass/fail hurdle – the student can only progress to real client work once they have shown a basic level of competence through selecting the 'right' answer. Under the York model a student can access the test online and take it as many times as they need to in order to pass.

There are, of course, limitations to this approach, but at the very least it requires the student to think about the outcome even if by a process of elimination.

Coursework

Again this traditional form of assessment used on many modules can be easily adapted for use in the clinic. This may consist of essay or problem questions in which the students address issues relevant to their clinical experience. Similar advantages and disadvantages to those identified above can be cited here.

As seen in the model module outlines contained in **Part 5.4**, selective use of essays – particularly when timed part-way through a module – can be a very effective assessment technique. Coursework can also be used to assess students who must carry out independent research and study as part of their degree. The clinic may be the setting for such research – for example, a detailed analysis of the law on disability discrimination and related practical considerations, arising out of a client case. Assessment of this activity may take the form of a research report or essay.[12]

---

11 For example, MCTs are currently on the Bar Professional Training Course and are likely to be part of the assessment regime for aspiring solicitors; see the proposals for the Solicitors Qualifying Examination, available at <https://www.sra.org.uk/home/hot-topics/Solicitors-Qualifying-Examination.page> accessed 23 August 2019.

12 This can extend to other forms of experiential and 'hands-on' learning, such as mooting and role play.

Presentations

As part of their clinical work, law clinic students are frequently called upon to present their findings and other aspects of their work. This may be done on an individual and/or group basis. Group presentations are, however, problematic in terms of assessment as the question arises of whose work is being assessed, although there are ways of addressing this.[13]

The presentations may be oral or written, may be submissions or reports, may make use of visual aids (such as posters) and/or may be e-technology based, including web postings, blogs and email exchanges. Of course, for anything that involves case-sensitive information students must ensure that client confidentiality is respected.

A presentation can also be used as part of students' clinical work to show the extent of their reflection on their engagement in their clinical work, and to consider the skills they have utilised during their time in the university or externally-based clinic.

Portfolios

One of the most common forms of assessment in clinics is the portfolio.[14] This device can be simply a collation of student work – for example, a collection of documents drafted by the student, materials they used (especially in their research) and entries maintained in a diary or journal detailing what they did in the clinic.

A portfolio may take on a strongly reflective nature where the student not only outlines what they did, but also goes on to set out how and why matters worked out as they did – and, importantly, what could have happened and what they learnt from that experience, particularly what they might do (or not do) next time in terms of improving performance. A portfolio might also include identifying shortcomings in the law and practice and how this might be reformed.

Assessment here might not only be based on the portfolio submission itself but can include the student's response to tutor feedback on the original submission.[15]

---

13   For an interesting discussion of the challenges and benefits of assessing group work, see D Williams, J Beard and J Rymer, 'Team projects: Achieving their full potential' (1991) *Journal of Marketing Education* 13, 45.

14   Using a medical setting, as is so often the case in academic writing on experiential learning, a very helpful discussion on the learning (and assessment) potential of portfolios can be found in M Jasper, 'The portfolio workbook as a strategy for student-centred nursing' (1995) *Nursing Education Today* 15, 446.

15   As practised, for example, in the law clinic at Strathclyde University.

Viva

Using an oral defence of a student's understanding is not common in law school assessment, at least not at undergraduate or Master's level. We suggest that this is an oversight and that the *viva voce* can be a very powerful and valuable assessment method. Personal experience suggests that individual *vivas* are somewhat intimidating for individual students and are time-consuming to conduct.[16] Rather a group *viva*, where all of those students who have worked on specific cases sit down with the examiners to discuss their experiences. Clearly the LOs need to be linked to this assessment technique and you need to think about the problems noted above and with assessing individual and group work.

One solution is to assess individual performances but to allow the 'conversation' to take place in a group setting. There are several advantages to this, including the logistical and the psychological, which are discussed in detail elsewhere.[17] The *viva* can avoid some of the problems caused by the tendency of students to 'retro-fit' evidence to suit assessment demands (deliberate or otherwise). It also allows the examiner to probe beyond initial responses and to more fully test the extent of a student's understanding. Such a face-to-face encounter also largely avoids the potential for plagiarism.

Casework performance

For obvious reasons, one tempting medium for assessment is the work that the student has actually done in the clinic, for example as evidenced by what appears on the client file. We suggest that while this may be an appropriate format for assessment it runs the danger of making the quality of what the student does in terms of casework the focus for assessment. Given that what is done for the client must be professionally competent, is it fair to set such a standard for the student who is not yet legally qualified? Of course, the clinic supervisor must ensure that the client receives a professionally acceptable service but it is not the student's responsibility to ensure this.

Unless the learning outcome requires demonstration of professional competence (for example, as a pre-qualification bar examination might) a student, for example at the undergraduate level, should be assessed on criteria other than competence. Again, depending on specific LOs, on an LLB degree credit should perhaps be given to students who reflect insightfully on their shortcomings rather than those who can draft a letter as a practising lawyer might. Being able to recognise what is good (or not so good) is an indicator of the depth of a student's understanding.

---

16   The use of the *viva* in clinical assessment is discussed in R Grimes and J Gibbons (**note 8**).
17   Ibid.

Finally, under this topic, assessing actual casework is also problematic in terms of equivalence. Assessing one student's casework will almost certainly and necessarily be different from another's, given the different case facts and legal issues involved in each case.[18]

Dissertation/thesis

In principle, there is nothing to prevent (and many reasons in favour) assessment of student performance by way of a substantial written submission on a topic relevant to the student's clinical studies.

For example, a student may have worked on a family law case where a client was seeking financial payments for herself and her children from her ex-husband. After advising the client the student may choose to consider the law on child support more generally and whether this is an area of law ripe for reform. The study may also involve a comparative element looking at the legal provision elsewhere, for example in the EU. If one of the LOs addresses law reform then submission of a dissertation on this subject may be an entirely valid form of assessment. Something less than a formal dissertation – a long essay or report – may also serve a similar purpose.

We can now consider assessment outside of the context of student performance.

Feedback from students

For several reasons the clinic lends itself to self-scrutiny. The interactive nature of clinical study and the reflective process it encourages and requires offers a unique opportunity for all participants – teachers, students and clients – to assess the value of what has taken place.

Post-case questionnaires for all concerned are a valuable way of eliciting such responses. Students might also be given clinic-experience opportunities to consider their perceptions and expectations, and use this to aid reflection during and after the clinical experience. An annual report can capture some of this feedback. **Part 5.5.4** contains an example of such a report from the University of Wolverhampton. Experience suggests that all concerned – staff, students and clients – greatly appreciate the work and value of the clinic.

Sample clinic experience questionnaires for students and clients are also contained in **Parts 5.4 and 5.5**.

---

18   For more on equivalence see **Part 2.8: Quality assurance: Higher education and clinical legal education**.

External feedback

Similarly, feedback can (and in the case of external examiners in UK universities, must) be sought from external sources. In particular, we recommend an advisory board. While having recommendatory powers only, such a body can be an invaluable source of help, especially if all relevant stakeholders are represented – including the local practising profession, the bar association/ law society, not for profit/NGO groups providing legal services, academic staff, students and relevant community groups. Not only will the board assist in the process of evaluation and the shaping of future strategy, but the involvement of the board will add credibility to and ensure a degree of ownership of the clinic in the wider world.

A forum for discussion

As we know well in the academic world, peer review is a frequently used and often highly valuable means of sharing views and enhancing the ultimate quality of what is produced, be that clinical practice or scholarship based on experiential learning.

To this end, clinic networks such as CLEO[19] in the UK and CLEA[20] in the USA are an invaluable and easily accessible conduit for the exchange of views and ideas, and for the sharing of proven good or 'best' practice. On the international stage, GAJE functions as a highly effective clinical network.[21]

Quality assurance is also promoted and to an extent guaranteed by the publication of articles and other manuscripts on clinical legal education. The *International Journal of Clinical Legal Education* (IJCLE) is one such outlet and has, in recent times, become a productive outlet for empirical and related research. The largely US-focused and based *Clinical Law Review* is also a very helpful source of relevant publications.

All of these fora promote and support critical evaluation and, in consequence, assessment of what is happening on the ground. More detail on CLE networks can be found in **Part 6** of this Handbook.

As a final comment under this section it should be noted that most, if not all, of the above methods of assessment can be delivered and assessed through electronic means, and increasingly both submission and assessment (and also feedback) can be carried out (and given) in e-format.

---

19   CLEO is the Clinical Legal Education Organisation (see the Glossary at **Part 6**).

20   The umbrella group for clinicians in the USA (which heavily influenced the formation of CLEO) is the Clinical Legal Education Association.

21   The Global Alliance for Justice Education (see the Glossary at **Part 6**).

Feedback

So far we have only mentioned feedback in passing. Reams have been published on the role and relevance of feedback, particularly since the rise and now prominence of the concept of student-centred learning.[22] In a clinical context many clinical faculty pride themselves on the quality of the teacher/student dynamic, particularly in terms of learning.

A law clinic readily lends itself to such a positive relationship. The extent of supervision required, the small group learning context and the high levels of motivation resulting from live client clinical work all contribute to a fertile feedback environment. In other modules feedback will principally be in the form of notations on student submissions (essays, in particular, and – but normally to a much lesser extent – examinations) but it is increasingly being given in e-format. The big difference in the clinic is that there is ample opportunity for feedback to be given to students, promptly and in detail, as client care (let alone good education) demands it.

Students can be given verbal and/or written feedback, to meet institutional requirements and address individuals' learning styles, both formally and informally. For example:

- a feedback pro forma developed as part of the client file that a student is assigned to
- an email that is then placed on the client file, serving also as an accurate and true record of feedback given as part of the supervisory process.

In using informal discussions as a means of providing feedback, students are encouraged to conduct self and peer assessment of their performances in the clinic – what they think they did well, what did not go to plan and what they need to improve on for the next time. This is best done relatively soon after the event, so the experience is fresh in the students' minds and they can then take the feedback away, reflect on it and develop their knowledge, skills and values for the next occasion.

Also, with much clinical work being conducted in small groups (hereafter referred to as student law firms (SLFs)), peer feedback is also an important component of the process, with feedback becoming an exchange of ideas and concepts, and one piece of feedback leading from and building on what has gone before. Regular meetings between student and case supervisor are also needed to ensure that the necessary discussions take place on case progress and – where issues of common interest arise that affect everyone in the

---

22   For an overview of this concept and a discussion of assessment in this context, see D Brandes and P Ginnis, *A guide to student-centred learning* (Simon and Schuster Education, 1986).

clinic, for example professional practice issues around client confidentiality or conflicts of interest – there need to be meetings of the whole clinic cohort. The regular SLF meetings are sometimes referred to as 'rounds', drawing on the medical analogy of the consultant and medical students touring wards to discuss symptoms, diagnoses and treatment.[23]

Even though it may not be formally recognised as such, all of this is feedback in the sense that it informs student understanding. Requiring students to assume responsibility for their cases (albeit closely supervised) encourages them to assume a degree of ownership and promotes learning, with teacher and learner interacting in a shared experiential context.

Finally, each institution is likely to have its own assessment/feedback rules and policies. This regime must be satisfied over and above the feedback described here, although the teacher should have ample evidence on which to base assessment and feedback given the interaction involved in clinic work.

Some have suggested, understandably, that the close relationship between clinical supervisor and student can skew the 'objectivity' of the assessment process. We put the word in inverted commas as it presupposes that any assessment process is objective. We suggest that this is not the case, unless perhaps the assessment format is a multiple choice question and there is a pre-defined 'right' answer with the marker sticking rigidly to matching the relevant answers. Anything short of this is relatively subjective. The safeguards against unacceptable degrees of bias include having clear and transparent LOs and assessment criteria, assessing in teams of two or more and having an internal and external moderation system.

Not all CLE activities are, however, formally assessed. Many clinics operate on an extra-curricular basis, as an opportunity for students to gain much-needed legal work experience and an exposure to the significance of pro bono services. In such circumstances, of course, there may be formative assessment – for example, detailed feedback on student performance – and the clinical work may have an impact on other aspects of the programme.

Practical legal skills are currently assessed as part of formal training on the way to becoming a barrister or solicitor. 'Practising' legal skills in a clinic should provide students with invaluable experience, the opportunity to engage in activities in a legal setting – such as conducting interviews or drafting correspondence – outside the confines of formal assessment, and to receive feedback on a one-to-one basis (perhaps in much more detail than they would do as part of their course). In turn, this should equip them better for a summative examination elsewhere on the degree or vocational course.

---

23   The use of 'rounds' is well discussed in S Bryant and E Milstein, 'Rounds: a "signature pedagogy" for clinical legal education' (2007) 14 *Clinical Law Review* 195.

Such opportunities will also allow the student to conduct self-assessment and increase the prospect of reflection prior to any formal examination, not to mention enhancing their CVs and giving them ammunition for use in future job interviews.

Future implications: informing the curriculum and the academic/professional regulators

The legal education world is in a state of flux. Some would say this is long overdue. The work and final report of the Legal Education Training Review (LETR)[24] set a new agenda, clearly highlighting diversity and access, ethics and professional responsibility and the value of work-based learning.

While many have criticised the report[25] its implications have been profound, with both the Solicitors Regulation Authority (SRA) and the Bar Standards Board – that respectively govern the admission of solicitors and barristers in England and Wales – actively involved at the time of writing in major reviews of the future of legal education and training. In the case of the SRA, the advent of the Solicitors Qualifying Examination (SQE) will remove the requirement for candidates to have completed a Qualifying Law Degree in order to be admitted as a solicitor.[26]

Strictly speaking, the remit of the LETR did not include undergraduate programmes but the quasi-regulatory body for the so-called academic stage of legal (and other) education – the Quality Assurance Agency (QAA) – has reached similar conclusions on the expected standards, achievements, qualities and aptitudes expected of a law graduate.[27]

It seems that in a post-LETR world there will be less specific regulation on law schools in terms of both content and form of the curriculum, but that what the universities and colleges produce will need to be outcome focused, although those outcomes will not be necessarily measured until after graduation, at

24   *Setting standards: The future of legal services education and training regulation in England and Wales*, (LETR, 2013) <https://www.letr.org.uk/wp-content/uploads/LETR-Report.pdf> accessed 14 July 2017.

25   For example, see A Sanders, 'Poor thinking, Poor outcome? The future of the law degree after the Legal and Education Training Review and the case for socio-legalism' in H Sommerland, S Harris-Short, S Vaughan and R Young (eds), *The futures of legal education and the legal profession* (Hart Publishing, 2015).

26   <https://www.sra.org.uk/home/hot-topics/Solicitors-Qualifying-Examination> accessed 23 August 2018.

27   QAA, Quality Assurance Agency for Higher Education in the form of the new *Benchmark Standard for Law* (2015) <https://www.qaa.ac.uk/docs/qaa/subject-benchmark-statements/subject-benchmark-statement-law.pdf?sfvrsn=b939c881_16> accessed 14 July 2017.

least in terms of routes to qualification as a legal professional.

One thing is certain: that, depending on LOs set and assessment regimes designed, clinics stand to tick many of the relevant boxes – be that an ability to apply doctrine and theory to practice, an understanding of the nature and extent of skills required to be a practising (and competent) lawyer and the meaning of being a legal professional and the role of a lawyer in modern society. As explored in **Part 2**, time spent in clinic may also form work experience that can be counted towards professional qualification.[28]

Thinking of assessment in its widest sense the clinic may also be highly relevant (and its impact measurable) in terms of contribution to legal service provision, recruitment and retention of students and the degree to which clinical experience enhances a student's employability. Having robust and demonstrable assessment may serve many purposes, from convincing an employer of a student's worth (having passed, for example, a programme in clinic that requires an understanding of professional practice rules), as well as leading to a credible and accepted form of qualification.

Assessment, therefore, is not to be regarded as an obstacle to be overcome or a commitment to be resourced: if taken in a constructive spirit, it is an important part of the legal education process.

---

28   See **Part 2.9: Clinical legal education as solicitor qualifying work experience**.

Part 4
Research on clinical legal education

Part 4
Research on clinical legal education: Unpacking the evidence

Tribe Mkwebu

Introduction

This section comprises of a literature review that identifies themes arising from research on clinical legal education. Existing evidence relating to clinical pedagogy is synthesised to create a web of knowledge. I also draw on insights gained from my doctoral research and my experience as a clinic supervisor within Northumbria Law School's Student Law Office.

An initial systematic literature search identified relevant factors that clinicians should take into consideration when planning to establish, develop and sustain clinical programmes. The results of this initial review led to the development of a map of the identified factors. The continued expansion of the global clinical movement and the need for clinic resources – such as a handbook on clinical legal education – necessitated a further review. The purpose here is to:

- determine the extent to which research has been undertaken in the field
- provide a rationale and justification for continued engagement, expansion and sustenance of all dimensions of research in the field
- assess what is known and outline what is not yet known.[1]

I have structured this section in terms of specific thematic examples gleaned from a review of clinical scholarship. While the establishment and sustainability of clinical programmes falls outside the purview of this section, you will find the consideration of certain influential factors in the establishment and sustainability of a clinic a common thread running through the section.

With that said, I briefly consider the importance of a clinical component within the legal education curriculum for the purposes of context. Reviewed clinical scholarship suggests that clinical programmes can help law students gain practical lawyering skills essential for legal practice, and at the same time provide a platform upon which members of the community can access free

---

1   Tribe Mkwebu, 'A systematic review of literature on clinical legal education: a tool for researchers in responding to an explosion of clinical scholarship' (2015) *International Journal of Clinical Legal Education* 22(3), 238–74.

legal advice.[2] The clinical scholarship I reviewed describes a global clinical movement in motion; sweeping across five continents and elucidating the increasingly important role that experiential learning plays in the education of students. In providing relevant information on the development of the global clinical movement, Bloch states the following:

> ... a momentum has begun to develop that has helped sustain existing clinical programs and ease the path toward institutionalizing clinical education. In other words, the global reach of clinical legal education has aided and facilitated its growth and acceptance.[3]

Encapsulated in this quotation is the fact that many, myself included, accept and firmly believe that the benefits of clinical legal education transcend borders. Many clinicians all over the world try to make legal academies and the legal profession more permeable to the advancement of social justice and the preparation of students for law practice. A great deal of clinical scholarship has focused on the importance of clinical legal education in educating future lawyers.

Clinicians, in the main, acknowledge the wisdom if not the necessity of integrating a clinical component within the mainstream legal education curriculum. Sometimes, it is easy to believe that we understand why clinics are formed and how they are developed, justifying our understanding by calling it common sense. Consequently, we end up not engaging in a systematic way[4] to understand our field and how the establishment and sustainability of clinical programmes can be influenced by a consideration of certain topical issues that I raise below.

The thematic literature review presented here is organised around five themes:

- First, universities have a responsibility to model curriculum requirements that should support a teaching and learning environment where our and our students' mental health and emotional wellbeing should be supported. With the wellbeing of students and staff located within the broader contemporary debates currently taking place within the sector, issues associated with wellbeing are addressed.

- Second, consideration of reflection and reflective practice within a clinical pedagogy is given to determine the extent to which this important

2   Tribe Mkwebu, 'Unpacking clinical scholarship: why clinics start and how they last' (2017) *Asian Journal of Legal Education* 4(1), 33–46.

3   Frank S Bloch (ed.), *The Global Clinical Movement: Educating Lawyers for Social Justice* (OUP 2011), xxiii.

4   Angela Boland, Gemma Gerry and Rumona Dickson (eds.), *Doing a Systematic Review: A Student's Guide* (SAGE Publications 2014).

element of clinical pedagogy can and should be situated within the cycle of experiential education. Considering the fact that reflection, by definition, is an intimately personal experience, the challenging nature of assessing reflection is highlighted and the question of whether or not reflection should be assessed within a clinic setting is addressed.

- Third, the scale at which the clinic nurtures a contemporary environment that is highly conducive to developing skills for clinic students is examined. The extent to which the clinic helps students to enhance their employability opportunities, while also providing them with practical, hands-on experience of the kind of activities they will be undertaking once they graduate and enter the professional world is reviewed.

- Fourth, the importance of clinic students being exposed to social justice is discerned and the inherent tension between the service and education missions of clinical legal education is discussed.

- Fifth, the extraordinary pervasiveness of regulation and the number of questions rising from the regulatory framework within a clinic setting is explored.

Emotional wellbeing of students and academic staff

Understanding and reacting to the emotional wellbeing of students and staff is a growing challenge, and one that needs greater consideration and exploration, as the evidence below shows.

Students may not find the transition to university life a straightforward one. For context, I refer to the contents of a House of Commons briefing paper,[5] the conclusions of a study undertaken in 2015 by a UK-based think tank,[6] the Institute for Public Policy Research, and the findings from a study by the Brain & Mind Research Institute (BMRI), University of Sydney.[7] I argue that the evidence gleaned from these studies should prompt universities, researchers and clinicians to dedicate a significant portion of their time – amid teaching commitments, research responsibilities and administration roles – to find out more about strategies to deal with emotional distress among students and staff. As highlighted below, such research insights would undoubtedly support detailed operational data from which the university and the law academy can

---

5   Carl Baker, Mental Health Statistics for England: Prevalence, Services and Funding, House of Commons Library (Briefing Number 6988, 25 April 2018).

6   Craig Thorley, 'Not by degrees: improving student mental health in the UK's universities, IPPR' (2017) <https://www.ippr.org/publications/not-by-degrees> (accessed 4 January 2019).

7   Norm Kelk, Georgina Luscombe, Sharon Medlow and Ian Hickie, *Courting the Blues: Attitudes Towards Depression in Australian Law Students and Lawyers*, BMRI Monograph 2009–1 (Sydney: Brain & Mind Research Institute 2009).

continually review and improve the emotional wellbeing and mental health needs operational processes and support services.

As a backdrop to the research to date on wellbeing, I explore certain factors in teaching and learning that I think might lead to decreased emotional wellbeing, resulting in mental health concerns such as stress, depression and anxiety. Next, I identify, review and appraise current research/evidence on this important topic, before proffering suggestions for further research on combating the scourge that mental health illness within higher education has become.

Students' wellbeing

In this section, I examine multileveled-intertwined interactions between a tutor and a student that can encourage imbalanced tutor-student power relations, leading to decreased emotional wellbeing of students, be it in other teaching and learning contexts or indeed within the clinic itself. I acknowledge that the relationship between a tutor and a student in a clinic is very different from other teaching and learning contexts. However, the case I make here is that the stricter the relations of social control or audit are in the law school, the more difficult it would be developing a pedagogy that incorporates a clinic element to it. This is more apparent in situations where a clinic supervisor's dominant function coincides with a clinic supervisee's most vulnerable and painful function.[8]

Based on my experience, my observations, interviews and document analysis from an empirical study I undertook as part of my PhD, arguably clinicians tend to bring out the best in students. However, where lines of deference are clearly marked students would certainly suffer more from the obstinacy and uncompromising attitude of a domineering supervisor, who may be convinced that they are right.

A relationship with clinic students can be stimulating and fruitful if students are allowed room for compromise and control of their casework, albeit under supervision. Clearly, the need for any clinic to deliver a service that meets the needs of clients will on occasions require a supervisor to intervene and take control. However, constantly picking through the shortcomings of clinic students is a recipe for distress.

Imbalanced tutor-student power relations without justification in terms of service delivery are a potential impediment to a clinic's creation and sustainability. It would be a fertile ground for emotional distress on the part of my students if I ignored their opinions on how they think they should conduct

---

8   Haider Ala Hamoudi, 'Toward a rule of law society in Iraq: introducing clinical legal education into Iraqi law schools' (2005) *Berkeley Journal of International Law* 23, 112–36.

their welfare benefits caseload. Being quite hierarchical in nature would create tension between students and staff and any attempts at trying to free up the processes required of universities to establish and sustain clinical programmes. Deference engenders a strong resistance and feelings of abhorrence on the part of students, potentially leading to emotional distress and mental health problems.[9]

In my welfare benefits law firms within the clinic, I make my students aware, from the beginning of their Student Law Office experience, that our clinic relationship will be based on an 'unwritten learning contract' over questions of content, pacing and their learning experiences. In addition, I make them appreciate the fact that their performance contributes to the clinic's overall ability to solve what is a difficult problem for a client. Little input from students regarding the nature of clinical legal education and the benefits such programmes bring to their legal training may cause feelings of isolation among students and may lead to emotional distress. As Lynn, a former clinic student at Northumbria, points out, 'clinical legal education is a partnership and allows us to learn from each other rather than the hierarchical approach that is typical of most learning'.[10] Lynn's quotation encapsulates one of the attributes a student working in a clinic must have, i.e. the ability and willingness to forge a student-supervisor partnership. From my own supervision I have observed that students who work in a clinic are generally enthusiastic about the experience: they are self-motivated and often highly committed to the work. Thus, such views held by students engaged in clinical programmes would help in reducing feelings of disenchantment.

Every student in the role of a legal representative must bear the practical responsibility for the resolution of their clients' cases, albeit under supervision, and such a responsibility can be overwhelming.[11] Thus, a clinic student who is invited into the relatively uncharted waters of taking instructions and giving advice must do so with a safety net of support structures, involving preliminary preparation and close supervision.[12] Students must not only be provided with the opportunity to take greater control of their future learning as they test for themselves the best ways to approach issues and problems in the cases they handle, but also be equipped to be resilient. In so doing, students will be able to develop a framework for how they would approach the need for ongoing

9   Serge A Martinez, 'Law clinics in Taiwan: can clinical legal education succeed in this civil law jurisdiction with an undergraduate legal system?' (2012) *National Taiwan University Law Review* 7, 343–84.

10   Mark Lynn, 'Student law office conference: a platform for student engagement with clinical legal education' (2005) *International Journal of Clinical Legal Education* 19, 69–73, at p. 73.

11   Jeff Giddings, 'Contemplating the future of clinical legal education' (2008) *Griffith Law Review* 17, 1–26.

12   Ibid.

learning and development while at the same time serving the best interests of the client.

Students' enthusiasm (or lack thereof) in clinic casework would normally have an impact on the development of clinical legal education.[13] Thus, input into clinic work,[14] the notion of practical experience,[15] disenchantment with the traditional method of teaching law,[16] (sometimes) lack of module credit, student autonomy[17] and inadequate time for client contact and work[18] have all been found to be influential in either promoting or impeding the creation and sustainability of clinical programmes – and may also add to emotional distress.

The enthusiasm of law students for taking clinical programmes may be negatively impacted if it is not offered as a credit-bearing module, the student–teacher ratio is too high and students are not involved in the selection of cases.[19] Students working at Rijeka Law Clinic lacked enthusiasm for the live client work carried out at the clinic because the clinical component was never incorporated into the grading scheme.[20] Students had less incentive to participate in a programme that would not contribute to the final grading of their law studies.

However, feelings of disenchantment caused by undertaking clinic work that has no credit bearing is not universal. Some students from non-credit-bearing clinic modules may find having undertaken such a module useful in gaining experience that they may find difficult to obtain outside of the clinic. Nicolson suggests that it is about providing opportunities for connecting the 'aspirations of law students with professional ideals (justice, service, fairness) ...' when students engage in clinic casework.[21]

---

13   Shelley AM Gavigan, 'Twenty-five years of dynamic tension: the Parkdale Community legal services experience' (1997) *Osgoode Hall Law Journal* 35, 443–74.

14   Lynn, 'Student law office conference' (**note 10**).

15   Lawrence Donnelly, 'Clinical legal education in Ireland: some transatlantic musings' (2010) *Phoenix Law Review* 4, 7–20.

16   Jason M Dolin, 'Opportunity lost: how law school disappoints law students, the public, and the legal profession (2007) *California Western Law Review* 44(1), 219–55.

17   Cath Sylvester, Elaine Hall and Jonny Hall, 'Problem based learning and clinical legal education: what can clinical legal educators learn from PBL?' (2004) *International Journal of Clinical Legal Education* 6, 39–63.

18   Bruce Lasky and MRK Prasad, 'The clinical movement in South East Asia and India: a comparative perspective and lessons to be learned', in Frank S Bloch (ed.), *The Global Clinical Movement: Educating Lawyers for Social Justice* (OUP 2011), 38–44.

19   Romulus Gidro and Veronica Rebreanu, 'Four years of a Romanian juridical clinic 1998–2002' (2005) *International Journal of Clinical Legal Education* 7, 49–57.

20   Steven Austermiller, 'ABA/CEELI's clinic programs in Croatia' (2003) *International Journal of Clinical Legal Education* 3, 58–66.

21   Donald Nicolson, 'Problematising competence in clinical legal education: what do we mean

Staff wellbeing

Having considered the emotional wellbeing of students, the mental health of clinic supervisors is equally important to explore too. From my own experience as a lecturer and a supervisor, positive affective states such as joy, happiness, vigour and positive mood contribute to improving my own emotional wellbeing. Staff members who have good levels of wellbeing would, generally, feel that life is in balance and that they can generally cope well with challenges. They feel motivated and engaged. They feel resilient and are able to deal effectively with daily troubles that come with academic life, as well as having the ability to bounce back from life's many challenges. When supervising students dealing with complex areas of law and juggling a multitude of different tasks and demands, it is important that we are given the right emotional and practical support so that we can in turn support and promote the emotional wellbeing of our students.

The view that clinical innovations within the broader traditional legal education curriculum are mere proxy for a money-generating scheme[22] is a typical constraint in the establishment and sustainability of a clinical pedagogy and can be frustrating for clinical staff. Schneider posits that the introduction of a new component into an existing curriculum normally creates tension within an educational establishment.[23] Krasnicka has noted that it is not always easy to establish a new clinical programme at a law school where it is difficult convincing authorities that clinical legal education is an excellent opportunity for the students to get a sense of law in practice.[24] Likewise, one of the impediments to the creation of the clinical programmes and the viability of existing ones is faculty inertia, in which some colleagues in the law academy may simply not have much interest and enthusiasm in a clinical pedagogy.[25] Resistance to clinical legal education by the traditional law faculty and the total control of the practice of law by the Bar Association Act 1972 in Jordan severely

---

by competence and how do we assess non-skill competences? Special issue: problematising assessment in clinical legal education' (2016) *International Journal of Clinical Legal Education* 23(1), 2.

22   Martha Skrodzka, Joy Chia and Eddie Bruce-Jones, 'The next step forward: the development of clinical legal education in Poland through a clinical pilot program in Bialystok' (2008) *Columbia Journal of East European Law* 2(1), 56–93.

23   Elizabeth Schneider, 'Political interference in law school clinical programs: reflections on outside interference and academic freedom' (1985) *Journal of College and University Law* 11(2), 179–214.

24   Isabela Krasnicka, 'Legal education and clinical legal education in Poland' (2008) *International Journal of Clinical Legal Education* 13, 47–55.

25   Peter Hoffman, 'Law schools and the changing face of practice' (2012) *New York Law School Law Review* 56(2), 203–32.

restricted the scope of clinical legal education in that jurisdiction.[26]

Thus, scepticism by university authorities and the traditional members of the academic staff, exacerbated by strong beliefs in the traditional lecture/seminar method as the single educational tool in the overall education of law students, can be an inhibiting and distressing factor when planning to set up a clinic. It has been suggested that the older the university is and the length of time one has taught at such an institution, the bigger the chance of having a faculty that sees clinical legal education as untested and unorthodox[27] and therefore justifying part of a faculty's resistance to change. The view that clinical programmes are new, untested, expensive[28] and merely money-generating projects would impede efforts to sustain clinical programmes that are already in existence – and efforts to foster new ones – and create fertile grounds for emotional distress among the clinical staff.

Writing about the law clinic at Seattle University, Mitchell states that:

> In the past years, this clinic was perceived as an appendage to the budget, and a very expensive appendage at that. Many saw the clinic as lacking intellectual rigour, smacking of the notion of a trade school, and serving as a refuge for the less academically capable who took the clinic in an effort to avoid the difficult courses.[29]

To some extent, the perception here is one that applies in particular to the United States of America where clinic often forms a key part of pre-qualification skills-based training. However, two complementary aims in clinical legal education are the promotion of professional skills training through the improvement of the quality of law practice, and the support of the law school involvement in the public service delivery in which the standards of professionalism and public responsibility are raised. According to Bloch:

> clinical programmes engage law students in experiential learning of various lawyering skills and values through active participation

---

26 Nisreen Mahasneh and Kimberly A Thomas, 'Learning from the unique and common challenges: clinical legal education in Jordan' (2012) *Berkeley Journal of Middle Eastern and Islamic Law* 5(1), 1–38.

27 Hamoudi, 'Toward a rule of law society in Iraq' (**note 8**). Referring to Iraq, Hamoudi noted that the dean of one of the targeted law schools and several faculty members expressed their belief that clinical legal education methodologies were untested and unorthodox and therefore not worthy of the university's high standards and expense.

28 Mutaz Qafisheh, 'The role of legal clinics in leading legal education: a model from the Middle East' (2012) *Legal Education Review* 22(1), 177–98.

29 John B Mitchell, 'And then suddenly Seattle University was on its way to a parallel, interactive curriculum' (1995) *Clinical Law Review* 2(1), 1–36, at p. 5.

in some type of public service activity, such as a legal aid clinic.[30]

It is therefore essential that the interpretation of the lawyering profession within a legal education curriculum pays critical attention to the interplay between theory and practice in educating future lawyers.[31]

Literature has revealed that sometimes the favourable opinions of the junior members of staff are not normally held in the same regard as those of their senior colleagues, particularly where legal academies are quite hierarchical in nature.[32] Efforts at preserving the status quo will stifle any efforts at establishing and expanding clinical programmes and may be a cause of distress among the reformists. The review demonstrates that where there is a strong belief among the more traditional academics in the traditional model of legal education – in which students learn in passive and non-interactive manner – the creation and sustainability of a clinical programme would be difficult and may lead to emotional distress on the part of clinicians.

Enthusiasm among the retained clinical staff is as important for the success and expansion of a clinical programme as getting sufficient resources and giving staff appropriate terms and conditions. Hiring conditions within an institution can easily extinguish the opportunity for enthusiasm, particularly when an inferior status is accorded to clinical staff.[33] The emotional wellbeing of clinic staff will be affected if they do not enjoy the same compensation, status, or job security as their *normal* law school or faculty academic colleagues.[34]

Law faculties may not have the necessary teaching staff to commit to the clinic on a full-time basis. Clinicians may still conduct their clinical programmes in addition to their regular teaching workload. This may lead to feelings of emotional distress and problems of mental health. Wilson has noted that clinical legal education requires smaller numbers of students per faculty member to provide quality supervision of student work and competent representation of the client.[35] Wilson's view suggests that due diligence in case handling requires

---

30   Frank S Bloch, 'The case for clinical scholarship' (2004) *International Journal of Clinical Legal Education* 4, 7–21, at p. 8.

31   Alexander Scherr, 'Lawyers and decisions: a model of practical judgement' (2002) *Villanova Law Review* 42(1), 161–279.

32   Hamoudi, 'Toward a rule of law society in Iraq' (**note 8**). Any attempts at trying to free up the processes required of universities to establish and/or sustain clinical programmes in a law school where deference to tradition is the norm would be met with a strong resistance and feelings of abhorrence, which might lead to emotional distress on the part of the clinician.

33   Dave Holness, 'Improving access to justice through compulsory student work at university law clinics' (2013) *Potchefstroom Electronic Law Journal* 16(4), 327–49.

34   Ibid., 335–36.

35   Richard J Wilson, 'Western Europe: last holdout in the world acceptance of clinical legal education' (2009) *German Law Journal* 10(6 and 7), 823–46.

close supervision of each student, from the initial attendance by a client, through the identification of the legal issues presented in the client's case, up to carrying out research to inform practical legal advice and representation.

Therefore, a low student-to-faculty ratio provides a good platform for these processes to be achieved successfully. It generates interest within the clinical faculty, allows a student to receive more individualised attention from their supervisor and inadvertently promotes performance and staff wellbeing. Conversely, a high student-to-faculty ratio caused by the large number of students entering law school classes may inhibit the successful establishment of clinical programmes within law schools.[36] Any efforts in creating a law clinic where there is already a high student–faculty ratio and an additional burden on the already substantially overtaxed members of the clinical faculty may be met with a lack of enthusiasm and a decrease in the emotional wellbeing of staff.

Lack of incentives, such as reduced teaching loads, for the appointed clinical staff has an impact on their enthusiasm[37] and may be a source of mental health problems for the clinician. The call for frequent publication and the requirement to have attained a PhD by a certain period should normally be viewed as one of the few methods available for every academic member of staff to demonstrate academic talent and boost opportunities for career progression. However, this can be problematic for certain members of the clinic team who may have just entered academia and have little or no training in undertaking research, and who may not have had the opportunity to publish work in academic journals while they were in legal practice. This may impact on the emotional wellbeing of clinicians and can cause substantial distress. Where an employer insists on members of the academic staff publishing articles in academic journals and attaining a PhD by a certain period, this may lead to anxiety and distress if clinicians interpret this as a *publish* or *perish*-type situation (though of course such requirements to *publish* and the resultant effect of *perishing* if the former is not accomplished are context-specific). However, even where such a requirement is rigidly enforced, there is absolutely no need for any clinician to feel isolated and to doubt their ability to write and publish.

Clinicians can still argue for a wider definition of scholarship than that of their traditional academic colleagues by pointing out in written articles not only the broad social and professional goals of their clinic but the richness and complexities of their clinical methodologies in addressing issues presented by their clinic clientele, legal education scholarship, legal practice, regulations, ethics, standards, law in context and indeed empirical legal research. If clinicians preoccupy themselves with trying to distinguish between writing about their

---

36   Hamoudi, 'Toward a rule of law society in Iraq' (**note 8**).

37   Margaret M Barry, 'Clinical legal education in the law university: goals and challenges' (2007) *International Journal of Clinical Legal Education* 7, 27–50.

clinical pedagogy and the traditional law teaching, and so do not publish, there is a likelihood that they would be overlooked at the time of promotion followed by an almost unavoidable second-class status, not only for them but also for their clinic. Thus, clinic supervisors are not and should not be solely limited to publish in traditional academic journals.

Researching the broad topic of wellbeing in clinical legal education without considering research in health and emotional wellbeing from the perspective of the wider general population, legal education and the legal profession risks running thin on evidence. This is due to the connectedness of the population, university students, education and the legal profession. I do not assume in this section that just because we have high levels of mental health problems generally in the UK and beyond, it therefore means that the high levels must be reflected in any clinic intake.[38] However, we must be mindful that the students we supervise in the clinic are drawn from the general population, as are the clinic supervisors. Clinic students are part of the wider university community, as are the clinic tutors. Clinic students are law students, first and foremost, whether or not they are or would be involved with the clinic. They may end up being in legal practice, just like some of their tutors who have been drawn into academia from the legal profession.

In their project, funded by the Legal Education Research Network (LERN), Wilson and Strevens assessed perceptions of wellbeing among law lecturers.[39] Their study provides evidence that changes in academia and the never-ending increasing expectations – of universities, of students and of academics – have an impact upon the perceptions of wellbeing in the study's respondents. In their study, a total of 185 UK academics completed a large survey, which included demographic questions such as age, academic qualifications and experience. Respondents also completed four questionnaires and a series of open-ended questions.[40]

Wilson and Strevens noted that:

> [a]lthough most reported depression, anxiety and stress levels within the normal range, those who reported high stress levels were significantly more likely to report lower hope scores and higher obstruction of values scores as well as significantly less environmental mastery and self-acceptance.[41]

---

38   Ann Macaskill, 'The mental health of university students in the United Kingdom' (2013) *British Journal of Guidance and Counselling* 41(4), 426–41

39   Clare Wilson and Caroline Strevens, 'Perceptions of psychological wellbeing in UK law academics' (2018) *The Law Teacher* 52(3), 335–49.

40   Ibid.

41   Ibid., 335.

They found that the issue of autonomy was profoundly important to law teachers. Further, they warned of the potential increase in levels of psychological distress and concluded by calling for further investigation into this very important aspect of academic practice. Wilson and Strevens also noted that:

> little research to date has explored the expectations of academic staff in dealing with stressed students or the implications for their own well-being

and argue that it is crucial for institutions to know exactly how staff understand and manage their own psychological wellbeing in order to support students and academics.[42]

Students undoubtedly worry about the future and such worry may extend to concerns about job prospects and the emotional requirements of the legal profession. It is therefore important to begin to think of the role of clinical legal education as a vehicle in the advancement of clinic students' understanding of the processes involved in managing feelings to fulfil the emotional requirements of the legal profession. A LERN-funded study at Sheffield Hallam University examined how clinical legal education influenced the clinic students' understanding of the legal profession in relation to emotional labour expectations.[43] Westaby's findings were that 'law clinics have had a profound effect on some of the participants' understandings of emotional labour expectations'.[44]

Currently, there is little empirical research on the emotional wellbeing of law students undertaking clinical legal education in the UK, and yet mental illness is a serious problem in the general population of the UK. According to a House of Commons briefing paper,[45] an estimated 1 in 6 people experienced a common mental disorder in England a week before the survey. Anxiety and depression were the most common disorders revealed by the study.[46]

This is worrisome and should indeed be a concern for any law academy and/or clinician running a law clinic or considering establishing a new one. According to the report, younger people, people living in deprived areas and people with

---

42   Ibid., 335.

43   Chalen Westaby, 'A qualitative study of the impact of law clinics on students' perceptions of emotional labour expectations' (2014) *The Law Teacher* 48(3), 248–80.

44   Ibid., 276.

45   Baker, Mental Health Statistics for England: Prevalence, Services and Funding (**note 5**). According to the report, the number entering treatment in 2016/17 stood at 281,000 women and 140,000 men in the 18–35 age groups. That level was almost matched by the next age group, 36–64, which had 283,000 women and 168,000 men. The total figure, which included figures for the under 18s and over 65s, indicates that around 1 million people received physiological therapy for a common mental disorder in just a single year.

46   Ibid.

disabilities are less likely than average to recover from their condition after psychological therapy. A million people were in contact with adult health services as of December 2017.[47] According to a study undertaken in 2015 by a UK-based think tank, the Institute for Public Policy Research, more than 15,395 UK domiciled first-year students disclosed a mental health condition.[48] The study also reported that this figure was nearly five times the number that was recorded in 2006. University student suicide deaths rose by 79 per cent during the same period, to a record 134 in 2015, and owing to mental health issues, university drop outs have also risen to record levels.[49]

As can be seen, psychological distress and mental health illness are, statistically, the greatest burden of disease in both adults and young people in England. The recent data from studies undertaken in the UK to look at the mental health of university students is broadly consistent with studies undertaken elsewhere. The report of the Brain & Mind Research Institute (BMRI), University of Sydney,[50] makes a significant contribution to the research, which I believe would lead to the development of ways that universities, law schools and clinicians can help to protect students from the development or exacerbation of depression and other mental illnesses.

The BMRI study disclosed that 35.4 per cent of the law students that the Institute surveyed were found to have high or very high distress levels, and almost 70 per cent had moderate to very high distress levels of 68.5 per cent. The report also disclosed that the law student distress proportions were higher than those of the other Australian law schools' students and higher than those of a sample of the general Australian population. In 2005, a survey of 5,000 students in all faculties at the University of New South Wales (UNSW) – to which 2,528 students responded – was carried out to investigate students' attitudes to their experience and expectations of their university education, so that teachers could respond effectively to those expectations.[51] When the data

---

47   Ibid.

48   Thorley, 'Not by degrees' (**note 6**).

49   Ibid. While it is less clear cut as to whether university students are under greater stress than their predecessors, the pressures bearing down on the student community in the UK include the burden of debt to pay annual tuition fees that surpass £9,000 a year. University students might be spending a great deal of time worrying about the uncertainty of their employment prospects upon graduation. Undoubtedly, social media now seems a natural part of our lives, if not the most important aspect of it, and sometimes such platforms may give the impression that everyone everywhere elsewhere is excelling in everything. This may have an effect on the emotional wellbeing of a clinic student who thinks they are not good enough compared to others within and outside the clinic.

50   Kelk et al, *Courting the Blues* (**note 7**).

51   Massimiliano Tani (ed.), *Report: On the Motivations, Expectations and Experiences of Students in Tertiary Education: Findings from a large survey carried out at the University of New South Wales* (2006) <https://www.academia.edu/27853897/On_the_motivations_expectations_and_experiences_of_students_in_tertiary_education_findings_from_a_large_survey_carried_out_at_The_University_of_New_South_Wales>.

was examined, the authors made startling observations:

> ... some unexpected differences between law students and other students appeared. Law students reported different reasons for their choice of course, seemed disproportionately concerned about their grades, less interested in team work, and had different ideas about employers' preferences for graduates when compared to students from other disciplines.[52]

What this quotation encapsulates is that law students may have certain personal characteristics including lack of autonomy and lack of social connectedness that might be indicators of depression or depressed thinking.[53] From my own experience and observations within a welfare benefits law firm within a clinic, some clinic students are perfectionists or tend towards perfectionism, coupled sometimes with relentless self-criticism; in my view their standards may be too high and are sometimes unrealistic. These characteristics may contribute to the psychological distress of law students and lawyers, leading to cases of mental illness.[54]

These figures and facts should therefore strongly inform any university, legal academy and/or clinician planning to establish a clinical programme and/or sustain an already existing one in developing policies pertaining to the emotional wellbeing and mental health needs of clinic students and supervisors.

Recently, calls have been made to revise the design of the legal education curriculum in England and Wales:

> to include programme learning outcomes that address the development of competencies of resilience and management of subjective wellbeing.[55]

Reform is long overdue. The time is nigh for legal education curriculum intervention. Likewise, as clinicians burdened with the tripartite role of teacher, consultant and counsellor within a clinic setting, clinic directors and supervisors need to reflect on their practice and be able to formulate, and vigorously incorporate within the clinical pedagogy, effective policies to deal with the mental health needs of students. Clinicians and clinic directors must not be blind to the fact that poor mental health and wellbeing can affect

---

52   Massimilliano Tani and Prue Vines, 'Law students' attitudes to education: pointers to depression in the legal academy and the profession?' (2009) *Legal Education Review* 19(1).

53   Michael Appleby and Judy Bourke, 'Promoting law student mental health literacy and wellbeing: a case study from The College of Law, Australia' (2014) *International Journal of Clinical Legal Education* 20, 461–98.

54   Paul Verkul, Terry Martin and Martin Seligman, 'Why lawyers are unhappy' (2005) *Deakin Law Review* 10(1), 49–66, at p. 54.

55   Caroline Strevens and Clare Wilson, 'Law student wellbeing in the UK: a call for curriculum intervention' (2016) *Journal of Commonwealth Law and Legal Education* 11(1), 44–56, at p. 44.

students' academic performance and their desire to remain in higher education. It is therefore important that clinicians develop an understanding of the emotional wellbeing of students and its relevance to a clinical pedagogy. The field will benefit from empirical studies that shape opportunities for students and enable them to develop resilience to stress, anxiety and similar barriers to achievement and success in higher education. Undertaking empirical research on emotional wellbeing should assist clinic students to develop their emotional competencies, which I hope would help students to not only survive in legal practice, but to also enjoy legal practice and achieve success.[56]

As can be seen, a sizeable literature has implicated several factors that might lead to decreased emotional wellbeing among students and staff in institutions of higher learning. Academic members of staff and university students are drawn from the general population. Clinicians are part of the academic staff within a university. Clinic students are part of the university community of students. My observations are that clinicians and non-clinicians are a surprisingly under-researched group. There is still need for further research that explores the expectations of academic staff in dealing with emotionally distressed students, and indeed research that examines the implications for the wellbeing of academic staff of dealing with stressed students. Currently, limited empirical data exist. More rigorous and theoretically informed research is needed before firm conclusions can be drawn on how best we can combat the scourge of decreased emotional wellbeing of students and staff, be it within the clinic or outside it.

Reflection and assessment

The benefits to clinic students of being given some opportunity to reflect on the work they do in the clinic is well documented in the field. The clinical scholarship I reviewed considers reflection to be an important ingredient of competence and good practice.

The role of reflection is frequently noted in the general education scholarship and in the empirical research that has been undertaken in areas which cover a wide range of professions, including medicine, nursing and psychology.[57]

---

56   Colin James, 'Seeing things as we are: emotional intelligence and clinical legal education' (2005) *International Journal of Clinical Legal Education* 8, 123–49.

57   Notable writers whose works assert that the emergence of reflective practice is part of a change that acknowledges the need for students to act and to think professionally as an integral part of learning throughout their courses of study, integrating theory and practice from the outset, include: Chris Argyris and Donald Schön, *Theory into Practice: Increasing Professional Effectiveness* (Jossey Bass 1974); David Boud, Rosemary Keogh and David Walker, *Reflection: Turning Experience into Learning* (Kogan Page 1985); Ronald M Epstein and Edward M Hundert, 'Defining and assessing

Reflection is viewed as an essential characteristic for professional competence such that students should be encouraged to improve their ability to be reflective in all aspects of their personal and professional lives.[58] Ogilvy and Czapanskiy have provided us with a rich bibliography of materials relating to reflection and a critique of clinical scholarship,[59] and in my view, Ogilvy's other edited book on reflection, among other topics, is an indispensable guide for clinicians.[60] The text focuses on reflection, with reflective lawyering taking centre stage within the text.

Encountering clients who really need help because of their less privileged positions in society can elicit different responses from clinic students.[61] Garcia-Añón has used his experience in clinical legal education in Spain as a backdrop to problematize assessment in clinical legal education.[62] Evans et al give an insightful narration of how reflection is an important element of clinical legal education.[63] Stuckey opines that reflection helps students learn how to learn from experience.[64] Milstein puts it more formally with his suggestion that the ultimate aim of clinical teaching is to develop reflective practitioners and lifelong learners.[65] Citing Stuckey,[66] Spencer posits that it is an accepted argument that reflection is an optimal experiential learning involving a circular sequence of experience, reflection, theory and practice.[67]

professional competence' (2002) *Journal of American Medical Association* 287, 226–35; Jennifer A Moon, *A Handbook of Reflective and Experiential Learning: Theory and Practice* (Routledge Farmer 2004); Donald Schön, *The Reflective Practitioner* (Jossey-Bass 1983); Donald Schön, *Educating the Reflective Practitioner* (Jossey-Bass 1987).

58   JP Sandy Ogilvy, 'The use of journals in legal education: a tool for reflection' (1996–7) *Clinical Law Review* 3, 55.

59   JP Sandy Ogilvy and Karen Czapanskiy, 'Clinical legal education: an annotated bibliography' Part IV (revised 2005) <http://center-hre.org/wp-content/uploads/2011/05/doc246-eng.pdf>.

60   JP Sandy Ogilvy, Leah Wortham and Lisa G Lerman (eds.), *Learning from Practice: A Professional Development Text for Legal Externs* (2nd edition.) (Thomson/West 2007).

61   Robert Rader, 'Confessions of guilt: a clinic student's reflections on representing indigent criminal defendants' (1994) *Clinical Law Review* 1, 299.

62   Jose Garcia-Añón, 'How do we assess in clinical legal education? A "reflection" about reflective learning' (2016) *International Journal of Clinical Legal Education* 23(1) 48–65.

63   Adrian Evans, Anna Cody, Anna Copeland, Jeff Giddings, Peter Joy, Mary Anne Noone and Simon Rice, *Australian Clinical Legal Education: Designing and Operating a Best Practice Clinical Program in an Australian Law School* (ANU Press 2017), available at <https://www.jstor.org/stable/j.ctt1q1crv4> (accessed February 2020).

64   Roy T. Stuckey et al, *Best Practices for Legal Education: A Vision and a Roadmap. Clinical Legal Education Association* (Clinical Legal Education Association 2007).

65   Elliot Milstein, 'Clinical legal education in the United States: in-house clinics, externships, and simulations' (2001) *Journal of Legal Education* 51(3), 375–80.

66   Roy T Stuckey, 'Teaching with a purpose: defining and achieving desired outcomes in clinical law courses' (2007–08) *Clinical Law Review* 13, 807.

67   Rachel Spencer, 'Holding up the mirror: a theoretical and practical analysis of the role of

Definition of *reflection*

As can be seen from the reviewed clinical scholarship, the emergence of reflection within the clinic is a part of a change that acknowledges the need for students and supervisors to think professionally at all times when dealing with clients. However, how the term *reflection* ought to be defined still poses some challenges in the field. Should there be a single, universally accepted definition? While considering what reflection is might seem too fundamental a question for this Handbook, I believe that examining how other scholars define reflection is an important start to appreciating the fact that reflection is complicated and challenging.

Since the definition of reflection is dependent upon the context in which the clinic is situated, there is a lack of consensus regarding the term's definition. As shall be seen below, others have even questioned whether reflection must be assessed at all.

So Dewey defines reflection as an:

> active, persistent and careful consideration of any belief or supposed form of knowledge in the light of the grounds that support it and the further conclusion to which it tends.[68]

While Boud et al define reflection as:

> a generic term for those intellectual and affective activities in which individuals engage to explore their experiences in order to lead to a new understanding and appreciation.[69]

And Moon describes reflection as:

> a form of mental processing with a purpose and/or anticipated outcome that is applied to relatively complex or unstructured ideas for which there is not an obvious solution.[70]

Although there is no single, universal definition of reflection, the term is generally accepted to mean an active, disciplined and deliberate strategy that is incorporated into the processes and activities of teaching and learning to help improve understanding. It is, therefore, much more than a review and justification of what has happened at the end of a period or activity.

---

reflection in clinical legal education' (2012) *International Journal of Clinical Legal Education* 18 181–216.

68   John Dewey, *How We Think: A Restatement of the Relation of Reflective Thinking to the Educative Process* (D.C. Heath & Co Publishers 1933), 9.

69   David Boud, Rosemary Keogh and David Walker, *Reflection: Turning Experience into Learning* (Kogan Page 1985), 19.

70   Moon, *A Handbook of Reflective and Experiential Learning* (**note 57**).

In dealing with live client welfare benefits casework within the Student Law Office at Northumbria University, I encourage my students to understand themselves as learners who must be concerned with the processes as well as the products of their learning, and to develop the awareness and strategies to be lifelong learners. In an endeavour to support independence and develop reflective practice skills among students, clinicians should seek to build on and develop students' knowledge and skills through a virtuous circle of reflection on practice involving research, evaluation and adaptation.

Reflective practice

Even though the concepts underlying reflective practice are much older,[71] the phrase *reflective practice* was originally minted by Schön to describe the ability to reflect on one's actions so as to engage in a process of continuous learning.[72] Schön's concepts – such as *reflection-on-action, reflection-for-action* and *reflection-in-action* – explain how professionals meet the challenges of their work with a kind of improvisation through practice.[73] Each of these reflective

---

71   Earlier in the 20th century, John Dewey was among the first to write about reflective practice with his exploration of experience, interaction and reflection (John Dewey, *How We Think*). Other researchers such as Kurt Lewin and Jean Piaget followed, and developed relevant theories of human learning and development. See Alice Y Kolb and David A Kolb, 'Learning styles and learning spaces: enhancing experiential learning in higher education' (2005) *Academy of Management Learning and Education* 4(2), 193–212.

72   Donald Schön, *The Reflective Practitioner: How Professionals Think in Action* (Basic Books 1983).

73   In order to effectively achieve the objectives of reflective practice in any area of practice and/ or pedagogy, several models and theories on reflective practice have been formulated to facilitate the process of reflection. Reflection has, over time, been divided into three main categories, namely reflection-on-action, reflection-for-action and reflection-in-action. Reflection-on-action refers to the retrospective contemplation of practice undertaken in order to uncover the knowledge used in practical situations, by analysing and interpreting the information recalled. Therefore, reflection-on-action would normally involve clinic students looking back after the event (such as, for example, an interview with a client) has occurred. It involves the turning of information into knowledge by use of a cognitive post mortem. It is also believed that this kind of reflection not only increases one's knowledge but also challenges the theories and concepts one holds. See Gillie Bolton, *Reflective Practice: Writing and Professional Development* (Paul Chapman Publishing 2001). Reflection-for-action involves the proactive use of these past reflections to inform future action (for instance, considering how new learnings from reflection upon an interaction with a live client might guide a clinic student or clinic supervisor's response to future encounters of a similar nature within a clinic setting). Reflection-in-action refers to thinking about what you are doing while you are doing it. It is typically stimulated by surprise, by something which puzzles the student or the clinician concerned (Jennifer Greenwood, 'Reflective practice: a critique of the work of Argyris & Schön' (1993) *Journal of Advanced Nursing* 27, 13–17). Accordingly, this gives the clinic student or clinic supervisor a chance to redesign what is being done while it is being done, and is therefore associated with making decisions and adjustments to our actions in a moment-to-moment fashion. See Donald Schön, *The Reflective Practitioner* (Basic Books 1983) and John Smyth, 'Developing and sustaining critical reflection in teacher education' (1989) *Journal of Teacher Education* 40(2), 2–9.

processes represents an important skill. Clinic students and their supervisors should develop the ability to engage in critical awareness of their experiences both during client casework and supervision.

Reflective practice involves paying critical attention to the practical values and theories by which everyday actions are informed through a reflectively examined practice that would ultimately lead to developmental insight,[74] itself an important aspect of clinical legal pedagogy. As such, a key rationale for reflective practice in a clinical setting is that experience alone involving the initial extraction of instructions from a client, undertaking practical legal research on the case and giving practical legal advice alone does not necessarily lead to students learning and being prepared for legal practice upon graduation.[75] Instead, a deliberate reflection on the experience of undertaking clinic casework, for example, would be essential.[76]

Reflecting on cases within a clinic setting advances the learning process of students. In the firms I supervise, I encourage my students undertaking casework in welfare benefits law to periodically step back to ponder the meaning – both to them and to their clients – of what has recently transpired in their immediate Student Law Office environment. By so doing, the students get involved in a process that illuminates what they and others have experienced, providing a basis for future action in the provision of services to indigent members of the community.

In particular, reflection privileges the process of inquiry in understanding the welfare benefits system in the UK, leading to an understanding of experience that the students might have overlooked in taking instructions from the client, in undertaking practical legal research and in providing practical legal advice. Viewed in this way, reflection is typically concerned with forms of experiential learning that 'seek(s) to inquire about the most fundamental assumptions and premises behind our practices'.[77] As such, clinicians must therefore create activities within their firms to promote reflection and evidence to support and inform this curricular intervention. Innovation must not just remain largely theoretical. Clinicians must be clear on which reflection approaches have impact in the supervision of clinic students.

---

74   Gillie Bolton, *Reflective Practice: Writing and Professional Development* (3rd edition) (SAGE Publications 2010 [2001]).

75   John J Loughran, 'Effective reflective practice: in search of meaning in learning about teaching' (2002) *Journal of Teacher Education* 53(1), 33–43.

76   Marilyn Cochran-Smith and Susan L Lytle, 'Relationships of knowledge and practice: teacher learning in communities' (1999) *Review of Research in Education* 24(1), 249–305.

77   Joseph A Raelin as cited in Steen Hoyrup & Bente Elkjaer, 'Reflection: taking it beyond the individual', in David Boud, Peter Cressey and Peter Docherty (eds.), *Productive Reflection at Work: Learning for Changing Organizations* (Routledge 2006), 36.

Models for reflection

Frameworks for reflection, commonly known as models or theories, encourage a structured process to guide the art of reflecting on an event, past or current. However, I do not intend to go into much detail here regarding reflective models, but suffice it to say that there is no single or right model. It is important to choose the model or a combination of models that best suits your local context and which will best assist clinic students to learn from their clinic experience. Often, it is appropriate to use one model of reflection as a basis, but use prompt questions from other models if they best fit a particular situation. Common reflection models I use in my clinic practice include, among others, those developed by Kolb,[78] by Gibbs,[79] by Driscoll[80] and by Moon.[81]

To evaluate the proposition by clinicians that reflection is an essential component of competence in clinical legal education, and to appraise the extent of research to date on this topic, I propose a review of certain reflective lawyering questions I believe to be pertinent in situating reflection in the cycle of experiential learning:

1. Do clinicians and clinic students engage in reflection when dealing with clinic casework?

2. What is the nature of the reflective thinking of the participating clinic students when engaged in clinic casework?

3. To what extent, if any, can reflection be developed within a clinic setting?

4. Would the development of reflection be impacted by the local context within which a clinical programme is situated?

5. What are the potential efficacious and inefficacious effects of promoting reflection within a clinical pedagogy?

78 David A Kolb, *Experiential Learning: Experience as the Source of Learning and Development* (Prentice Hall 1984). Kolb's Learning Cycle has four elements of a loop which you can start at any point, though normally you start with an experience.

79 In 1988, Graham Gibbs developed his reflective cycle based upon each stage of David A Kolb's 1984 experiential cycle (Graham Gibbs, *Learning by Doing: A Guide to Teaching and Learning Methods* (Further Education Unit, Oxford Polytechnic 1988)). He suggested how a full structured analysis of a situation could take place using prompt questions at each stage. It is probably the most cited model by healthcare professionals but does not contain the number or depth of prompt questions contained in some other model.

80 John Driscoll, 'Reflective practice for practise' (1994) *Senior Nurse* 13, 47–50. Terry Borton's three stem questions: 'What?', 'So What?' and 'Now What?' [Terry Borton, *Reach, Touch, and Teach* (1st edition) (McGraw-Hill 1970)] were developed by John Driscoll in 1994, 2000 and 2007. Driscoll matched the three questions to the stages of an experiential learning cycle, and added trigger questions that can be used to complete the cycle.

81 Moon, *A Handbook of Reflective and Experiential Learning* (**note 57**).

6.   To what extent, if any, can reflection be assessed?

For want of space, I do not intend to go into much detail regarding questions 1–5 before considering next the topical issue of assessing reflection. However, a forum for addressing such questions has been published and the reader is referred to this.[82]

Assessing reflection

Arguably, many examinations in traditional subjects in different faculties within a university will usually include the covert assessment of reflection upon other material because they assess critical thinking skills. For example, students undertaking History and English Literature examinations may be required to reflect upon sources of information and literary excerpts that sometimes involve the need to evaluate them in multiple respects to gauge the level of the students' reflective thinking.[83]

Reflective journals record self-reflection during the course of the semester. Recording reflective thinking in such a manner has a positive impact on students' overall metacognitive and other critical thinking skills.[84] When writing in their reflective journals, clinic students should record their reflections as they occur, or as soon as possible afterwards, when they have had them. This would help students avoid the pitfalls of relying on memory to retrieve information after the internal authentic reflective process has already happened, for example an interview they have had. This approach reduces a student's temptation to falsify information as a way of making up for the information that the mind no longer remembers and in the process threatening the purpose and cogency of having this type of assessment in the first place. Journals 'help the law student to maintain a sense of self throughout the process of professional socialization that takes place in law school'.[85]

Ledvinka[86] offers an insightful consideration of the educational theory underlying reflection in clinic, raises issues concerning assessment of reflection and considers whether it is appropriate to assess reflection at all; and if so, how

---

82   See Special Issue of *The Law Teacher*, September 2019.

83   The classic opener *'Compare and contrast …'* in some assessments at university usually requires students to reflect in this sense. Similarly, science assessments at higher institutions of learning may require students to reflect upon the outcomes of experiments when interpreting their scientific findings.

84   Jessica L Naber and Tami H Wyatt, 'The effect of reflective writing interventions on the critical thinking skills and dispositions of baccalaureate nursing students' (2014) *Nurse Education Today* 34(1), 67–72.

85   Ogilvy, 'The use of journals in legal education', 81 (**note 58**).

86   Georgina Ledvinka, 'Reflection and assessment in clinical legal education: do you see what I see?' (2006) *International Journal of Clinical Legal Education* 9, 29–56.

fair and how consistent that assessment might be given its inherently subjective nature. The author makes an argument that the reason clinicians assess reflection is to check the learning journey by students as they work with cases. Garcia-Añón[87] has postulated that reflective learning is a part of assessment in clinical pedagogy, albeit given formatively. Sylvester argues[88] that a one off/end of year nature of assessing reflection is not entirely a good way of evidencing reflective practice. Using Kolb's model of reflection as a backdrop and drawing from Moon's focus on the role of reflection in learning that embeds reflection into the learning process, Sylvester posits that:

> Whilst we might be able to assess the degree to which the student sees the links to the bigger picture it is considerably harder to draw from these isolated examples of reflection an approach to mental processing in line with the learning cycle.[89]

Further, Sylvester has drawn from Van der Vleuten's longitudinal utility model for assessment of medical training[90] in medicine and has suggested that 'competencies can be tracked at different levels'.[91] In focusing on the assessment of experiential learning in the context of students learning and supervisors teaching students through the use of hands-on, interactive and reflective methods, Grimes and Gibbons posit that the importance and value of assessment from both formative and summative perspective is desirable and requires a balance.[92] They suggest the use of group oral examinations to unpick reflection in the context of a clinic and to mitigate against the shortcomings of individual assessments. The global clinical movement is still a developing phenomenon whose theoretical frameworks are yet to be entrenched alongside theoretical frameworks in other established fields. In my view, I do not think that there is any harm in borrowing from existing frameworks despite differences in disciplines.

McNamara and Ruinard have advised that in designing new assessment frameworks in clinical legal education, clinicians must not shy away from drawing on concepts of assessment of professional competence in fields such as medicine and other health professional fields.[93] As can be seen, these

87   Garcia-Añón, 'How do we assess in clinical legal education?' (**note 62**).

88   Cath Sylvester, 'Through a glass darkly: assessment of a real client, compulsory clinic in an undergraduate law programme: problematising assessment in clinical legal education' (2016) *International Journal of Clinical Legal Education* 23, 32–47.

89   Ibid., 45.

90   Cess van der Vleuten and LWT Schuwirth, 'Assessing professional competence: from methods to programmes' (2005) *Medical Education* 39(3), 309–17.

91   Sylvester, 'Through a glass darkly' (**note 88**).

92   Richard Grimes and Jenny Gibbons, 'Assessing experiential learning – us, them, and the others' (2016) *International Journal of Clinical Legal Education* 23(1), 107–36.

93   Judith McNamara and Elizabeth Ruinard, 'Evaluation of collaborative assessment of work

papers on the assessment of reflection suggest that reflection can be assessed in a clinical pedagogy using different assessments methods. Different levels of reflection can be discerned. Further, there is a clear demonstration in the reviewed papers on reflection correlating with reflection in other fields in ways that are undoubtedly theoretically consistent.

Students do not only have to be assessed once at the end of their clinical module for reflective practice in authentic settings, and therefore some questions remain regarding whether what is being measured in the end of year reflective report is a valid indicator of reflective activity, when one considers that students benefit from formative assessment throughout their learning. Despite these concerns, failure to assess reflection and reflective thinking within a clinical pedagogy may imply to learners a lack of real value for this activity in the provision of legal services. While there is no doubt about the explosion of clinical scholarship dispersed across several concepts and aspects of a clinical pedagogy, the literature on reflection and reflective practice is still in development and largely theoretical. Nonetheless, the literature offers a useful insight on reflection and reflective practice and their usefulness in clinical legal education. There is, therefore, an obvious discernible implication for clinical practice that the global clinical movement members may consider when planning to establish and sustain clinical programmes within their legal academies.

Clinicians must be mindful of the fact that:

> the purpose of assessing reflection is to communicate the value of the ongoing process of assimilating new learning and to instil it as a lifelong approach to learning.[94]

However, there is dearth of scholarship that specifically addresses the particularly challenging nature of assessing reflection in clinic. Studies that clearly articulate how reflection should be assessed are needed in the field since reflection is meant to be an intimately personal experience. If this is so, does it mean that we have to alter the personal experience aspect of reflection by simply defining standards for assessment? Surely, doing so would make reflection a less personal and externally imposed process.

Assessment of reflection is either oral or in written form. This may well disadvantage clinic students who are less familiar with the conventional or context-specific linguistic expectations in a manner that has nothing to do with their being able to engross in reflection. This may well become a barrier. Native speakers who have autism, for example, may find it difficult to write a reflective piece of work if this is the way in which reflection is assessed. Where

---

integrated learning' (2016) *International Journal of Clinical Legal Education* 23, 5–31.

94   Sylvester, 'Through a glass darkly', 45 (**note 88**).

reflection is assessed orally, the same may be true of an international student who is a non-English language speaker or who comes from a background with less exposure to common academic linguistic forms.

Modelling reflection in practice

A closer look at the clinical scholarship reviewed in relation to the questions posed above suggests that we must not ignore the assertion that reflection, with all its firm utility and role in clinical pedagogy, may not be obvious to clinic students, particularly where there are challenges in the caseload they are running and managing. It is therefore incumbent upon clinic supervisors to model reflection in their own practice as lawyers. Modelled in this way, the reflective tasks or activities clinic supervisors set for their students should become more explicit and easy to complete.

Reflection must at all times be viewed not only as an individual experience but also as a collaborative exercise between a clinic student and a supervisor. For clinic supervisors, it is not enough to be able to read, learn and write, and incorporate the theoretical frameworks on reflection in their practice without reflecting on how well they are developing their students' skills to reflect. As with any other skills that law graduates must acquire during their legal training, clinic students may need a structure to guide the reflective activities they undertake during their time in the clinic, right at the beginning of their clinical practicum.

At the time when they are guided in developing their critical thinking and relational competencies, clinic students would certainly require feedback on both the content and the process of reflecting on the work they have done, as proffered by Schön in his three forms of reflective practice.[95] Where feedback is given on these forms of reflection, this process enables clinic students take stock of their strengths and weaknesses to determine how best to proceed in their learning. By so doing, clinicians and their students find themselves engaging with a process that opens up opportunities for self-appraisal and encouragement.

While clinical scholarship has suggested clinic supervisors must provide

---

95   In 1983, Schön distinguished among three forms of reflective practice. First, reflection-on-action involves making sense of an event that has already taken place for example, reflecting upon an event with a client after an interview has finished. Second, reflection-for-action involves the proactive use of these past reflections to inform future action (for instance, considering how new learnings from the reflection upon which a clinic student interacted with a clinic client might guide their response to future encounters of a similar nature either within a clinic setting or indeed in practice. Finally, reflection-in-action encompasses engagement in reflection as a relational event is unfolding, making decisions and adjustments to our actions in a moment-to-moment fashion. See note 73 for further discussion on this point.

structure, guidance and supervision to promote the role of reflective thinking in clinic, it is important too to consider the environment for teaching and learning about reflection. In some respect reflection and its utility can only be well understood if relative to a certain environment and context. If the culture and environment within which a clinical programme is located does not value and legitimize this important aspect of education, reflection and reflective practice will not feature in clinical pedagogy and clinic students will not experience the benefits of this innovative tool of learning. Subsequently, negative experiences or uncertainties within a clinical setting will continue unabated.

As shown in the clinical scholarship I reviewed, there has been a recent increase in interest in describing the competencies for effective lawyering within a clinical programme. One of the most important mechanisms for enabling the acquisitions of competencies in the provision of legal services is reflection and reflective practice, in tandem of course with clinic supervision. This particular section has taken the position – based on the review of the relevant scholarship on reflection and my own experiences – that the role of reflection in clinical programmes has indeed stimulated considerable articulation of reflective stories across the global clinical movement. To a certain extent, clinical scholarship on reflection provides the clinical movement with a direction for future work in research and legal practice. A key assumption underlying the literature on reflection is that it enhances competence and enhances the learning of clinic students.

Skills development and student employability

Helping students develop their essential professional skills while they are still at university is essential, and clinics should find ways of incorporating skills within their clinical programmes that enhance employability opportunities for students. The book by Kerrigan and Murray on clinical legal education[96] aims at enhancing the skills of interviewing, research, writing, drafting and advocacy. The chapter on interviewing skills is very insightful as it gives generic advice on how to conduct an interview, before focusing on the specific types of interview that a clinic student should be familiar with and use. Examples include the use of open-ended and closed questions.

The authors go further into exploring the nature of empathy and how this should be developed. According to Kerrigan and Murray,[97] related to the notion of skills development in clinical pedagogy is the equally important acquisition

---

96   Kevin Kerrigan and Victoria Murray (eds.), *A Student Guide to Clinical Legal Education and Pro Bono* (1st edition) (Palgrave Macmillan 2011).

97   Ibid.

of practical knowledge by the clinic student that is attractive to employers and helpful for any workplace. The necessity for and the benefits of a pedagogy that bridges the gap between legal education and professional skills are well documented.[98]

Critical to graduate employability for students is the development of the mind, behaviours, work ethic and professional identity through experiential learning.[99] A widely accepted definition of graduate employability, and the one I think we should promote in clinical pedagogy, is the achievement of:

> the skills, understandings and personal attributes that make an individual more likely to secure employment and be successful in their chosen occupations to the benefit of themselves, the workforce, the community and the economy.[100]

Using the Graduate Employability Indicators prepared by Oliver et al[101] as a theoretical grounding to gather and triangulate the perceptions of clinic graduates, Cantatore undertook a study with a group of law students before and after their clinical programme experience.[102] The findings were that a legal education that has a clinical component within it presents considerable learning opportunities for students and enables them to acquire skills. Alexander and Boothby recently undertook a qualitative study that sought to find:

> insights into the role clinical legal education can play in preparing students for their transition from university into graduate careers.[103]

98   Richard Grimes, 'Legal skills and clinical legal education' (1995) *Web Journal of Current Legal Issues* 3; Judith Dickson, 'Clinical legal education in the 21st century: still educating for service?' (2000) *International Journal of Clinical Legal Education* 1, 33–46; Philip F Iya, 'Fighting Africa's poverty and ignorance through clinical legal education: shared experiences with new initiatives for the 21st century' (2000) *International Journal of Clinical Legal Education* 1, 13–32; David A Binder and Paul B Bergman, 'Taking lawyering skills training seriously' (2003) *Clinical Law Review* 10, 301; Robert MacCrate, 'Yesterday, today and tomorrow: building the continuum of legal education and professional development' (2004) *Clinical Law Review* 10(2); James Marson, Adam Wilson and Mark Van Hoorebeek, 'The Necessity of clinical legal education in university law schools: A UK perspective' (2005) *International Journal of Clinical Legal Education* 7, 29–43; Evans et al, *Australian Clinical Legal Education.*

99   Mantz Yorke and Peter T Knight, *Embedding Employability into the Curriculum.* Learning & Employability Series 1 (The Higher Education Academy 2006).

100 Ibid., 8.

101 Beverley Oliver, Barbara Whelan, Lynne Hunt, Sara Hammer, Sandra Jones, Amanda Pearce and Fiona Henderson, *Introducing the Graduate Employability Indicators* (Australian Learning and Teaching Council 2011).

102 Francina Cantatore, 'The impact of pro bono law clinics on employability and work readiness in law students' (2018) *International Journal of Clinical Legal Education* 25(1), 147–72.

103 Jill Alexander and Carol Boothby, 'Stakeholder perceptions of clinical legal education within an employability context' (2018) *International Journal of Clinical Legal Education* 25(3), 53–84.

Their findings were that at the point of recruitment, having undertaken clinic modules at the university does not appear to have an automatic advantage in securing employment for clinic students.

Such research findings demonstrate that even though the automatic ticket to employment may not be readily available to a clinic student entering the employment market, clinical programmes do still play an important role in the provision of legal services to indigent members of the community. Many clinicians believe that the clinic experience is a source of confidence for clinic students who have at least spent a semester or a year bridging the academic skill of thinking like a lawyer to the professional skill of lawyering.

However, there are evidential gaps in assessing the exact impact of a clinical pedagogy on the skills development and employability of clinic students. There is particular need for more robust evidence involving not only students but also other different stakeholders, such as employers and clinicians, using the guidelines for conducting graduate employability research set by Oliver et al.[104]

Currently, there is very little rigorous research on the impact that clinic experience has on students when they settle into their newly found real-life jobs after graduation. This is particularly the case in post-clinic experience where more knowledge is needed about whether employability skills gained through a clinical programme assist the graduates to keep and hold their jobs. If we are truly committed to supporting our institutions in revaluating and reforming teaching and learning outcomes, and in implementing clinical programmes that promote skills development and graduate employability opportunities for our students, we need to continue enhancing our research to ensure that these evidence gaps are filled.

Social justice mission

There has been an increasing interest and attention paid to two specific missions of clinical legal education – social justice and education – for the simple reason that there is an important connection between legal education, public service and social justice.

Much of the clinical scholarship I reviewed propagates that in addition to bridging the gap between legal education and lawyering skills, the exposure to a social justice mission limb of a clinical pedagogy gives students an intellectual footing and a long-lasting engagement with social justice.[105] It is therefore no

104 Oliver et al, *Introducing the Graduate Employability Indicators* (**note 101**).

105 Rose Voyvodic and Mary Medcalf, 'Advancing social justice through an interdisciplinary approach to clinical legal education: the case of Legal Assistance of Windsor' (2004) *Washington University Journal of Law and Policy* 14, 101–32.

surprise to see clinical scholarship propounding that clinical programmes:

> meld legal theory with lawyering skills, and students learn lawyering values by providing legal assistance to clients who would otherwise lack access to justice.[106]

In addition to the increased awareness of these two objectives, the tension between them has become increasingly visible, which has become the subject of intense scrutiny and debate among clinicians and scholars. The ongoing discussions on the education and social mission goals of clinical pedagogy may be of interest to those planning to set up clinical programmes or those involved in the sustenance of programmes that already exist. The reviewed literature provides evidence of the importance of striking a balance between these two objectives.

There is an argument that the 'service expectations that will inevitably be linked to external funding need to be balanced with maintaining the focus on student learning'.[107] This means that when providing an intense and productive clinical experience for students to serve there is also a need to focus on their education. However, sentiments to the effect that through a clinical pedagogy law students learn on the backs of the poor, sum up perpetual tensions between conflicting clinical legal education objectives related to student learning, community service and the legal professional responsibilities of supervisors.[108]

Experiential learning provides students with an opportunity to learn how to question and practise law within a broader social justice framework. However, it is also apparent from literature reviewed that if the opportunity to place law in its social milieu were not balanced with the educational needs of students, setting up or sustaining clinics would undoubtedly be faced with some challenges. Some clinicians have warned of students' interests in clinical pedagogy fading if the mission and ideology of the law school's clinical programmes remain entrenched in the concept of social justice lawyering 'that is heavily dependent on rights-based strategies and traditional, hierarchical conceptions of the lawyer-client relationship'.[109] The implication of this approach for law clinics, as noted by Macfarlane, is that the greater our emphasis on the social justice mission of clinical programmes, the less emphasis is on the education objective, and hence the greater the impediment such an approach would impose on efforts to convince institution leaders to create clinical programmes.

---

106 Margaret M Barry, Jon C Dubin and Peter A Joy, 'Clinical education for this millennium: the third wave' (2000) *Clinical Law Review* 7(1), 1–75. 14.

107 Giddings, 'Contemplating the future of clinical legal education' (**note 11**), 8.

108 Gavigan,'Twenty-five years of dynamic tension' (**note 13**).

109 Julie MacFarlane, 'Bringing the clinic into the 21st century' (2009) *Windsor Yearbook of Access to Justice* 27(1), 35.

A recent study by Nicolson shows that one of the longest and most persistent traditions in clinical legal education is seeing the creation of an array of social justice clinicians as a principal pedagogical goal.[110] This is not surprising. Bloch and other contributing authors have made a rallying call for the global clinical movement to educate lawyers for social justice through the inculcation of social skills and ethos among the students.[111] The question is, whether social justice values can be taught through clinical legal education.[112] McKeown has sought to take exception to some of the beliefs in the field about ethical discussions and challenged the suppositions about social justice; he argues that:

> social justice has a plurality of meaning and that rather than teaching a set of values, law schools can provide the framework in which students can themselves (de)construct values.[113]

McKeown and Hall acknowledge that '[t]here is a natural symbiotic relationship between clinical legal education, social justice and public service'[114] although it should be added perhaps that a social justice or public service objective is not a necessary requirement for a clinical programme. They also accept that there is an indigent community and groups of marginalised and unrepresented individuals who may be desperately in need of legal assistance but may be unable to afford to pay for such services, and would of course turn to the clinic for free advice and representation.

However, McKeown and Hall also caution against taking an idealistic perspective as to the relationship between clinical legal education, social justice and public service. They warn against clinicians imposing their own set beliefs on clinic students and argue that imposing beliefs 'may be particularly dangerous in assessed legal clinics where students believe that they must tell their clinical supervisor what they believe they want to hear'.[115]

For those planning to set up law clinics it is important to acknowledge the inherent conflict between clinical legal education's main objectives of providing quality education to students and the provision of a legal service. Given the inherent tension between the two missions of a clinical programme, failing to

---

110 Donald Nicolson, 'Our roots began in (South) Africa: modelling law clinics to maximize social justice ends' (2016) *International Journal of Clinical Legal Education* 23(3), 87–136.

111 Bloch, *The global clinical movement* (**note 3**).

112 Paul McKeown, 'Can social justice values be taught through clinical legal education?', in Chris Ashford and Paul McKeown (eds.), *Social Justice and Legal Education* (Cambridge Scholars Publishing 2018), 84–110.

113 Ibid., 3.

114 Paul McKeown and Elaine Hall, 'If we could instill social justice values through clinical legal education, should we?' (2018) *Journal of International and Comparative Law* 5(1), 143–80, at p. 180.

115 Ibid., 180.

balance them may be an obstacle to the establishment and sustainability of a clinical programme, particularly where there 'is the pressure on law school clinics to maximise the numbers of indigent persons they represent'.[116] The problem seems to be more prevalent in certain parts of the world. Maisel has noted that all legal clinics that provide free representation to indigent persons face serious caseload pressures, but this issue is magnified in developing countries, such as South Africa, where most of the population live in abject poverty.

Although the reviewed clinical scholarship has identified an inherent tension between the two missions of clinical legal education, there have been very few empirical studies to date on this important topic. There is a need for a realist synthesis of our clinical programmes to answer two research questions I think are pertinent in aiding a deeper understanding of this inherent tension:

- What are the key factors that clinicians need to consider to achieve a balance between the education and service objectives of their clinical programmes?
- In what ways does a consideration of such factors enable or inhibit this balance within a law clinic setting, for whom and in what circumstances?

It is submitted that if these two questions were explored further in research, the results would reveal the most common factors for balancing the educational and the service goals of clinical legal education, and indeed the most common contexts in which certain factors are effective in balancing the two missions. Findings from such research would extend existing clinical scholarship in this topic, provide recommendations for the development of the law clinic practice and highlight the need for further research using much more informed and nuanced methodologies that seem to be currently lacking. I hope that it would be at this stage that the question of necessity in striking a balance between the two missions would be answered, if it can be at all.

Regulatory framework

Within the field of legal practice, adhering to the codes of conduct required in the provision of legal services cannot be wished away. **Part 2** of this Handbook addresses the need to increase an awareness of regulation and compliance by universities that employ solicitors and barristers to provide legal services through law school clinics. I do not intend to repeat the contents of **Part 2**, which deal with the regulatory status of university law school solicitors and

116 Peggy Maisel, 'Expanding and sustaining clinical legal education in developing countries: what we can learn from South Africa' (2007) *Fordham International Law Journal* 30(2), 374–420, at p. 414.

barristers and the various legislative and regulatory rules with which they must comply. Suffice it to say that regulatory bodies, such as the Solicitors Regulation Authority and the Bar Standards Board for England and Wales, require those that provide legal advice and representation to be qualified to do so and have necessary authorisations or exemptions in place before they can provide certain legal services.

Although the literature is sparse, it is important that we familiarise ourselves with the provisions of the Legal Services Act 2007 from which the regulatory framework is derived, as well as other prevailing legislation which governs the way that clinics can and should provide their services. This is important because it ensures that the work carried out in the clinic is to a certain standard and that only qualified people can do it. Clear guidance, however, still lags far behind available knowledge and research, resulting in wide interpretations of the regulatory framework. Moreover, even with an extensive reading of the rules, an understanding of the intricacies of the legislative and regulatory framework may be challenging and sometimes feel like a daunting enterprise.

One way to mitigate the impact of the varying understanding of this framework is through consultation and seeking the knowledge of those who have been in the field for a while. It is important to emphasise the importance of networking and consultation among clinicians so as to consolidate knowledge and understanding of how to meet legal requirements[117] pertaining to university law clinics, including the restrictions and limitations the framework imposes.[118]

Without exception, a basic component of learning how to operate within the rules involves being exposed to the fundamentals of reading the rules correctly and with a deeper understanding. Thus, unpacking the rules through the research can help universities and clinicians know what to do or what to promote in ideal or less than ideal situations. Further research on the regulatory and legislative framework is required to empower universities and clinicians, by providing information and practical strategies for embracing the possibilities and avoiding the pitfalls of providing a service outside the confines of the regulation.

---

117 Linden Thomas, 'Law clinics in England and Wales: a regulatory black hole' (2017) *The Law Teacher* 51(4).

118 LawWorks' Response to Legal Services Board Consultation: 'Are regulatory restrictions in practicing rules for in-house lawyers justified?' (LawWorks, 5 June 2015) <https://www.LawWorks.org.uk/solicitors-and-volunteers/resources/LawWorks-response-legal-services-board-consultation-are> (accessed 18 April 2019).

Conclusion

The clinical scholarship reviewed for this part of the Handbook has shown that empirical research on the wellbeing and mental health needs of clinic students and members of staff engaged in clinical pedagogy; reflection and assessment; skills development and student employability; social justice and regulation is still underdeveloped. Notwithstanding, certain findings in the studies reviewed were quite consistent across clinical programmes even though they are largely theoretical. However, I believe that as the clinical movement continues to grow and develop its scholarship on these important themes in clinical legal education, there will be more studies in the future. In my hope to stimulate further discussion on the issues raised in this section, I end by restating some of the topical issues I believe still need further exploration in our field.

Wellbeing

Regarding the wellbeing of students and staff, where should the lines be drawn between clinic supervision and pastoral support for clinic students with wellbeing issues considering that members of staff in some institutions are not clinically trained to deal with mental health concerns? Where a situation arises in which a member of staff has to offer immediate support to a distressed clinic student, what are the implications of dealing with such for the wellbeing of the clinic staff?

Reflection

Regarding reflection in the clinic, should we concern ourselves with the process of reflection, the products of reflection or indeed both? Does reflection on how and what students experience and learn within the clinic lead to improvements in their final assessments? If reflection is meant to be an intimately personal experience for clinic students, how do we define the standards for assessment without making reflection a less personal and externally imposed process?

Reflection is assessed orally or in a written form. How might this affect those students who are less familiar with the context-specific linguistic expectations in a way that has absolutely nothing to do with their ability to participate in reflective practice? Where the tool of assessing reflection is a written piece, pause and think of students with high functioning autism spectrum disorder who find it difficult to perform writing tasks and/or to engage with the expected thinking process.

Employability skills

The literature review revealed that a law clinic is widely considered instrumental in equipping new law graduates with the required employability skills to function effectively in the work environment. It appears there seems to be a changing paradigm in the job sector as employers, now more than ever, seek to employ graduates whose education has had a focus on the interventions of technology. This calls for us to collectively reflect, debate and discuss some of the questions that face the sector and indeed our field as we try to keep up with the influence of technology in legal practice. For example, how does our current curriculum afford us the opportunity to innovate and prepare our students to become technologically savvy and future-ready for the professional world?

It is incumbent upon us to engage in the digital age discourse to discuss and understand some of the complex and disruptive changes brought about by technologically mediated practices. However, how do we examine the discourse of technology to reorient a clinic and make it fit for a technologically driven delivery of services? See in particular **Part 2.13**, which provides an analysis of the issues associated with virtual lawyering and technology.

Social justice and education

The literature reviewed on the two missions of clinical legal education indicates that there is a tension between the need to focus on students' development as lawyers and the expectation that students will help to meet a (previously unmet) legal need. How do we address the conflict and work towards striking a balance between the two mission objectives, if ever there is a need to do so? To what extent is there a danger of clinicians imposing their own social justice values by focusing on this aspect of clinics, or can the focus on such issues enable students to develop their own understanding and awareness of social justice?

Regulation

Although the literature is sparse on the issue of operation of the clinic within the prevailing regulatory and legislative environment in the UK, there has been an emphasis on the importance of dialogue between university law schools and the regulator. Without exception, there is an argument that the regulatory restrictions under which law clinics currently operate require clinicians to engage proactively with the regulator. To this end, what sort of information and practical strategies do clinicians need to have to embrace the possibilities and avoid the pitfalls of operating outside the ambit of regulation?

It is my hope that future empirical research will use meticulous methodological models to address these questions. Perhaps for those us who have for years intuitively felt that clinical legal education has both huge pedagogic benefits and promotes social justice, such research may persuade a wider audience of the need for the further development of what we have come to know as the global clinical movement.

Part 5
Precedent documents and resources

This part of the Handbook contains a bank of precedents and resources which have kindly been shared by clinicians from a number of different institutions.[1] The documents have been anonymised[2] and, although liability for accuracy and legal compliance remains with individual clinics, they are intended to offer practical examples of documents that may be useful in clinics. They are not intended to be definitive or exhaustive and will need to be tailored to reflect an individual clinic's requirements and in response to legislative and regulatory developments. Not all clinics will consider that they need all of the documents provided here and some clinics will find that they need documents for which no template has been provided.

In some instances, we have included more than one template of the same type of document in order to demonstrate the different approaches taken by different clinics. For example, we have included three different types of student agreements/contract.

Some of the precedents provided here will have been adopted and tailored from other sources, in some cases a many years ago. Original sources are not always known and therefore cannot be credited.

5.1 Contracts and handbooks

5.1.1 Student handbooks

5.1.2 External supervisor handbook: Option 1

5.1.3 External supervisor handbook: Option 2

5.1.4 Student agreement: Option 1

5.1.5 Student agreement: Option 2

5.1.6 Student agreement: Option 3

5.1.7 Client information agreement

5.1.8 Third party confidentiality agreement

---

1   Our thanks in particular goes to Richard Grimes, Ann Thanaraj and Mike Sales, the University of Birmingham, the University of Essex, Northumbria University, Queen Mary's University London and the University of Wolverhampton for sharing their resources.

2   With the exception of the University of Wolverhampton Legal Advice Centre Annual Report, which is contained in the 'useful resources' section.

5.2   Policies and procedures

5.3   Checklists and practice documents

5.4   Learning and teaching

5.5   Other useful resources

Part 5.1
Contracts and handbooks

5.1.1 Student handbooks

It is good practice for clinics to have a handbook for student volunteers which outlines the way that the clinic operates and sets out the expectations of all clinic participants.

The precise content of the *Student handbook* will vary from clinic to clinic, depending upon the type of service the clinic provides, the way that it operates and the policies it has in place. You may have a number of different handbooks within your clinic, each tailored to reflect the different processes involved in different projects that you are running.

Precedent student handbooks

There are some excellent materials freely available to download that provide a good starting point for preparing the *Student handbook* for your clinic.

- Law Works has a *Student handbook* available to download at: <http://www.lawworks.org.uk/solicitors-and-volunteers/resources/template-student-handbook>
- The London South Bank University Legal Advice Clinic Team also published an operational manual specifically for drop-in clinics, which is available to download at: <https://www.lawworks.org.uk/solicitors-and-volunteers/resources/sample-drop-university-clinic-handbook>
- A version of York University's Streetlaw handbook is available at: www.gaje.org/abstract-richard-grimes/

You may wish to adapt and incorporate a number of the documents contained elsewhere in **Part 5** of this Handbook into your *Student handbook*. You may notice that some of those documents have been taken from the above resources and edited to suit individual clinic requirements.

5.1.2 External supervisor handbook: Option 1

Supervisor handbook

Important information and contact details

Client enquiry line

Email

Telephone

Address

Staff

Name

Email

Telephone

Important note about contact

- **Email**: It is best to use the [*clinic@university*].ac.uk email address to ensure your email is dealt with. All [*clinic/centre*] staff check this account regularly.
- **Phone**: It is best to use the direct number [*insert*]. The [*clinic/centre*] public line is extremely busy and highly likely to direct you straight to voicemail, which could result in a delay.

Contacting student advisers

Students should not email you directly from their own [*personal*] email addresses. Any emails sent to you about a case should come from the student email account:

[*email*]@[*university*].ac.uk

If you need to speak to a student over the phone, please contact [*insert name*] and we can arrange a call with the student adviser.

Opening times

Client appointment sessions take place on [*day*] between [*time*] and [*time*].

The office is open: [*specify hours*]

Location and directions: [*specify location and directions*]

Areas of law covered at the [*clinic/centre*]: [*specify areas*]

Advising process [*amend as necessary*]

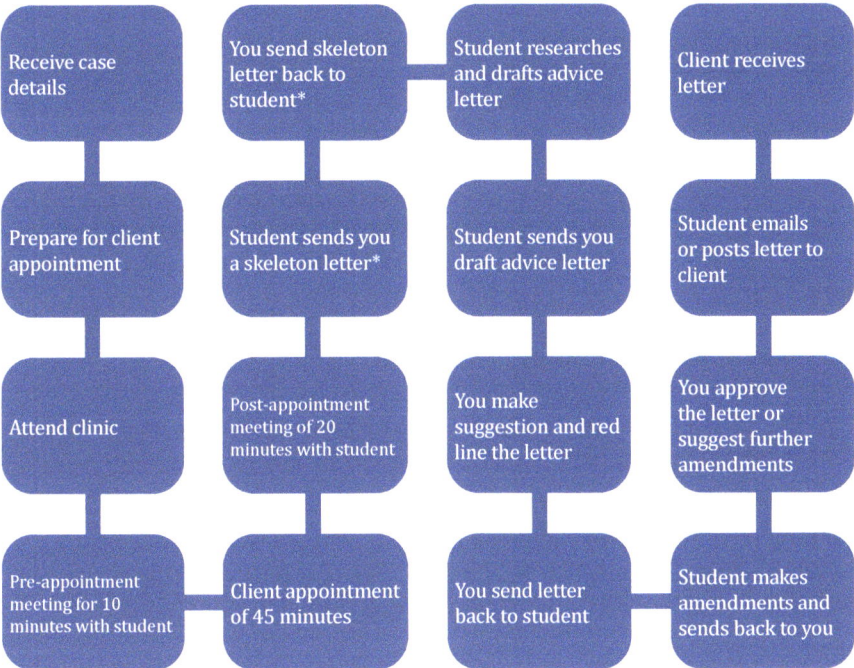

* If you would prefer to complete the skeleton with the student adviser during the post-interview meeting, then please skip these steps in the process.

Appointment schedule [two-appointment schedule]

[*Specify time*] Appointments	[*Specify time*] Appointments
[*Specify time*] You arrive.	[*Specify time*] Pre-interview meeting between the supervisor and the student to discuss their research and what they plan to ask the client.
[*Specify time*] Pre-interview meeting between the supervisor and the student to discuss their research and what they plan to ask the client.	[*Specify time*] Interview with client.
[*Specify time*] Interview with client.	[*Specify time*] Post-interview meeting between the supervisor and student to de-brief and discuss what the student will research and the letter structure.
[*Specify time*] Post-interview meeting between the supervisor and student to de-brief and discuss what the student will research and the letter structure.	[*Specify time*] Client appointments end and [*centre/clinic*] closes
[*Specify time*] First student team leaves.	

*[During [*specify months*] there will be no student advisers, which means you will be interviewing and advising the client. You may have an observer who can note-take but cannot assist with the case or drafting the letter of advice.]

Key information for the appointment sessions

- **Oral feedback:** After the appointment there is scheduled time for you to give feedback to the student. We ask that you give them some feedback on their interview technique/client rapport, etc. and that you discuss the future advice letter with them.
- **Feedback form:** After the session you will be asked to complete short feedback forms on the students. These are vital to their development and to the student adviser competition. The form will be given to you by the receptionists. Please do not leave without completing these forms.
- **Firm name:** The clients should not be told which firm you work for – otherwise they may try to contact you there.
- **Greeting the client:** The students will greet the client in reception and bring them into the appointment room. They will introduce you as their

'supervisor'.

- **Giving advice:** During the session it is important that advice is not given to the client by student or supervisor.

- **Student-led appointments:** Please do let the student lead the interview unless you feel that there is a specific need to intervene. You may find the client tries to speak to you when they find out you are the supervisor. If this happens you may find it easier to make a note to avoid eye contact and to move back your chair slightly.

- **Data protection notice:** As a data processor for the university you will be asked to sign a data protection form by the receptionists. You will only need to sign this form once.

- Please refer to the Law Society guidance on Data Protection: www. lawsociety.org.uk/advice/practice-notes/data-protection.

Client documents

The 14-day advising period will begin once we have all relevant documents from the client. Clients are asked to bring all documents with them to the interview or provide them to us in advance of their appointment. If they fail to provide us with all their documents seven days after the interview, their case will be closed (discretion will be used where appropriate).

If necessary you are able to remove a copy of the client documents from the [*clinic/centre*]. These documents will not be redacted. It will be your responsibility to ensure that any documents you remove from the [*clinic/centre*] are shredded once the advice letter has been sent to the client. If you are taking documents away, you will be asked by the receptionist to sign a book which indicates that it is your responsibility to shred the documents in a timely manner. There will also be a reminder sticker placed on the documents.

If you need to request further documents from a client, please ask them to send the documents to [*email*]@[*university*].ac.uk.

If you would prefer an electronic copy, we can scan the client documents and email them to you the day after the client appointment.

Deadlines

You can decide whether you would prefer to complete the skeleton outline with the student adviser during the post-interview meeting or whether you would like them to write it up and send it to you for approval. If you choose the former option, please go straight to Step 3.

Step 1: Receiving the skeleton letter (one day after the client interview)

The skeleton is designed to be a useful tool to ensure letters have focus and structure. Sometimes a student may include an area of law in the skeleton which is irrelevant and realise this during the research and drafting stages. For this reason there may be times when you leave an area in the skeleton but make the observation in the comments section that this may prove irrelevant when the final letter is completed, and state the reason. It is easier to take information out of a draft letter than include it. If the student has included paragraph numbers and you do not like this you may wish to say, and vice versa. The skeleton should have different headings which a student will use within the letter and the relevant subheadings. The facts section should be as full as possible at this stage. Each letter will be different: some will have a series of IRACs for different legal issues around the same problem; some letters will just have one.

- Please note: You can also complete the skeleton with the student adviser in the post-interview meeting. If you choose to do this, you can go straight to Step 3.

Step 2: Skeleton will be returned to your student adviser (two days after the interview)

Your student adviser will expect to receive a checked skeleton from you that outlines whether their research areas and structure are correct.

Step 3: First draft of the letter from your student adviser (seven days after the interview)

- The letter **should not** contain any of the client's personal details.
- There should be an accompanying bibliography; if there is not, please request one.

Step 4: Returning the first draft to your students (10–11 days after the interview)

- If you require the students to do further research or drafting, you should return the first draft before the stated deadline.
- If you are unhappy with the spelling, punctuation or grammar, we again ask that you notify [*specify centre supervisor*] in good time so this can be addressed with the students.
- 'Track changes' is the easiest way for the students to see and address the changes/suggestions you have made. It also avoids issues with handwritten notes and allows for a thorough review of the students' work.

- In addition to track changes, there is also a section at the end of the letter where we ask you to mark some set criteria as **excellent**, **good**, **average** or **poor**. There is space for you to add some more general comments and observations.
- We check every advice letter before it is posted for spelling, grammar and presentation, but when you return it to us, you are confirming the legal information is correct.
- Trainees should have their letter approved by their supervisor before it is returned to us.
- Your email to the students with the letter attached must state whether you approve its posting.
- We appreciate you have a busy schedule but ask that if there is going to be a delay, you inform us immediately. It is important to the reputation of the [*clinic/centre*] that we are able to manage the client's expectations of our service.
- If you send the letter back after this deadline we request that the letter is returned ready to post to avoid further delay to the client.

Step 5: Sending the letter to the client (14 days after the interview)

- The letter will be emailed (or posted if this has been specifically requested by the client) from the [*clinic/centre*] at **1pm** on the stated deadline.
- Unless you inform us in advance that there will be a delay the client will expect to receive the letter 14 days after their appointment.

What are clients expecting?

Client information

Clients are provided with the following information before the interview:

- The [*clinic/centre*] is a preliminary advice centre and we cannot represent the client or provide ongoing advice.
- If they cancel their appointment with less than 24 hours' notice, do not attend or arrive 15 minutes or more late, they will not be offered another appointment.
- They need to bring all documents with them to the interview or provide them to us in advance of their appointment. The 14-day advising period will begin once we have all relevant documents.
- We are unable to provide ongoing assistance. In some instances, clients will have further questions or want to clarify points in the letter after

it has been sent to them. If this is the case, we may contact you to see if there is any scope for answering those questions and ask the student adviser to draft a response for you to review (provided the questions are not extensive, relate to the letter and are not outside the scope of the advice sought). If this is the case, and you are happy to review the student adviser's response do let us know, but you are under absolutely no obligation to do so.

Client expectations

The client will expect the following service from the [*clinic/centre*]:

- To receive the advice letter within 14 days of their appointment at the [*clinic/centre*].
- To be informed of any delay and to be provided with a new date by which they can expect to receive their advice letter. If you are busy and there will be a delay to the client, we understand this, but we must let the client know in advance and manage their expectations.
- A template letter to the opponent. Wherever possible the students should draft a template letter(s) for the client to use. These letters can arise in a number of situations and circumstances. For example, it may be a letter to the opponent in a case, or some draft text that they can use to send to a relevant person. Template letters/pieces of text should be provided to a client on the very clear understanding that we do not represent the client, we only advise. As a result the letter must be sent by them and they must not purport in any way that we have sent the letter. It is not unusual for the names and addresses, etc. to be left blank for the client to complete, for example [*insert name here*].

What are the student advisers expecting?

Pre-appointment meeting

The students are likely to be nervous as they will not have dealt with clients before. They may need guidance on the types of questions they should ask. The students should have researched the area of law beforehand and have drafted their questions or topics for questioning.

Appointment

The students should be given every opportunity to ask the client their questions. If you would like the client to repeat some information or clarify a point for your notes then you may intervene. If, at the end of the interview, you feel the students have missed any points you should ask the client these questions. The students should give you the opportunity to ask any questions once they have finished.

Post-appointment meeting

The students benefit from your advice on the research they need to complete and the structure of the advice letter, particularly as each supervisor requires a different approach. A lot of supervisors find that the more time spent discussing the structure and research areas at this stage, the less time is needed later when the letter is sent to them.

Student adviser training

The students have received training on the following areas:

- [*Clinic/centre*] procedures
- Interviewing a client (open questions, followed by more specific closed questions)
- Drafting
- Researching
- Subject-specific training for each subject area that will arise in their project.

Key information

Student roles

The student adviser will lead the client interview, research and draft the letter. They are expected to have done research before the client interview and contribute heavily in the pre and post-interview meetings.

There will also be a note-taker in attendance at the client interview. Their role is to simply take notes at the appointment, but they can contribute to the pre and post-interview meetings as well. The case details will have been sent to the note-taker in advance of the appointment but they are not expected to have done any research and will not be involved in writing the advice letter.

Conflict of interests

A conflict of interest check is done before the client is seen; therefore no issues of conflict should arise during the client interview. If problems do arise, please inform the session supervisor.

Your details

To ensure that our processes are as smooth as possible it is essential that we have the correct contact details for you. For this reason, when you attend we will ask you to confirm your email address and contact number. This is to ensure we are always up to date and there are no unnecessary delays when sending emails.

Outlook reminders

You will receive Outlook reminders to inform you of your deadlines.

Referrals

Referrals to the Free Representation Unit, the Bar Pro Bono Unit and LawWorks can be made through the [*clinic/centre*] if the client is in need of representation. Ask the session supervisor for more information.

Security

The students are trained to bring the client into the room and direct them into the chair that is furthest from the door. This is a security precaution.

There are panic buttons in each advising room located on the walls (box with a red top). The button is the red part of the box on the top. In most of our interview rooms these panic alarms are located near the chair furthest from the door and therefore where the client usually sits. For this reason a student in each interview will be wearing a portable panic alarm around their neck.

In addition, at each advice session there is a porter/commissionaire on hand for assistance. They have security training and can immediately contact security if necessary. They are located [*insert location*].

Most of our advising rooms are used as offices during the day. For security reasons we make a special effort to ensure that they are tidy and that there are not unnecessary objects lying around the rooms when they are being used as interview rooms.

If during a session you have any concerns about a client, please stop the interview and inform the session supervisor.

You do need to be aware of the security precautions taken by the [*clinic/centre*]. The students will be shown where the panic buttons are before the client appointment sessions.

[Annexes A to C contain example documents you may wish to use]

Annex A: Case details form

Date	Request taken by	Type of appointment	Client number
First name:	Salutation:	Address:	Email:
Last name:	Staff, student or public:	Phone number:	
How did you hear about the [clinic/centre]?	What is your employment status?	If a company, what is your annual turnover?	
Are you/your partner members or ex members of the Forces?	If employed, what job do you do?	How many people in your household?	
Special arrangements, i.e. contact restrictions or disability requirements?	Have you had advice on this issue before?	Are there any deadlines?	Area of law:
	If so, from where?	Dates:	Project:
	Is it still ongoing?	Details of deadline:	
Client would like advice on:			
Details of case:			
What documents have you asked the client to bring with them?			
Opponent name:	Opponent affiliated to [university]? Yes / No		
Time of appointment:	Student advisers:		Date of appointment

Annex B: Skeleton

Facts of the case

Outline the facts of the case to make sure that you have covered them all and everyone agrees what was heard in the interview.

Use the IRAC method:

- **Issues**: as agreed with your supervisor in the post-interview meeting.
- **Rules**: state and explain the relevant legal rule.
- **Application**: apply the rule to your facts.
- **Conclude**: by explicitly answering the question or taking a position on the issue.

Annex C: Advice letter template for students

Client reference number: [*Insert client number*]

[*Insert date*]

Privileged & confidential

[*Insert client name and address*]

Dear [*Insert client title and surname*]

Re: Your appointment with the [*clinic/centre*] on [*insert date of appointment*]

Thank you for attending your appointment with us and using the services of the [*clinic/centre*]. Although we cannot provide you with representation in any proceedings and do not hold ourselves out to be a firm of solicitors, our advice is free and we aim to provide the same high standard of service expected by a law firm.

Our advice is based on the following documents you provided:

- [*insert titles of documents*]

[Please use the IRAC method for your structure]

We hope that the information above provides you with a comprehensive understanding of the legal questions you asked us to address. Should you require any assistance in the future in any other matters, please do not hesitate to contact us.

[EITHER:]

[IF YOU ARE EMAILING THE LETTER:]

We would be extremely grateful if you could take a few moments to complete this short form, as your feedback is important to the development of our services: [*insert link*].

[OR]

[IF YOU ARE POSTING THE LETTER:]

Please find a Client Questionnaire enclosed; we would be extremely grateful if you could take a few moments to complete this short form, as your feedback is important to the development of our services.

Yours sincerely

[*Insert your name*]

Student Adviser

Ensure that the Director/Coordinator/Administrator has checked the letter

Note to supervisor: please could you complete the feedback below.

Feedback to student adviser

When providing feedback, please take into consideration that student advisers are either second or final-year students and that this is their first opportunity to write in a non-academic practical environment. Therefore, feedback should be supported with constructive suggestions that enable them to develop their skills for the future.

- Structure of the letter
- Grammar
- Spelling
- Understanding of the law
- Delivery of advice
- Overall standard
- Do you have any further comments and suggestions that may help the student adviser develop their skills?

5.1.3 External supervisor handbook: Option 2[1]

[Insert name of clinic]

A law clinic operated by [*insert name of university and external partners*]

SOLICITOR HANDBOOK[2]

[INSERT YEAR]

---

1   This handbook is developed from a template provided by LawWorks.

2   This handbook was developed for a clinic that relies upon external solicitors from one firm that partners with the university in the delivery of the pro bono clinic.

Contents

1.   Introduction

1.1   Thank you for volunteering your time to take part in [*insert name of clinic*]. [*Insert name of clinic*] is a pro bono scheme which was launched [*insert date*] by [*insert details of partners*] in conjunction with the Law School at the [*insert name of university*].

1.2   [*Insert name of clinic*] involves [*insert name of law firm*] solicitors supervising students in the provision of free legal advice to people in the local community who would not normally be able to access it.

1.3   The aims of [*insert name of clinic*] are:

(a)   to provide free legal advice for members of the local community

(b)   to provide law students with practical legal experience.

1.4   [*Insert name of clinic*] is one of the ways our firm ensures we discharge our responsibility for improving access to justice and upholding the rule of law.

2.   Key people

2.1   [*Insert key contacts for the clinic within the law firm that provides supervising solicitors*]

2.2   Law School

[*Insert name*] is responsible for [*insert name of clinic*] at the law school and [*his/her*] contact details are:

[*Insert details*]

2.3   Please remember to copy in [*insert email address*] into all correspondence (internal and external).

3.   How [*insert name of clinic*] works

A flow chart of the [*insert name of clinic*] process can be found at Schedule 1.

(A)   Stage 1: Query received from client

1.   [*Insert name of clinic*]'s clients are members of the local community. [*Insert name of clinic*] is advertised in public places within the community, e.g. community centres, GP surgeries, etc.

2.   All contact with clients is handled by the law school's student committee. Clients contact [*insert name of clinic*] by telephoning [*insert number*] or emailing [*insert email*].

3.   The law school's student committee speaks to the client and completes a pro-forma that contains information about the client and preliminary details of their query. If the query is something that they know our firm can supervise, they will provide the client with a provisional appointment. All clients will be seen by appointment only.

4.   [*Insert name of clinic*] appointments will take place on [*insert day[s]*] evenings between [*insert times*] at the university. However, there can be some flexibility in exceptional circumstances. [*Insert name of clinic*] is a term-time only project. It will not operate during university holidays or the examination period. The term dates [*insert name of clinic*] will operate in [*insert academic year*] are:

        Autumn term   [*insert dates*]

        Spring term   [*insert dates*]

5.   The law school committee will send the pro-forma to the [*insert firm name*] committee members who are on a rota (committee members are on duty for one week on a rota basis). The [*insert firm name*] committee member will ask the secretaries to undertake a conflict check and determine whether the query is something that [*insert firm name*] can assist with.

6.   The [*insert firm name*] committee member will have responsibility for the matter throughout the process. The [*insert firm name*] committee member is responsible for good record-keeping and should therefore be copied into all emails between [*insert firm name*] volunteers and students.

7.   If [*insert firm name*] cannot assist the client, the [*insert firm name*] committee member will inform the law school committee. The matter will be referred to another firm if it is within their expertise.

(B)   Stage 2: Allocation of query

1.   If [*insert firm name*] can assist the client, the [*insert firm name*] committee member will identify which specialism is required and which volunteer is next on the rota for that specialism.

2.   The [*insert firm name*] committee member will then approach the relevant [*insert firm name*] volunteer with the client pro-forma and ask if the provisional date for the interview is convenient, and if not, ask them to suggest alternatives.

3.   If the [*insert firm name*] volunteer confirms they can take on the matter the [*insert firm name*] committee member will email the law school committee to confirm:

        (a)   that [*insert firm name*] can take on that particular enquiry

(b)   that they are the committee member with responsibility for the client

(c)   the details of the [*insert firm name*] volunteer

(d)   whether the [*insert firm name*] volunteer can attend the proposed date for the interview OR suggest a date and time for the interview to be rearranged.

4.   The law school will appoint two students to be responsible for the client. The law school students will undertake initial research and email the [*insert firm name*] volunteer with:

(a)   their name and contact details

(b)   their opinion as to the key issues raised by the client

(c)   their provisional questions to be covered during the client appointment.

5.   The [*insert firm name*] volunteer will need to read the outline provided by the students and discuss this with the students either via email or telephone or on the day of the appointment during the pre-appointment briefing. The students are aware that individual solicitors will approach this in the way that best suits them. In all cases there will still be a pre-appointment briefing.

(C)   Stage 3: Client appointment

1.   On the date of the client appointment, the [*insert firm name*] volunteer will need to attend:

[*Insert address*]

From the meeting point the [*insert firm name*] volunteer will be guided by one of the student committee to a room in the law school where the client interview will take place. (A map is attached at Schedule 2. The Law School building is [*insert number*] on the map.)

2.   [*Insert firm name*] volunteers will be expected to get to the law school for the client appointment. Available transport options are:

[*Insert details*]

Expenses: [*Insert firm name*] volunteers may reclaim travel expenses in the usual way by [*insert details*].

3.   A law school committee member will meet the [*insert firm name*] volunteer at the entrance to the law school.

4.   If [*insert firm name*] volunteers have any difficulties getting to the appointment, please call the student coordinators on [*insert number*]. If you cannot get through then you should call [*insert details*].

5.   In the unlikely event that an emergency should arise during a clinic

session (for example, a client or student falling ill) you should call the university's Security Control team on [*insert number*]. One of the student committee should then contact the Clinic Director on their mobile.

6.   On the day of the appointment, the [*insert firm name*] volunteer should **arrive 30 minutes beforehand** to enable a pre-appointment briefing to take place with the law school students. During this briefing you should liaise with the law school students about which questions they should ask the client, advise them as to the most pertinent issues in the client's case and suggest the best way to handle the appointment as a whole.

7.   **No advice** should be given during the client appointment. All advice must be given in writing. The client will receive a letter of advice within two weeks of the appointment.

8.   The student team will consist of two students who will be expected to lead the appointment. The appointment should usually last no longer than 30 minutes. Ideally the [*insert firm name*] volunteer should only need to observe the appointment to ensure the students are asking the right questions, getting the right level of information and are not providing any face-to-face legal advice. If it is necessary to intervene, we would ask that the reasons for doing so are clearly explained to the students in the post-appointment briefing so that they can learn from the experience as much as possible.

9.   After the appointment, the [*insert firm name*] volunteer will need to conduct a post-appointment briefing with the law school students. Ideally this should take place immediately after the appointment has ended and should not take more than 30 minutes. The law school students should be provided with an outline of the key issues they need to focus on in their research (if relevant) and in their letter of advice. The students should be reminded that they must send their attendance note and draft letter of advice to the [*insert firm name*] volunteer **within seven days** of the appointment. Please remember to copy [*insert email address*] into all correspondence with the law school students.

10.   The [*insert firm name*] volunteers should only be supervising the work of the law school students. They are not being asked to take on that work themselves. The law school students retain responsibility for the work for each client, although the [*insert firm name*] volunteer has ultimate responsibility for the content of the advice given.

(D)   Stage 4: Drafting letter of advice to client

1.   The law school students will conduct any further research and draft a letter of advice to the client. The law school students may ask a relevant law lecturer at the university to check any aspects of the law that they refer to in their letter of advice. For reasons of confidentiality, the specific

facts of the case and the identity of the client will not be disclosed to the law lecturer who helps the student with research issues. [*Insert name*] should check the format of the letter before it is forwarded to [*insert firm name*].

2. Once the draft letter of advice is completed, the law school students will forward it to the [*insert firm name*] volunteer who will finalise and approve it or provide feedback and invite the students to redraft. This process can be facilitated by the [*insert firm name*] committee member; however, in practice we have found that the [*insert firm name*] volunteer often prefers the direct contact with the law school students.

(E)   Stage 5: Approval of letter of advice to client

1. The [*insert firm name*] volunteer will need to review the draft letter of advice. Ideally the [*insert firm name*] volunteer will suggest changes and allow the students to make those changes, rather than amend the letter themselves. This will allow the students to learn more effectively from the experience. However, due to the **two-week deadline** for the client to receive the letter after the appointment, the [*insert firm name*] volunteer may need to occasionally take a more active role.

2. The [*insert firm name*] committee member is there to assist the [*insert firm name*] volunteer with undertaking further research, amending the letter and liaising with the law school students.

3. The [*insert firm name*] volunteer or, if the volunteer has less than three years' PQE, someone with more than three years' PQE in the appropriate area of law will need to approve the final draft of the letter. The [*insert firm name*] committee member will email the approved letter to the Clinic Director.

4. **The [*insert firm name*] volunteer and [*insert firm name*] committee member should complete a feedback form with regard to the students' performance** (see the Law school student feedback form at Schedule 3).

(F)   Stage 6: Sending letter of advice to client

1. The Clinic Director will sign the letter of advice on behalf of the law school and send it to the client.

2. There will be no ongoing legal representation by the law school students or the [*insert firm name*] volunteer on behalf of the client. The letter of advice may signpost the client to other sources of assistance.

3. The client will be sent a feedback form by the law school regarding [*insert name of clinic*].

4.   Time-keeping

Any time spent on [*insert name of clinic*] by [*insert firm name*] staff should be recorded under file number [*insert*]. Time spent on [*insert name of clinic*] is deemed to be valuable time by [*insert firm name*].

5.   Record-keeping

5.1   While each case is ongoing, the client's file will be securely kept in the law school pro bono room. Students have been trained on confidentiality requirements.

5.2   All emails or documents [*insert firm name*] receive or create should be e-filed on the [*insert name of clinic*] folder (matter number: [*insert*]) under the correct client. The client folder will be called the client first initial and the first three letters of their last name (e.g. A KET).

5.3   The folder looks like this:

[*Insert image*]

Please ask a committee member if you need any assistance. They will file all client emails and documents into which they are copied. So please remember to copy them into all emails between you and the law school students.

5.4   Please make sure the following documents are e-filed:

(a)   Client pro-forma.

(b)   Summary of issues and questions prepared by the law school students.

(c)   Draft letter of advice provided by the law school students.

(d)   Final letter of advice approved by [*insert firm name*] volunteer.

5.5   The [*insert firm name*] committee member will ensure that a spreadsheet is kept up to date throughout the matter (document number [*insert*]).

6.   Further information

If you have any questions about [*insert name of clinic*] please contact: [*insert details*].

Schedule 1: Flowchart of the [*insert name of clinic*] process

For emails you send to the university, please remember to copy in: [**insert email address**]

Stage 1: Query received from client

- Student committee receives client query and completes pro-forma.
- Student sends pro-forma to [*insert firm name*] committee member on rota.
- If the matter falls within our expertise, secretaries undertake conflict checks.
- [*Insert firm name*] committee member approaches [*insert firm name*] volunteer in relation to their capacity and availability.

Stage 2: Allocation of query

- [*insert firm name*] committee member allocates query to [*insert firm name*] volunteer and sends pro-forma.
- File number for time recording and e-filing: [*insert*].
- **Within seven days of receipt of query:** [*Insert firm name*] committee member contacts student committee to confirm [*insert firm name*] volunteer and convenient appointment time.
- **Seven days before client appointment:** Students undertake initial research and send proposed questions to [*insert firm name*] volunteer.

Stage 3: Client appointment

- [*Insert firm name*] volunteer attends university for client appointment.
- [*Insert firm name*] volunteer to arrive 30 minutes beforehand for pre-appointment briefing.
- Students interview client for 30 minutes with supervision from [*insert firm name*] volunteer.
- [*Insert firm name*] volunteer and students have post-appointment debrief.

Stage 4: Letter of advice to client

- Students conduct further research and draft letter of advice to client.
- Draft letter reviewed by lecturers (re law) and Clinic Director (re format).
- **Within seven days of client appointment:** Students forward draft letter to [insert firm name] volunteer.

Stage 5: Approval of letter of advice to client

- [Insert firm name] volunteer reviews letter of advice and suggests/ makes any changes.
- [Insert firm name] committee member assists where possible.
- [Insert firm name] volunteer (or someone with three years' PQE in relevant area of law) approves letter.
- [Insert firm name] committee member emails approved letter to Clinic Director.
- [Insert firm name] volunteer send the approved letter to committee member to e-file.
- [Insert firm name] volunteer and committee member complete Law school student feedback form.

Stage 6: Sending letter of advice to client

- **Within 14 days of client appointment:** Clinic Director signs letter on behalf of law school and sends to client.
- There is no ongoing relationship with client.
- Client sent a feedback form from law school in relation to [insert name of clinic].

Schedule 2: Map of the Law School [*insert map*]

Schedule 3: Law school student feedback form

Professional volunteer feedback

Student volunteers

Professional volunteer

Professional committee member/Clerk

Client reference

Date of appointment

1.   With 10 being the highest score and 1 the lowest, please rate the students in respect of the following:

  Preparation for client meeting

  Conducting client meeting

  Undertaking appropriate research

  Drafting letter of advice

  Keeping within agreed timetable

2.   Was there anything that the students did particularly well?

3.   Is there anything that the students should aim to improve upon?

Signed:_____

Professional volunteer/Professional committee member/Clerk

(Delete as appropriate)

Dated:_____

Once completed, please email to [*insert email address*].

Schedule 4: Money laundering guidance

[Insert your clinic's guidance on money laundering procedures here. There is an example at Part 5.2.4].

5.1.4 Student agreement: Option 1

Participant contract

This contract is between you, a participant in the [*insert clinic name*], and [*insert clinic name*]. It sets out your primary obligations to the [*insert clinic name*] and our commitment to you. You will find further details of the procedures you must follow during your work in the [*insert clinic name*] Handbook.

1.   General principles

The [*insert clinic name*] undertakes a range of pro bono activities. All activities carried out in the name of the [*insert clinic name*] will be insured against usual risks and this includes professional indemnity cover.

Participants in the [*insert clinic name*] undertake a designated induction and training programme and must enter into this contract as a pre-requisite to participation in the [*insert clinic name*].

All of the [*insert clinic name*] activities are supervised by professionally qualified personnel and the [*insert clinic name*] is managed by a Director who meets current Solicitors Regulation Authority (SRA) supervisory requirements.

The clinic activities take place at such times and in such places as shall be notified, following consultation where possible with participants.

The activities are designed to provide a legal service that meets expected professional standards and complies with regulatory requirements. The activities provide participants with a sound and structured educational experience. In the event that any of the activities do not serve this educational aim the [*insert clinic name*] reserves the right, subject to professional obligations, to withdraw from the activity in question. However, if professional obligations conflict with educational aims then our professional duty will prevail.

Every participant will, so far as is possible, receive detailed feedback on all aspects of his or her contribution to the [*insert clinic name*]. Some participants will be assessed on their performance in the [*insert clinic name*] while others will participate on a pro bono basis. The operational rules will be the same for both.

Upon successful completion of the allocated time in the [*insert clinic name*] participants will be awarded a Certificate of Participation.

2.   Organisational matters

In order to serve the professional and educational aims of the [*insert clinic name*] all participants must comply with the following:

2.1   Attend punctually for any scheduled [*insert clinic name*] session.

2.2   If unable to attend, inform [*insert clinic name*] staff according to the procedures set out in the [*insert clinic name*] Handbook.

2.3   Dress in a manner appropriate to working in a solicitor's office at any time when meeting clients face to face.

2.4   Work involving contact with clients is to be undertaken only at times when a member of [*insert clinic name*] staff is available, unless prior authorisation is given.

2.5   No advice of any kind can be given without first getting approval from a [*insert clinic name*] solicitor. Advice may only be given in writing. You must never give oral advice.

2.6   No correspondence of any nature can be sent out without a member of the [*insert clinic name*] staff's counter signature. Advice letters must be counter-signed by a [*insert clinic name*] solicitor.

2.7   You must tell clients that the [*insert clinic name*] is supervised by a qualified solicitor with a practising certificate.

2.8   There must always be at least two participants in attendance during any face-to-face client contact.

2.9   All casework where a client's personal details or the nature of the case affecting the client could be identified must be carried out either in the [*insert clinic name*] office or in other premises approved by [*insert clinic name*] staff.

2.10   To preserve the confidentiality of the [*insert clinic name*]'s cases, you must not receive personal visitors or personal telephone calls on premises being used by [*insert clinic name*].

2.11   No documentation relating to a case, whether in hard or electronic copy, shall be kept in any place other than the [*insert clinic name*] office or other place approved by [*insert clinic name*] staff. For example, no documentation relating to a client's case may be kept on a participant's own computer or mobile devices.

2.12   In order to enable you to actively reflect on your experience and so that you can share your experiences with other participants you must attend a weekly firm meeting and a weekly meeting with all clinic participants and [*insert clinic name*] staff. This is an essential part of your participation in the [*insert clinic name*] and will ensure that you and other participants get the most out of the experience.

2.13   All participants must provide a copy of their up-to-date study timetable, contact address and telephone number to [*insert clinic name*] staff. This is because [*insert clinic name*] staff may need to contact you and therefore must know where you are and how to do so.

3.   Professional and ethical matters

In order that we meet the professional standards set by the SRA and our other obligations as ethical lawyers we must observe the following:

3.1   Everyone working within the [*insert clinic name*] must be familiar with the rules regulating the work of solicitors, in particular the Solicitors Regulation Authority Standards and Regulations. A copy of the relevant Standards and Regulations, and guidance to them, is available in the [*insert clinic name*] office and on the SRA website: www.sra.org.uk.

3.2   We are unable to take or continue any action on behalf of a client against [*insert university name*], its governors, subsidiaries, employees or current students, any former client or in any other circumstance where a conflict of interest has arisen or might arise. In such cases and where possible, the client will be referred elsewhere, after the reason for our inability to act – conflict of interest – has been explained.

3.3   Participant(s) must ensure that at all times their conduct is in accordance with the profession's regulatory framework and the [*insert clinic name*]'s Equal Opportunities policy. This applies to all conduct – conduct of the case, conduct when dealing with clients, [*insert clinic name*] staff and third parties and conduct between participants.

3.4   A breach of professional conduct may result in the offending participant being removed from the [*insert clinic name*].

3.5   Participants must ensure that their files are managed in accordance with the [*insert clinic name*] protocols. A failure to do so may be treated as a breach of required professional standards. It may also mean that the file will be taken over by other participants or [*insert clinic name*] staff and no Certificate of Participation in the [*insert clinic name*] will be issued to the offending participant. [*Insert clinic name*] staff will advise how relevant protocols can be met and the operational rules are set out in the [*insert clinic name*] Handbook.

3.6   No decision to remove a participant from the [*insert clinic name*] programme will be made without the participant being given the opportunity to explain his or her behaviour. The Director will then discuss the matter with [*insert clinic name*] staff before making a decision. If a participant is removed from the [*insert clinic name*] a right of appeal will lie to the [*insert law school name*] Head of School who will conduct the appeal as he or she shall think fit, subject to rules of natural justice.

3.7   For reasons of confidentiality, you must not discuss or disclose to any persons other than other participants, or [*insert clinic name*] staff, matters confidential to the [*insert clinic name*] and its clients.

3.8   For reasons of confidentiality, files must not normally be removed from the [*insert clinic name*] office or other authorised premises. If it is necessary to take a file from the [*insert clinic name*] office or other authorised premises you must first obtain permission to do so from [*insert clinic name*] staff and the file must be signed out and returned as soon as the purpose for its removal has been met.

3.9   Your duty not to discuss or disclose to any unauthorised person matters confidential to the [*insert clinic name*] or any other matters which may come to your knowledge through your clinical work, continues **after** you have ceased to participate in the [*insert clinic name*].

3.10   In order to comply with professional rules and procedures and principles of good practice, all advice given and work done by participants must be carried out under the overall supervision of a solicitor with a practising certificate.

3.11   It is a breach of these rules to do any of the following without [*insert clinic name*] staff authority:

   –   see or contact a client

   –   send out any material of any sort, whether on headed or un-headed paper, in connection with any matter the [*insert clinic name*] is actually or potentially handling, or has handled

   –   agree to take any other step for a client.

3.12   In order to comply with professional rules, **all** correspondence, incoming and outgoing, must be seen and checked by [*insert clinic name*] staff. A [*insert clinic name*] solicitor must approve and counter-sign all advice letters.

3.13   The decision as to whether the client can be offered advice will only be taken with the agreement of [*insert clinic name*] staff, after consultation with you.

3.14   No individual participant may continue to deal with a case if it appears that he or she may have any personal involvement or vested interest in the client's problem. If any such involvement is identified, the student must consult a member of the [*insert clinic name*] staff before discussing the matter further with the client.

4.   Payment in money or kind

Due to the nature of the [*insert clinic name*]'s work and structure there are restrictions imposed on payments for and to the [*insert clinic name*]. These are:

4.1   We do not charge clients for our services.

4.2   We do not handle clients' money and no payment of any kind should be taken from or for a client.

4.3   The offer of any gift by a client or any other person in connection with [*insert clinic name*] work may be permissible but must be referred to a [*insert clinic name*] solicitor for approval.

5.   Assistance under the Access to Justice Act 1999

Even though, mainly for resource reasons, we do not normally represent clients beyond initial advice, and even if we do not currently use public funding for legal services, we are professionally obliged to:

5.1   Inform all clients of the possibility of assistance under the Act (known as 'legal aid').

5.2   Give clients a copy of the *Information for clients* leaflet which contains reference to the legal aid scheme.

6.   Client care

There are strict obligations on us in terms of ensuring requisite standards of client care. To comply with these we must ensure the following:

6.1   All clients advised by the [*insert clinic name*] are given a copy of the *Information for clients* leaflet. This should be given to the client at the commencement of the first interview. The contents of this should be explained clearly to the client.

6.2   Clients may only be given advice in writing and only after proper consideration and research and with the approval of a [*insert clinic name*] solicitor.

6.3   No casework can be undertaken unless the client has signed the *Information for clients* leaflet.

6.4   It is essential that you complete work in accordance with the timescales set out in the Handbook or agreed with [*insert clinic name*] staff. You must let [*insert clinic name*] staff know immediately if this is not going to be possible.

6.5 Where an appointment for a client is made, participants will be expected to keep that appointment. In the event of a participant not being able to keep an appointment, for example due to illness, he or she must inform [*insert clinic name*] staff in accordance with the procedure laid down in the Handbook.

The above rules and requirements are there for good reason. We now ask you to sign this contract to indicate your agreement and commitment.

We hope that you enjoy the experience of working in the [*insert clinic name*]. You should find that if you follow the procedures your learning will be greatly enhanced and you will make a very valuable and much appreciated contribution to unmet legal need.

Please read the following and, if you agree to be bound by it, sign the form where indicated.

Thank you for your interest and anticipated involvement.

Declaration

I have read, understand and accept the terms of this contract so far as it relates to me and undertake to respect the confidentiality of the [*insert clinic name*] and its clients at all times. I acknowledge that I may be removed from the [*insert clinic name*] if I fail to attend a meeting with a client or any firm or case management meeting without good reason or if I breach the rules of professional conduct. I undertake to read the [*insert clinic name*] Handbook and abide by its procedures.

Signed by participant   ....

Name of participant   ....

Date   ....

Signed by [*insert clinic name*]

Director   ....

Name of Director

[*insert director name*]   ....

Date   ....

5.1.5 Student agreement: Option 2

Student volunteer contract[1]

This contract is between you and [*insert name of university*]. It sets out only your primary obligations. You will find further details of the procedures that you must follow during your work with [*insert name of clinic*] in the *Student handbook*, the policies referred to in this agreement and other documentation provided to you by [*insert job title*[2]].

Organisational/internal matters

1.1   Advice clinic sessions

1.1.1   Clients will telephone [*insert name of clinic*] for an appointment which will be held on days fixed in advance by the Clinic Director[s].

1.1.2   Where allocated to a client case as a student volunteer, you will respond promptly to [*insert name or job title*] to confirm that you are able to attend your allocated appointment.

1.1.3   To ensure the smooth running of the client appointment you must arrive at [*insert venue*] at least 45 minutes before the scheduled appointment.

1.1.4   After the appointment you will need to allow at least one hour for your post-appointment review with the professional volunteer (supervising solicitor or barrister), follow-up work and paperwork. All client files must be maintained in accordance with the procedures laid down in the *Student handbook*. Written notification will be given of any changes.

1.1.5   You must attend punctually during the agreed hours.

1.1.6   If you are unable to attend as agreed, it is your responsibility to inform [*insert name*] according to the procedure set out in the *Student handbook*.

1.1.7   You are expected to dress in a manner appropriate to working in a law firm.

---

1   This agreement describes a clinic run by a university in which students are supervised on some cases by external lawyers acting on a voluntary basis.

2   For example, Clinic Director.

1.2   Contact with clients

1.2.1   No advice of any kind can be given without first checking with the professional volunteer. Advice may only be given in writing. You must never give oral advice.

1.2.2   Before a client leaves the interview, you must ensure, so far as is possible, that you have checked that all relevant information has been obtained. This includes a signed [*Client information agreement*][3] and the required identification documents. All documentation should be stored on the paper file in a locked filing cabinet.

1.2.3   No correspondence of any nature can be sent out without the professional volunteer's authorisation and a Clinic Director's signature.

1.2.4   You must tell clients that [*insert name of clinic*] is supervised by professional volunteers who are qualified solicitors and barristers with practising certificates.

1.2.5   The decision as to whether any advice on a case can be given will be made by the professional volunteer in consultation with you. In the event of disagreement, the professional volunteer will make the final decision.

1.2.6   You must never include any information that could identify the client or the case in the body of an email. All such information should be included in password-protected Word documents. You should never state what the password is in the email to which the document is attached.

1.3   To preserve the confidentiality of [*insert name of clinic*]'s affairs, you must not receive personal visitors or personal telephone calls in the clinic office.

1.4   You must comply with the university's Data Protection policy and Information Security policy at all times.[4] You must also:

1.4.1   complete the mandatory data protection training required by the Clinic Director[s] prior to participation in the clinic

---

3   Different clinics will have different names for this document: client care letter, terms of engagement, etc.

4   You may wish to include links to these policies.

      1.4.2   comply with any instructions that you are given by the Clinic Director[s], administrator(s) and/or professional volunteer(s) in relation to data protection

      1.4.3   ensure that you comply with the clinic's Privacy Notice[5] when handling client data.

      Please read the documents referred to in this section carefully prior to your participation in [*insert name of clinic*]. Please note that these documents may be updated from time to time and therefore you should check you are familiar with the most recent version.

1.5   In order to enable you to reflect on what you have learnt you will be invited to a meeting to discuss your experience. This is an essential part of your participation in the clinic.

1.6   Working in pairs is also an essential part of your [*insert name of clinic*] experience. It develops communication skills and confidence, and means responsibility and workloads are shared and work double-checked.

1.7   A student feedback form must be completed at the end of each case.

1.8   All student volunteers working in [*insert name of clinic*] must provide a copy of their most up-to-date telephone number to the Clinic Administrator. This is because we may need to contact student volunteers about the case they are working on.

Professional and ethical matters

2.1   We are unable to take any action on behalf of a client against the [*insert name of university*], any of its branches or subsidiaries, its governors, employees, current students or any former client of [*insert name of clinic*]. The client may be signposted elsewhere, after the reasons for our inability to act have been explained.

2.2   Professional responsibilities and confidentiality

      2.2.1   The duty of confidentiality extends to all [*insert name of clinic*] matters.

      2.2.2   Everyone working within [*insert name of clinic*] must be familiar with the Solicitors Regulation Authority's Standards and Regulations. In particular, the SRA Principles and the parts of the SRA Code of Conduct for Solicitors, RELs and RFLs on confidentiality. A copy of the Standards and Regulations is available [*insert location*].[6]

5   You may wish to include a link to this.

6   As set out elsewhere in this handbook, the new SRA Standards and Regulations came into

2.2.3   Student volunteers must ensure that at all times their conduct is in accordance with the profession's conduct rules. This applies to all conduct – conduct of the case, conduct when dealing with the professional volunteer and [*insert name of clinic*] staff, and conduct as between student volunteers.

2.2.4   A breach of professional conduct may result in the student volunteer being removed from [*insert name of clinic*]. This is a matter for the Clinic Director[s] [in conjunction with the professional volunteer where appropriate].

2.2.5   Student volunteers must ensure that their client file is managed in accordance with the [*insert name of clinic*] protocols. A failure to do so will be treated as a breach of the professional conduct rules. It will also mean that the client file cannot be signed off as closed. The Clinic Director[s] can advise how relevant protocols can be met.

2.2.6   For reasons of confidentiality you must not discuss or disclose to any persons, other than your fellow student volunteer(s), the professional volunteer, the Clinic Coordinator(s), the Clinic Administrator(s) or Clinic Director[s], matters confidential to [*insert name of clinic*] and its clients.

2.2.7   For reasons of confidentiality, client files and any documents relating to a client's case must not normally be removed from the clinic office. You agree that you will only undertake work relating to the client's case in the clinic office, using the computers available and in accordance with the provisions of the *Student handbook*. You further agree that you will only save electronic documents in the electronic folder set up for your case on the secure clinic drive.

2.2.8   For reasons of confidentiality you must only use your university email address to send and receive any communications relating to your case. You must switch off any automatic forwarding and/or links from the university account to personal accounts.

2.2.9   Your duty not to discuss or disclose to any other

force on 25 November 2019. The link in this paragraph will need to be updated whenever new versions are published on the SRA website.

persons matters confidential to [*insert name of clinic*], its clients, or any other matters which may come to your knowledge through your work, continues after you have ceased to participate in [*insert name of clinic*].

Supervision

3.1   All advice given and work done by student volunteers must be under the overall supervision of their assigned professional volunteer (supervising solicitor or barrister).

3.2   It is a breach of these rules to do any of the following without the authority of the professional volunteer:

    3.2.1   See or contact a client

    3.2.2   Send out any material of any sort, whether on headed or non-headed paper, in connection with any matter [*insert name of clinic*] is actually or potentially handling, or has handled

    3.3.3   Agree to take any other step for a client.

3.3   All correspondence and outgoing documentation must be authorised by the professional volunteer and signed by a Clinic Director.

3.4   The decision as to whether the client can be offered advice will only be taken with the agreement of the professional volunteer, after consultation with the student volunteer.

3.5   No individual student volunteer may continue to deal with a case if it appears that they may have any personal involvement or vested interest in the client's problem. If any such involvement is identified, the student volunteer must consult the professional volunteer before discussing the matter further with the client.

Money

4.1   We do not charge clients for our services.

4.2   No payment should be received from or on behalf of a client.

4.3   The offer of any gift by a client or any other person in connection with [*insert name of clinic*] must be referred to the professional volunteer and the Clinic Director[s].

4.4   We have a professional duty to inform all clients of the possible availability of the assistance under publicly funded advice and representation (formerly known as 'legal aid'). This is covered in the *Client information agreement*.

Client care

5.1 All clients advised at [*insert name of clinic*] must be given a copy of the *Client information agreement*. A copy of this document will have been sent to the client, along with the letter confirming their appointment. The client will be asked to bring the document with them. However, you should have a spare copy with you in case they forget. The contents of the *Client information agreement* should be explained clearly to the client at the start of the first appointment.

5.2 Clients may only be given advice in writing and only after proper consideration and research and with the approval of the professional volunteer.

5.3 No casework can be undertaken unless the client has signed the *Client information agreement* and provided the required identification documentation.

5.4 It is essential that you complete work in accordance with the timescales set out in the *Student handbook* or agreed with the professional volunteer. You must let the professional volunteer and Clinic Director[s] know immediately if this is not going to be possible.

5.5 Where an appointment for a client is made, the student volunteers must keep that appointment. In the event of a student volunteer not being able to keep an appointment, they must inform the Clinic Director[s] and the professional volunteer in accordance with the procedure laid down in the *Student handbook*.

I have read and accept the terms of this contract and undertake to abide by those terms and to respect the confidentiality of [*insert name of clinic*] and its clients at all times.

I consent to my personal data, including my name and contact details, being shared with the client and with the [*insert name of clinic*] partner firms and chambers.

I understand I will be removed from [*insert name of clinic*] if I fail to attend an appointment with a client or any case management meeting without good reason or if I breach the rules of professional conduct or any of the rules contained within this agreement.

I further understand that if I breach the university's conduct rules in the course of my involvement with [*insert name of clinic*] I may be subject to the university's student disciplinary procedure[7] and that if I breach the rules on client data that are contained in the *Student handbook* and the *Privacy notice* that may lead to the university having to notify the Information Commissioners

---

7   You may wish to insert a link to that here.

Office, which could result in significant fines and reputational damage for the university.

I undertake to read the [*insert name of clinic*] *Student handbook* and abide by its procedures.

Name of student   ....

Signed   ....

Date   ....

5.1.6 Student agreement: Option 3

[*Insert name of clinic*]: Clinic membership rules

By joining the [*insert name of clinic*], I agree to:

1. Be an active member of the clinic until there is formal intimation that I no longer wish to take part in clinic activities, graduate or am removed from clinic membership in terms of its rules and procedures.

2. Uphold and protect the confidentiality of all clients without exception. In particular, this means that confidential details of cases should only be discussed with law clinic staff and other members on a need-to-know basis.

3. Act with respect to clients, members of the public, one another, and clinic staff.

4. Complete all required casework diligently and expeditiously.

5. Give reasonable notice or find suitable replacements if I cannot make an appointment with a client.

6. Check my university email every day and respond timeously to emails about clinic matters.

7. Ensure that I uphold all my clinic obligations, most importantly (but not only) to clients, and if I am not going to be able to do so to give ample notice to my fellow case advisor and relevant clinic staff.

I declare that I have read and understood the above.

Signed:

Full name:

Date:

5.1.7 Client information agreement[1]

1.   About [*insert name of clinic*]

1.1   The [*insert name of clinic*] enables students studying at the [*insert name of university*] to obtain practical legal experience. Students are not professionally qualified but will be supervised by solicitors or barristers holding practising certificates. The [*insert name of clinic*] Director, [*insert name*] and/or a student [*insert name of clinic*] coordinator will also be in attendance on appointment days.

1.2   The solicitors supervising [*insert name of clinic*] cases are regulated by the Solicitors Regulation Authority (SRA) and the barristers are regulated by the Bar Standards Board (BSB). This means that [*insert name of clinic*] must meet all of the relevant standards about managing a law office, conducting casework professionally and otherwise looking after its clients. If you would like to see what these rules are in detail, you can do so by visiting the SRA website at: http://www.sra.org.uk and clicking on 'SRA Standards and Regulations' and by visiting the BSB website at: http://www.barstandardsboard.org.uk and clicking on 'BSB Handbook'.

2.   What you can expect from [*insert name of clinic*]

2.1   Upon receiving your request for advice from [*insert name of clinic*] you will be asked to provide some personal details that will be shared via email with the supervising solicitors and barristers in [*insert name of clinic*] before an appointment can be arranged.

2.2   An appointment will be made for you to attend [*insert name of clinic*] where you will be interviewed by two student volunteers. The student volunteers will not be able to give you any advice at this appointment. After your appointment the student volunteers will discuss the case with a supervising solicitor or barrister. If at this stage it appears that we will be unable to give you advice, due to the nature of the case, pressure of time or complexity, you will be informed in writing. In such cases, you will, wherever possible, be given information on other organisations that may be able to help you.

2.3   If [*insert name of clinic*] is able to offer advice the letter of advice will normally be sent to you by post within 14 days of the appointment. If

---

1   This agreement includes clauses drawn from the LawWorks' *Student handbook*, Practice guidance from the Law Society of England & Wales and the Solicitors Regulation Authority, SRA Standards and Regulations guidance for the not for profit sector (23 July 2019) <https://www.sra.org.uk/newregs/> accessed 26 July 2019.

for any reason it is not possible for us to meet this deadline, you will be informed either in writing or by telephone.

3. What service can [*insert name of clinic*] offer?

3.1 [*Insert name of clinic*] provides an advice-only service. This means that we cannot represent you in court or at any other hearing. However, where possible [*insert name of clinic*] will signpost you to an appropriate body or organisation. We do not offer assistance beyond initial advice, for example we cannot do any letter-writing or form-filling on your behalf.

3.2 Should you need to contact [*insert name of clinic*] at any time please email [*insert email address*] or call [*insert number*] and leave a message. A member of our team will get back to you as soon as possible. Please note that [*insert name of clinic*] is not open during weekends.

3.3 You may end your instructions to us in writing at any time. Once we have agreed to take on your case, we may decide to stop acting for you only with good reason. We must give you reasonable notice that we will stop acting for you.

4. What will it cost?

4.1. [*Insert name of clinic*] does not charge for its services. However, you should be aware of the following points:

4.1.1 You may be eligible for publicly-funded help and representation to pursue or defend your claim (formerly known as 'legal aid'). [*Insert name of clinic*] can signpost you to a solicitor or barrister who may be able to obtain such assistance for you. If you are eligible to receive assistance you may be liable to pay a contribution. You may also be liable to repay your costs from any money or property recovered.

4.1.2 If you decide to pursue court or tribunal proceedings you may be ordered to pay the costs of your opponent if you lose your case.

4.1.3 [*Insert name of clinic*] cannot brief barristers on your behalf.

5. Insurance

5.1 [*Insert name of clinic*] has insurance cover provided by the [*insert name of university*], [*insert names of any partner organisations that provide lawyers to supervise*] who supervise [*insert name of clinic*].

5.2   The university's insurance policy is held with: [*insert details*]. Their address is: [*insert address*]. Our policy number is: [*insert number*]. The cover is for up to [*insert amount*] for any one claim. If we do fall short of the expected standard we are obliged to advise you of this and of your right to complain and seek advice and possible compensation. Details of insurance cover held by [*insert names of partner organisations*] are available upon request. If the university or any of the other parties named above have to make a notification under the terms of their insurance policy, information about you and your case may be seen by our insurers.

6.   What we expect of you

As our client, we expect you to be cooperative, frank and truthful about all aspects of your case and to tell us as soon as possible about any changes in your circumstances as they affect your case.

7.   What if I wish to make a complaint?

7.1   We hope you will be satisfied with the service provided by [*insert name of clinic*]. If you are unhappy please ask to see a [*insert name of clinic*] Director and talk things over to see if you can solve the problem. If you wish to complain in writing, you should address your complaint to:

[*Insert details*]

We have a written procedure in place that details how we handle complaints which is available upon request from [*insert name*], [*insert name of clinic*] Director, who can be contacted on [*insert number*].

We have eight weeks to consider your complaint. If we have not resolved it within this time you may complain to the Legal Ombudsman.

If you are not satisfied with our handling of your complaint you can ask the Legal Ombudsman to consider the complaint. The Legal Ombudsman can be contacted as follows:

–   By post: PO Box 6806, Wolverhampton WV1 9WJ

–   By telephone: 0300 555 0333 or 0121 245 3050

–   By email: enquiries@legalombudsman.org.uk

Normally, you will need to bring a complaint to the Legal Ombudsman within six months of receiving a final written response from us about your complaint or within six years of the act or omission about which you are complaining occurring (or if outside of this period, within three years of when you should reasonably have been aware of it).

The Solicitors Regulation Authority could also help you if you are concerned about our behaviour. This could be for things like dishonesty, taking or losing your money or treating you unfairly because of your age, a disability or other characteristic. You can raise your concerns with the Solicitors Regulation Authority via its website or by calling 0370 606 2555.

If you are unhappy about the way we manage your personal information you have a right to object to the Information Commissioner, Wycliffe House, Water Lane, Wilmslow, Cheshire SK9 5AF (Tel: 0303 123 1113)/ https://ico.org.uk/make-a-complaint/ [2]

8.   Student advisers and supervisor

8.1   Your student advisors are: [*insert names*]

They are being supervised by: [*insert name of supervising lawyer*] of [*insert name of university or name of organisation of supervising lawyer if different*] who has overall responsibility for supervision of your matter.

9.   Data protection

9.1   All cases are treated in the strictest confidence in accordance with best practices of the legal profession. This means your case will normally only be discussed by you, the student volunteers, university staff and students involved in the operation of [*insert name of clinic*] and staff from the partner law firm or chambers involved in your case. Information obtained during these discussions on or in relation to your case will be deemed 'personal information' as it relates to yourself and or your associates as identifiable individuals.

9.2   [*Insert name of clinic*] complies with the Principles set out in the Data Protection Act 2018 and the General Data Protection Regulation (GDPR). Personal information shall be processed in accordance with the *Privacy notice* contained at Appendix 1 of this agreement by university students and staff working within [*insert name of clinic*] and by staff from [*insert name of any partner organisations that provide supervising lawyers*] for the purpose of providing legal services to you, and for the purpose of case management and service delivery. Personal information will not be disclosed to third parties except as above, in accordance with the *Privacy notice* set out at Appendix 1 and:

2   Depending on the service offered by your clinic, you may also need to insert details of available regulatory redress schemes (such as the Office of the Immigration Services Commissioner or the Financial Conduct Authority). See the SRA Standards and Regulations guidance for the not for profit sector' (**note 1**) for more details on this.

- where you have explicitly requested or consented to the personal information being shared with a named third party

- where disclosure of personal data is required by law and where such disclosure is not protected by professional legal privilege and does not first require consent to be obtained

- where parties conduct audit or quality checks on our practice. These parties are required to maintain confidentiality in relation to your case

- where it is required by our regulators, the Solicitors Regulation Authority or the Bar Standards Board

- where it is required under the Proceeds of Crime Act 2002 which imposes a duty on lawyers to report certain information to the authorities, where, for example, it seems that some assets in your case were derived from a crime. If we have to make a report we may not be able to tell you that we have done so.

External firms or organisations may conduct audit or quality checks on our practice from time to time. They may wish to audit/quality check your file and related papers for this purpose. It is a specific requirement imposed by us that these external firms or organisations fully maintain confidentiality in relation to any files and papers which are audited/quality checked by them.

10.   Storage of personal information

In providing services to you, [*insert name of clinic*] shall store documents relating to your case in hardcopy and/or electronic format. We shall have in place technical and security measures which shall be of a standard generally observed in the legal profession. We shall store client records containing personal information securely for a period of not less than six years after the date on which your letter of advice is sent, unless there is an explicit requirement to destroy the information before that period, or retain the information for longer.

11.   [Proof of identity

11.1   The law requires solicitors to get satisfactory evidence of the identity of their clients and sometimes people related to them. This is because solicitors who deal with money and property on behalf of their client or advise clients on matters relating to money can be used by criminals wanting to launder money.

11.2   To comply with the law, we need to get evidence of your identity as soon as possible. Details of the documents that you will need to provide us with were set out in our letter to you dated [*insert date*].[3] If you cannot provide us with the specific identification requested, please contact us as soon as possible to discuss other ways to verify your identity. We will not be able to provide any advice to you until you have provided the identification we require.]

I confirm that I have read the above and accept the terms set out above and I hereby consent to [*insert name of clinic*] handling my case on the basis described in this document.

I consent to members of [*insert name of clinic*], namely [*insert name of university*], [*insert names of partner organisations providing supervising lawyers*] using, sharing and processing my personal data (including sensitive personal information) in the ways explained above and in the *Privacy notice* at Appendix 1 and in order to undertake identity and conflict of interest checks, to comply with statutory reporting obligations including those in respect of money laundering and fraud, and in order to deal with my request for advice. Such personal data will be safely stored in accordance with current data protection legislation at all times.

I consent to my information being shared between [*insert name of university*], [*insert names of any partner organisations providing supervising lawyers*] by email.

Name of client: ....

Signed :   ....

Date: ....

---

3   Where identity information is required (see **Part 2.5: Anti-money laundering** for more detail on this) details of what the client needs to provide can be listed in a letter to the client, along with confirmation of other details of their appointment

Appendix 1: Privacy notice [*insert* Privacy notice]

See 5.2.2 and 5.2.3 for examples.

5.1.8 Third party confidentiality agreement[1]

I acknowledge that during my visit to [*insert name of clinic*], I may have access to confidential information and personal data belonging to clients of [*insert name of clinic*] ('confidential information').

I shall not, either during my visit to [*insert name of clinic*], or at any time thereafter, use or disclose to any third party (save for the student volunteers and supervising lawyers allocated to the case to which the confidential information relates or to the Clinic Director[s]) any confidential information.

This restriction does not apply to:

(a)   any use or disclosure authorised by the client or required by law; or

(b)   any information which is already in, or comes into, the public domain otherwise than through my unauthorised disclosure.

Name: _____

Signature: _____

Date: _____

---

1   From time to time you may welcome visitors to your clinic, such as: colleagues from other departments in your own institution; guests from other universities; and visitors from the third sector. It is important to ensure that they are obliged to keep any information relating to the clinic confidential. Where a visitor wishes to sit in on a client meeting, the client's consent should be sought in advance of the meeting.

Part 5.2
Policies and procedures

5.2.1 Data protection and records retention policy[1]

Background

1. The [*insert name of clinic/centre*] is part of [*insert name of university*] and as such [*university*] is the data controller of personal data processed by the [*clinic/centre*]. The [*insert name of clinic/centre*] adheres to the [*university*] *Data protection policy*.[2]

Client information

2. Details of client enquiries are recorded in both hard and electronic copies.

3. Details of client enquiries are retained for up to one year unless the enquiry proceeds to being a case. This period starts from the end of the academic year when the client enquiry was made to the [*clinic/centre*].[3]

4. If an enquiry proceeds to be a case, the [*case summary form*] and all other documents relevant to the case will be kept for six years as part of the client case file. This period starts from the end of the academic year when the client enquiry was taken. If the enquiry does not become a case, the [*case summary form*] is deleted at the end of the academic year.

5. All client answerphone messages that come to the client telephone answer machine are deleted as soon as they are logged on the [*clinic/centre*] system.

6. All emails containing client enquiries are deleted at the end of each academic year.

Case files

7. Hardcopy case files are made when a case has been booked for an appointment. They are retained for the duration that the case is active [*or for one additional academic year if the case relates to an assessment document*].

---

1 This policy will need to be checked against the university's policy from time to time. Some time periods specified will be a matter of discretion for the specific clinic/centre.

2 Insert location of the *Data protection policy*.

3 An academic year starts on 1 September of each calendar year.

8. When the case has been electronically saved and archived, the hard copy of the file is destroyed (unless it is part of an assessment as stated above).

9. Electronic client files are retained for six years in password-protected files that only [*clinic/centre*] staff have access to. This period starts from the end of the academic year when the case was dealt with.

10. The [*client emails/contents of a client email folder*] forms part of the correspondence of the client file. As such it is kept for six years.

Appointment information

11. An electronic appointment list is kept outlining all the appointments that are booked in for [*clinic/centre*] appointments and contain details of who has worked on the case. This contains basic client contact information and details of the opponent in the case. This version is kept in [*specify university data storage system*] [*indefinitely*] [*for six years. This period starts at the end of the academic year when the appointment was held.*] This is for the purposes of client case records and to ensure client conflict checks are carried out for new clients.[4]

Student information (appointments and projects)

12. Hard copies of student applications that are made for the purposes of selection are shredded at the end of the academic year.

13. All registers taken at training events or other events are scanned into the university hard drive and hard copies are shredded. Electronic versions are kept for six years and then deleted. This period starts from the end of the academic year when they were taken.

14. Student applications are held on the university hard drive for six years. This period starts from the end of the academic year that they relate to.

15. Lists of student advisers (including contact details) are kept for six years. Student names are also kept on the appointment list for six years. These periods start from the end of the academic year that they relate to. This is for the purposes of reference writing and in the case of a complaint/query relating to a case.

16. Student references are saved on the [*specify university data storage system*] and saved for six years.

17. Student applications are submitted via [*specify method and any*

---

4   Clinics should consider whether any information should be kept beyond the six year period to ensure professional regulatory requirements are met (for example, conflict checking) and ensure this is reflected in this policy.

encryption]. These are password-protected. [*Specify staff*] have access to these, which are retained for two years and then deleted. This period starts from the end of the academic year that they relate to.

18.   Scanned copies of student Disclosure and Barring Service (DBS) certificates are kept on the [*specify university data storage system*] for six years.

19.   [*Include details of other student groups and data control time limits*].

Supervisor information

20.   Hard copies of a volunteer supervising lawyer's information (supervisor) is not kept.

21.   Supervisor details are kept in the [*specify relevant project spreadsheet*] and retained for six years. This period starts from the end of the academic year that the document relates to.

22.   Supervisor details are kept on a [*specify data storage location*] on the university's [*specify data storage system*]. The information is kept for six years. This period starts from the end of the academic year that it relates to.

External organisations and schools

23.   Details of [*schools/external organisations*] enquiring or taking part in [*specify project*] are retained for six years electronically on the [*specify university data storage system*].

24.   Feedback forms for [*specify project*] are retained for six years. This period starts from the end of the academic year that they relate to.

Miscellaneous

25.   Incident records are kept electronically for six years. This period starts from the end of the academic year that they relate to.

26.   Anonymous equality and diversity data is kept for ten years electronically on the [*specify university data storage system*]. This period starts from the end of the academic year that it relates to.

27.   Data processor forms are retained for six years on the university hard drive. This period starts from the end of the academic year that it relates to.

For data retention or protection queries please contact [*specify person*] at [*insert email address*]. For [*university*] data retention or protection queries please contact [*specify person if required*] at [*insert email address*].

5.2.2 Privacy notice: Option 1

[*Insert name of clinic*]: Privacy notice[1]

This *Privacy notice* provides information about how the university uses the personal data we collect where you engage with our [*insert name of clinic*]. It supplements the page on our website [*insert link to university's webpage setting out how the institution uses data*].

The [*insert name of clinic*] is run by the law school at [*insert name of university*]. It [*insert brief description of the work done by your clinic*]. [Much of this work is done under the supervision of volunteer lawyers from law firms and barristers chambers.]

Please read the information set out below carefully before requesting assistance from [*insert name of clinic*]. Please feel free to contact [*insert name and job title of appropriate contact*] at [*insert email address and telephone number*] if you do not understand any part of the information, or ask a friend or relative or other person known to you or otherwise (such as a translator) to assist you with the information.

How does this *Privacy notice* relate to other privacy notices?

If you are also a current student or alumni of [*insert name of university*] then our *Current students* or *Alumni and supporters* privacy notices will also apply to you.

[Sometimes another organisation will also be a data controller of your personal data, for example one of the partner law firms or barristers' chambers that we work with which may provide supervision for our students when they are working on your case. These organisations should have their own privacy notices explaining how they use your data.[2]]

What personal data will be processed?

If you approach us to ask us for advice, we will process biographical and contact details, as well as information that you provide to us about your legal query such as the problems you are facing and the other people involved.

Depending on your query we might need to ask you for and use information about you which is of a sensitive nature, for example information about your health and finances.

---

1   This template was provided by a university that had incorporated into its draft some of the LawWorks template Privacy Notice contained in its GDPR Toolkit.

2   This may be relevant where volunteer lawyers are involved in supervising the work done by the students in your clinic on behalf of their own firms or chambers.

What is the purpose of the processing?

We will use your information to help you in connection with the legal problem you have come to see us about. We will also use it in the first instance in order to determine whether your query is a matter that we are able to assist you with. For example, some legal queries will be too complex for a student law clinic to advise on, or we may find that we, or one of our partner firms, has already provided advice to another party involved in your query and are therefore unable to take on your case due to a conflict of interest.

You do not have to provide us with any information, or give your consent for us to share your personal information. However, our ability to act on your behalf might be affected if you do not.

What is the legal basis of the processing?

Normally, we process your data with explicit consent. Sometimes we do so because it is necessary for:

- The performance of our agreement to provide you with legal advice or in order to take steps at your request before entering into an agreement with you to provide legal advice. This will include:
  - determining whether your query is one that we are able to assist you with
  - determining whether we can find a volunteer lawyer to supervise your case
  - providing legal advice and assistance to you.
- Compliance with a legal obligation (for example, identity checks under money laundering legislation) or regulatory obligation (for example, reporting to the Solicitors Regulation Authority).
- The performance of tasks we carry out in the public interest (for example, the educational benefits for our students of giving legal advice).
- For the purposes of an external organisation's legitimate interests (for example, to enable your access to external services such as the supervision from our partner law firms and chambers).

We will only process your special category data with your explicit consent or if it is necessary:

- for the establishment, exercise or defence of legal claims
- very occasionally, to protect your or another person's vital interests and you are not capable of giving your consent (for example, in an emergency)
- in the substantial public interest.

Who will your personal data be shared with?

Within the university, your data is shared with only those university staff and students who need to be able to access it for the purpose of running our pro bono services and advising you on your case.

Before we agree to take on your case we may need to share your information (including special category personal information, for example relating to your racial or ethnic origin, political opinions, religious or philosophical beliefs, or trade union membership) with the law firms and barristers' chambers that assist with our cases in order to try and find a volunteer lawyer to supervise your case. We will inform you in advance where we need to convey information about you to a third party and will only share information about you where we have obtained your prior consent either verbally or in writing. Your information may also be shared with third parties:

- where you have explicitly requested or consented to the personal information being shared with a named third party
- where disclosure of personal data is required by law and where such disclosure is not protected by professional legal privilege and does not first require consent to be obtained
- as part of audit or quality checks on our practice carried out by external firms or organisations. They may wish to audit/quality check your file and related papers for this purpose. It is a specific requirement imposed by us that these external firms or organisations fully maintain confidentiality in relation to any files and papers which are audited/quality checked by them
- where it is required by our regulators, the Solicitors Regulation Authority or the Bar Standards Board
- under the Proceeds of Crime Act 2002, which imposes a duty on lawyers to report certain information to the authorities, where, for example, it seems that some assets in your case were derived from a crime. If we have to make a report we may not be able to tell you that we have done so.

If we need to obtain any information about you from a third party for the purpose of assisting you we will only do so once you have provided us with your consent.

We ensure we have appropriate data sharing agreements in place before sharing your personal data with any other data controllers.

Your personal data is shared as is necessary, on a considered and confidential basis, with several external organisations that assist with processing your information. These organisations act on our behalf in accordance with our instructions and do not process your data for any purpose over and above what we have asked them to do. We make sure we have appropriate contracts in place with them. Sometimes your personal data is processed by these organisations outside the European Economic Area (EEA) (for example, because they use a cloud-based system with servers based outside the EEA), and if so, we make sure that appropriate safeguards are in place to ensure the confidentiality and security of your personal data.

We do not share your data with external organisations for marketing their products or services. We do not sell your personal data to third parties under any circumstances, or permit third parties to sell on the data we have shared with them.

How long is your data kept?

We will only keep your personal information for as long as necessary, which will depend on the type of information held and the reason for holding it.

We will keep information about you only for as long as we need it in order to:

- comply with any legal requirement concerning your information
- be able to respond in the event that a complaint is made
- ensure that information about you is accurate and up to date
- undertake research and statistical analysis.

Where you make an enquiry with us but we are not able to take on your case, we will not keep your details for longer than 12 months.

Where we have given you legal advice, we will have to retain some basic personal information about you (such as your name, address, basic details about the nature of your query and the other parties involved) indefinitely, in order to comply with regulatory requirements that we do not take on any cases for other clients in the future where there might be a conflict of interest with your case. We will delete all other information seven years after our letter of advice is sent to you.

Your rights in relation to your data

Details about your rights are set out on the website page [*insert link to university webpage*]. This also explains how to ask any questions you may have about how your personal data is used, exercise any of your rights or complain about the way your data is being handled.

5.2.3 Privacy notice: Option 2

Privacy notice

1. Who we are

The [*insert name of university*] ('we' or 'us') are a 'data controller' for the purposes of the data protection legislation (including the Data Protection Act 1998 and the General Data Protection Regulation (GDPR)) and we are responsible for, and control the processing of, your personal information.

2. Your privacy

We are committed to protecting your privacy. This notice explains how the university and [*insert name of clinic*] collect and process your personal information for the purposes of providing general legal advice.

3. Information we collect

We obtain personal information about you from the following sources.

Information provided by you:

Personal information during initial interview with [_____], whether online or in person	
Personal information through one of our websites, i.e. through our online enquiry form	
Completed and/or returned surveys or response/feedback forms such as equality and diversity monitoring form and post-interview questionnaire	
Registered to attend an event	
Personal information as part of discussions with any of our team or representatives, such as a drop-in enquiry	
Other (please state)	

We may process the following personal information about you:

(a) Your title, full name (including former name or alias), gender, date of birth.

(b) Your contact information (home/term-time address, telephone number(s), email address).

(c) Your business details, including positions, organisation, professional memberships and qualifications.

(d)   Your outside interests and memberships.

(e)   Your financial information (including your bank/building society details).

(f)   Information available through the media or the world wide web.

(g)   Your family/next of kin details, including your spouse/partner.

(h)   Other information you share with us.

Personal information we collect about you may include 'special categories' data, such as information about your racial or ethnic origin, religious or other beliefs, physical or mental health and criminal offences/proceedings.

'Special categories' data would only be processed where you have provided it yourself (with your consent), for example during discussions with any of our representatives or where such is recorded for the purposes of assessing accessibility requirements arising as a result of a disability, or where this information has already been made public or processing is required by law.

The [insert name of university] uses cookies to improve the content and experience of its website users, but rest assured that these do not allow for us to identify you personally. More information on how to manage cookies can be found [insert].

4.   How we use your data

We collect your personal data solely for the purpose of providing you with general legal advice concerning the issue that you have visited us about; such information will only be shared between those supervisors and students whom are working on your case. Occasionally our supervisors will be solicitors in practice whom are external to our organisation.

In relation to special categories data, we collect personal information to enable us to deliver these services and to better understand our community so that we can better meet your needs and improve our services. This data is shared periodically with LawWorks anonymously.

We may process your personal information for the following purposes:

(a)   Due diligence

        Should you choose to make a gift or donation to the university, we may process your personal information for due diligence purposes and in line with our Corporate fundraising policy [insert link].

(b)   Communications

        We may, from time to time, contact you by email, post or telephone to pursue the purposes mentioned above and in particular for the following reasons:

- to keep you up to date with the progress of your legal matter
- to invite you to events that may be of interest to you
- to invite you to support our fundraising activities
- to keep you up to date with other relevant information, which we think may be of interest to you.

If you would like to opt out of the above communications, please let us know. See **9. How to contact us** below for further information.

5. Who your information may be shared with

Your personal information is held in a secure location (locked filing cabinet) and may also be held on a cloud-based client management system. We will not disclose your personal data to other companies within our group, third parties working in partnership or on behalf of the university, and/or government agencies unless required to do so by law.

We do not transfer your personal information to third parties outside the European Economic Area (EEA) or to territories without adequate levels of protection. Where personal data is processed by a third party, we take reasonable steps to ensure that the data is processed strictly according to the instructions of the university, for the relevant purposes only and securely destroyed or returned upon completion/termination. We take reasonable steps to ensure that third party processors are subject to written legal obligations in respect of data protection and the duty of confidentiality.

We do not sell or rent any personal information or data supplied by you. We may compile aggregate statistics and provide them to third parties, but we do not include personal information that identifies individual users.

6. Retention

We may retain your personal information for a period of six years or as long as necessary and in line with our statutory/regulatory obligations where appropriate.

If you wish to request for any of your records to be removed from our database, or would like to opt-out of any or all communications from the [*insert university name*], please see **9. How to contact us** and **7. Rights of data subjects** below for further information.

7. Rights of data subjects

(a) Right to request a copy of your information

You can request a copy of your information which we hold (this is known as a subject access request). If you would like a copy of some or all of it, please visit [*insert link to relevant university webpage*].

(b)   Right to correct mistakes in your information

You can require us to correct any mistakes in your information that we hold free of charge. If you would like to do so, please write to us (see **9. How to contact us** below) and provide us with enough information to identify you, as well as inform us of the information that is incorrect and what it should be replaced with.

(c)   Right to ask us to stop contacting you with direct marketing

If you would like to amend your mailing subscriptions or unsubscribe you can do so by emailing [*insert email address*].

8.   Lawful basis for processing

The university may rely on one or multiple grounds for processing your personal data including:

(a)   You have provided consent for the processing.

(b)   There is a contractual commitment to provide the services and, therefore, processing is necessary to meet those contractual obligations.

(c)   The information is available to the public at large.

(d)   The processing is necessary for the purposes of legitimate interests of the university or other third parties and does not affect the fundamental rights and freedoms of the individuals concerned.

9.   How to contact us

[*Insert contact details*]

If you have any concerns or believe that your personal information is being handled in a manner which is contrary to statutory requirements, you may wish to contact the university's Data Protection Officer via [*insert email address*] or complain to the Information Commissioner's Office via www.ico.org.

10.   Revisions to the privacy notice

We may revise this privacy notice at any time in response to changes in the law or other factors. We encourage you to periodically visit this page to review the most current policy, or obtain a copy by contacting us directly.

5.2.4 Client identification policy[1]

[*Insert name of clinic*]: Guidance

It is essential that ***every*** client who comes to [insert name of clinic] has been properly identified before any advice is given to them. This note explains why that is the case and describes how identification must be carried out.

Why must we identify clients?

There are a number of reasons why we must verify the identity of a client. The most important of those are as follows:-

1.   Are they who they say they are? We must be sure that a client is who they say they are and that any documents that they would like us to review (during their interview or afterwards) rightfully belong to them and have been legitimately obtained.

2.   Is the client applying undue pressure on another party? Verifying a client's identity may help to alert us to the possibility that the client or some other person is being taken advantage of.

       (For example, perhaps a son might bring documents belonging to his mother and ask to receive advice in respect of them in order to coerce his mother into taking some particular action that would be beneficial for him).

3.   Are we at risk of committing (or being party to) a criminal offence? Money laundering legislation requires us to verify a client's identity if that client is seeking advice which falls within the 'regulated sector'. The reason for this is to prevent law firms and other organisations from unwittingly committing or becoming complicit in money laundering activity. Failure to comply with this requirement is a criminal offence.

       The **'regulated sector'** includes:

- Participation in financial or real property transactions concerning:
    - Buying and selling of real property or business entities;
    - managing of client money, securities or other assets;
    - opening or management of bank, savings or securities accounts;

1   This policy assumes all clients will be subject to identity checks. For more information on the legal requirements on clinics see **Part 2.5: Anti-money laundering**. This precedent outlines documents that would be required from clients that are individuals, trustees of a trust and partners in a partnership. If your clinic is likely to advise companies then you should consider covering the identify requirements for companies in your policy too.

- organisation of contributions necessary for the creation, operation or management of companies; or
- creation, operation or management of trusts, companies or similar structures.
- Provision of advice about the tax affairs of a client.
- Formation of companies or other legal persons.
- Acting or arranging for another person to act:
  - as a director or secretary of a company;
  - as a partner of a partnership; or
  - in a similar position in relation to other legal persons.
- Provision of a registered office, business address, correspondence or administrative address or other related services for a company, partnership or any other legal person or arrangement.
- Acting or arranging for another person to act:
  - as a trustee of an express trust or similar legal arrangement; or
  - as a nominee shareholder for a person other than a company whose securities are listed on a regulated market.

(It is participating in a transaction to assist in the planning or execution of the transaction or otherwise acting for or on behalf of a client in the transaction).

Even if the subject matter that a client is seeking advice on does not appear at first to fall within the regulated sector at the outset, it may end up straying into the regulated sector and sometimes this can be very early on. For example, advice on the process of divorce might stray into divorce settlement advice and thus into the provision of tax advice. Another example is when advising on employment issues.

For that very reason, most law firms now choose to verify the identity of all clients at the outset of a matter, whether or not it appears at that stage to fall within the regulated sector. The Solicitors' Regulation Authority ('SRA') encourages that approach.

4.   Are there any other risks? Even where none of the above apply and the advice sought is definitely not within the regulated sector, additional potential risks still exist; sham litigation, for example, may amount to money laundering.

[Insert name of clinic]'s Policy

For all of the reasons above, according to [insert name of clinic]'s policy you must obtain certain documents to check the identity of all clients whether or not regulated sector work is involved.

Under no circumstances must any legal advice of any kind (most importantly, any tax advice) be provided to a client before identify documents have been produced by the client.

What documents do I require from the client?

If the client is an individual, we require either:

- one document from list A; **or** if this is unavailable
- one document from list B and another from list C
-

List A: Photo ID
Valid passport
Valid photocard driving licence with current address on
Valid government issue identity card (for non-UK resident individuals only)

List B: Proof of name
Valid full driving licence (with no photo) that includes current address
Birth certificate (with relevant marriage certificate or deed poll if your name has changed)
A bank, building society or credit card statement (but not an internet statement) dated within the last three months

List C: Proof of current home address
A utility bill – gas, electricity, water or telephone (but not a mobile telephone bill or online bill) –dated within the last three months
Current council tax bill (but not an online bill): **UK ONLY**
Current house or motor insurance certificate

For trustees of a trust

If the client is a trustee, we must verify the identities of a minimum of two trustees and identify who (by knowing their names and contact details) the ultimate beneficial owners of the trust are.

For each trustee, we require:

- one document from list A; **or** if this is unavailable
- one document from list B and another from list C

List A: Photo ID
Valid passport
Valid photocard driving licence with current address on

List B: Proof of name
Valid old-style driving licence with current address on
Birth certificate (with relevant marriage certificate or deed poll if your name has changed)
A bank, building society or credit card statement (but not an internet statement) dated within the last three months

List C: Proof of current home address
A utility bill – gas, electricity, water or telephone (but not a mobile telephone bill or online bill) – dated within the last three months
Current council tax bill (but not an online bill)
Current house or motor insurance certificate

The ultimate beneficial owners of the trust are:

- the settlor;
- the trustees;
- the beneficiaries;
- where the individual (or some of the individuals) benefiting from the trust have not been determined, the class of persons in whose main interest the trust is set up, or operates;
- any individual who has control over the trust.

Control means power (whether exercisable alone, jointly, with another person or with the consent of another person) under the trust instrument or by law to:

- dispose of, advance, lend, invest, pay or apply trust property;
- vary or terminate the trust;
- add or remove a person as beneficiary or to or from a class of beneficiaries;
- appoint or remove trustees or given another individual control over the trust; or
- direct, withhold consent to or veto the exercise of a power mentioned in the bullet points above.

A protector of a trust is likely to be an ultimate beneficial owner.

To identify the ultimate beneficial owners you should see the original, or original certified copy of the trust document and ask the trustees whether anyone else (other than those mentioned in the trust document) exercise control over the trust or benefits from the trust.

For partners in a partnership

If the client is a partner in a partnership, we must verify the identities of a minimum of two partners and identify who the other individuals who would fall within the definition of ultimate beneficial ownership are. For each partner, we require:

- one document from list A; **or** if this is unavailable
- one document from list B and another from list C.

List A: Photo ID
Valid passport
Valid photocard driving licence with current address on

List B: Proof of name
Valid old-style driving licence with current address on
Birth certificate (with relevant marriage certificate or deed poll if your name has changed)
A bank, building society or credit card statement (but not an internet statement) dated within the last three months

List C: Proof of current home address
A utility bill – gas, electricity, water or telephone (but not a mobile telephone bill or online bill) – dated within the last three months
Current council tax bill (but not an online bill)
Current house or motor insurance certificate

An ultimate beneficial owner of a partnership is anyone who:

- exercises ultimate control over the management of the partnership;
- owns or controls (whether directly or indirectly) more than 25% of the partnership assets, or voting rights – this will include anyone who is entitled to more than 25% of the partnerships profits; or
- anyone else who controls the partnership.

To identify the ultimate beneficial owners of a partnership you should examine the original partnership agreement (if there is one) and ask the partners to explain the ownership and control structure.

What do I do with the documents once I have them?

The documents should be obtained from the client before their interview begins. Once you have the necessary documents you must take a photocopy, which you must then certify and file on the [insert name of clinic] system.

In order to certify a document:

- write "Certified to be a true copy of the original seen by me" on the face of the document;
- sign and date (with today's date) the document (never back date a certification); and
- print your name and "[insert name of clinic]" underneath your signature.

What if the client does not bring the documents to the interview?

At the time when you agree the date and time of the interview with a client, you should inform them of the need for them to bring their identity documents with them and stress that legal advice cannot be provided without those documents.

You should then remind the client:

- when you send them a letter confirming their appointment; and
- when you call them 24 hours before their interview.

In the event that a client forgets to bring the documents with them, the interview can still go ahead but no letter of advice can be released to the client under the identity documents have been produced. You are reminded that the interview is a fact-finding exercise ONLY and no legal advice (oral or otherwise) is to be given during any interview in any event.

If the client attempts to provide at the interview, or subsequently sends you, a photocopy of the original document as opposed to the original document itself, that will not be sufficient. Also, in order to be able to certify a copy of a document as a true copy of the original you must have seen the original. Do not be tempted to certify a photocopy as a true copy of the original when you have seen the original at some point in the past. You should certify the photocopy as soon as you have copied the original.

What do I do if I think this policy has been breached?

If at any time you become aware of any breach or possible breach of this policy you should disclose details as soon as possible to a member of staff in the clinic.

5.2.5 Complaints procedure

[Insert clinic name]

At the [*insert clinic name*] we endeavour to provide a high quality service to all of our clients. If for any reason you are dissatisfied with the service you have received, or the way your case is being conducted, please take the steps below.

Stage 1: Informal resolution

You should normally try to resolve your complaint with [*insert job title and name of staff member[1]*]. You can contact them in writing or by telephone using the details below:

[*Insert contact address and telephone number*]

Whether or not a resolution is reached at an informal stage, a record will be maintained of your concerns and our response.[2] We will inform you in writing of the outcome of this stage of the process.

Stage 2: Formal investigation

If your complaint is not resolved at the informal stage of the process, you should contact [*insert name of staff member or job title[3]*], who has ultimate responsibility within the Law School for complaints. They can be contacted using the details below:

[*Insert contact address and telephone number*]

[*Insert name of staff member of job title*] will carry out an investigation, or will appoint someone to do so on their behalf. This may involve inviting representations from all concerned, including you. The person carrying out the investigation will compile and provide a report, including conclusions and a proposed way forward. If you remain unsatisfied, you may proceed to the external stage.

---

1   Consider who the most appropriate staff member is to name here as the initial point of contact for dealing with complaints.

2   You may wish to cross refer to your *Privacy notice* here.

3   This should be someone more senior than the person assigned to deal with initial complaints. For example, it might be the Head of School or the Clinic Director.

Stage 3: External stage: The Legal Ombudsman[4]

If you are not satisfied with our handling of your complaint you can ask the Legal Ombudsman to consider the complaint. The Legal Ombudsman can be contacted as follows:

- By post: PO Box 6806, Wolverhampton, WV1 9WJ
- By telephone: 0300 555 0333 or 0121 245 3050
- By email: enquiries@legalombudsman.org.uk

Normally, you will need to bring a complaint to the Legal Ombudsman within six months of receiving a final written response from us about your complaint or within six years of the act or omission about which you are complaining occurring (or if outside of this period, within three years of when you should reasonably have been aware of it).

[[5]Referral to partner organisations

If, at any stage in the complaints process, the university considers that your complaint relates to an area that falls within the remit of one of our partner organisation[s] [*insert name(s) of partner organisations*[6]] then we will refer the matter to the relevant partner to be dealt with in accordance with their own complaints procedures, details of which will be provided upon referral. The university's own process may continue alongside the partner's complaints process or may be delayed pending the outcome of that process.]

---

4   Note that the SRA Code of Conduct for Solicitors (2019), Regulation 8.4 provides that if a client's complaint has not been resolved to the client's satisfaction within eight weeks following the making of a complaint, they should be informed in writing of any right they have to complain to the Legal Ombudsman. The Regulation also contains details of information that should be provided to a client where your complaints procedure has been exhausted. Further guidance on complaints and information that must be given to clients is contained in the SRA Standards and Regulations guidance for the not for profit sector (23 July 2019) <https://www.sra.org.uk/newregs/> accessed 26 July 2019.

5   This clause may be appropriate where your clinic is run with the support of lawyers from an external organisation, such as a law firm or barristers' chambers.

6   For example, Joe Bloggs LLP.

5.2.6 Social media policy

[Insert name of clinic/centre]

For the purposes of this document, social media includes, but is not limited to, the following:

- Facebook
- Snapchat
- Twitter
- LinkedIn
- Instagram
- WhatsApp
- Tinder

or any similar platforms.

Client enquiries

The [*clinic/centre*] does not take client enquiries from social media platforms. Clients who contact the [*clinic/centre*] on social media platforms should be told to make an enquiry via [*telephone/email/our online enquiry form: edit as appropriate*]. The [*clinic/centre*] does not handle any client communication through social media.

The same policy applies for enquiries relating to [*clinic/centre*] projects.

Contact between students working together

Students working on cases in the [*clinic/centre*] should avoid communicating with each other via social media unless this is essential (for example, to communicate the fact that one member of a team may be late/unable to attend a session). No discussion of client cases on social media should take place and, in particular, there must be no mention of any information that could identify a client.

Contact between students and clients

Students should not contact clients on social media or in any way accept their 'friend requests' or similar invitations while they are working at the [*clinic/centre*].

Students should not contact school students or other contacts made through [*specify clinic/centre project*] on social media.

Students will use their name on the bottom of client advice letters and in other [*clinic/centre*] projects. Students should be aware when they are presenting themselves on social media (especially when using their name), that clients or other [*clinic/centre*] project stakeholders may search for them.

If a client, or other person connected with using the [*clinic/centre*] services, contacts a student on social media, students should immediately draw this to the attention of the [*specify staff member*] and not respond.

Contact between students and [*clinic/centre*] staff

Students should not contact [*clinic/centre*] staff on social media while they are working on projects at the [*clinic/centre*]. All queries should be directed to the [*clinic/centre/staff shared email address* (*specify@specify*.ac.uk)] or a staff member's individual professional email address if the matter is of a personal nature.

Failure to comply with this policy may result in disciplinary action.

5.2.7 Student disciplinary code[1]

1. Introduction

The [*insert name of clinic*] is committed to creating an environment where all clinic members and staff are able to perform their duties to the best of their ability. However, the [*insert name of clinic*] also recognises that there may be occasions when disciplinary and/or performance problems arise, and that it needs to ensure confidential and quality services to its clients and uphold its reputation for doing so.

The purpose of this policy is to ensure that, if problems do arise, they are dealt with fairly and consistently. This policy sets out the action that shall be taken when problems occur.

2. Overarching principles

Any disciplinary action to which a clinic member is subject shall be underpinned by the following principles:

The procedure is designed to establish the facts quickly and to deal consistently and confidentially with disciplinary issues.

At every stage, the clinic member shall be advised in writing (which includes email) of the nature of the complaint and shall be given the opportunity to state their case in a meeting before any decision is taken on whether to impose a warning or other disciplinary sanction.

At every stage, complainants and those subject to complaint can be expected, as far as possible, to be dealt with confidentially and with respect for their privacy. However, any person who is the subject of complaint will be advised, and an appropriately redacted copy of the concern or complaint and any associated evidence will normally be copied to them, in order that they are given the opportunity to respond. It may also be necessary to disclose information to others in order to deal with the concern or complaint and, in these circumstances, the parties concerned will be informed of such a disclosure.

The clinic member shall be given the opportunity to be accompanied by another clinic member at any disciplinary meeting.

When a decision has been made regarding whether or not disciplinary or any other action is justified, the clinic member shall be informed in writing.

There is a right to appeal against any disciplinary action taken against a clinic member.

---

1   Some clinics may introduce their own disciplinary policy, such as this, to manage student misconduct. Others may wish to (or be required to) rely on university-wide policies.

3.   Identifying a problem

If any clinic member, staff or volunteer becomes concerned that another clinic member has acted:

(a)   in breach of the membership rules as signed on joining the clinic or practice rules as contained in the *Law clinic handbook*; or

(b)   in a manner deemed contrary to the interests of the clinic

they should bring this to the attention of the Clinic Director, Deputy Director or a Clinic Supervisor. Complaints received anonymously will not normally be accepted, except where there are compelling reasons, supported by evidence, for the matter to be investigated.

For the avoidance of doubt, acting in a manner deemed contrary to the interests of the clinic includes but is not limited to:

- Failing to adhere to, without good reason, any law clinic policy.
- Breach of confidentiality.
- Bringing the law clinic into disrepute.
- Breach of the university's policies on harassment, bullying, etc.
- Not responding to emails/communication relating to clinic business within 24 hours (48 hours on the weekend).
- Once a case is allocated by a firm manager, the clinic member must accept/decline the case within 24 hours. If declining, a reason must be given.
- Acting inappropriately in the clinic or while representing the clinic in the community.
- Misuse of clinic space; this includes but is not limited to unauthorised printing, using the clinic space for non-clinic activities, giving out the clinic door code to non-clinic members, etc.
- Not completing a case without good reason and without providing adequate notification to the supervisor.
- Not submitting casework (this includes attendance notes and advice letters) within the deadline set out by the supervisor.
- Repeatedly not submitting advice letters to the expected clinic standard.
- Not declaring a conflict of interest as soon as you become aware of it.
- Being unfit for work through alcohol or illegal drugs.
- Deliberate damage to law clinic property.
- Any criminal conviction which calls into question suitability to be a clinic member.

- Failure to notify the law clinic of any criminal conviction, in any jurisdiction, whether spent or otherwise.
- Failure to notify the law clinic of any criminal proceedings ongoing in this or any other jurisdiction.
- Any other criminal acts.

4.   Initial informal investigation

Upon being made aware of a concern that a clinic member has acted:

(a)   in breach of the practice rules; or

(b)   in a manner deemed contrary to the interests of the clinic

the issue should be investigated by the relevant case supervisor if it relates to the conduct of a case or by the Director or Deputy Director if it relates to any other issue, who may decide:

- that there is no substance to the alleged complaint
- that the matter is not sufficiently serious or is otherwise not suitable for disciplinary action
- to attempt to resolve the matter by informal discussion with the clinic member where the allegation is of minor misconduct.

In all these cases no disciplinary action shall take place, nor shall any record be made against that clinic member.

5.   Formal investigation by the Management Committee

If the matter is regarded by the Director/Deputy Director or supervisor as serious or otherwise suitable for disciplinary action, it should then be formally investigated by a Disciplinary Subcommittee of the Management Committee, comprising of two non-student members of the Management Committee, chaired by the Director or Deputy Director, but excluding the member who conducted the initial informal investigation.

At the outset of the investigation, the clinic member shall be sent a letter which shall contain:

- details of the complaint against the clinic member
- arrangements for an investigatory meeting
- the right to be accompanied by another clinic member
- copies of any relevant documents being relied on.

The Disciplinary Subcommittee shall first speak with the initial investigator and any other persons who may have relevant information, such as the person who first raised the issue being investigated.

Subsequently, the Subcommittee will invite the clinic member under investigation to attend a meeting at which the allegations can be discussed. The meeting should take place as soon as is reasonably possible, but with sufficient time for the clinic member to consider their response to the information contained in the letter and no later than ten working days after notification of the complaint to the clinic member. The clinic member under investigation will have the right to be accompanied by another clinic member.

If, in the course of its investigations, the Disciplinary Subcommittee discovers further potential instances where the clinic member has acted:

(a)   in breach of the practice rules; or

(b)   in a manner deemed contrary to the interests of the clinic

the Disciplinary Subcommittee may, where appropriate, consider this conduct together with the conduct which was the subject of the initial investigation and the member shall be notified accordingly.

6.   Decision by Disciplinary Subcommittee

After considering all relevant information, the Subcommittee may decide to:

- dismiss the allegation, in which case no record of the proceedings will be kept
- decide that the clinic member requires further training
- issue a written warning to the clinic member about their future conduct
- terminate clinic membership, but only if the clinic member has had prior written warning of their conduct or their conduct is deemed by the Disciplinary Subcommittee to be sufficiently severe to warrant immediate termination of membership. For the avoidance of doubt, conduct sufficiently severe to warrant termination of membership without prior written warning includes, but is not limited to:
  - commission of a crime of dishonesty
  - assault against another clinic member or member of the public
  - intentional breach of confidentiality without good cause
  - deliberate failure to gain the necessary supervisor authorisation for action in relation to cases such as letters to clients and third parties, pleadings, etc.

In making a decision to issue a warning or to terminate membership, the Disciplinary Subcommittee shall consider:

- all previous written warnings
- the length of time since any previous warnings
- the conduct of the clinic member in the intermediate period.

Once the majority of the Disciplinary Subcommittee has reached a decision, it shall inform the Management Committee of its decision before communicating it to the clinic member.

The clinic member shall receive a letter from the Chair of the Disciplinary Subcommittee outlining:

- an overview of the investigation
- findings in fact
- any findings that the clinic member has acted in breach of the constitution or practice rules, or that the member has acted in a manner deemed contrary to the interests of the clinic
- what decision has been taken
- reasons for that decision
- nature of the right to appeal.

If a clinic member receives more than two warnings within a 12-month period, the clinic member can have their membership instantly terminated if the Disciplinary Subcommittee feels that this is the more appropriate course of action.

7.   Appeals

If a clinic member wishes to appeal against any disciplinary decision, they must appeal in writing to the Head of the Law School within seven days of the disciplinary decision being communicated to them, who shall hear the appeal within four weeks of receipt of the appeal, and the clinic member will be invited to a meeting with the Head of School and will have the right to be accompanied by another member of the clinic to the appeal meeting.

The decision of the Head of School will be final.

Part 5.3
Checklists and practice documents

5.3.1 Appointment confirmation letter

Date: [*insert date*]

Ref: [*File number*]

Private and confidential

[*Name of client*]

[*Address*]

Dear [*name*]

Appointment confirmation

Further to your telephone conversation with [*insert name/role*], I write to confirm that the following appointment has been arranged:

Day: **[*day*]**

Date: **[*DD MM YYYY*]**

Time: **[*00:00*]**

The appointment will take place at [*insert location*] where your student adviser will meet you. Please find directions enclosed for your convenience.

Please also find enclosed a document entitled the *Client information agreement*.[1] This explains how [*insert name of clinic*] works, what you can expect from [*insert name of clinic*] and the documentation you are required to bring to your appointment. **Please ensure that you read and sign this document, returning it to us on the day of your appointment.**

---

1   This may alternatively be called *Client care letter*, *Terms of engagement*, etc.

[Insert one of the following three options regarding identification documents depending upon whether the client is an individual, a trustee or a partner in a partnership. Delete the other options as appropriate.[2]]

[*For a client who is an individual*]

For identification purposes, please bring to your interview either:

- One document from List A

OR (if this is unavailable)

- One document from List B and another from List C.

List A: Photo ID
Valid passport
Valid photocard driving licence with current address on
Valid government-issue identity card (for non-UK resident individuals only)

List B: Proof of name
Valid full driving licence (with no photo), which includes current address
Birth certificate (with relevant marriage certificate or deed poll if your name has changed)
A bank, building society or credit card statement (but not an internet statement) dated within the last three months

List C: Proof of current home address
A utility bill – gas, electricity, water or telephone (but not a mobile telephone bill or online bill) – dated within the last three months
Current council tax bill (but not an online bill) *UK ONLY*
Current house or motor insurance certificate

[*For a client who is a trustee*]

For identification purposes, please bring to your interview either:

- One document from List A

OR if this is unavailable

---

2   If your clinic is likely to advise companies then you should consider including the identity requirements for companies in this document too.

- One document from List B and another from List C.

(Please note: We will need to see these identification documents in respect of **both yourself and at least one other trustee.**)

List A: Photo ID
Valid passport
Valid photocard driving licence with current address on

List B: Proof of name
Valid old-style driving licence with current address on
Birth certificate (with relevant marriage certificate or deed poll if your name has changed)
A bank, building society or credit card statement (but not an internet statement) dated within the last three months

List C: Proof of current home address
A utility bill – gas, electricity, water or telephone (but not a mobile telephone bill or online bill) – dated within the last three months
Current council tax bill (but not an online bill)
Current house or motor insurance certificate

[*For a client who is a partner in a partnership*]

For identification purposes, please bring to your interview either:

- One document from List A

OR if this is unavailable

- One document from List B and another from List C.

(Please note: We will need to see these identification documents in respect of **both yourself and at least one other partner.**)

List A: Photo ID
Valid passport
Valid photocard driving licence with current address on

List B: Proof of name
Valid old-style driving licence with current address on
Birth certificate (with relevant marriage certificate or deed poll if your name has changed)
A bank, building society or credit card statement (but not an internet statement) dated within the last three months

List C: Proof of current home address
A utility bill – gas, electricity, water or telephone (but not a mobile telephone bill or online bill) – dated within the last three months
Current council tax bill (but not an online bill)
Current house or motor insurance certificate

We will not be able to provide you with any advice until we have received the proof of identification documents required.

Please note that we will contact you by telephone 24 hours before your appointment to confirm that you are still available to attend. If you have not heard from us, please contact us by no later than 10am on the day of your appointment to confirm your attendance.

If we cannot get hold of you and we have not heard from you by 10am on the day of your appointment, then your appointment will be cancelled. We cannot guarantee that the appointment will be rearranged.

If you have a disability and require any reasonable adjustments to be made in order to assist you during your appointment or in the provision of our advice, please let us know by calling [*insert number*]. If you leave a message a member of our team will call you back.

Should you be unable to attend your appointment for any reason, we would be grateful if you could notify us as soon as possible. Otherwise, we look forward to meeting you shortly. Should you have any queries, please do not hesitate to contact us on [*insert number*].

Yours sincerely

[*Insert name*]

[*Insert name of clinic*] Director

5.3.2 Client appointment confirmation

Client name: [*insert name*]

Reference number: [*insert reference*]

Appointment date: [*insert date*]

Appointment time: [*insert time*]

Purpose of the law clinic

[*Insert clinic/centre name*] has been established to enable law students at the university to obtain practical legal experience while providing a service to the local community. Everyone working in the law clinic, except the Director, Deputy and Coordinators, are volunteers.

Our service

You will receive a maximum 45-minute appointment with two student advisers and their supervising solicitor. Sometimes there may be two supervising solicitors with the students. Fourteen working days after the appointment you will receive a letter of advice outlining the strength of your case and the choices that may be available to you. We are unable to provide representation at court or tribunal but we can refer you to other organisations for free representation. They have their own assessment process so we cannot guarantee they will take on your case.

We are a preliminary advice service allowing you to assess the strength of your case before you pursue it further. Unfortunately, we are unable to provide follow-up advice but will be able to provide you with details of where you can receive this.

Advice process

Please note that this process takes 14 working days. If there is a delay we will notify you.

Cancellations

If you:

- do not provide us with 24 hours' notice that you cannot attend your appointment
- do not attend your appointment
- are more than 15 minutes late to your appointment
- cancel your appointment twice

we will not be able to offer you another appointment in the future. Discretion will be used where appropriate.

This is due to the high demand for our services. We are only able to help a small number of clients each week and therefore missed appointments are a lost opportunity for another person in need of free legal advice. The lawyers and the students give their expertise and time voluntarily, free of charge and spend time prior to the interview preparing. A missed appointment is a waste of their time and our resources.

What you need to bring

We are unable to offer you advice until you have provided us with photocopies of the following documents [*delete those that are not relevant*]:

- Employment contract
- Employee handbook
- Pay slips
- Correspondence with employer, i.e. letters, emails, etc.
- Notice of dismissal
- ET1
- ET3
- Notice of hearing
- Job description
- Tenancy agreement
- Inventory
- Correspondence with landlord, i.e. letters, emails, etc.
- Receipts
- Contract
- Terms and conditions
- Leasehold
- Freehold
- Correspondence with opponent, i.e. letters, emails, etc.
- Information which will assist you to understand their work
- Parental responsibility agreement
- Partnership certificate
- Visa information
- Charge sheet
- Summons

- Court date letter
- Court papers
- Business plan
- Articles
- Board minutes
- Shareholders' resolutions
- Accounts
- General terms and conditions of business
- Tax forms/correspondence with HMRC
- Companies House forms
- Banking documents/security/guarantees
- [*Insert other documents as appropriate*]
- Any other relevant documents or correspondence

You should provide photocopies of these documents before your appointment.

If you provide this information at a later date, the 14-day period will begin from the date of receipt.

If two weeks have passed from your initial interview and we have not been provided the relevant documents, your case will be closed. We may not rebook your appointment until it is clear you are able to provide the previously requested documents.

Queries and complaints

If you have any queries about your appointment or our services please call or email us.

Please direct complaints to the Deputy Director [*insert name*] at [*insert email address*].ac.uk. If you feel that your complaint has not been dealt with adequately it will be directed to the [*insert clinic/centre*] Advisory Panel.

Data protection information

[*Insert details of data protection/privacy policy as appropriate*]

Entry

[*Insert travel/other directions for getting to the clinic/centre*]

[**Drafting note**: This document can be used prior to a client interview but will not constitute a *Terms of engagement* letter. See **Part 5.1.7** for a *Client information agreement.*]

5.3.3 Attendance form: Interview

[*Insert name of clinic*]

1.   Personal and general details

Date: ……………..………………. Case/File number.……………………………………………

Time interview commenced ………………………….…finished ………………….………………

Name(s) of client(s) ………………………………………………………………………………

Address ………………………………………………………………………………………………

………

………

Tel no: mobile ………………………….………... daytime ………………………………………

Email address …………………………………………………………………………………………

Law clinic supervisors:

Academic……………………………………………………………………………………………………

Solicitor ……………………………………………………………………………………………………

Student advisers:

(1) ……

(2)……

Brief description of client's matter …………………………………………………………………

………

………

………

………

Interviewed by…………………………………………………………………………………………

Has client consulted a solicitor previously on this matter? Yes   □ No □

If **Yes**, name of solicitor/firm and address………………………………………………………

………

………

Details of opponent(s) (full name and address) ....

....

....

Is there a conflict of interest? Yes □ No □

Details and action required: ....

....

....

2.   Pre-interview checklist

Have you:

Introduced yourself, your role and course of study?	Yes □	No □
Explained the purpose of today's interview?	Yes □	No □
Explained the nature of the service?	Yes □	No □
Provided information as to costs?	Yes □	No □
Given information regarding confidentiality?	Yes □	No □
Informed the client about the complaints procedure?	Yes □	No □
Completed the client's personal and general details?	Yes □	No □
Completed the *Equality and diversity monitoring form*?	Yes □	No □
Provided the *Client information agreement* to the client, and received signed copy back?	Yes □	No □
Asked the client if they are happy and ready to proceed with the interview?	Yes □	No □

If you have answered **No** to any of the above questions, please justify:

....

....

....

3. Interview details

....
....
....
....
....
....
....
....
....

Please continue on a separate sheet if necessary.

4. Post-interview

Action to be taken (indicating who by and when) ....
....
....
....
....
....

5. Advice session

Date: .... Time commenced: .... Time finished: ....

Present: ....

Summary of advice given:

....
....
....
....
....
....
....
....
....
....
....

6.   File closure

Did the client attend for their follow-up advice session?   Yes □   No □

If **No**, was a second appointment offered?   Yes □   No □

If not, why? ....

Has an advice letter been sent to client?   Yes □   No □

Date: ....

Has the file been marked as closed?   Yes □   No □

If **Yes**, date: ....

Has this file been reviewed?   Yes □   No □

If **Yes**, date: ....

If the answer to any of the above questions is **No**, please provide details:

....
....
....
....

5.3.4 Interview aide memoire

[*Insert name of clinic*]

You will need to follow your aide memoire, and obtain first instructions from your client.

1.   Meet and greet the client

- Confidence
- Handshake
- Formal greeting
- Put the client at ease
- Introduce yourself

2.   Obtaining personal information

- Name
- Address
- Contact numbers
- Email address
- Best time to contact them?
- Seen a solicitor about this matter previously?

3.   Formalities

- Explain purpose of interview
- Explain nature of the service
- Provide information as to costs
- Inform client re rules of confidentiality
- Provide the *Client information agreement*
- Ask the client if they are happy to proceed

4.   Interview details

- Ask open question to get information from the client
- Summarise instructions
- Obtain further information by asking closed questions

- Take notes: have you got everything down?
- Have you asked for copies of relevant documents?
- Have you identified the client's concerns?
- Have you checked with your fellow student volunteer/supervisor that you have all of the necessary information?

5. Closing the interview

- Advise the client of next steps:
  - What will you do?
  - What do they need to do? (e.g. provide copies of documents, notify us of their availability for next appointment)
- Would they prefer a follow-up appointment or written advice?
- Is there anything else that has been missed?
- Ask the client to complete the *Equality and diversity monitoring form*
- Say goodbye appropriately

5.3.5 Client equality and diversity monitoring form: Option 1

Disability

The Equality Act 2010 defines disability as 'a physical or mental impairment which has a substantial & long term adverse effect on a person's ability to carry out normal day to day activities'.

Do you consider yourself to have a disability?

Yes   ....   No   ....   Prefer not to say ....

Age

Please indicate which category you fall into:

Under 20	....
20–25	....
26–35	....
36–45	....
Over 46	....
Prefer not to say	....

Ethnicity

Please indicate your ethnicity group:

White British	
White Irish	
White Other	
Black or Black British African	
Black or Black British Caribbean	
Black or Black British Other	
Asian or Asian British Indian	
Asian or Asian British Pakistani	
Asian or Asian British Bangladeshi	
Chinese	

Mixed White and Black Caribbean	
Mixed White and Black African	
Mixed White and Asian	
Mixed Other	
Asian or Asian British Other	
Unknown	
Prefer not to say	

Gender

Do you identify yourself as:

Male   ....

Female   ....

Non-binary/third gender   ....

Prefer to self-describe   ....

Prefer not to say   ....

Household income

Please indicate which income bracket your household falls into:

Less than £17,900 per year   ....

£17,901–£32,000 per year   ....

More than £32,000 per year   ....

Prefer not to say   ....

Legal issue

Please indicate which area of law your legal issue falls within:

Business law (including partnership matters	
Contract law	
Employment law	
Housing/Property law	
Negligence	

Probate matters	
Other (please state)	

We would be grateful if you could comment on the service you have received today, and how useful you feel it was for you:

....
....
....
....
....
....
....
....

Thank you for taking the time to complete this form. The data collected will be used to assist in monitoring the effectiveness of the [*insert name of clinic*] and related clinics, and in order to analyse and evaluate which sectors of the community we have served, and how we can widen this in the future.

Please note that the data may also be shared with LawWorks, a registered charity, who operate, assist and enable access to free, independent, pro bono legal advice in England and Wales.

5.3.6 Client equality and diversity monitoring form: Option 2

Date: _____

The data you provide will assist us in monitoring the effectiveness of our equality and diversity policies. It will also assist us in any funding applications we make in the future. The collection of this information complies with the General Data Protection Regulation 2018 and is in accordance with our privacy policy, which you can access at [*insert link/details of address where policy available*]. This information will only be used to prepare analyses and aggregated statistical reports and to develop policies [*insert any other use*].

1. Which of the following applies to you?	2. What is your employment status?	3. Gender
[University] Staff ☐ [University] Student ☐ Member of the public ☐	Employed ☐ Self-employed ☐ Unemployed ☐ Disability benefits ☐ Full-time student ☐ Pensioner ☐ Full-time parent ☐ Prefer not to say ☐	Male ☐ Female ☐ Non-binary/third gender ☐ Prefer not to say ☐ Is the gender indicated the same as your gender at birth? No ☐ Yes ☐ Prefer not to say ☐
4. Age	5. What is your nationality?	6. What is your postcode?
7. Sexual orientation Heterosexual/straight ☐ Gay man ☐ Lesbian/Gay woman ☐ Bisexual ☐ Other ☐ Prefer not to say ☐		8. Do you consider yourself to have a disability? Yes ☐ No ☐ Prefer not to say ☐

9. What is your ethnic group?		
White English ☐ European ☐ Irish ☐ Northern Irish ☐ Scottish ☐ Welsh ☐ Other ☐ Please specify	**Mixed** White and Black Caribbean ☐ White and Black African ☐ White and Asian ☐ Other ☐ Please specify	**Any other ethnic background** Please specify
Asian or Asian British Indian ☐ Pakistani ☐ Bangladeshi ☐ Chinese ☐ Japanese ☐ Other ☐ Please specify	**Black or Black British** African ☐ Caribbean ☐ Other ☐ Please specify	Prefer not to say ☐

5.3.7 Case close-down checklist

Client ref: ....

Date letter sent: ....

Date file submitted: ....

Submitted on time: Yes/No: ....

Action	Completed
Interview notes are in the client's file.	
Client documents: copies of all case documents are in the client's file and duplicates have been shredded.	
Advice letter has been sent to the client by email or by post.	
Advice letter has been saved in the client's electronic file as 'Advice letter' in both Word and PDF format.	
Thank you card has been written to your external supervisor, with envelope addressed and sealed, and passed to a member of the [*insert name of clinic*] team. Please ensure the envelope is addressed and stamped as per the template.	
White board has been ticked off.	
The following are in your client folder: • [*Client appointment confirmation leaflet*] • Certified identity documents • Client information agreement (signed by client) • All correspondence in date order (emails and attendance notes of any conversations on the telephone to your supervisor, your client and [*clinic/ centre*] staff • Billing/time recording sheet • Notes from the client appointment, any other working notes and research • Copies of all draft advice letters (showing tracked changes) • Final advice letter [*and accompanying email*].	

Signing this form confirms the above actions are complete. Ensure a member of staff has signed off this file. **Please leave completed and signed form at the top of your client file.**

Student name: ....   Staff name: ....

Signature: ....   Signature: ....

Date: ....   Date:..

Part 5.4
Learning and teaching

5.4.1 Model module outline for a law clinic including assessment: Option 1

Name of module: Law Clinic

Programme: LLB

Module leader: [*insert name*]

Credit rating: 20 (at levels 5 and 6)

Duration and terms: The module is delivered in one term and is offered in both the Autumn and Spring terms. The timing of individual student activity may vary and is likely to be compressed into shorter periods to reflect caseloads and client contact opportunities.

Students will be expected to complete their casework by the end of either Term 1 or Term 2 depending on which term they have been allocated to. Students will work on clinic cases in groups known as student law firms (SLFs).

Teaching programme: This will consist of weekly workshops for the whole clinic cohort, a weekly meeting for each SLF, meetings as case management requires and other occasional, plenary sessions.

Procedural requirements: Students must comply with professional behaviour requirements, including attendance at meetings and conduct of casework. Failure to observe such requirements may result in removal from the module.

Student numbers: For supervisory reasons this module is limited to an annual cohort of 50 students from Years 2 and 3. Selection is based on option first choices and in the event of over-subscription, a 'lottery' draw.

Module content and delivery: This module gives students the opportunity to participate in 'real' cases for clients across a range of identified areas of unmet legal need including: social security benefits claims; housing problems; consumer issues; employment and family cases; and advice for small businesses.

Through this participation students will be able to develop and apply their theoretical understanding of substantive law, procedure, legal and related skills, and professional values and ethical considerations, in a practical setting.

Clients may be individuals or organisations who require advice and possibly representation, or who are seeking more general assistance including help with legal research or advice on law reform. All students will get the opportunity of working in the in-house clinic based at the [*insert university name*] Law School and in external projects involving particular specialisms.

All student work will be supervised by suitably qualified and experienced members of staff. Students will work on allocated cases and take part in both individual tasks and collective work as part of their SLF activity.

Outcomes and assessment

Module learning outcomes (MLOs)

After completing the module all students should be able:

- Through a critical analysis of at least one aspect of substantive law encountered during the module, to demonstrate a clear understanding of the legal principles involved, as evidenced by documented research and subsequent advice given.
- With reference to a range of clinic-related experiences, to identify the fundamental principles underpinning the skills that lawyers need to have to effectively carry out their work.
- In complying with applicable standards of professional conduct and client care requirements, to show a sound appreciation of the constraints on and expectations of a university-based legal service provider.
- (For Year 3 students only): With reference to one aspect of law, procedure or other regulatory matter encountered during the module, to identify the relevant merits or shortcomings of that provision including, if relevant, a critical reflection on how that law, procedure or regulatory provision might be improved.

Assessment method

Assessment is structured and weighted as follows:

MLO 1: An advice letter to a 'client', based on a given scenario, supported by fully documented legal research (40 per cent of the overall module weighting). The assessment task is to be completed in Week 1 of the term following study of the module.

MLO 2: An oral examination (*viva*) based on the student's understanding of the nature and extent of the skills necessary for a lawyer to effectively carry out their work (30 per cent). The *viva* is held in Week 9 of the term of study.

MLO 3: A group mark (for the work of each SLF) based on the extent to which all of the case files handled by that SLF meet professional practice requirements (10 per cent) and (for Year 2 students only) a reflective report (up to 1,500 words) on whether and to what extent tension exists between the educational aims of a clinic and the legal service needs of clients (20 per cent). The group mark will be determined by Week 1 of the term following study of the module and the critique is to be submitted by Week 6 of the term of study.

MLO 4 (For Year 3 students only): A critique (up to 1,500 words) of the relative merits or shortcomings of one aspect of the law, procedure or other regulatory provision arising in the context of work carried out in the clinic (20 per cent). The critique is to be submitted by Week 2 of the term following study of the module.

Recommended reading

The following texts are recommended:

- Kevin Kerrigan and Victoria. Murray (eds), *A student guide to clinical legal education and pro bono* (Palgrave Macmillan, 2011).
- Frank Bloch (ed), *The global clinical movement: Educating lawyers for social justice* (Oxford University Press, 2010).
- Hugh Brayne, Nigel Duncan and Richard Grimes, *Clinical legal education – active learning in your law school* (Blackstone Press, 1998) (currently out of print but excerpts on the university intranet and hard copy available in the clinic).

Additional reading will be referred to during the module. The intranet Clinic pages contain a set of helpful additional materials, including academic writings and sample portfolios and feedback.

5.4.2 Model module outline for a law clinic including assessment: Option 2

Name of module: Practical Legal Skills

Programme: LLB

Module leader: [*insert*]

Credit rating: 20 (level 6)

Module description

This module provides students with the opportunity to develop practical legal skills and ethical awareness through one of the following:

(A)   Participation in the Legal Advice Centre where students will have the opportunity to offer legal advice, under the supervision of a qualified solicitor, to members of the public.

(B)   Participation in mooting. Mooting is the process by which students will be able to argue cases in a mock trial and thereby develop their advocacy skills.

(C)   Undertaking a placement approved by the university. This will normally be with a firm of solicitors or the local council.

Students will have a choice, subject to their course requirements and to the number of places available, to study the law in practice in one of the above elements of practical legal skills.

Mooting will allow students to develop their advocacy and presentation skills. Participation in the Legal Advice Centre and undertaking a placement with a solicitors' firm or other relevant legal placement will complement the students' academic legal studies with practical skills and problem solving.

Learning outcomes

Students should be able to:

1.   Recognise and distil complex arguments from factual or hypothetical information and prioritise them in terms of their relevance and importance, as well as presenting arguments concisely, persuasively and to a high standard to either clients or a mock court.

2.   Show preparedness and presence of mind to respond orally or in writing to complex questions on points of law.

3.   Conduct in-depth independent study of an area of substantive law involved in practical legal skills, demonstrating research skills.

Teaching programme

This module will run in Semester 1 as a compulsory module. For Weeks 1–5 (Weeks 6–10 of the university's academic calendar) students will attend, per week:

- 1 x 2-hour lecture
- 1 x 2-hour seminar.

Students will be placed in seminar groups based on which practical legal activity they have been assigned to.

From Week 6, the student will be placed on their practical legal activity, which they must participate in on a weekly basis for six weeks. Students are expected to undertake a minimum of four contact hours per week on their allocated activity.

Module assessment

Assessment No.1

Learning Outcomes met: LO1 & LO2

Weighting: 25 per cent

Assessment type: Oral presentation (5 minutes)

Assessment No.2

Learning Outcomes met: LO3

Weighting: 75 per cent

Assessment type: Research (3,000 word report)

Book resources/recommended reading

Author	Year	Title	Publisher	Compulsory/ Recommended reading
E Finch and S Fafinski	2019	*Legal skills*	OUP	Compulsory reading
F Boyle, D Capps, P Plowden and C Sandford	2013	*Practical guide to lawyering skills*	Routledge	Recommended reading
C Maughan and J Webb	2005	*Lawyering skills and the legal process*	CUP	Recommended reading
J Hill	2009	*A practical guide to mooting*	Palgrave	Recommended reading

5.4.3 Model module outline for a law clinic including assessment: Option 3

Module title: Legal Advice Centre

Short module title: Legal Advice Centre

Module code: [*insert*]

Credit value: 30.00

Credit level: Academic Level 6

Department: Law School

Semester/year-long : Autumn & Spring Session

Details of accreditation by professional, statutory or regulatory body: N/A

Module leader: [*insert name*]

Module appraisers: [*insert names*]

Module pre-requisites (module code/s only): N/A

Maximum student numbers on module (if applicable): N/A

Module description (including outline content)

Key to this module will be the development of the law student's practical legal skills. The module is a vehicle for the study of law through the application of theory to practice.

Students will have the opportunity to enhance their employability skills by interviewing clients, researching the relevant law and drafting legal documents. It is also an opportunity to gain internships with law firms and Citizens Advice.

Learning outcomes

- Develop the ability to work in a team and consider the law applicable to the client.
- Research and analyse the relevant laws and highlight the various legal options available to the client.
- Demonstrate the ability to draft legal documents.
- Demonstrate the ability to manage a case file from the initial interview with the client through to closure of the file.
- Demonstrate the ability to conduct professional interviews in a structured and 'client-centric' manner.

- Demonstrate an ability to present complex legal information in a manner appropriate to the specific client.

- Gain an appreciation of client care issues such as client confidentiality and legal ethics.

- Develop an understanding of the law in other common law and civil law jurisdictions.

Assessment

Assessment will be by a portfolio consisting of evidence of:

- practical legal research
- drafting of legal documents
- a reflective diary/journal.

Late submission of coursework

Tutors will advise students of the date the coursework has to be handed in. A student must normally submit their coursework by the deadline. However, in exceptional circumstances a student may be able to negotiate an extension with the Extensions Tutor provided this is done before the deadline for submission. The decision to grant an extension is at the discretion of the Extension Tutor and is not an automatic right to which the student is entitled.

If a piece of work is submitted up to 14 days after the deadline or the agreed extension, no mark above 40 per cent will be awarded except where an agreed extension is in place. Where a piece of work is submitted after 14 days following the deadline or agreed extension, the work will receive a zero mark.

Assessments and learning outcomes

The detail of the assessments, which will vary from year to year, will ensure that the students always have an opportunity to achieve the Learning Outcomes for the module.

Reassessment

When a student fails to obtain an overall pass mark considering all the elements of assessment, they will be required to re-present themselves, unless agreed otherwise by the Law Assessment Board. This will be in the form a second submission of the portfolio. It will involve student engagement with their supervisor to identify any inaccuracies in the student's law, drafting and interviewing skills.

Expected methods of delivery

The teaching methods used on this module will be varied, using a selection of lectures, workshops, guest lectures and Blackboard facilities as a learning space. Module delivery will consist of a small number of introductory and other occasional plenary sessions, attendance at a firm's meeting and attendance in the Centre and at other venues as and when required by casework demands.

Delivery of this module will be conducted via a combination of academic-led, non-academic-led and self-directed learning. The assessed coursework focuses on practical legal skills and the ability to demonstrate a capacity for reflection on the legal skills and the legal process with all its attendant ethical and professional demands.

Teaching and supervision will be held primarily at the Centre's offices located in the [*insert*].

Students will be supervised during the client interview, after which they will receive feedback from their supervisor. The teaching space will be used for the students to conduct their practical legal research and drafting.

5.4.4 Model module outline for a Streetlaw module including assessment: Option 4

Streetlaw[1]

Teaching and learning profile

Aims of the module (i.e. the broad educational purposes)

Streetlaw is a vehicle by which the public can be made more aware of their rights and responsibilities. This module educates students about public legal education, pro bono work, street law and clinical legal education.

Students learn specific areas of law and run three Streetlaw projects designed to educate different groups in the community on that area of law. Strategy, reflection, feedback and principles of teaching/engaging audiences will be key features of each Streetlaw project.

Students taking this module will:

1.   Gain knowledge of the theories of public legal education and practice delivering public legal education.

2.   Specifically learn three substantive areas of law to a standard where students can deliver the Streetlaw projects and answer questions from the community.

3.   Develop the skills of teamwork, reflection, organisation, time management, teaching and communication.

Learning outcomes (i.e. knowledge, skills and attributes to be developed through completion of this module)

On completion of the module, students will be able to do the following.

Academic content

1.   Demonstrate an understanding of and an ability to engage in the theories of Streetlaw and public legal education.

2.   Explore and apply legal rules, doctrines and concepts in specific and real contexts.

---

1   Street Law™ was originally developed by law students in Georgetown University, Washington DC. The trademark has been registered in the USA by Street Law Inc of Washington DC, USA. The term Streetlaw has been adapted for use in the UK and is used in this context with Street Law Inc's knowledge.

Disciplinary skills

1.   Comprehend complex legal topics, and effectively communicate the information to different community groups from different backgrounds.

2.   Demonstrate enhanced legal research skills.

Attributes

1.   Use legal knowledge to design, manage and participate in a group to deliver public legal education initiatives.

2.   Self-reflect and assess self-progress.

3.   Identify the information needs appropriate to different professional groups and community groups and tailor the public legal education project accordingly.

Module contents

> In essence, Streetlaw is a vehicle by which the public can be made more aware of their rights and responsibilities. [...] the law students learn a great deal more than the law they teach – about the communities they serve and the role that law and lawyers have in addressing the legal needs of the public.
>
> (Richard Grimes, David McQuoid-Mason, Ed O'Brien and Judy Zimmer, 'Street Law and social justice education' in Frank S Bloch (ed), *The global clinical movement: Educating lawyers for social justice* (Oxford University Press, 2011.)

This module is a unique opportunity to work with different community groups to inform their knowledge of the law. The module covers the theory and history of Streetlaw as well as public legal education more widely. Students will also learn academic content (relating to community activities) and develop communication skills, organisation skills, an ability to undertake teamwork and creativity.

Other advice about the module

Lectures

The course will be taught through a mixture of seminars and preparation for community projects. Some community activities may be outside of the scheduled seminar times.

Independent private study

This module requires a significant amount of private study. This includes reading preparation for each class and independent/group work preparing for community-based workshops.

All students need to undertake Disclosure and Barring Service (DBS) checks prior to the module starting and have satisfactory clearance. [*Insert name of appropriate person/team*] will assist with this.

Miscellaneous

This module involves working on clinical legal education projects at [*insert name of clinic*]. This includes interacting with the public (including school-aged pupils). Students on the module must abide by the rules and procedures of the [*insert name of clinic*]. Any breach of these rules may result in the student being removed from practical work with the community which may mean that they are not able to complete part of the assessment.

Assessment profile

Summative assessment	50%: Assessed reflective essay (2,500 words)
	50%: Presentation and accompanying PowerPoint (or equivalent) document.
Formative assignments (not counting towards final module mark but important for your progress)	Three community-based workshops

5.4.5 Learning diary[1]

Your details

Projects you are a student adviser on:

Areas of law you have/will advise on:

Dates of client appointments:

1.

2.

3.

4.

5.

What do you hope to achieve from being a student adviser?

1.

2.

3.

4.

5.

Training

What training have you completed? (please tick)

---

1   This might be used in an extra-curricular clinic to encourage students to reflect on what they have learnt over their time in the clinic, or in an assessed clinic to encourage students to keep contemporaneous notes of their learning journey.

Introduction ☐

Drafting training ☐

Research training ☐

Interview training ☐

Computer training ☐

Subject-specific training 1 ☐

Subject-specific training 2 ☐

Subject-specific training 3 ☐

Any other training undertaken? ☐

Key notes from training sessions

Please reflect on each of your training sessions.

What were the five most important things you learnt in each session?

LAC introduction

[*Leave sufficient blank space for notes*]

Interview training

[*Leave sufficient blank space for notes*]

Drafting training

[*Leave sufficient blank space for notes*]

Research training

[*Leave sufficient blank space for notes*]

Computer training

[*Leave sufficient blank space for notes*]

Subject-specific training 1

[*Leave sufficient blank space for notes*]

Subject-specific training 2

[*Leave sufficient blank space for notes*]

Subject-specific training 3

[*Leave sufficient blank space for notes*]

Other training notes

[*Leave sufficient blank space for notes*]

Client case 1

Date: **Time:**

Supervisor: **Note-taker:**

Client number: **Project:**

Case facts and summary of issues

[*Leave sufficient blank space for notes*]

Did your case have any ethical issues?

[*Leave sufficient blank space for notes*]

What feedback did you get from your supervisor on the night of the appointment?

[*Leave sufficient blank space for notes*]

Summarise the feedback given to you by your supervisor from your first and (where relevant) second draft.

[*Leave sufficient blank space for notes*]

What have you learnt from completing this case?

[*Leave sufficient blank space for notes*]

What are you going to work on in your next case?

[*Leave sufficient blank space for notes*]

Interesting points raised at debrief session:

[*Leave sufficient blank space for notes*]

[Repeat the above for each case the student will be assigned to]

Reflection on [*clinic/centre*] experience

Did you meet the learning outcomes you wrote down at the beginning of this diary?

If not, what was different? Why do you think this was the case?

[*Leave sufficient blank space for notes*]

The top five skills you learnt from working in the [*clinic/centre*]:

1.

2.

3.

4.

5.

Key aspects to mention on job applications or during interviews about your [*clinic/centre*] experience:

1.

2.

3.

4.

5.

The five areas you need to work on most are:

1.

2.

3.

4.

5.

Areas/skills were you good at during the year:

1.

2.

3.

4.

5.

Notes

[*Leave sufficient blank space for notes*]

5.4.6 Student evaluation form: Option 1

This student evaluation form has two sections and requires completion for every case.

Section 1 focuses on your experiences dealing with your clients and associated casework, and section 2 upon the supervision and support you received.

Student views are important to us as they help us improve the education we offer to our students and the service we give to the public.

Section 1: Case evaluation

Student name (optional):

File number:

Nature of case:

[You must fill out the file number and nature of case prior to submission in all cases]

1. Please provide a synopsis of your case

2. Legal research

To what extent did the research required for this case improve your legal research skills?

Very little									*A great deal*
1	☐	2	☐	3	☐	4	☐	5	☐

3. Substantive law

Did your participation increase your understanding of the law, applicable to the case(s) you were involved in?

Very little					A great deal
1 ☐	2 ☐	3 ☐	4 ☐	5 ☐	

4. Problem-solving

Did your participation in this case increase your capacity to apply the law to practical problems?

Very little					A great deal
1 ☐	2 ☐	3 ☐	4 ☐	5 ☐	

5. Other skills

Did your participation in this case increase your understanding of the skills that lawyers use in their day-to-day work?

Very little					A great deal
1 ☐	2 ☐	3 ☐	4 ☐	5 ☐	

6. Ethics and professional responsibility

Did your participation in this case increase your awareness of the ethical and professional issues affecting a lawyer in practice today?

Very little					A great deal
1 ☐	2 ☐	3 ☐	4 ☐	5 ☐	

7. Overall impression

Do you consider the experiences gained dealing with this case, or in the clinic, to be a valuable part of your legal education?

Very little					A great deal
1 ☐	2 ☐	3 ☐	4 ☐	5 ☐	

8. Your experience

What did you enjoy the **most** about this case and the [*clinic*] module?

What did you **least** enjoy about this case and the [*clinic*] module?

In your opinion, how could the [*clinic*] module be improved?

9. **On average, how many hours' work did you spend on your case and on the [*clinic*] module?**

10. **Support: Do you feel that you received enough support?**

From [*clinic*] staff

From the members of your [*student law firm*]

Other [*clinic*] students

11.   Is the workspace in the [*clinic*] satisfactory?

If you believe improvements are needed or could be made, please tell us about them.

12.   Would you like more training?

If you would, please tell us what you think is missing or could be improved upon.

```
┌─────────────────────────────────────────────────────────────┐
│                                                             │
│                                                             │
│                                                             │
│                                                             │
│                                                             │
│                                                             │
└─────────────────────────────────────────────────────────────┘
```

13.   What aspects of the [*clinic*] module have been the most beneficial for your legal education?

Please tell us about them.

```
┌─────────────────────────────────────────────────────────────┐
│                                                             │
│                                                             │
│                                                             │
│                                                             │
│                                                             │
│                                                             │
└─────────────────────────────────────────────────────────────┘
```

14.   Is there anything else you would like to tell us about?

```
┌─────────────────────────────────────────────────────────────┐
│                                                             │
│                                                             │
│                                                             │
│                                                             │
│                                                             │
│                                                             │
│                                                             │
└─────────────────────────────────────────────────────────────┘
```

Section 2: Supervision evaluation

Name of supervisor:

[*You must fill out the supervisor's name prior to submission in all cases*]

Please read the following before you complete this section of the form.

Only use this form to comment on the supervision **you** received in the [*clinic*] as we place great importance on the quality of the supervision **you** received when participating in the module and on your view of such supervision. As the information contained within this form may affect your supervisor's career and development, please complete it as accurately and fairly as you can.

Clinic staff will use the information on this form in order to reflect on what you found helpful about their supervision and in what way it can be improved, so it would be helpful if you could always explain your answers.

1. **How do you rate the effort/level of commitment YOU have made overall in the clinic, including the preparation of your case, your attendance at meetings with clinic staff and participation in your firm?**

Very poor   *Very good*

1 ☐   2 ☐   3 ☐   4 ☐   5 ☐

2. **How do you view the performance/approach by the CLINIC STAFF in the supervision of your casework? Please provide a mark for each of the following questions:**

Encouraging ALL members of the [*student law firm*] to participate:

Very poor   *Very good*

1 ☐   2 ☐   3 ☐   4 ☐   5 ☐

Creating an open and cooperative atmosphere during clinic meetings:

Very poor   *Very good*

1 ☐   2 ☐   3 ☐   4 ☐   5 ☐

Providing you with constructive feedback on your work:

Very poor   *Very good*

1 ☐   2 ☐   3 ☐   4 ☐   5 ☐

Making it easy for you to ask questions in clinic meetings:

Very poor   *Very good*

1 ☐   2 ☐   3 ☐   4 ☐   5 ☐

Dealing effectively with questions in clinic meetings, including responding to questions which needed to be taken away from the meeting:

Very poor				*Very good*
1 ☐	2 ☐	3 ☐	4 ☐	5 ☐

Dealing effectively with questions asked outside of your scheduled clinic meetings:

Very poor				*Very good*
1 ☐	2 ☐	3 ☐	4 ☐	5 ☐

Being well informed on the subject matter:

Very poor				*Very good*
1 ☐	2 ☐	3 ☐	4 ☐	5 ☐

Being enthusiastic in their dealings with you:

Very poor				*Very good*
1 ☐	2 ☐	3 ☐	4 ☐	5 ☐

Discussing the subject matters, emails received or alterations to letters and putting them into a practical context:

Very poor				*Very good*
1 ☐	2 ☐	3 ☐	4 ☐	5 ☐

Improving your understanding of the legal process:

Very poor				*Very good*
1 ☐	2 ☐	3 ☐	4 ☐	5 ☐

Effectively managing their supervision time:

Very poor				*Very good*
1 ☐	2 ☐	3 ☐	4 ☐	5 ☐

Effectively managing their supervision so that you derived maximum educational benefit from your participation in the [*clinic*] module:

Very poor				*Very good*
1 ☐	2 ☐	3 ☐	4 ☐	5 ☐

3.   **Please use the space below to:**

(a)   Explain and provide details of why you feel your supervisor has performed below average in any of the areas defined in question 2.

AND/OR

(b)   Make any constructive suggestion that you feel would improve the supervision provided by clinic staff.

It would be helpful if you could provide as much detail as possible

4.   **Please tell us about times when the clinic staff have made your supervision and experience of clinic work well for you. It would be helpful if you could give as much detail as possible, and where you are providing feedback on a member of clinic staff who is not your supervisor that you advise us of whom you are referring to:**

5.   Taking into account your responses and replies to the questions above, how do you rate the QUALITY OF SUPERVISION by clinic staff overall?

Very poor   *Very good*

1   [ ]   2   [ ]   3   [ ]   4   [ ]   5   [ ]

Thank you for completing this form: please email it to your supervisor, leave it their in-tray or email [*insert name*] direct.

It will be returned to you for your own reflection.

5.4.7 Student evaluation form: Option 2

Date: **Present:**

Was this: **An interview session**   ☐   **An advice session**   ☐

(a)   [*To be completed by supervisor*] **What did the student do well and why, in relation to:**

Meet and greet:

Communication:

Empathy:

Listening:

Summarising and clarifying:

Other:

(b)   [*To be completed by supervisor*] **What can the student improve for next time and why?**

(c)   [*To be completed by student*] Peer/self-assessment of how the interview/advice session went

(d)   [*To be completed by student*] Set aims for the future

For example:

1.   *I will make an effort to speak slower in order to improve communication and professionalism.*

1.

2.

3.

Part 5.5
Other useful resources

5.5.1 Client feedback questionnaire: Option 1

Please complete this questionnaire to give us your views. This will help us to improve our service to our clients. (Where appropriate, please mark the boxes provided with a cross.)

1. Why did you decide to use the [*name of clinic/centre*] at [*specify university*]?

2. Was the explanation of how the [*clinic/centre*] works:

   Excellent ☐

   Good ☐

   Poor ☐

   How can we improve our explanation?

3. How well do you feel that your advice letter explained the law and legal practices? It was:

   Excellent ☐

   Good ☐

   Poor ☐

4. Did you have confidence in the advice given to you?

   Yes ☐

   No ☐

If **No**, what could we have done to improve?

5.   Was the service overall:

        Excellent   ☐

        Good   ☐

        Poor   ☐

        What could we have done to improve?

6.   Would you use [*name of clinic/centre*] again?

        Yes   ☐

        No   ☐

        If **No**, why not?

7.   Would you recommend [*name of clinic/centre*] to friends and family?

        Yes   ☐

        No   ☐

8.   After receiving the letter of advice, have you taken further steps to resolve your matter?

9.   Is there anything else you would like to add?

10.   If you thought our service was worth using, would you be able to provide us with a quote we can use for promotional materials and funding applications?

11.   If you completed Question 10 may we add your name? If so, what is your name?

Thank you for completing this form.

Please [*use the attached pre-paid envelope to*] return it to: [*name and address of clinic/centre*] or return electronically to: [*clinic/centre email address*]

5.5.2 Client feedback questionnaire: Option 2

File number:

Client feedback is appreciated and we would like to hear if you have any comments or suggestions about the service we gave you as it will help us improve our service to clients in the future.

We would be grateful if you could complete and return this questionnaire; if you require a stamped addressed envelope or would prefer an electronic version, please let us know as we will be happy to oblige.

Where appropriate, please mark the appropriate boxes with a cross like this:

| X |

Please provide as much detail on the form as possible.

1.   How did you know about the clinic?

Online search   []   Local library   []

Citizens Advice   []   Newspaper advert   []

Other   [   ]

2.   Did you consider going elsewhere for legal assistance?

Yes   []   No   []

If **Yes**, where did you think about going?
[   ]

3.   Why did you decide to use the clinic?

[   ]

4.   Before you attended your interview at the clinic, did you view
      the fact that your firm members were to be students rather than
      qualified lawyers as:

Helpful   [   ]   Unhelpful   [   ]   Unimportant   [   ]

For the following five questions, please rate how well we did on a scale of:

5 (Very well/happy/good) – 1 (Very badly/unhappy/bad)

5.   How clearly did we explain to you how the clinic works?

Very badly   *Very well*
1   [   ]   2   [   ]   3   [   ]   4   [   ]   5   [   ]

6.   How well were you kept informed by the clinic about the progress
      of your case?

Very badly   *Very well*
1   [   ]   2   [   ]   3   [   ]   4   [   ]   5   [   ]

7.   How clearly were law and legal procedures explained to you?

Very badly   *Very well*
1   [   ]   2   [   ]   3   [   ]   4   [   ]   5   [   ]

8.   How happy were you with the speed with which the clinic dealt
      with your case?

Very unhappy   *Very happy*
1   [   ]   2   [   ]   3   [   ]   4   [   ]   5   [   ]

9.   How was the service we gave you overall?

Very bad   *Very good*
1   [   ]   2   [   ]   3   [   ]   4   [   ]   5   [   ]

10.   Did you have confidence in the students advising you?

Yes   [   ]   No   [   ]

11.   Would you use the clinic again?

Yes   [   ]   No   [   ]

12.   Would you recommend the clinic to someone else?

Yes   [   ]   No   [   ]

13.   Is there anything we could have done better in your case?

14.   Is there anything else that would help us to improve our service?

15.   Are there any other comments that you would like to make?

16.   What is your name (you do not have to give it)?

Thank you very much for taking the time to complete this form.

Please return it to: [*insert postal and email address for clinic*]

5.5.3 Law School Clinic Advisory Board: Terms of reference

University of [*insert name*]

Terms of reference for the Advisory Board to [*insert name*] Law School Clinic:

- To receive, and comment upon, an annual report on the work of the [*insert name*] Law School Clinic.
- To share intelligence on matters relevant to the Clinic, including developments in the discipline, business and community relationships, research opportunities and wider policy developments that might affect the work of the Clinic and the Law School.
- To share good practice about the promotion of the Clinic and Law School to key external audiences.
- To foster good industry/professional links.
- To support initiatives that assist in the employability of graduates.
- To assist in identifying teaching, research and knowledge exchange activities.
- To meet twice annually.

5.5.4 Legal Advice Centre: Annual report[1]

University of Wolverhampton

Synopsis

This report intends to inform the reader how the Legal Advice Centre (LAC) has developed over the past academic year, and in particular how it has added value to the Law School within the Faculty of Social Sciences at the university, and how it has contributed to the local community and promoted the university in a positive way.

It will explore ways in which the LAC can improve in its delivery of offering legal services, and by way of providing clinical legal education to undergraduate and postgraduate students, and how the activities of the LAC can be extended and further promoted within the Wolverhampton area.

Author: Beverley Rizzotto

Date: 2 August 2016

---

1   This report, kindly provided by the University of Wolverhampton, may serve as a useful template for those wishing to capture the annual performance of their own clinics.

Introduction

The Legal Advice Centre (LAC), which operates from a unit within the Mander Centre in Wolverhampton City Centre, was established in 2011. In May 2015, a Centre Manager was appointed with a view to re-establishing the Centre, and to fully utilise the service and structure developed to maximise the benefit to the students of the university, and the local community.

Since September 2015, the Legal Advice Centre has opened for a minimum of 16 hours a week during term-time, and four hours per week outside of term-time (summer). The Centre has engaged students (both undergraduate and postgraduate), academic staff from within the Law School and local solicitors in practice.

This report provides an overview of the work of the Legal Advice Centre during the past academic year (2015/16), and puts in place proposed changes and plans for the future.

How the Legal Advice Centre works

Students from levels 4, 5, 6 and 7 volunteer at the Legal Advice Centre for a minimum of two hours per week. They are given a designated slot, which is determined by their availability to fit in with their studies and other commitments, and also taking into account demand by the community.

Students are encouraged to take responsibility in their role and must open up and close the Centre, and take walk-in enquiries, referring to the LAC Manager or supervisor if they are unable to deal with the enquiry alone. Students are supervised during their sessions at the LAC at all times.

The students' duties include:

- Working in the Legal Advice Centre, taking enquiries from the general public and liaising with the LAC Manager.
- Signposting members of the public to other agencies in the instance that we cannot help.
- Taking meetings with clients to take instructions, and find out about their legal problem or issue, and take detailed notes.
- Writing up attendance notes for client meetings.
- Researching legal problems, and summarising the law applicable, providing generic solutions and options available. This is in written format, which is sent to the case supervisor to be checked.
- Holding 'advice meetings' with the clients to provide them with the information and legal knowledge gained during the period of research.

- Working under the supervision of a member of staff, the LAC Manager or a solicitor in practice.
- Liaising with academic staff, solicitors in practice and the LAC Manager in relation to advice, legal research, attendance notes and arranging sessions.

Application process

All LLB students and LPC students were provided with a talk by the LAC Manager during welcome week in September/October 2015, with regards to opportunities at the Legal Advice Centre. Students must submit a CV and covering letter detailing why they want to volunteer at the Centre, prior to attending a short interview with the LAC Manager.

This process gets students familiar with the job application process they may encounter when applying for employment during or after their degree at the university, and provides them with experience in submitting such applications. It is hoped that they will gain confidence and proficiency in writing job application letters and CVs. The application process also allows the LAC Manager to assess suitability and commitment at an early stage, as students must make an effort in applying to volunteer.

Training

Student volunteers are currently provided training in relation to the following:

- Legal Advice Centre Process
- Solicitors' Code of Conduct: Client Care, Confidentiality and Conflict of Interest
- Interviewing and Advising
- Overview of Duties of Student Volunteers and LAC Documents.

The training is spread out across four hours, in two, two-hour sessions, which must be completed prior to commencing volunteering at the Centre. The training is intended to be interactive rather than solely lecture style, to engage the students, get them working in pairs or small groups, and to begin to think about the service users and obligations that they must uphold, both as a student volunteer and in the future as a legal professional.

Supervision

In the past academic year, supervision has been provided by the LAC Manager, with supporting academics. We have also maintained and established new contacts within the legal profession, who assist the Centre in providing solicitors to supervise matters on a pro bono basis. The firms that have engaged are:

- FBC Manby Bowdler
- Martin Kaye Solicitors
- Talbots
- Irwin Mitchell (training purposes only).

File maintenance and record keeping

We use standard pro-formas for telephone enquiries and drop-in enquiries, and every client who attends an appointment has their own file, of which a paper copy is kept, and an electronic copy used to provide to students and supervisors.

Documents that are kept include:

- 'Information for clients' form (information re costs, complaints, confidentiality)
- File attendance record
- Equality and diversity monitoring form
- Client care letter
- Student confidentiality waiver
- Attendance note
- Preparation note
- Telephone message
- Drop-in message
- Appointment diary.

Students are encouraged and required to complete as much of the documentation as possible, and this is overseen by the LAC Manager.

File reviews are conducted in keeping with SRA guidelines.

Feedback for students

This is provided by the LAC Manager, and given to students to encourage and improve performance during interview and advice sessions in the future.

Services we offer

The Legal Advice Centre serves members of the local community in providing general legal advice in relation to the following areas of law:

- business law
- contractual/consumer disputes
- housing/property law
- law of negligence
- employment law
- probate.

The LAC does not provide representation to clients.

No further advice is provided after the advice session and follow-up letter.

Generally, no specific referrals are made, but clients can be signposted to organisations, websites or places where they may be able to get further assistance. We work closely with other agencies – for example, Citizens Advice, Welfare Rights Service (Law Student Representation Project) and Wolverhampton Legal Companions (WLC) – in making referrals and accepting referrals.

If we cannot assist, we also utilise the Wolverhampton City Council Welfare Rights Service information booklet in order to connect with other local agencies where service users may be able to receive advice.

The LAC does not currently deal with clients who have legal issues in relation to the following:

- crime related matters
- debt matters
- finance related matters (taxation, investment)
- family matters (divorce, domestic violence, child custody).

Clients do not receive advice 'on the spot' – this allows time for the students to discuss the legal issue and research the matter, prior to delivering the advice in a follow-up appointment or in a letter.

Currently, all clients receive a letter regardless of whether they attend for an advice appointment. This serves to re-confirm the advice given, and also to ensure compliance with the SRA Code of Conduct. Students are encouraged to complete a first draft of the letter using a standard precedent. Where this does not happen, the LAC Manager is then responsible for completing this letter. This can be time-intensive.

Events and activities

Birmingham Legal Walk

The Birmingham Legal Walk took place on Monday 6 June 2016 and the Legal Advice Centre entered a team to complete the 10km route.

The University of Wolverhampton Law School was among 22 other teams – consisting of chambers and legal professionals, law firms and education institutions – that walked 10km through the streets of Birmingham.

We assisted in raising funds for free legal advice charities in Birmingham and around the Midlands. The Legal Advice Centre raised over £450, and Law School staff were joined by volunteers from the Centre. In participating in this event, the profile of the university and the Legal Advice Centre was raised within the legal profession and the local community.

BBC Radio West Midlands

In August 2015, we were invited to attend the BBC at The Mailbox in Birmingham to participate in the Danny Kelly show, to discuss the work of the Legal Advice Centre, and changes to legal aid since the introduction of the Legal Aid, Sentencing and Punishment of Offenders Act 2012. Attending were Beverley Rizzotto and Sana Niazi Butt, a student volunteer at the Centre.

Again, such exposure not only raised the profile of the university, but also served to inform the community of the Legal Advice Centre, and the services that we offer.

Statistics and analysis

Student volunteers

- Semester 1: **17 student volunteers**
    - 4 LPC students
    - 11 UG students (5 x 3rd year, 4 x 2nd year, 2 x 1st year)
    - 1 CILEx student
    - 1 GDL student
- Semester 2: **25 student volunteers**
    - 2 LPC students
    - 20 UG students (4 x 3rd year, 5 x 2nd year, 10 x 1st year, 1 x ERASMUS student)
    - 2 CILEx students
    - 1 GDL student

There was only one returning student from academic year 2014/15.

Since the beginning of Semester 1 in October 2016, the number of student volunteers at any one time has remained consistent, while the contact hours they had with the LAC were higher in Semester 1. This takes into account the closure of the LAC for the Easter break, the exam period in May 2016 and the summer period. The number of student contact hours is largely based on the LAC being open for between 14 and 18 hours per week, with 2–3 students in attendance at any one time.

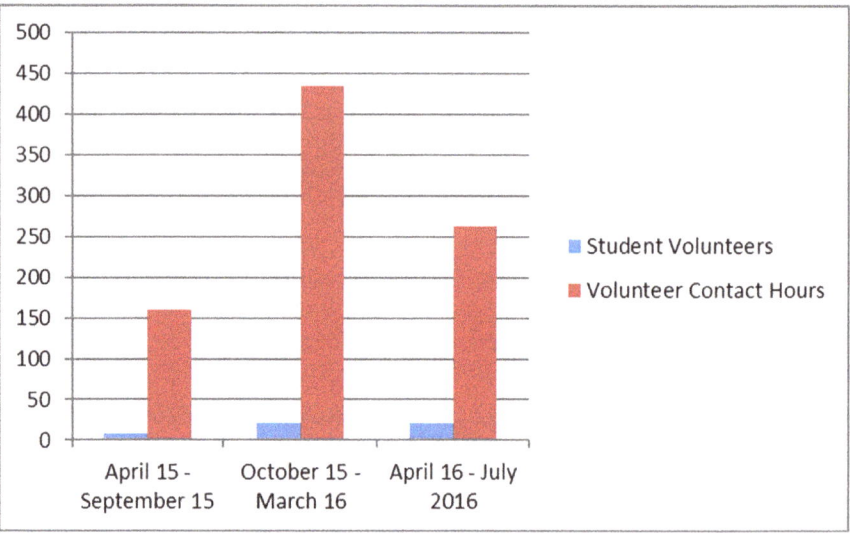

It is therefore manageable, in the future, to expand the opening hours of the LAC to cater for a larger number of student volunteers, if this situation was to present itself due to clinical legal education being embedded in the university curriculum, or simply if a higher number of students wished to volunteer at the LAC. It would also be possible for the number of student volunteers present at any one time to be increased, although a maximum of four students would be sufficient to manage the LAC and to ensure that it was staffed appropriately. More experienced student volunteers could also be left alone at the LAC without constant supervision by a member of staff (for example, if there are no appointments booked), if the number of students were between three and four for each session.

Community involvement

The response from the community has been overwhelming, and demand is always high.

By way of summary:

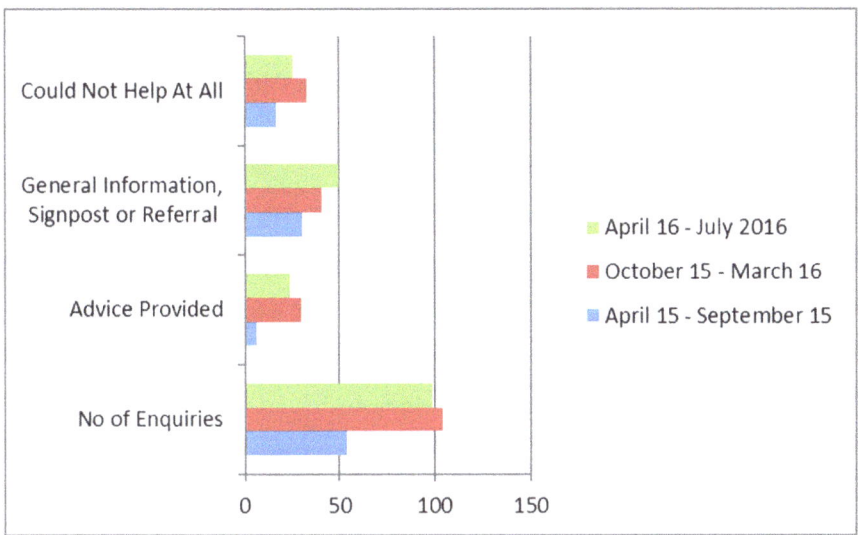

This shows the general trend for demand in the community for the services of the Legal Advice Centre. The number of enquiries in the last year has risen considerably. Month by month, demand in respect of online and email enquiries has remained stable and consistent; however, there is more fluctuation in the number of drop-in enquiries received from service users. This reflects the closure of the Legal Advice Centre for the Easter break, the exam period in May 2016 and the summer period. One may expect to see the number of enquiries received via phone, email and online form during such periods increase.

The university website is updated regularly to provide up-to-date opening hours, and a notice is always visible on the front of the Legal Advice Centre, with details of how to make an enquiry using the web form. This shows us the habits of potential service users, in that those who may visit the Centre are not necessarily encouraged to contact us via other means if we are closed. While we can only speculate why this is, if we wanted to increase the number of enquiries – and thus appointments and volume of legal advice provided – we need to look to adopt different methods of capturing this group of people. This could be done by a simple course of action such as leaving our leaflets with contact details outside of the LAC during closed periods, and also to distribute them from information points within the Mander Centre and city area.

Areas of law

This shows the general trend in respect of demand by service users for each area of law, including those we do not cover. Within the 'Other' category, many of such enquiries relate to family law matters, which we do not deal with.

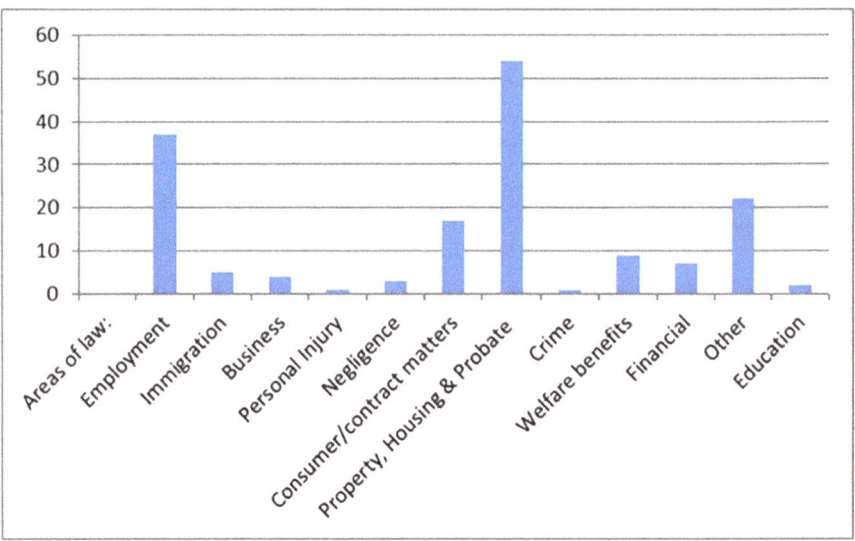

*This data includes both enquiries received between April 2016 and July 2016, and appointments for legal advice only, offered between April 2015 and March 2016. Therefore, it does not reflect the total number of enquiries received, but is largely representative of the demand in each area of legal expertise.

Feedback

Student volunteer feedback

All student volunteers who have dedicated time over the past academic year were asked to complete a short questionnaire about their experience at the Legal Advice Centre, and to comment on changes for the future.

While it is appreciated that the sample only reflects the views of a small proportion of the law student population as a whole (and is therefore arguably not truly representative), the trends set by responses to the questions asked were very clear:

- Students enjoyed volunteering at the Legal Advice Centre.
- Students believed that it had assisted them in their studies, predominantly for three reasons:

- – it provided them opportunities to research different areas of law relevant to their degree, and better equipped them with skills to do so
- – it assisted their understanding of legal concepts and issues learnt as part of their degree, in putting such information into a practical context
- – it provided them with the opportunity to gain wider legal knowledge in a practical environment.
- Students would welcome a module in clinical legal education being made available to them as an elective as part of their degree, and would be likely to opt for such a module.
- Students felt adequately supported by the LAC Manager and supervisors.

Plans for the future

- To continue to operate the Legal Advice Centre for the benefit of students studying within the Faculty of Social Sciences at the University of Wolverhampton.
- To encourage students from all levels (undergraduate and postgraduate) to volunteer at the Centre, to enhance their studies, and to increase employability.
- To maintain all continuing, existing students who have volunteered at the Legal Advice Centre in order to maximise continuity, allow students to further develop skills, maintain the smooth running of the Centre by utilising experienced student volunteers, and to assist with a new cohort of students.
- To develop a potential scheme of work and module syllabus in an attempt to embed clinical legal education into the curriculum at the University of Wolverhampton.
- To re-launch the Legal Advice Centre in keeping with the start of the next academic year, to raise awareness within the university and local community of the work we do and the services we offer.
- To continue to liaise with other agencies, in particular with other employability initiatives that the university runs (Wolverhampton Legal Companions and the Law Student Representation Project), to ensure that the local community is sufficiently supported by the schemes, and to inform one another of the services provided, to make effective signposting and referrals.
- To continue to engage with local businesses and charities, in particular law firms who have previously supported the Legal Advice Centre in supervising students giving advice to clients, and charities such as

Citizens Advice and the Wolverhampton Advocacy Service to gain access to the local community in accepting referrals.

- To maintain current levels of training and support to student volunteers, including 'refresher' training for those students returning to the Centre.

- To build relationships and contacts within the LawWorks network, and fully utilising services that they offer, in respect of staff training and training for student volunteers, and to ensure effective management of the Legal Advice Centre.

- To further explore the possibility of using the free online client management system at the Legal Advice Centre to ensure that SRA regulations are complied with, and to assist with case management, client care and meeting deadlines. This will also be available to student volunteers, who will benefit from using such systems as they are similar to those used in practice.

- To continue to keep watch on any funding opportunities, and liaise with the university's business development team, in order to submit successful bids.

5.5.5 Data audit

[*Insert date*]

[*Insert name*] University Law Clinic

Project/ Activity	What data do we hold?	Why is it processed?	It is necessary?	How long is it necessary to retain?	Who is the data shared with?	Are we allowed to hold this data?	Are we the controller or a processor?	How is data held/ processed?
Student application process for participation in clinic	Name. University email address. Mobile number. Details given on application form regarding past experience, suitability for role, etc.	In order to enable selection of student participants.	Yes: in order to select applicants. Then to provide feedback and respond to queries about applications.	12 months	Law School staff involved in pro bono. Current student committee members who assist with recruitment and selection.	Yes. Explicit consent given in application form.	Controller	Application forms submitted by students to university email address. Upon receipt they are saved electronically on university drive – access available to small number of Law School staff only. Hardcopies printed and stored in locked filing cabinet in clinic office. Reviewed by a small number of staff and student committee members. All work on hardcopy versions done in clinic office. Applications may not be removed from the office by students.
Clinic student volunteers	Name. Contact details (phone number/email address).	So that students can be contacted about their clinic project. Name and the fact of students' participation in pro bono retained to inform content of references at a later date.	Yes: it is essential that we can contact students about their pro bono work. It is also important for students that we are able to provide accurate references detailing the nature of students' participation in pro bono activities, sometimes several years after they have graduated.	Contact details/ application forms, etc. are retained for seven years from date of application. Name and details of participation are retained indefinitely.	Law School staff involved in pro bono. External pro bono partner organisations that provide support and supervision for clinic projects. Student names are also shared with clients.	Explicit consent given in application form. Explicit consent also contained in student volunteer agreements.	Controller	Details saved electronically on university drive – access available to small number of Law School staff only.

Project/ Activity	What data do we hold?	Why is it processed?	It is necessary?	How long is it necessary to retain?	Who is the data shared with?	Are we allowed to hold this data?	Are we the controller or a processor?	How is data held/ processed?
Legal Advice Clinic	Personal client data (including sensitive data), e.g.: Name. Address. Contact details. Potentially information on race, gender, religion, etc. Potentially details regarding health if relevant to query. Personal legal issues (family law, employment, etc.). We may also hold some personal data (names, etc.) of other parties involved in the client's query.	Reasons for collecting client data can be divided into five categories: Data included in client's initial query to clinic by phone or email. Data collected by clinic volunteers in order to process initial request for advice and determine whether we are able to take on the client's case (conflict checks, area of law query falls into, etc.).	Clients not taken on – it is necessary to retain for a short period of time in case they contact us again. Clients taken on – it is necessary to collect and retain names and contact details from clients (client's own details and those of other interested parties) in order to comply with regulatory requirements for conflict checking, etc. It is also necessary to retain case details for seven years in order to ensure the university would be able to respond to any potential claims arising from the advice given by the clinic.	Details of potential clients where case not taken on are retained for one year from date query received Details of clients and their cases where case taken on – full file retained for seven years from date of advice. Basic client details (e.g. name, address, date of birth, basic information about query) retained indefinitely for ongoing conflict checking purposes.	Law School staff involved in running the clinic Student volunteers Professional volunteers and supporting staff at partner firms/ chambers that provide supervision – these are currently [insert names] With LawWorks for the Better Information project (charting impact of pro bono advice) where client signs separate consent form to agree to this.	First contact is always initiated by client. Links to/referrals to privacy policy are included on clinic website, in automated email response and in answerphone message. Verbal consent is obtained to collect basic details in order to process enquiry and share with professional partners for purpose of conflict checking. Form is completed by student coordinators and contains a checkbox to indicate consent given.	Controller	Email queries received by a small list of recipients via university email addresses. All staff and students are required to use university email (students sign a written agreement to confirm they will do this). Client and case details (including emails) saved on secure university drive with restricted access (given only to university staff involved in the clinic and students currently allocated to volunteer on the project). Microsoft documents are password protected.

Project/ Activity	What data do we hold?	Why is it processed?	It is necessary?	How long is it necessary to retain?	Who is the data shared with?	Are we allowed to hold this data?	Are we the controller or a processor?	How is data held/ processed?
		Once case taken on, in order to advise client. Client name and contact details retained permanently in order to enable conflict checks to be carried out. Case details are also retained for seven years to account for limitation periods on potential claims.				Where case is taken on, client's written consent is obtained (via client information agreement).		Client and case details are shared with partner organisations via email using password protected documents. Hardcopy documents are stored in locked filing cabinets in the locked pro bono office. Only two members of staff are keyholders to the office. There is one other key which students must sign out via reception. When returning key out of hours it is dropped off in a locked mailbox. Written agreements, which include clauses on data sharing, are in place with all partner organisations
Externship clinic run in partnership with Law Centre	No client data controlled or processed by the university. All held at Law Centre and Law Centre systems used.							
Streetlaw	No personal data collected from participants.							

Project/ Activity	What data do we hold?	Why is it processed?	It is necessary?	How long is it necessary to retain?	Who is the data shared with?	Are we allowed to hold this data?	Are we the controller or a processor?	How is data held/ processed?
Homeless shelter drop-in advice clinic: ran from 2013–15	This clinic no longer runs. However, we still hold personal client data (including sensitive data) on file, e.g.: Name. Address. Contact details. Potentially information on race, gender, religion, etc. where relevant to query. Potentially details regarding health if relevant to query. Personal legal issues (e.g. debt).	In order to: Carry out conflict checks. Advise clients.	Clients taken on: it is necessary to collect and retain names and contact details from clients (client's own details and those of other interested parties) in order to comply with regulatory requirements for conflict checking, etc. It is also necessary to retain case details for seven years in order to ensure the university would be able to respond to any potential claims arising from the advice given by the clinic.	See previous box	When clinic was running, data was shared with participating student volunteers and supervising solicitor and support staff from [insert firm name].	Yes, written client consent obtained.	Controller	All staff and students are required to use university email (students sign a written agreement to confirm). Client and case details (including emails, attendance notes) saved on secure university drive with restricted access (given only to university staff involved in the clinic and students currently allocated to volunteer on the project). Microsoft documents are password-protected. Client and case details are shared with partner organisations via email using password-protected documents. Hardcopy documents are stored in locked filing cabinets in the locked pro bono office. Only two members of staff are keyholders to the office. There is one other key which students must sign out via reception. When returning key out of hours it is dropped off in a locked mailbox. Written agreements, which include clauses on data sharing, are in place with partner organisations.

5.5.6 Digital and IT resource list

To accompany **Part 2.13: Lawyering in a digital age: Reflections on starting up a virtual law clinic**, Ann Thanaraj and Michael Sales have kindly provided the following annotated bibliography of readings that may be helpful for those looking for further insights into the emerging technological developments in legal practice and in the administration of justice in the UK and globally.

- Society of Computers and Law (SCL):
  https://www.scl.org
- This is an educational charity that seeks to shape and direct discussions and training around technology and law.
- American Bar Association, Online Legal Services:
  https://www.americanbar.org/groups/delivery_legal_services/reinventing_the_practice_of_law/topics/online_legal_services/
- This is a rich resource bank of ethical, professional and regulatory matters relating to the delivery of online legal services. It draws upon expert opinion from leaders in the field and differentiates between informative websites with legal information and the actual practice of law online.
- Richard Granat is an online legal services consultant, lawyer and expert in this field. He co-chairs the ABA's ELawyering Task Force of the Law Practice Management Division and serves on the Standing Committee on the Delivery of Legal Services of the ABA. He blogs regularly in this area:
  https://www.richardgranat.com/single-post/2019/03/26/Call-for-an-Association-for-the-Advancement-of-Legal-Product
- The House of Lords Select Committee on Communications published a parliamentary report titled *Regulating in a digital world* (April 2019):
  https://publications.parliament.uk/pa/ld201719/ldselect/ldcomuni/299/299.pdf
- Guido Noto La Diega, Claire Bessant, Ann Thanaraj, Cameron Giles, Hanna Kreitem and Rachel Allsopp, '"The internet: to regulate or not to regulate?" Submission to House of Lords Select Committee on Communications' inquiry' (2018):
  http://insight.cumbria.ac.uk/id/eprint/3836/
- This co-authored work explains how the regulation of the Internet should be improved, and whether online platforms have sufficient accountability and transparency. The paper sought to explore if adequate processes are in place to moderate content effectively, proposing a

number of mechanisms to improve regulations – including effective user education – while identifying the power imbalance between the platform and the user, as well as the insufficiency of an approach to compliance centred on long and opaque Terms & Conditions that nobody reads, let alone understands.

- The research took an evidence-based and holistic approach to a multidisciplinary challenge that will inform the Digital Authority, a new body whose creation has commendably been recommended by the House of Lords. Other areas of technological impact include the possibility that the judicial role might become augmented by technology (see Nikolaos Aletras et al, below).

- HM Courts & Tribunal Services and the SCL, 'The cutting edge of digital reform' conference 3 and 4 December 2018, International forum on online courts:

  https://www.gov.uk/guidance/international-forum-on-online-courts-3-and-4-december-2018

- HM Courts & Tribunal Service, 'New routes to justice: Richard Susskind and Susan Acland-Hood reflect on digital courts and the progress of the reform programme' (2 May 2019):

  https://www.gov.uk/government/news/new-routes-to-justice-richard-susskind-and-susan-acland-hood-discuss-reform-of-courts-tribunals

- SCL, 'Courts and Tribunals (Online Procedure) Bill receives first reading in House of Lords' (May 2019):

  https://www.scl.org/news/10529-courts-and-tribunals-online-procedure-bill-receives-first-reading-in-house-of-lords

- Deloitte, 'Privacy by design: Setting a new standard for privacy certification':

  https://www2.deloitte.com/content/dam/Deloitte/ca/Documents/risk/ca-en-ers-privacy-by-design-brochure.PDF

- PricewaterhouseCoopers Legal LLP, 'GDPR: Data protection by design and by default' (2016):

  https://www.pwc.lu/en/general-data-protection/docs/pwc-gdpr-data-protection-by-design.pdf

- SCL, 'Automated decisions based on profiling: Information, explanation or justification – that's the question!' (April 2018):

  https://www.scl.org/articles/10247-automated-decisions-based-on-profiling-information-explanation-or-justification-that-s-the-question

- SCL, 'Understanding how AI and automation will impact on legal workflow' (January 2018):

https://www.scl.org/articles/10119-understanding-how-ai-and-automation-will-impact-on-legal-workflow

- SCL, 'AI: Making the UK ready willing and able' (May 2018): https://www.scl.org/articles/10209-ai-making-the-uk-ready-willing-and-able

- Solicitors Regulation Authority (SRA), 'Technology and legal services' (December 2018): https://www.sra.org.uk/risk/risk-resources/technology-legal-services/

- Legal Services Consumer Panel, 'Lawtech and consumers' (May 2019): https://www.legalservicesconsumerpanel.org.uk/wp-content/uploads/2019/06/LSCP-Technology-Paper-2019.pdf

- The paper reports on the discussion around ethical, regulatory and professional requirements of the use of lawtech in delivering services.

- Roger Smith, OBE, *Digital delivery of legal services to people on low incomes* (Legal Education Foundation, Annual Report, May 2016): https://www.thelegaleducationfoundation.org/digital/digital-report

- A series of reports commission by the Legal Education Foundation to evaluate how technology is being used to support the access to justice agenda, with the most recent updated report published in February 2019.

- Law, Technology and Access to Justice blog: https://law-tech-a2j.org/

- A resource for all those interested in the use of technology to advance access to justice around the world.

- Blair Janis, 'How technology is changing the practice of law' (2014) 31 *GPSolo Magazine* (American Bar Association: Solo, Small Firm & General Practice) May/June: http://www.americanbar.org/publications/gp_solo/2014/may_june/how_technology_changing_practice_law.html

- An argument is made for lawyers to remain risk averse and ensure that the actual services they provide – and the manner in which they provide them – will not in some way increase the risk of breaching important professional standards of the work, while questioning the role artificial intelligence could play in the manner in which legal services are delivered.

- Nikolaos Aletras, Dimitrios Tsarapatsanis, Daniel Preoţiuc-Pietro and Vasileios Lampos, 'Predicting judicial decisions of the European Court of Human Rights: A natural language processing perspective' (2016) 2

PeerJ Computer Science, 93 (October):
https://peerj.com/articles/cs-93

- The paper discusses a study on how artificial intelligence and predictive coding can be utilised to predict the outcome of cases tried by the European Court of Human Rights based solely on textual content. It finds that the coding model used is 79 per cent accurate on average.
- 'Legal revolution: The "future normal" for law firms', 17 *Managing Partner* (March 2015):
  http://entrepreneurlawyer.co.uk/wp-content/uploads/2010/03/
  MP_March-2015_Technology_EntrepreneurLawyer.pdf
- Discussion centre around the advancement of artificial intelligence and the need for stronger and regulated ethical guidance and regulation for inventions and its use in legal practice.
- Civil Justice Council, Online Dispute Resolution Advisory Group, 'Online dispute resolution for low value civil claims' (February 2015):
  https://www.judiciary.gov.uk/wp-content/uploads/2015/02/Online-
  Dispute-Resolution-Final-Web-Version1.pdf.
- The Council was chaired by Professor Richard Susskind, OBE and IT Adviser to the Lord Chief Justice, who called for a radical change in the way that the court system of England and Wales handles low value civil claims, through the introduction of online dispute resolution (ODR).
- UK Ministry of Justice, *Ministry of Justice Digital Strategy* (December 2012; last edited 7 January 2013)
  https://www.gov.uk/government/publications/ministry-of-justice-
  digital-strategy
- The Digital Strategy offers a roadmap on how the Ministry of Justice will set out to provide legal services which are accessible, effective and economical in meeting the Cross-Government 'Digital by Default' agenda.
- Association of Chief Police Officers (ACPO), *ACPO Good practice guide for computer-based electronic evidence* (2012):
  https://www.digital-detective.net/digital-forensics-documents/ACPO_
  Good_Practice_Guide_for_Digital_Evidence_v5.pdf
- The focus here is the regulatory and compliance guidance on the recovery of evidence from digital/electronic platforms and devices.
- Susan Monty, 'E-disclosure predictive coding' (2016) *Law Society Gazette*, 14 March:
  https://www.lawgazette.co.uk/practice-points/e-disclosure-
  predictive-coding/5054119.article

- The case of *Pyrrho Investments Ltd v MWB Property Ltd* [2016] EWHC 256 (Ch) has set the precedent for the use of predictive coding in electronic disclosure, which was judicially approved for the first time in the UK legal system.

- UK Ministry of Justice, *Transforming our justice system: Summary of reforms and consultation* (September 2016):
  https://consult.justice.gov.uk/digital-communications/transforming-our-courts-and-tribunals/supporting_documents/consultationpaper.pdf

- The court reform focuses on how technology can help make legal services more accessible while acknowledging that more support is necessary for those who require help in using online tools.

- Matthew Terry, Dr Steve Johnson and Peter Thompson, *Virtual Court pilot: Outcome evaluation* (December 2010) Ministry of Justice Research Series 21/10:
  https://www.justice.gov.uk/downloads/publications/research-and-analysis/moj-research/virtual-courts.pdf

- This innovative Virtual Court pilot study explores how technology could be used to speed up the criminal justice system and make it more efficient. In the pilot, the defendant appeared by way of video link at court while remaining in the police station, allowing flexibility for where the lawyers were appearing from. Enhanced online systems facilitated confidential transfer of files and documents between parties and agencies.

- Cara E Greene, Esq. 'Do lawyers have an ethical duty to understand technology?', Paper presented at the American Bar Association Section of Labor & Employment Law, National Symposium (21–23 Apr 2013)
  http://www.americanbar.org/content/dam/aba/events/labor_law/2013/04/aba_national_symposiumontechnologyinlaboremploymentlaw/16_greene.authcheckdam.pdf

- In the Model Rules of Professional Conduct, the American Bar Association acknowledged that 'competent lawyers must have some awareness of basic features of technology' while clarifying as a minimum that a lawyer should keep updated on the new developments in IT, including 'the benefits and risks associated with technology'.

- Canadian Bar Association Legal Futures Initiative, 'Futures: Transforming the delivery of legal services in Canada' (2014) § 7.4:
  http://www.cba.org/CBAMediaLibrary/cba_na/PDFs/CBA%20Legal%20Futures%20PDFS/Futures-Final-eng.pdf

- The Canadian legal profession is embracing the development and adoption of technology-driven platforms and service and delivery models for legal services, although it remains reserved on how lawyers are educated and trained, and how they are regulated to maintain professional standards while protecting the public.
- Vicky Kemp, Tine Munk and Suzanne Gower, 'Clinical legal education and experiential learning: Looking to the future' (2016) Report commissioned by the University of Manchester School of Law:

  http://hummedia.manchester.ac.uk/schools/law/main/news/Clinical-Legal-Education-Final-Report28.09.2016.pdf
- This paper examines the current innovations in law schools and provides insight into how institutions are addressing challenges and trends.
- In 2001 Marc Prensky proposed the idea that people are either 'digital natives' or 'digital immigrants', depending on when they were born. See Marc Prensky, 'Digital natives, digital immigrants Part 1' (2001) 9 *On the Horizon* 1:

  http://www.emeraldinsight.com/doi/
  pdfplus/10.1108/10748120110424816
- A highly criticised concept due to assumptions made on digital literacy and proficiency of demographics. A different take on this can be found in David S White and Alison Le Cornu, 'Visitors and Residents: A new typology for online engagement' (2011) *First Monday* – a framework for exploring the various ways in which individuals engage with digital technology:

  http://firstmonday.org/article/view/3171/3049
- Nate Lord, 'Law firm data security: Experts on how to protect legal clients' confidential data' (2016) *Digital Guardian*, 21 June:

  https://digitalguardian.com/blog/law-firm-data-security-experts-how-protect-legal-clients-confidential-data
- This blog offers useful guidance from several practising lawyers and data security experts on how to keep data confidential and secure online. It ask the question: 'What technologies and/or processes are in place to protect your clients' sensitive information?'
- Richard Susskind, OBE, *The end of lawyers?: Rethinking the nature of legal services* (Oxford University Press USA, 2010), revised edition.
- Susskind offers a challenging commentary on the future of legal services. He invites the reader to consider what aspects of their role can be undertaken with ease, speed and more economically using technology. He offers his views on how technology will be used and is currently being used in general legal practice, including in the courtroom, while

urging the reader to appreciate how technological systems can deliver a number of lawyering tasks – such as providing advice and problem-solving – at a more efficient and cheaper rate, and consequently minimizing some of the work lawyers will do in the future.

- Seth L Laver and Jessica L Wuebker, 'Home is where the office is: Ethical implications of the virtual office' (2014) 27 March:
  https://www.americanbar.org/groups/litigation/committees/professional-liability/articles/2014/spring2014-home-is-where-the-office-is-ethical-implications-of-the-virtual-office/

- The article explores the professional duties imposed on lawyers and the ethical implications of working.

- New York City Bar Association, Committee on Small Law Firms, 'The cloud and the small law firm: Business, ethics and privilege considerations' (November 2013):
  http://www2.nycbar.org/pdf/report/uploads/20072378-TheCloudandtheSmallLawFirm.pdf

- This paper offers safeguards and guidance on protecting client and firm electronic information, and guidance on using electronic devices for confidential work. It discusses ways lawyers can become aware and gain the required knowledge and skills required for online working.

- G M Filisko, 'Lawyers' definitions of virtual practice vary, but not when it comes to finding success' (2014) *ABA Journal*, 1 April:
  http://www.abajournal.com/magazine/article/lawyers_definitions_of_virtual_practice_vary_but_not_when_it_comes

- The ABA eLawyering Task Force issued suggested minimum requirements for virtual lawyers in 2009, followed by guidelines for the use of cloud computing in 2011.

- LawWare, 'Cloud security for solicitors: A best practice guide for UK law firms':
  https://lawware.co.uk/the-cloud/cloud-security-considerations/

- A website that provides cloud security solutions and resources for consideration on data security, privacy and space.

- Barry Reingold and Ryan Mrazik, 'Cloud computing: The intersection of massive scalability, data security and privacy (Part I)' (2009) *Cyberspace Law*, June, at 2:
  https://www.perkinscoie.com/images/content/1/7/v2/17961/ps-09-06-cloud-computing-article.pdf

- This article discusses the capabilities, challenges and limitations of cloud computing and associated privacy and data security concerns.

- Kristin J Hazelwood, 'Technology and client communications: Preparing law students and new lawyers to make choices that comply with the ethical duties of confidentiality, competence, and communication' (2014) 83 *Mississippi Law Journal* 245:

  http://uknowledge.uky.edu/cgi/viewcontent.
  cgi?article=1293&context=law_facpub

- The paper reviews how a lawyer meets their duties to communicate with the client, to protect the confidentiality of that communication, and to provide competent representation when using technology for legal services.

- Legal Cloud Computing Association, 'Legal Cloud Computing Association publishes response re: ABA Commission on Ethics 20/20 Issues Paper Concerning VLOs' (2011) 30 July:

  http://www.legalcloudcomputingassociation.org/legal-cloud-
  computing-association-publishes-response-re-aba-commission-on-
  ethics-2020-issues-paper-concerning-vlos/

- The LCCA advises that legal professionals should be educated about security and confidentiality issues related to the use of technology in law practice.

- American Bar Association, Law Practice Division, 'Guidelines for the use of cloud computing in law practice' from eLawyering Task Force:

  https://conferences.law.stanford.edu/futurelaw2015/wp-content/
  uploads/sites/14/2016/09/EP024500-relatedresources-cloudcomput
  ingguidelines05.30.2011.pdf

- National Cyber Security Centre:

  https://www.ncsc.gov.uk/

- Law Society, *The future of legal services* (2016) January:

  https://www.lawsociety.org.uk/news/documents/future-of-legal-
  services-pdf/

- This report identifies drivers for change to the solicitors' profession and the impact of those changes.

- IT Governance, EU General Data Protection Regulation (GDPR):

  https://www.itgovernance.co.uk/data-protection-dpa-and-eu-data-
  protection-regulation

- The GDPR has been introduced to accommodate and protect data and information held digitally and electronically, becoming more extensive in its scope and application than the Data Protection Act.

- IT Governance, 'EU General Data Protection Regulation – A compliance guide':

https://www.itgovernance.co.uk/resources/green-papers/guidance-for-achieving-compliance-with-the-eu-gdpr

- The EU General Data Protection Regulation (GDPR) requires personal data held about EU residents must be compatible with the regulation from 25 May 2018. This green paper provides information on the changes proposed and what organisations need to do to become compliant.
- IT Governance, Webinars:
https://www.itgovernance.co.uk/webinars/eu-gpdr-webinar
- A range of free webinars on the GDPR, implementation and compliance.
- Canadian Bar Association Ethics and Professional Responsibility Committee, 'Legal ethics in a digital world' (2014–15):
http://www.cba.org/getattachment/Sections/Ethics-and-Professional-Responsibility-Committee/Resources/Resources/2015/Legal-Ethics-in-a-Digital-World/guidelines-eng.pdf
- Similar to the UK or the English and Welsh jurisdiction, the lawyers' codes of conduct in Canada do not dictate any specific ethical or professional regulations for the use of technology. However, the CBA has interpreted some of its existing ethical obligations for its appropriate regulation over the use of technology in legal services.
- J Cabral et al, 'Using technology to enhance access to justice' (White Papers from the Legal Services Corporation Technology Summit, June) (2012) *Harvard Journal of Law & Technology* 26, 1, Fall:
http://jolt.law.harvard.edu/articles/pdf/v26/26HarvJLTech241.pdf
- This article comprises six papers featuring the use of technology to improve access to justice, barriers to using technology, the use of mobile technology and the financial, economic and ethical considerations on automation and technology.
- Stephanie Kimbro, *Online legal services for the client-centric law firm* (Ark Group, 2013).
- This guide provides advice on implementation, matters for consideration when identifying service providers, selection of appropriate technology and best practice in online delivery.
- Stephanie Kimbro, *Virtual law practice: How to deliver legal services online* (ABA, 2011) (2nd edn, 2015).
- With alternative methods of legal practice, this practical guide teaches lawyers how to set up and run a virtual law firm, using case studies and scenarios of how technology is being used for various purposes.
- Richard Susskind, *Tomorrow's lawyers: An introduction to your future* (Oxford University Press, 2013) (2nd edn, 2017).

- Susskind offers his vision of a new and emerging legal landscape with changing and new roles for lawyers, law firms, virtual hearings and online dispute resolution.
- ABA Standing Committee on the Delivery of Legal Services: https://www.americanbar.org/groups/delivery_legal_services.html
- The ABA Standing Committee on the Delivery of Legal Services site provides resources, discussions and updates on improving access to justice initiatives in the US.
- Jordan Furlong, 'The evolution of the legal services market: Stage 5' (2012) *Law 21*, 9 November: https://www.law21.ca/2012/11/the-evolution-of-the-legal-services-market-stage-5/
- This blog discusses the creative and innovative futures and careers that lawyers could have because of the trends in technology development for legal practice.
- Ann Thanaraj and Michael Sales, 'Lawyering in a digital age: A practice report on the design of a virtual law clinic at Cumbria' (2015) *International Journal of Clinical Legal Education*, 22(3), pp. 334–61, available at: http://journals.northumbria.ac.uk/index.php/ijcle/article/view/471
- A Thanaraj, 'Internationalizing education: Evaluating the growth of intercultural communication and competency in students through an international negotiation project using an online law office' (2015) *Journal of Pedagogic Development*, available at: http://insight.cumbria.ac.uk/id/eprint/2490/
- A Thanaraj, 'Identifying students' perspectives on skills and attributes gained from working in a virtual law clinic to create an impact on "the whole lawyer": A grounded theory study' (2017) *US-China Law Review* 14, 137: http://www.davidpublisher.org/Public/uploads/Contribute/5927cc6bd693a.pdf
- Research on some of the benefits of the VLC training initiative and curriculum.
- A Thanaraj, 'Understanding how a law clinic can contribute towards students' development of professional responsibility' (2016) 23 *International Journal of Clinical Legal Education* 4, available at: http://www.northumbriajournals.co.uk/index.php/ijcle/article/view/521
- A Thanaraj, 'Evaluating the potential of virtual simulations to facilitate

professional learning in law: A literature review' (2016) 6 *World Journal of Education* 6, available at:

http://www.sciedu.ca/journal/index.php/wje/article/view/10607

- Research on some of the areas for improvement in the design and learning construct embedded into the VLC.
- A Thanaraj and S Williams, 'Supporting the adoption of technology enhanced learning by academics at universities' (2016) *Journal of Teaching and Learning with Technology* 5(1), 59–86, available at:

  http://jotlt.indiana.edu/article/view/18985

- A Thanaraj, 'Making the case for a digital lawyering framework in legal education' (2017) 3 *International Review of Law*, 17:

  https://insight.cumbria.ac.uk/id/eprint/3324/1/Thanaraj_MakingTheCase.pdf

Part 6
Glossary of clinical legal education networks

Part 6.1
Glossary of clinical legal education networks

There are clinical legal education networks around the world that provide forums for clinicians to come together and share good practice, discuss new ideas and offer peer support. This Handbook would not have happened without such networks and we would encourage clinicians new and old to make use of these connections. The clinical community is a generous and welcoming one.

Details of many such networks and key organisations that work with and support them are set out below.[1]

Europe

Organisation	Description	Contact details
Clinical Legal Education Organisation (CLEO): UK	CLEO is a UK-based charitable organisation aimed at fostering, promoting and developing clinical legal education in all its forms, including education, training, collaboration and research. It frequently holds events and workshops for clinicians and offers a mentoring scheme. CLEO offers individual membership and is free to join.	Email: info@cleo-uk.org Website: http://www.cleo-uk.org/
European Network for Clinical Legal Education (ENCLE): Europe-wide	ENCLE is a European Network of people committed to achieving justice through education. It aims to bring together people from different countries, who exchange perspectives and work collaboratively from a variety of legal, educational and organisational settings in order to promote justice and increase the quality of law teaching through clinical legal education. Offers individual and institutional/organisational membership and is free to join.	Email: encle.info@gmail.com Website: http://encle.org/

---

1   Note that the organisations detailed here have a specific connection to, or focus on, clinical legal education and pro bono. Broader legal education networks and associations such as the Association of Law Teachers, the Socio-Legal Studies Association, the Society of Legal Scholars and the Legal Education Research Network may also hold events and facilitate conference streams that will be of particular interest to clinicians.

Organisation	Description	Contact details
LawWorks (the Solicitors Pro Bono Group): England and Wales	LawWorks is a charity working in England and Wales to connect volunteer lawyers with people in need of legal advice, who are not eligible for legal aid and cannot afford to pay, and with the not-for-profit organisations that support them. Its aim is to support lawyers in developing the knowledge and confidence to provide competent pro bono legal advice and to keep abreast of developments in the pro bono sector. Many university clinics register as part of the LawWorks network.	Website (which includes a contact form): www.lawworks.org.uk
Scottish University Law Clinic Network (SULCN)	The Scottish University Law Clinic Network works for the promotion of access to justice and to raise awareness of student law clinics and their activities.	Twitter: @SULCN For enquiries contact Rebecca Samaras: rebecca.samaras@ed.ac.uk
Streetlaw UK and Ireland Best Practices: UK and the Republic of Ireland	An informal network that holds annual conferences dedicated to sharing best practice in the teaching and delivery of Streetlaw/public legal education. Its events are advertised via CLEO.	For enquiries contact Linden Thomas: l.thomas@bham.ac.uk

Worldwide

Organisation	Description	Contact details
Association for Canadian Clinical Legal Education (ACCLE): Canada	ACCLE is a group of individuals and clinics who have come together to provide a forum for legal educators across Canada to share best practices, pedagogies and other information related to clinical legal education, and to encourage the promotion and improvement of clinical legal education in Canadian law schools. Individual and clinic membership is available for a small fee.	Email: info@accle.ca Website: http://accle.ca/

Organisation	Description	Contact details
Clinical Legal Education Association (CLEA): USA	CLEA exists to advocate for clinical legal education as fundamental to the education of lawyers. Among other things, CLEA and its members seek to foster excellent teaching and scholarship by clinical educators, and to integrate clinical teaching and extend its methods into the legal education program of every law school. Offers full membership, associate membership and group membership options for a small fee.	Email the President: clea@cleaweb.org Email about membership: membership@cleaweb.org Website: https://www.cleaweb.org/
Global Alliance for Justice Education (GAJE): Worldwide	GAJE is a global alliance of persons committed to achieving justice through education. GAJE holds worldwide conferences and engages in other activities that are aimed at promoting the exchange of information and experience among persons involved in justice education around the world. Clinical education of law students is a key component of justice education, but GAJE also works to advance other forms of socially relevant legal education involving practising lawyers, judges, non-governmental organisations and the lay public. Membership is free although there is an option to pay a voluntary fee.	Website (which includes a contact form): https://www.gaje.org/
International Journal of Clinical Legal Education (IJCLE): Worldwide	The *International Journal of Clinical Legal Education* is an international peer reviewed open access journal devoted to the innovative field of clinical legal education. The journal organises an annual conference which takes place in a different country each year.	Website: https://www.northumbriajournals.co.uk/index.php/ijcle
Network of University Legal Aid Institutions Nigeria	NULAI Nigeria is a non-governmental, non-profit and non-political organisation committed to promoting clinical legal education, legal education reform, legal aid and access to justice. Offers individual and institutional membership for a small fee. Applications can be made via the website.	Website: www.nulai.org

Organisation	Description	Contact details
South East Asia Clinical Legal Education Association (SEACLEA)	SEACLEA is a Southeast Asian Network of people and institutions committed to improving the quality of legal education and achieving justice in part through the use of clinical legal education. It aims to bring together people from different countries, who will exchange perspectives and work collaboratively from a variety of legal, educational and organisational settings in order to increase the quality of law teaching and improve justice through CLE.	Facebook: 'South East Asia Clinical Legal Education Association' Website: https://www.babseacle.org/southeast-asia-clinical-legal-education-association-seaclea/
Street Law Inc	Street Law Inc is a global, non-partisan, non-profit organisation with more than 40 years of experience developing classroom and community programs that educate young people about law and government. Street Law Inc works in the USA and around the globe.	Website: www.streetlaw.org
Street Law South Africa	Street Law South Africa deals with public legal education, human rights and democracy education programmes at South African universities and works extensively internationally. The project provides preventative legal education to both formal and informal communities, promoting fundamental rights, freedoms, participation and democratic cultures.	Facebook: @ StreetLawSouthAfrica

Part 7
Postscript: 'Things I wish I'd known before I started doing clinical legal education'

Words of wisdom from experienced clinicians on what they wish they'd known at the start of their clinical careers

Part 7.1
Professor John Fitzpatrick

I hope that a reflection on my experience of the law clinic at Kent will convey the enthusiasm I feel about clinical legal education and my warm encouragement to anyone thinking of getting involved.

I cherish the fortunate circumstance that a public university is able to combine a free legal service to those who need but cannot afford one, with an extraordinarily rich educational opportunity for its students. Staff and students working together can help people obtain, for example, due entitlement to welfare benefits, secure and safe housing, refugee status, compensation for unfair dismissal, the minimum wage, resolution of family disputes, advice for those in prison, access to public rights of way and greens, and can bring immigrant families together. They can spread the benefits to client groups by lessons disseminated and legal precedents gained, and all in the course of learning and teaching at relatively little extra cost – a law clinic invariably attracts students and enhances the reputation of a university.

A thrilling learning curve awaits students who choose to participate under supervision in a clinical legal practice. They are required to engage with the law and its unfolding application in real time, and also with the people who are immediately and intimately affected by it. Vocational skills are acquired, and a sense of public service. But in its educational dimension the practical activity is primarily a means to an academic end, namely a better knowledge of law, and an improved ability to reflect critically on law and its application in practice. Thus students are required to report upon their casework, to research matters arising and to submit substantial written work on relevant law, doctrine, procedure, theory and policy – and the lives of others.

Respect is due to the agency of the client, and the conduct of the case is driven by their instructions. If a first class service is delivered, and casework and study become a joint enterprise, then law clinic students can truly deepen and broaden their knowledge of law and society, and refine their ability to think about it.

In a clinical legal practice a strong camaraderie usually arises among students and staff, and an independent spirit in a collective endeavour. There is enjoyment, and also shared gratification when it occurs that staff and students have been able, using the law that they are learning, to make a difference for the better.

Professor John Fitzpatrick
Emeritus Professor of Law
University of Kent

Part 7.2
Dr Richard Grimes

In 1984 Anthony Amsterdam wrote, with more than a touch of prophesy and irony, his seminal article on legal education in the 21st century. The basic stance he takes is that now we all do 'clinic': what was all the fuss about?[1]

My own involvement in experiential learning began in the early 1990s after making the switch from being a partner in a provincial legal practice to a 'lecturing' post in academia. I had not heard of clinical legal education (CLE) but intuitively used case studies and role play in my teaching. The words 'simulation clinic' were unknown to me.

It was one of my students who mentioned what we now call live client law clinics and suggested that we visit something called the Student Law Office at Northumbria. That trip, coupled with the willingness of my then Dean to fund an extensive trip to the USA to look at clinical legal education provision, set me on a mission to understand and develop this pedagogy at my law school. The rest, as they say, is history!

I have been asked to write here about things I wish I'd known before I started doing CLE. I find this hard to do, as in all 'learning by doing' the lessons are more a result of application and reflection than prior knowledge. What I can say in the space available here is that for anyone establishing a clinic or expanding provision there are some fundamental principles that, if adopted, are likely to promote sustainability, maintain requisite quality, enhance the students' education and to serve a wider community purpose, including addressing aspects of unmet legal need.

These can be briefly summarised as follows:

- Be clear on the purpose of any clinic: learning outcomes, extent of any public service, where it sits within the overall curriculum.
- Be realistic in terms of available resources: the more 'hard' (law school/ university) funding can be relied upon the better ('soft' money, from outside of the educational institution, as attractive as it is can make the clinic vulnerable).
- Be well-structured: having clear operational rules (for example, in a clinic handbook) and lines of responsibility means that the clinic should function smoothly and expectations can be more easily managed.

---

1   Anthony Amsterdam, 'Clinical legal education – a 21st century perspective' (1984) *Journal of Legal Education* 34, 612.

- Capture the 'teachable moment': most of what happens in a clinic has learning value. The use of templates to record what the student does and thinks about what they do can help, as will regular and frequent meetings (referred to as 'rounds' in the literature) to discuss what has happened, what could happen and what now needs to happen. This will all aid the reflective process and necessary case management.

- Subject to the requirement for confidentiality, record and publicise the work of the clinic, for example in newsletters and reports.

- Use an advisory board with representatives from relevant stakeholders, including legal practice and the not-for-profit advice sector: they can become your champions.

- Enjoy your learning and teaching: whoever said that legal education should not be fun as well as instructive – just feel the buzz when you go into a clinic.

As Amsterdam clearly infers, through CLE everyone is a winner – the student, the client, the law school, the university and wider society – providing the clinic meets the applicable educational and legal practice standards.

Richard Grimes
Visiting Professor
Charles University, Prague

Part 7.3
Dr Jane Krishnadas

Is clinical legal education a choice? CLOCK, in times of crisis

There was a time (as I remember from a Law School meeting), when the concept of clinical legal education was considered by some to be a distinct choice. It was presented in terms of either prioritising time that enable academics to engage in critical social and legal research, compared to the time required to supervise and train students to give free legal advice to enhance and widen access to professional experience, as an addition to legal advice by the publicly funded legal aid sector.

My research on rights in times of crisis was based in India, where the majority of the public does not have access to funded legal advice or representation, and active research is considered to be not a choice but a duty of public universities to understand local needs as a method to transform local communities and national policy.[1]

The Law in Action module developed with Professor Rosie Harding at Keele University created a bridge between research and education, while marking the distinction between law in books and law in action. It was only through listening to our local communities that the impact of the significant withdrawal of legal aid in 2013 became realised, when Sharon from 'Voices of Experience' recited her story that when faced with leaving a 'torturous island of abuse' or entering the 'shark-infested legal waters', without a bridge, there is no choice.[2] Legal professionals had started to pull up the drawbridge from seemingly unnavigable and desiccated waters. Legal aid practices were no longer able to sustain legal aid contracts, or offer opportunities for training contracts in family, housing and welfare law. This diminished the resources for research and development in these specialist areas, which in turn would restrict the collation of robust evidence to inform social and legal policy reforms.

A transformative methodology, based upon the voices of those in need, informed how to reach out beyond the university, to build bridges with the local community – with law firms, Citizens Advice Bureaux, domestic and sexual violence services, and housing associations – and to develop an innovation: the Community Legal Outreach Collaboration (CLOCK). CLOCK

---

1   Jane Krishnadas, 'Rights as the intersections: Rebuilding cultural, material and spatial spheres – A transformative methodology' in Rohee Dasgupta (ed), *Cultural practices and political possibilities* (Cambridge Scholars Publishing, 2008).

2   Maria Whatton, *Beaten down, rising up, standing tall* (Voices of Experience, 2010).

is an interlocking network of legal actors, in which law students are the key.[3] Trained as Community Legal Companions, the students have assisted more than 4,000 people by signposting to legal aid and charitable services or, where not available, assist directly in court in the McKenzie role, to assist/ monitor fair proceedings. Many of these students have since graduated to secure training contracts in local family legal aid law firms, and CLOCK has now been cascaded across law schools around the country. The clock.uk.net portal has collated robust research data to inform the post implementation review of the Legal Aid, Sentencing and Punishment of Offenders Act 2012, on, for example, the means test for domestic violence cases and specifically to reinstate legal aid where children are at significant risk of harm.

Arendt's 'On humanity in dark times',[4] illustrates 'when the times become so extremely dark for certain groups of people that it is no longer up to them, their insight or choice, to withdraw from the world'. Moving forward from a point of crisis cannot be an individual choice, but is interdependent upon each actor as an agent of change. In today's times of crisis, each litigant in person, the profession, the judiciary and academia is a cog – an integral part of a critical mechanism for CLOCK – within the wider clinical legal education movement to transform access to justice.

Dr Jane Krishnadas
Keele University

---

3   Jane Krishnadas, 'CLOCK: "The community legal companion" as an agent of change: A transformative methodology' in Linden Thomas, Steven Vaughan, Bharat Malkani and Theresa Lynch (eds), *Reimagining clinical legal education* (Hart Publishing 2018).

4   Hannah Arendt, 'On humanity in dark times', in Hannah Arendt, *Men in Dark Times* (Harcourt, Brace & World 1968 [1955]), p. 13.

Part 7.4
Professor Donald Nicolson

The key to a clinic's success is its people: Take your time selecting students and work colleagues. Ensure that both are committed to the ideas of social justice and client service, and that they are collegial. As regards staff, look for optimists and people with a sense of humour. Both are going to be necessary when you face challenges. Things will always go wrong. People make mistakes. There are always crises. The ability to see things in perspective and the funny side of mistakes will help in riding the inevitable bumps of law clinic work.

Never underestimate students. Over the years, I have never ceased to be amazed at the confidence and abilities of students: students as young as 17 arguing (and winning) in court and tribunals, appearing on radio, chairing clinic meetings, developing case management systems and websites ... the list is endless. At the same time, don't believe all you are told by students wanting to join a clinic. I have also come across – and unfortunately increasingly so – students who speak eloquently about their motivation to help others but end up being only interested in putting something on their CVs and are not even bothered to reply to emails, turn up for appointments, conduct their research, etc.

Look after yourself. If you are not employed as a dedicated clinician, ensure that you are given sufficient time to manage your clinic responsibilities as well as your teaching, administration and research responsibilities. Otherwise, you (and indeed all clinicians) may end up working pro bono yourself. This is a great role model for students and is not necessarily a bad thing if you have the time, but it comes at a cost of your wellbeing and your work-life balance, while just being taken for granted by your institution. Do not put your life and soul into your clinic and lose precious time with your children that cannot be regained, only for university priorities to change. No matter how much we know that clinics contribute to the community and to an excellent legal education, university management (and even some law school heads) tend to see clinical legal education as an optional extra when compared with research, increasing student numbers, and whatever latest neo-liberal Damoclean sword is being dangled over academic heads.

Take risks. Don't let the perfect be the enemy of the good. If you have a good idea for helping those most in need, don't get hung up about excluding every potential risk no matter how small. If you have insurance and good quality assurance systems, do not let the desire to ensure a perfect service get in the way of enhancing access to justice for those most in need. Rather than Rolls-Royces for the few, provide economy cars for the many.

Professor Donald Nicolson
University of Essex

Part 7.5
Professor Julie Price

Once upon a time, there was no clinical legal education or real client work at Cardiff University's Law School. Then, a keen but naïve former high-street solicitor and Legal Practice Course tutor was given a blank sheet to 'come up with something relevant to Cardiff'. A spectacular absence of due diligence and an abundance of (now spent) energy later, and there is a whole suite of clinical activity at Cardiff. A fairy tale journey? Of course not. Magical? Sometimes. Happy ending? Definitely!

What tips would I give my young(er) eager self?

- Make sure that the department, and central university, understands – **really understands** – that any clinical activity takes significant extra resources, especially people's time. With real clients and casework, you are not only teaching and managing students, but you have a professional responsibility to clients, which at least doubles the workload. Have difficult conversations with decision-makers to agree a meaningful commitment before you expend too much time creating some fantastic clinical proposal that might go nowhere as soon as the cheque book is requested. At the outset, I wish I had appreciated how much universities operate as businesses, even with their community engagement agenda hats on.

- Keep an accurate time record of the various aspects of your activities. Just because something isn't conventionally recorded on a template workload allocation model doesn't mean it shouldn't be. Evidence is essential for informed investment decisions where business cases have to be made.

- Be bold about calculating the indirect financial value of your work to the department/university. Students pay our salaries. Students like (want, need) clinical experience. We all know that a clinic is a teaching/learning innovation with bells on. But we should also embrace calling upon it to substantiate our scholarship and engagement activities, or whatever other benchmarking/criteria our universities use in promotion/review procedures and the like. A clinic is many different things in different packages, so don't be shy about selling yourself and your clinical achievements flexibly and creatively. We are worth it!

- Try more partnership activity, and fewer labour-intensive schemes. Traditional clinics that replicate law offices are fantastic, but relentless. Aim for term-time only activity to avoid problems with vacation clinic cover.

- If you want to start an Innocence Project-type clinic, do full due diligence first, and then do it again. This is the most challenging of all clinical work, with many pitfalls. Having said that, the marvel of having two convictions overturned by the Court of Appeal – and extensive media interest in the very real problems with the criminal justice system – is unbeatable. Decades on, those many emails, calls and visits from past students, now friends, who gave so much of their time to fighting injustice, and learning bucketloads along the way, are invaluable. They are guaranteed to put a smile on my face every time.

- Don't forget how wonderful many of our students are, and how clinical experiences can genuinely shape their lives as well as their careers. You may feel unappreciated at times, but you will find that the clinical legal education world of friends (old and new) is hugely supportive. If you want to scream, just reach out and someone will have survived your particular unique-to-you crisis before – guaranteed!

- Finally, make sure that the department, and central university, understands … Oops – done that one already. But it's so important that I'm indulging myself by saying it again!

Professor Julie Price
Head of Pro Bono and Clinical Legal Education
Cardiff University's School of Law and Politics

Index

Lightning Source UK Ltd.
Milton Keynes UK
UKHW020825050620
364394UK00003B/5